BLOODY MONDAY

VOLUME 3

Story by Ryou Ryumon
Art by Kouji Megumi

Translated by Mari Morimoto
Lettered by Karl Felton

KC
KODANSHA
COMICS

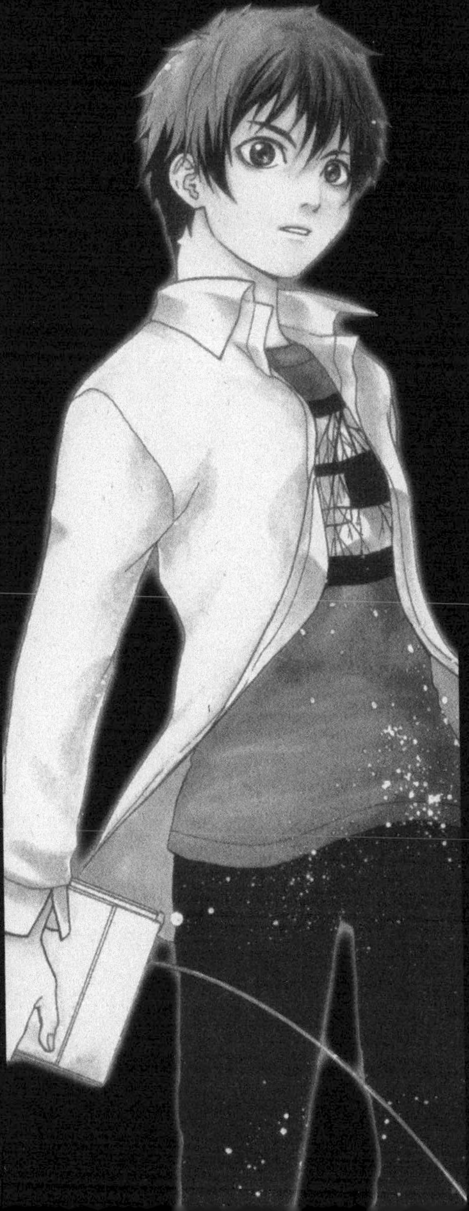

AUTHORS' NOTES

Have you ever heard the name "Echelon"? It refers to a search and monitoring system, said to operate mainly on behalf of America, which can intercept all types of communications, including phone calls and electronic mail, around the world. While it aids in preventing terrorism by continuously monitoring for terrorist terms such as "nuclear," "poison gas," and "bomb," it may also be scanning our everyday e-mails and phone calls. I wonder if e-mails written by female high school students in Japan that include the phrase, "...... just kidding~ (nuclear explosive laughter)!" are intercepted just to be safe.

—RYUMON

Once, while reading the news on my break, I happened upon an article titled, "Clean bombs possessing the most destructive power in the world, even greater than nuclear weapons". Some might think that human technology has reached its saturation point, but I feel that it, like viruses, will continue evolving, I thought to myself while chomping on an onigiri. [NOTE: Megumi's thoughts can be quite rambling]

—MEGUMI

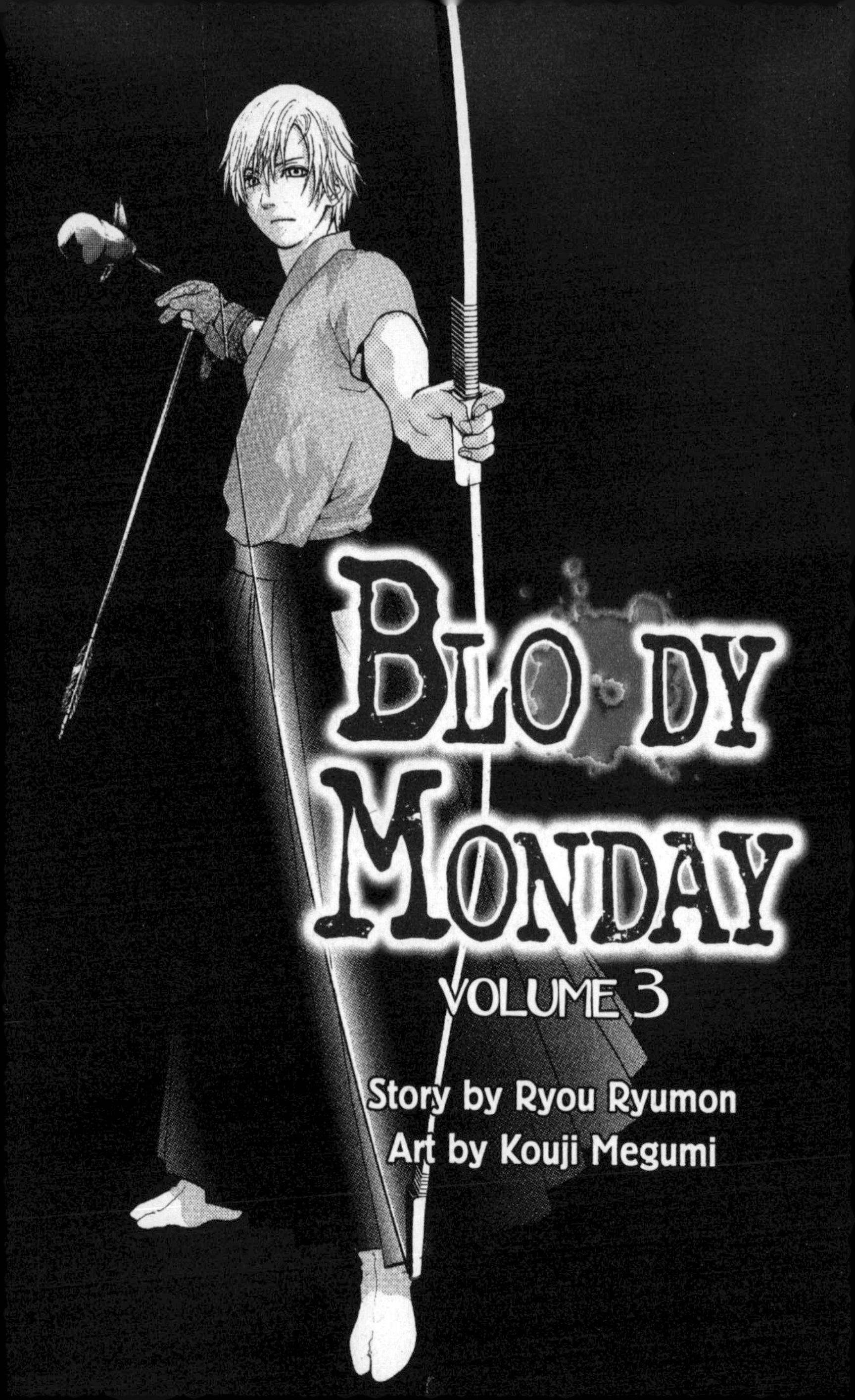
BLOODY MONDAY
VOLUME 3
Story by Ryou Ryumon
Art by Kouji Megumi

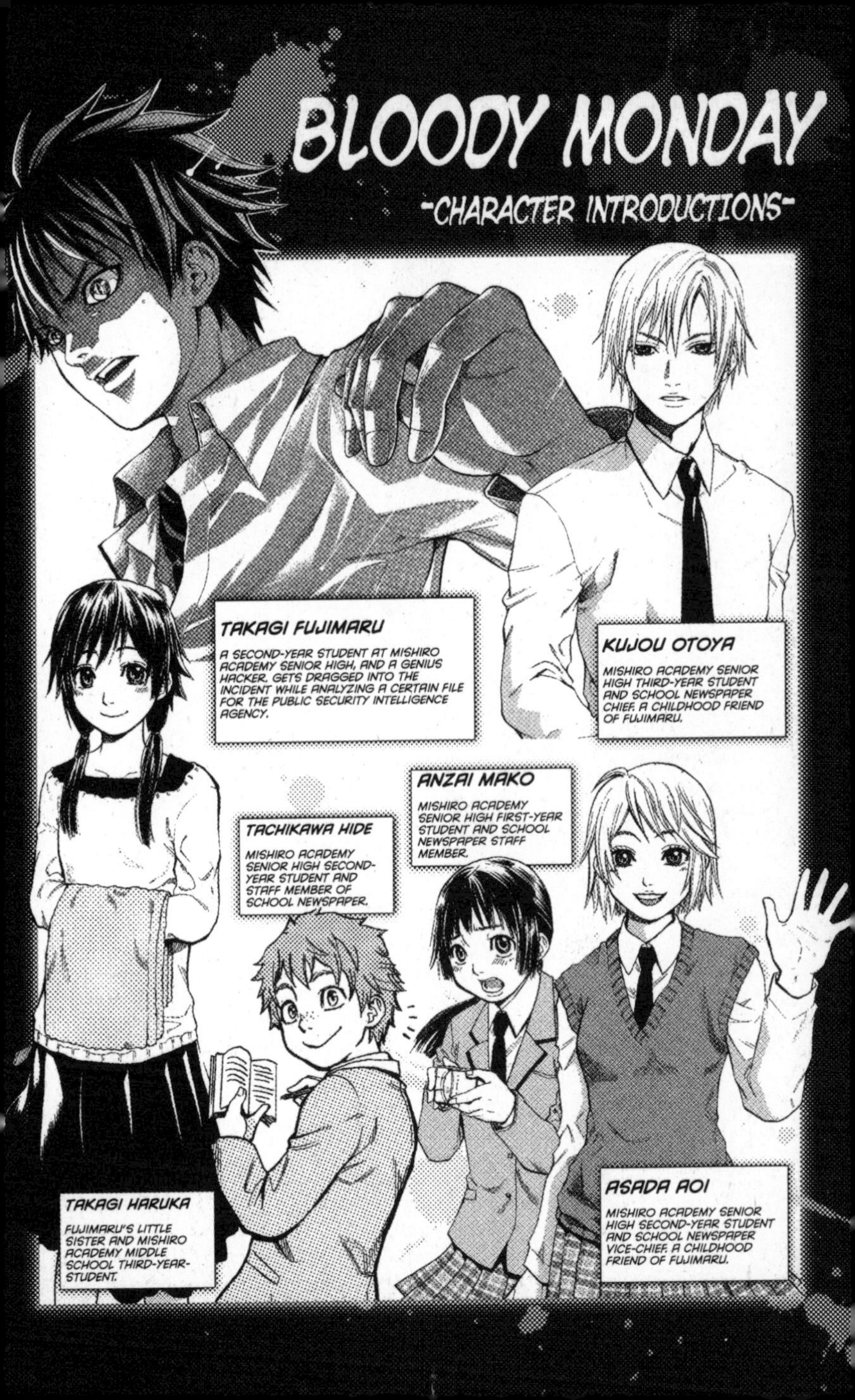
BLOODY MONDAY
-CHARACTER INTRODUCTIONS-
KUJOU OTOYA
MISHIRO ACADEMY SENIOR HIGH THIRD-YEAR STUDENT AND SCHOOL NEWSPAPER CHIEF. A CHILDHOOD FRIEND OF FUJIMARU.
TAKAGI FUJIMARU
A SECOND-YEAR STUDENT AT MISHIRO ACADEMY SENIOR HIGH, AND A GENIUS HACKER. GETS DRAGGED INTO THE INCIDENT WHILE ANALYZING A CERTAIN FILE FOR THE PUBLIC SECURITY INTELLIGENCE AGENCY.
ANZAI MAKO
MISHIRO ACADEMY SENIOR HIGH FIRST-YEAR STUDENT AND SCHOOL NEWSPAPER STAFF MEMBER.
TACHIKAWA HIDE
MISHIRO ACADEMY SENIOR HIGH SECOND-YEAR STUDENT AND STAFF MEMBER OF SCHOOL NEWSPAPER.
ASADA AOI
MISHIRO ACADEMY SENIOR HIGH SECOND-YEAR STUDENT AND SCHOOL NEWSPAPER VICE-CHIEF. A CHILDHOOD FRIEND OF FUJIMARU.
TAKAGI HARUKA
FUJIMARU'S LITTLE SISTER AND MISHIRO ACADEMY MIDDLE SCHOOL THIRD-YEAR-STUDENT.

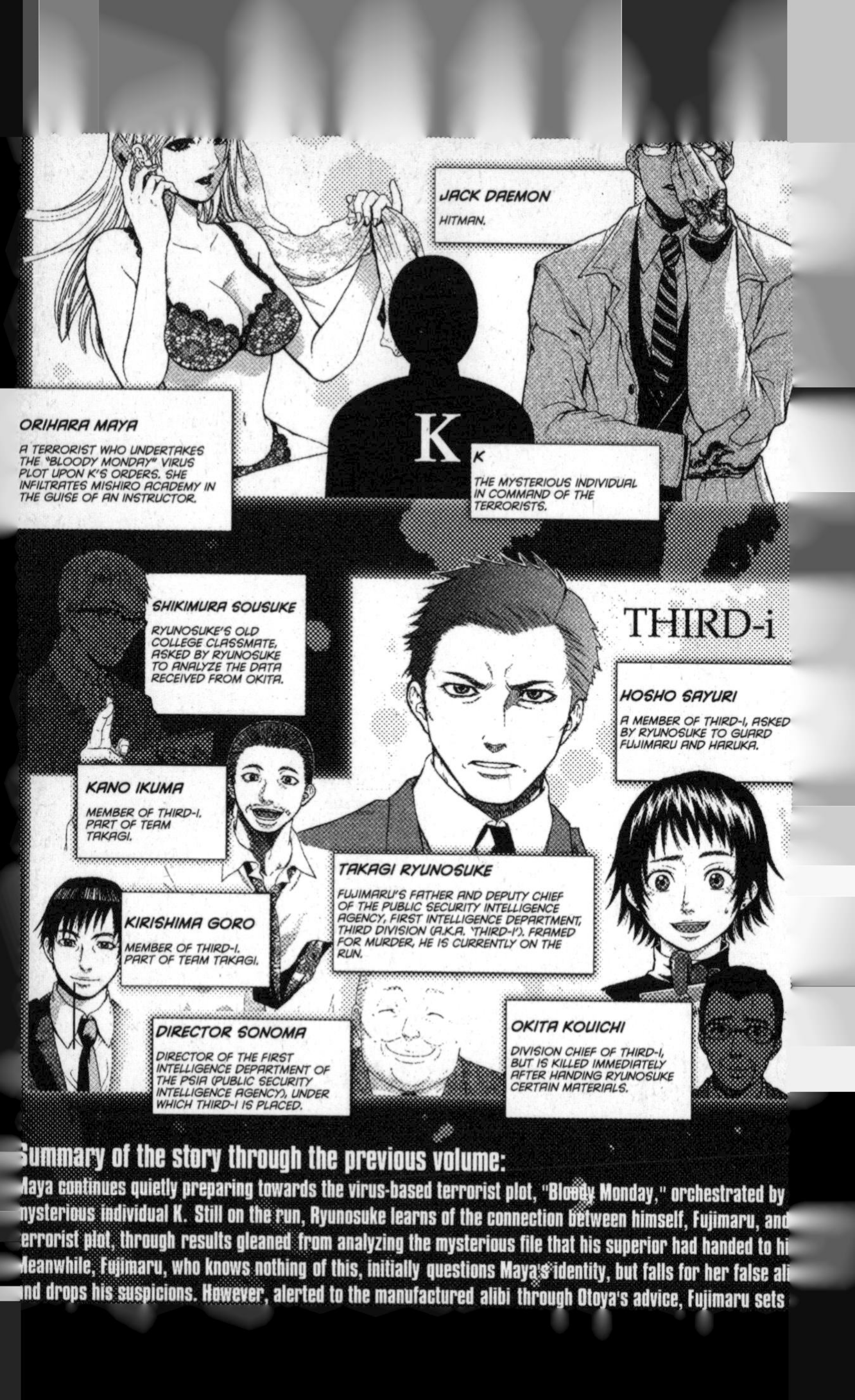
JACK DAEMON
HITMAN.
K
K
THE MYSTERIOUS INDIVIDUAL IN COMMAND OF THE TERRORISTS.
ORIHARA MAYA
A TERRORIST WHO UNDERTAKES THE "BLOODY MONDAY" VIRUS PLOT UPON K'S ORDERS. SHE INFILTRATES MISHIRO ACADEMY IN THE GUISE OF AN INSTRUCTOR.
THIRD-i
HOSHO SAYURI
A MEMBER OF THIRD-I, ASKED BY RYUNOSUKE TO GUARD FUJIMARU AND HARUKA.
SHIKIMURA SOUSUKE
RYUNOSUKE'S OLD COLLEGE CLASSMATE, ASKED BY RYUNOSUKE TO ANALYZE THE DATA RECEIVED FROM OKITA.
TAKAGI RYUNOSUKE
FUJIMARU'S FATHER AND DEPUTY CHIEF OF THE PUBLIC SECURITY INTELLIGENCE AGENCY, FIRST INTELLIGENCE DEPARTMENT, THIRD DIVISION (A.K.A. 'THIRD-I'). FRAMED FOR MURDER, HE IS CURRENTLY ON THE RUN.
KANO IKUMA
MEMBER OF THIRD-I. PART OF TEAM TAKAGI.
KIRISHIMA GORO
MEMBER OF THIRD-I. PART OF TEAM TAKAGI.
OKITA KOUICHI
DIVISION CHIEF OF THIRD-I, BUT IS KILLED IMMEDIATELY AFTER HANDING RYUNOSUKE CERTAIN MATERIALS.
DIRECTOR SONOMA
DIRECTOR OF THE FIRST INTELLIGENCE DEPARTMENT OF THE PSIA (PUBLIC SECURITY INTELLIGENCE AGENCY), UNDER WHICH THIRD-I IS PLACED.

Summary of the story through the previous volume:

Maya continues quietly preparing towards the virus-based terrorist plot, "Bloody Monday," orchestrated by mysterious individual K. Still on the run, Ryunosuke learns of the connection between himself, Fujimaru, and errorist plot, through results gleaned from analyzing the mysterious file that his superior had handed to hi Meanwhile, Fujimaru, who knows nothing of this, initially questions Maya's identity, but falls for her false ali nd drops his suspicions. However, alerted to the manufactured alibi through Otoya's advice, Fujimaru sets

Contents

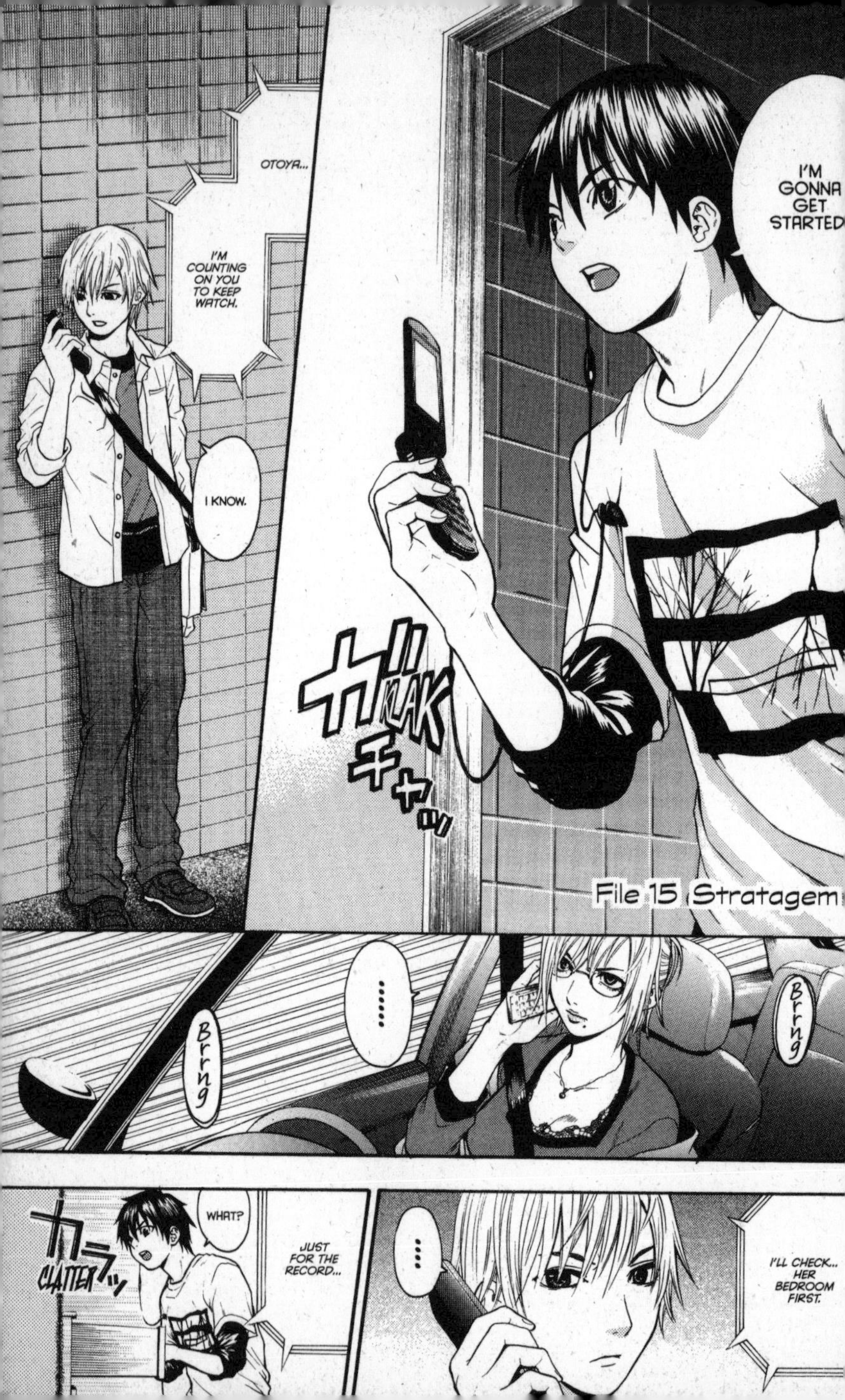
I'M GONNA GET STARTED
カチャッ
KLAK
File 15 Stratagem
OTOYA...
I'M COUNTING ON YOU TO KEEP WATCH.
I KNOW.
Brrng
......
Brrng
I'LL CHECK... HER BEDROOM FIRST.
....
JUST FOR THE RECORD...
WHAT?
カラッ
CLATTER

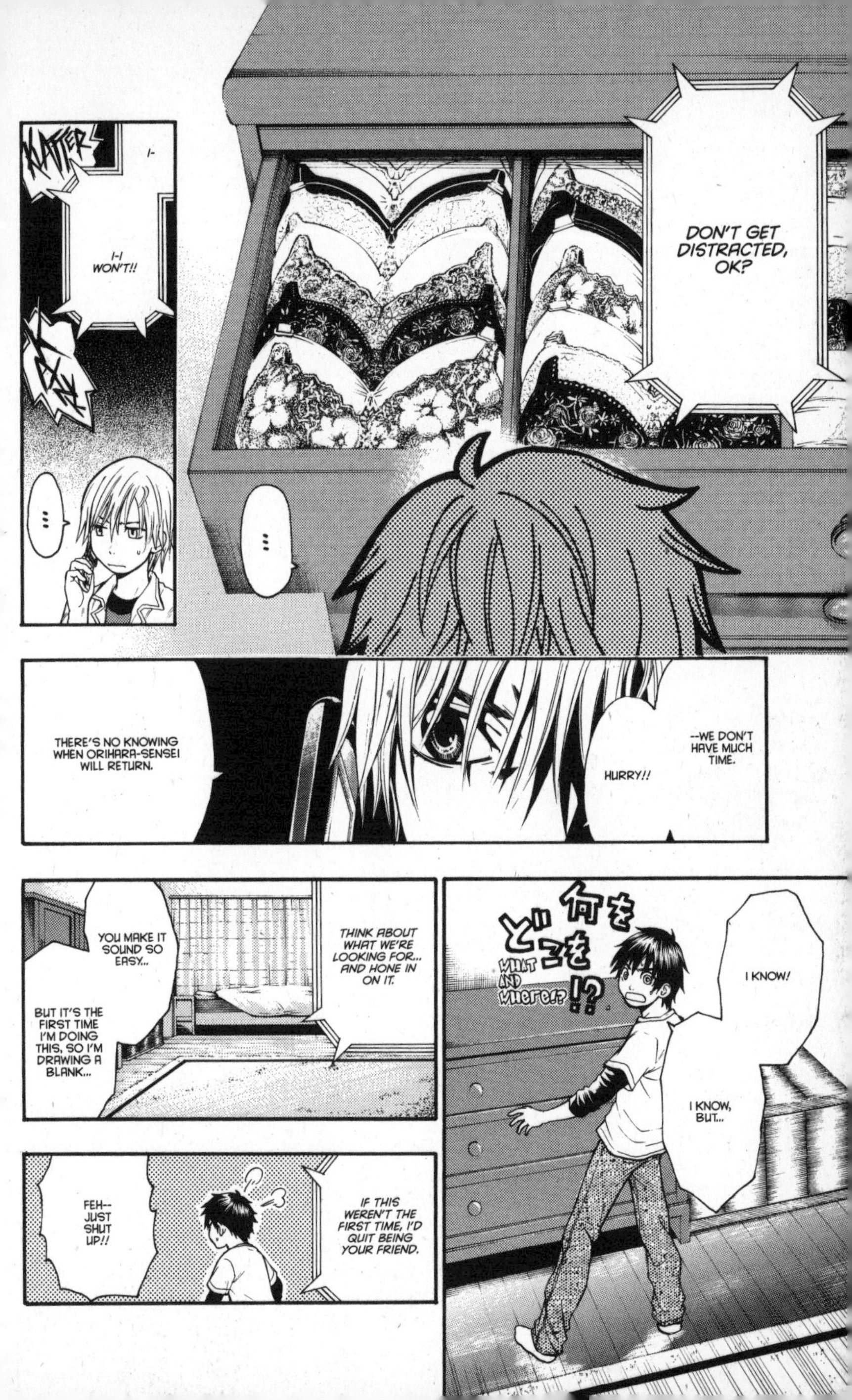
DON'T GET DISTRACTED, OK?
...
I-
KLATTER
I-I WON'T!!
...
--WE DON'T HAVE MUCH TIME.
HURRY!!
THERE'S NO KNOWING WHEN ORIHARA-SENSEI WILL RETURN.
何をどこを!?
WHAT AND WHERE!?
I KNOW!
I KNOW, BUT...
THINK ABOUT WHAT WE'RE LOOKING FOR... AND HONE IN ON IT.
YOU MAKE IT SOUND SO EASY...
BUT IT'S THE FIRST TIME I'M DOING THIS, SO I'M DRAWING A BLANK...
IF THIS WEREN'T THE FIRST TIME, I'D QUIT BEING YOUR FRIEND.
FEH-- JUST SHUT UP!!

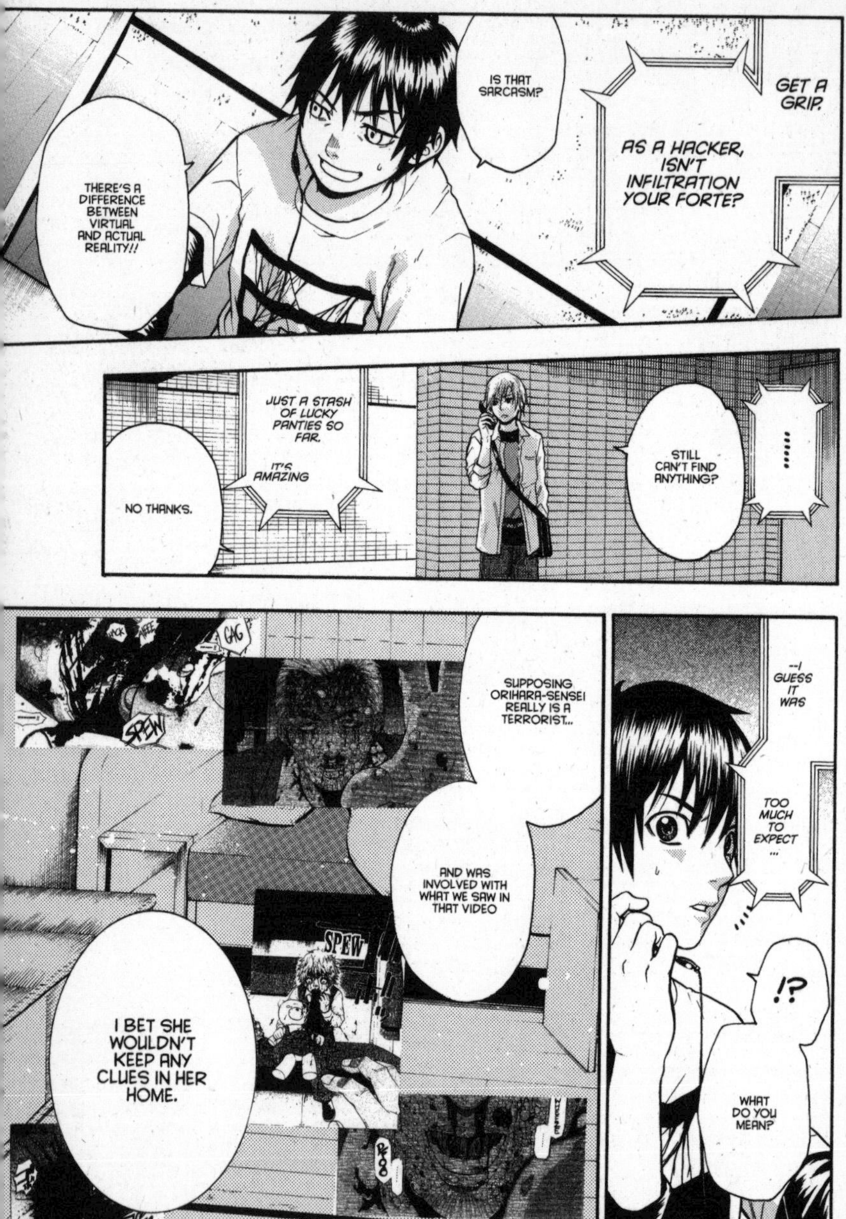
GET A GRIP.
AS A HACKER, ISN'T INFILTRATION YOUR FORTE?
IS THAT SARCASM?
THERE'S A DIFFERENCE BETWEEN VIRTUAL AND ACTUAL REALITY!!
......
STILL CAN'T FIND ANYTHING?
JUST A STASH OF LUCKY PANTIES SO FAR.
IT'S AMAZING
NO THANKS.
--I GUESS IT WAS
TOO MUCH TO EXPECT ...
...
!?
WHAT DO YOU MEAN?
SUPPOSING ORIHARA-SENSEI REALLY IS A TERRORIST...
AND WAS INVOLVED WITH WHAT WE SAW IN THAT VIDEO
GAG
SPEW
SPEW
I BET SHE WOULDN'T KEEP ANY CLUES IN HER HOME.

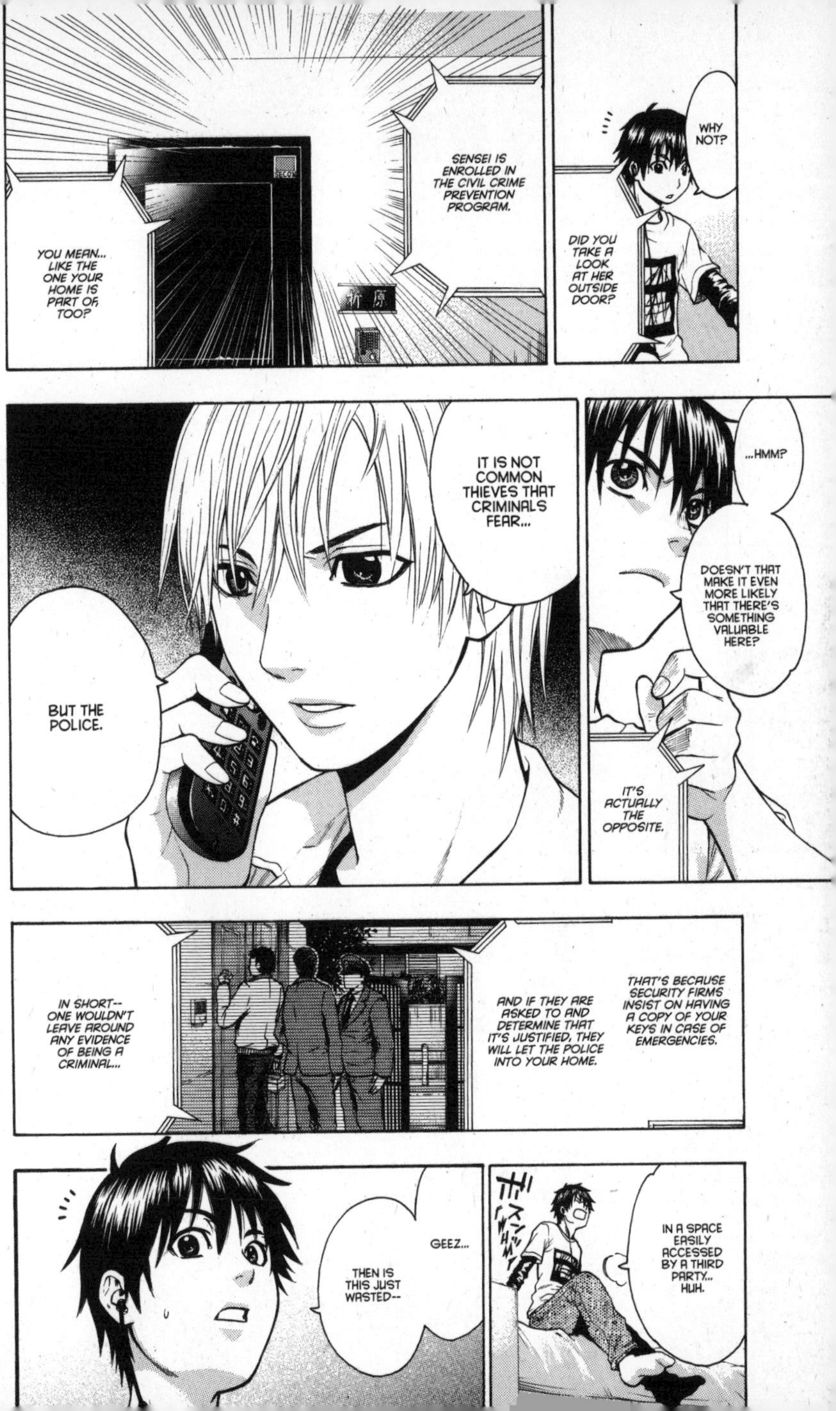
WHY NOT?
DID YOU TAKE A LOOK AT HER OUTSIDE DOOR?
SENSEI IS ENROLLED IN THE CIVIL CRIME PREVENTION PROGRAM.
YOU MEAN... LIKE THE ONE YOUR HOME IS PART OF, TOO?
...HMM?
DOESN'T THAT MAKE IT EVEN MORE LIKELY THAT THERE'S SOMETHING VALUABLE HERE?
IT'S ACTUALLY THE OPPOSITE.
IT IS NOT COMMON THIEVES THAT CRIMINALS FEAR...
BUT THE POLICE.
THAT'S BECAUSE SECURITY FIRMS INSIST ON HAVING A COPY OF YOUR KEYS IN CASE OF EMERGENCIES.
AND IF THEY ARE ASKED TO AND DETERMINE THAT IT'S JUSTIFIED, THEY WILL LET THE POLICE INTO YOUR HOME.
IN SHORT-- ONE WOULDN'T LEAVE AROUND ANY EVIDENCE OF BEING A CRIMINAL...
IN A SPACE EASILY ACCESSED BY A THIRD PARTY... HUH.
GEEZ...
THEN IS THIS JUST WASTED--

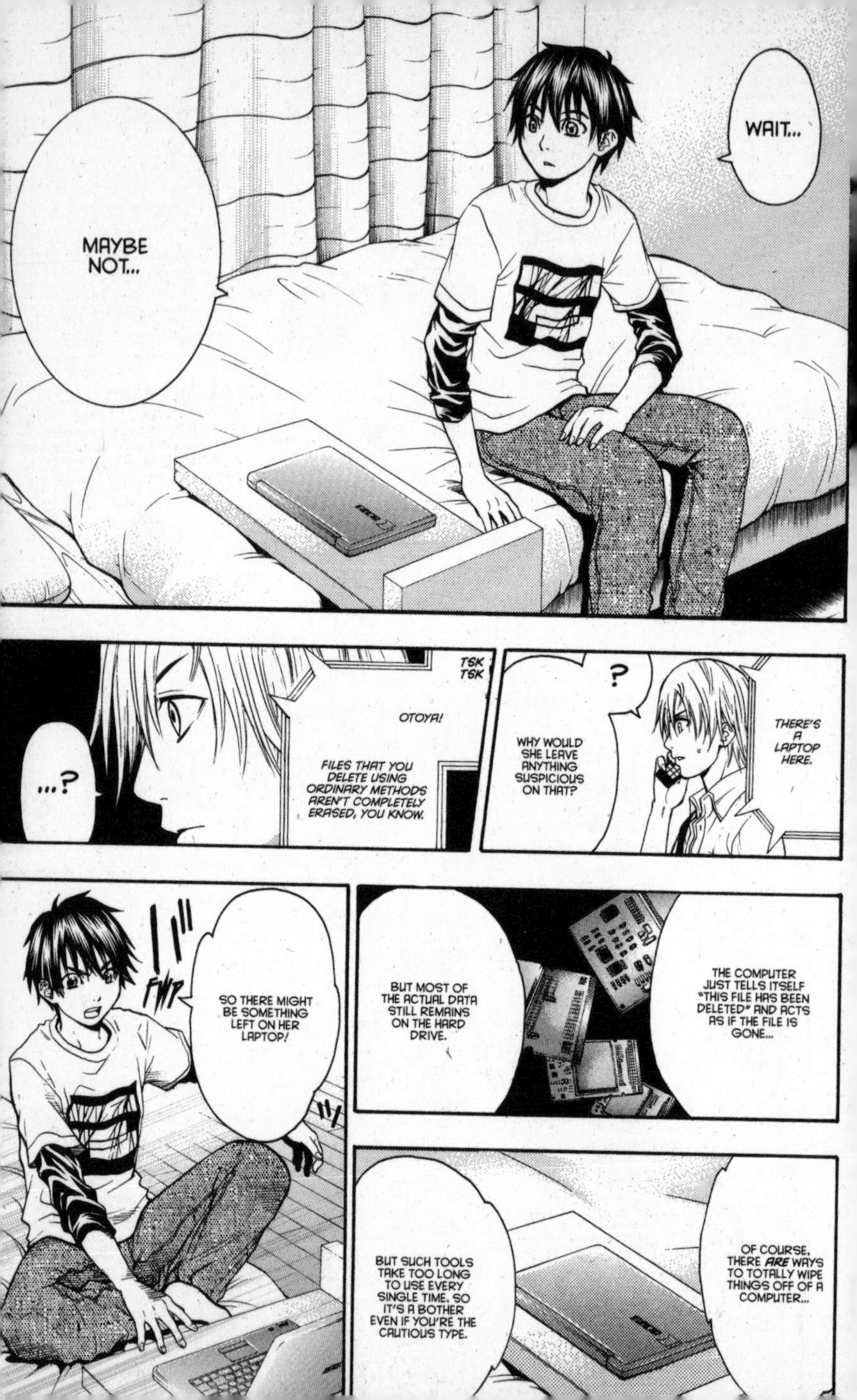
WAIT...
MAYBE NOT...
THERE'S A LAPTOP HERE.
?
WHY WOULD SHE LEAVE ANYTHING SUSPICIOUS ON THAT?
TSK TSK
OTOYA!
FILES THAT YOU DELETE USING ORDINARY METHODS AREN'T COMPLETELY ERASED, YOU KNOW.
...?
THE COMPUTER JUST TELLS ITSELF "THIS FILE HAS BEEN DELETED" AND ACTS AS IF THE FILE IS GONE...
BUT MOST OF THE ACTUAL DATA STILL REMAINS ON THE HARD DRIVE.
OF COURSE, THERE *ARE* WAYS TO TOTALLY WIPE THINGS OFF OF A COMPUTER...
BUT SUCH TOOLS TAKE TOO LONG TO USE EVERY SINGLE TIME, SO IT'S A BOTHER EVEN IF YOU'RE THE CAUTIOUS TYPE.
FWP
SO THERE MIGHT BE SOMETHING LEFT ON HER LAPTOP!

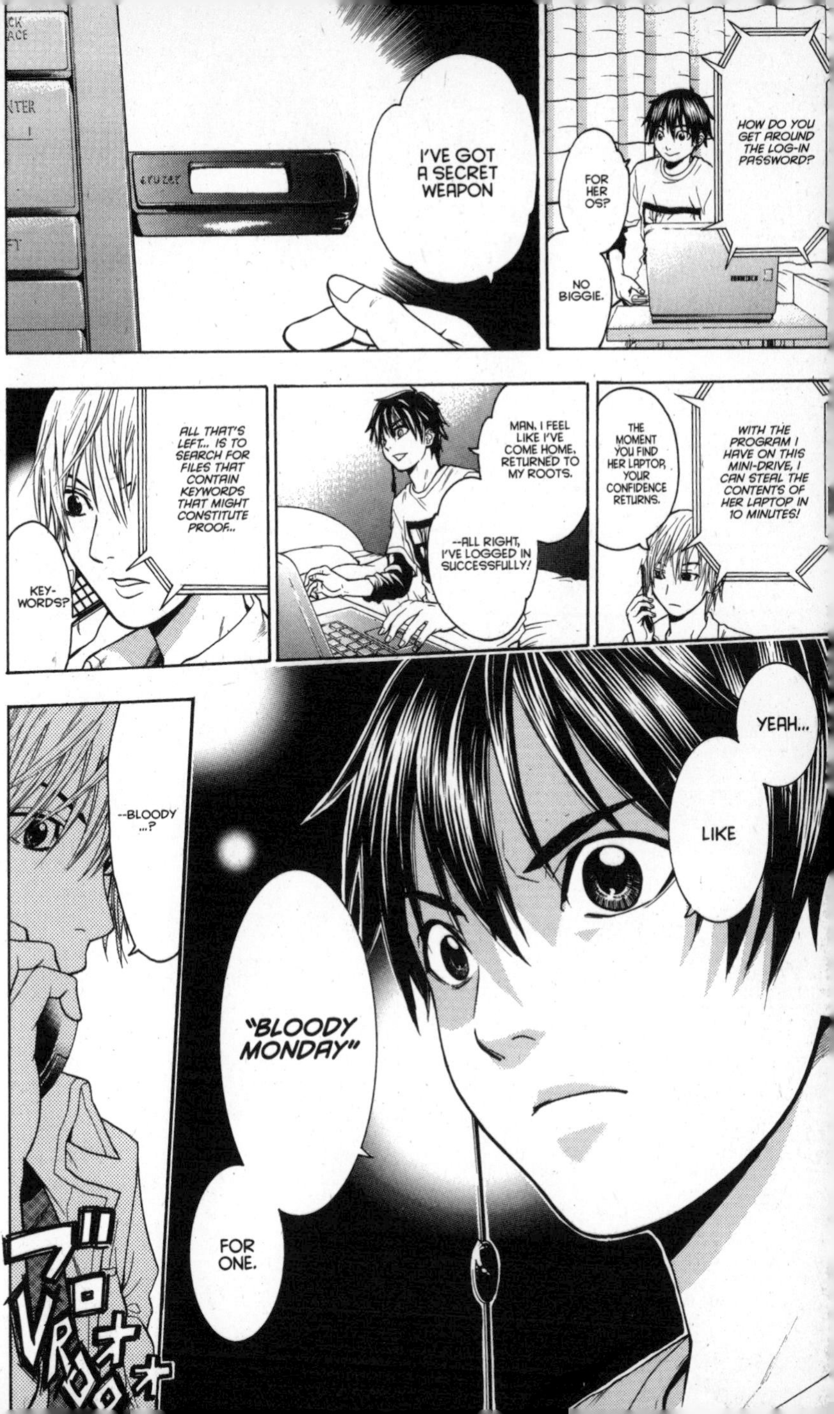
HOW DO YOU GET AROUND THE LOG-IN PASSWORD?
FOR HER OS?
NO BIGGIE.
I'VE GOT A SECRET WEAPON
WITH THE PROGRAM I HAVE ON THIS MINI-DRIVE, I CAN STEAL THE CONTENTS OF HER LAPTOP IN 10 MINUTES!
THE MOMENT YOU FIND HER LAPTOP, YOUR CONFIDENCE RETURNS.
MAN, I FEEL LIKE I'VE COME HOME, RETURNED TO MY ROOTS.
--ALL RIGHT, I'VE LOGGED IN SUCCESSFULLY!
ALL THAT'S LEFT... IS TO SEARCH FOR FILES THAT CONTAIN KEYWORDS THAT MIGHT CONSTITUTE PROOF...
KEY-WORDS?
YEAH...
LIKE
"BLOODY MONDAY"
FOR ONE.
--BLOODY ...?
ブロオオ
VROOO

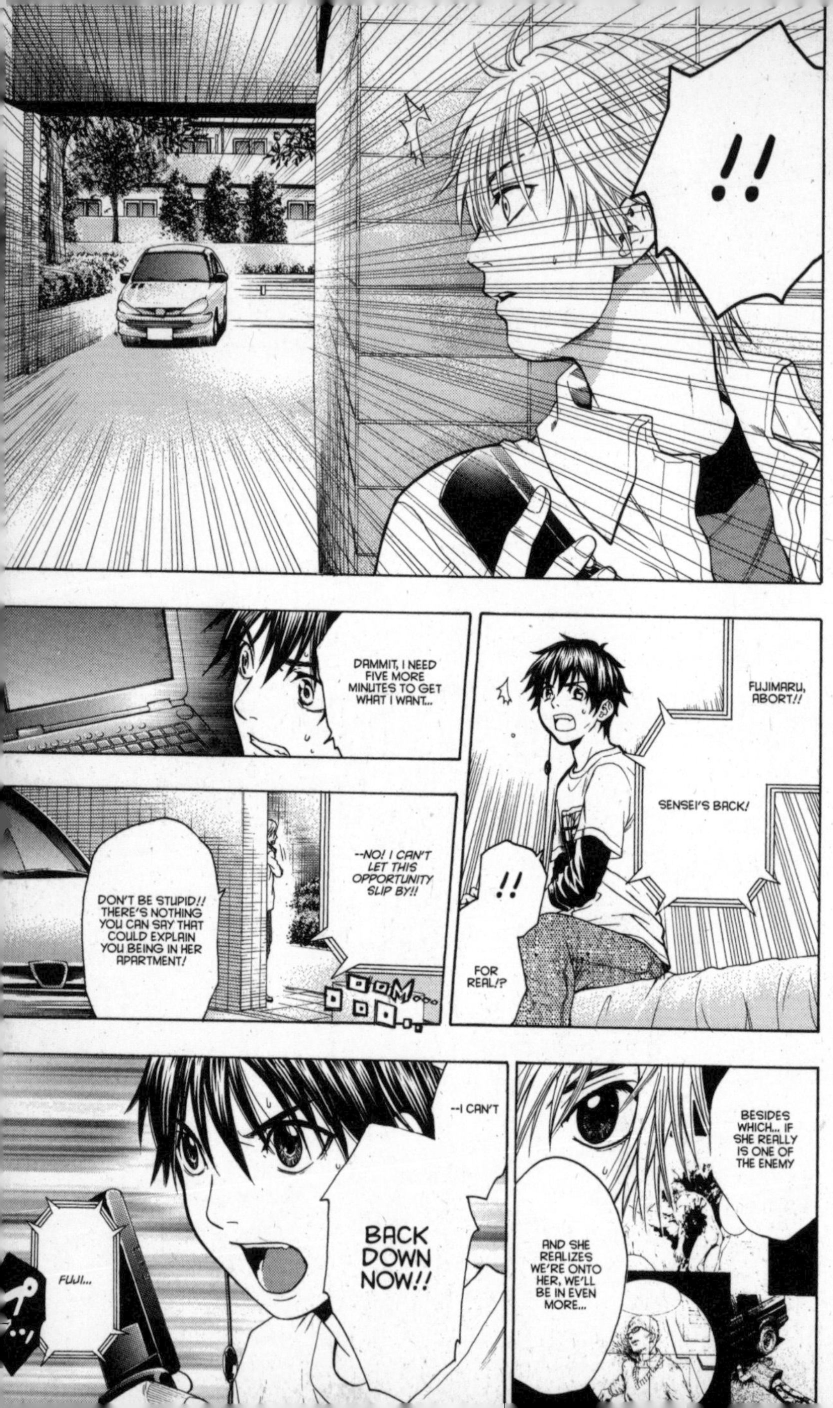
!!
FUJIMARU, ABORT!!
SENSEI'S BACK!
!!
FOR REAL!?
DAMMIT, I NEED FIVE MORE MINUTES TO GET WHAT I WANT...
--NO! I CAN'T LET THIS OPPORTUNITY SLIP BY!!
DOOM...
DON'T BE STUPID!! THERE'S NOTHING YOU CAN SAY THAT COULD EXPLAIN YOU BEING IN HER APARTMENT!
BESIDES WHICH... IF SHE REALLY IS ONE OF THE ENEMY
AND SHE REALIZES WE'RE ONTO HER, WE'LL BE IN EVEN MORE...
--I CAN'T
BACK DOWN NOW!!
FUJI...

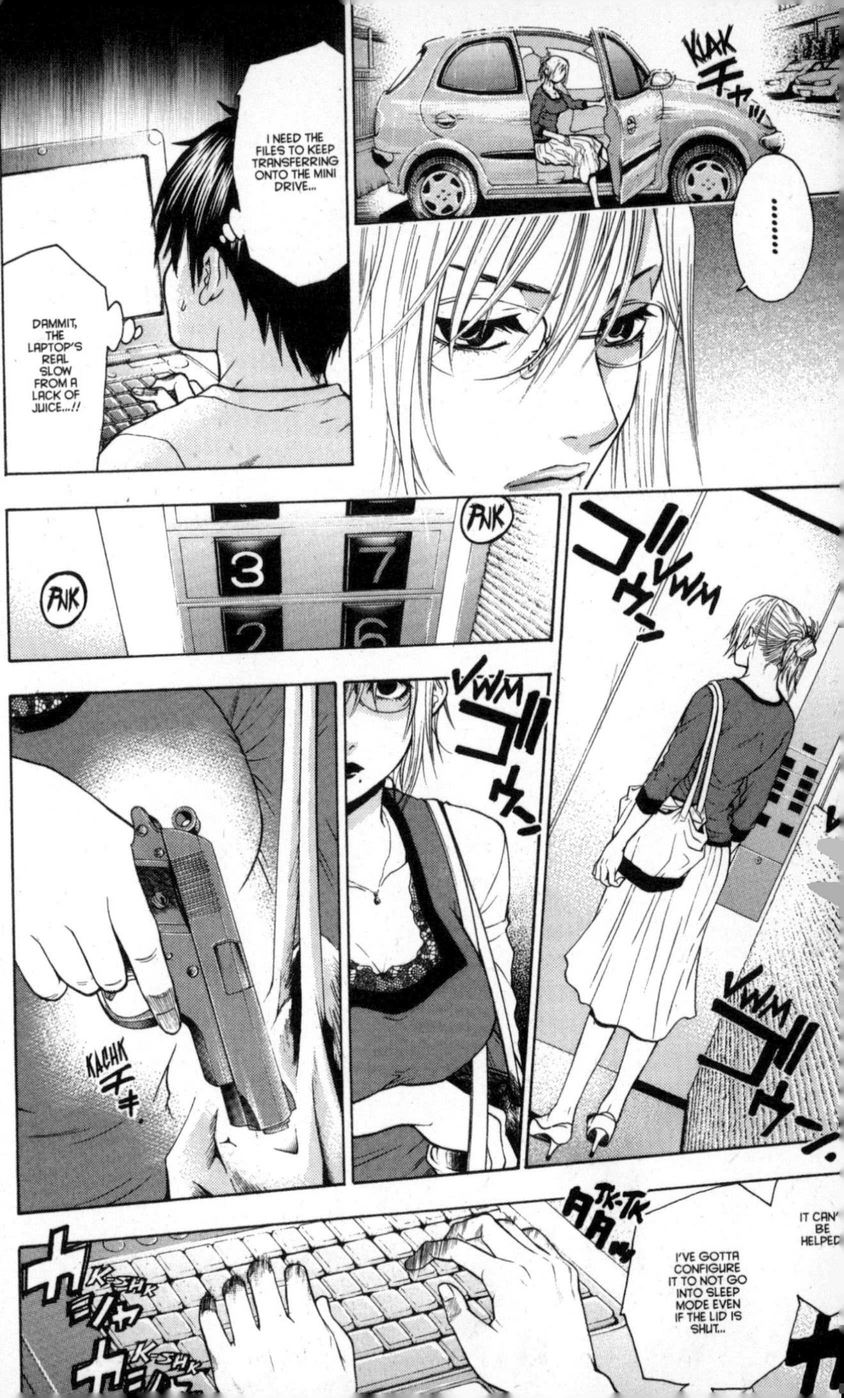
KLAK
......
I NEED THE FILES TO KEEP TRANSFERRING ONTO THE MINI DRIVE...
DAMMIT, THE LAPTOP'S REAL SLOW FROM A LACK OF JUICE...!!
VWM
VWM
VWM
PNK
PNK
VWM
KACHK
IT CAN'T BE HELPED
I'VE GOTTA CONFIGURE IT TO NOT GO INTO SLEEP MODE EVEN IF THE LID IS SHUT...
TK-TK
K-SHK
K-SHK

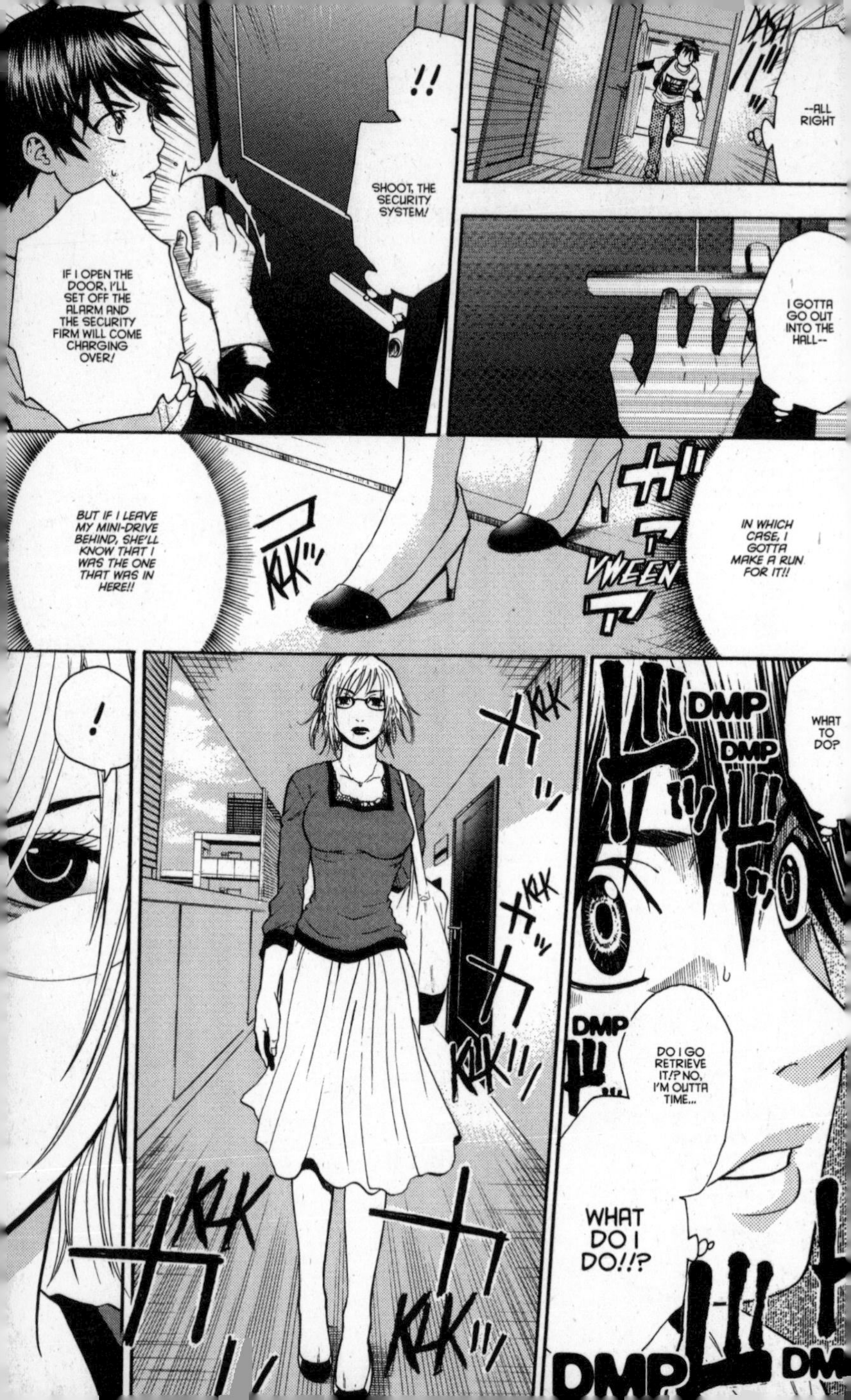
DASH
--ALL RIGHT
I GOTTA GO OUT INTO THE HALL--
!!
SHOOT, THE SECURITY SYSTEM!
IF I OPEN THE DOOR, I'LL SET OFF THE ALARM AND THE SECURITY FIRM WILL COME CHARGING OVER!
IN WHICH CASE, I GOTTA MAKE A RUN FOR IT!!
VWEEN
KLK
BUT IF I LEAVE MY MINI-DRIVE BEHIND, SHE'LL KNOW THAT I WAS THE ONE THAT WAS IN HERE!!
DMP
DMP
WHAT TO DO?
DMP
DO I GO RETRIEVE IT!? NO, I'M OUTTA TIME...
WHAT DO I DO!!?
DMP
DM
KLK
KLK
KLK
KLK
KLK
!

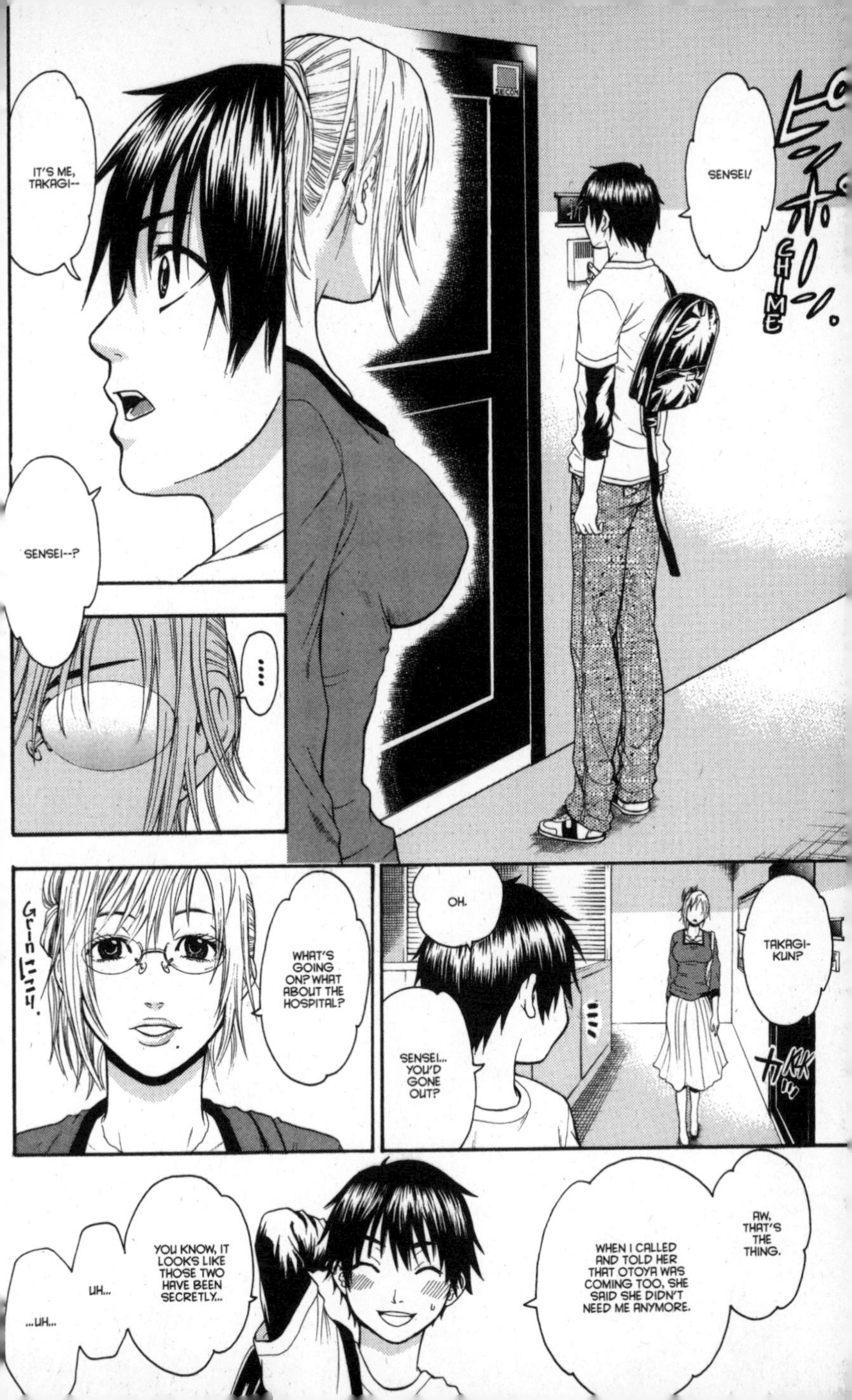
CHIME
SENSEI!
IT'S ME, TAKAGI--
SENSEI--?
....
TAKAGI-KUN?
KAKK
OH.
SENSEI... YOU'D GONE OUT?
WHAT'S GOING ON? WHAT ABOUT THE HOSPITAL?
Grin
AW, THAT'S THE THING.
WHEN I CALLED AND TOLD HER THAT OTOYA WAS COMING TOO, SHE SAID SHE DIDN'T NEED ME ANYMORE.
YOU KNOW, IT LOOKS LIKE THOSE TWO HAVE BEEN SECRETLY...
UH...
...UH...

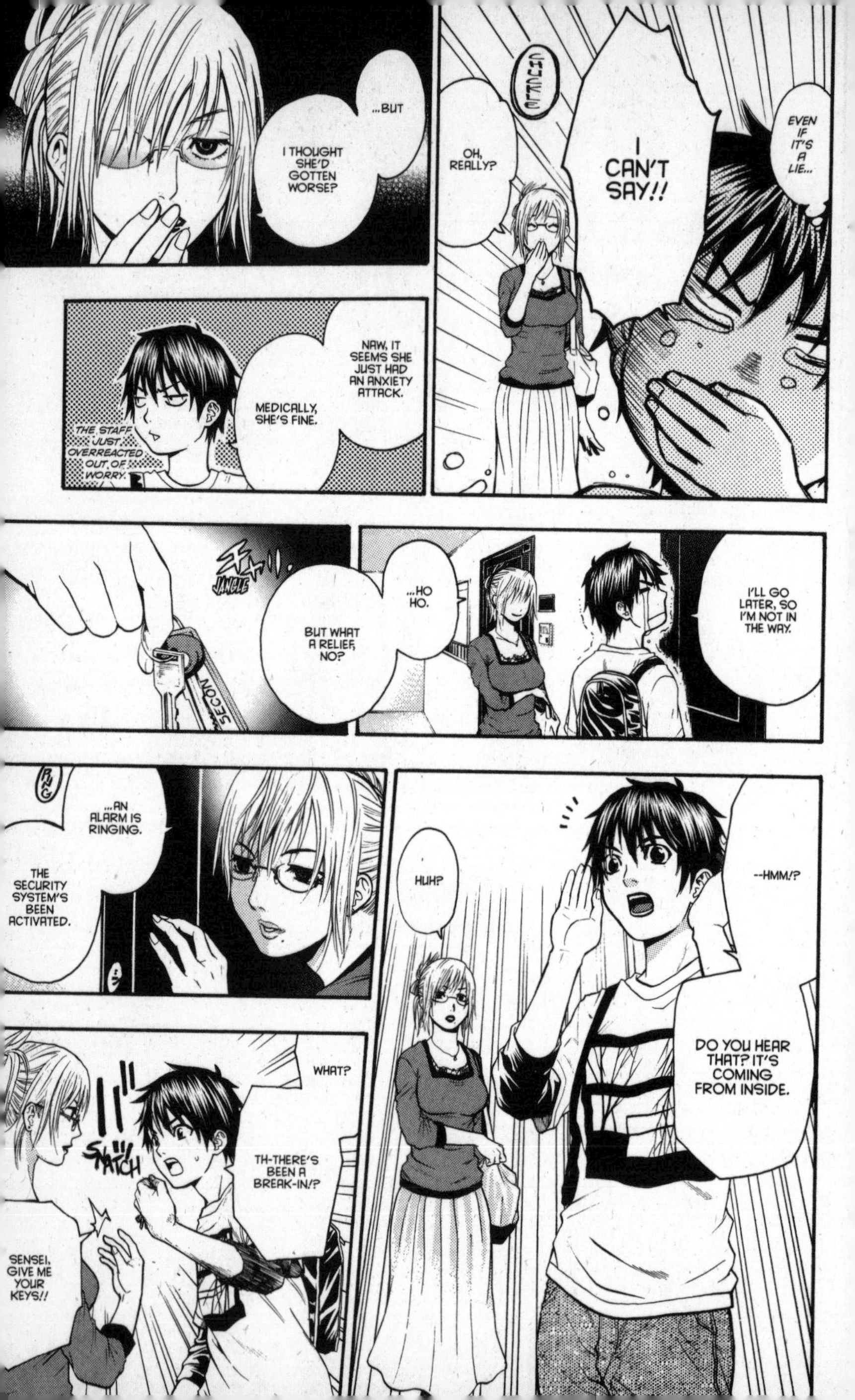
EVEN IF IT'S A LIE...
I CAN'T SAY!!
CHUCKLE
OH, REALLY?
...BUT
I THOUGHT SHE'D GOTTEN WORSE?
NAW, IT SEEMS SHE JUST HAD AN ANXIETY ATTACK.
MEDICALLY, SHE'S FINE.
THE STAFF JUST OVERREACTED OUT OF WORRY.
I'LL GO LATER, SO I'M NOT IN THE WAY.
...HO HO.
BUT WHAT A RELIEF, NO?
チャリ
JANGLE
SECOM
--HMM!?
HUH?
DO YOU HEAR THAT? IT'S COMING FROM INSIDE.
RING
...AN ALARM IS RINGING.
THE SECURITY SYSTEM'S BEEN ACTIVATED.
WHAT?
TH-THERE'S BEEN A BREAK-IN!?
SNATCH
SENSEI, GIVE ME YOUR KEYS!!

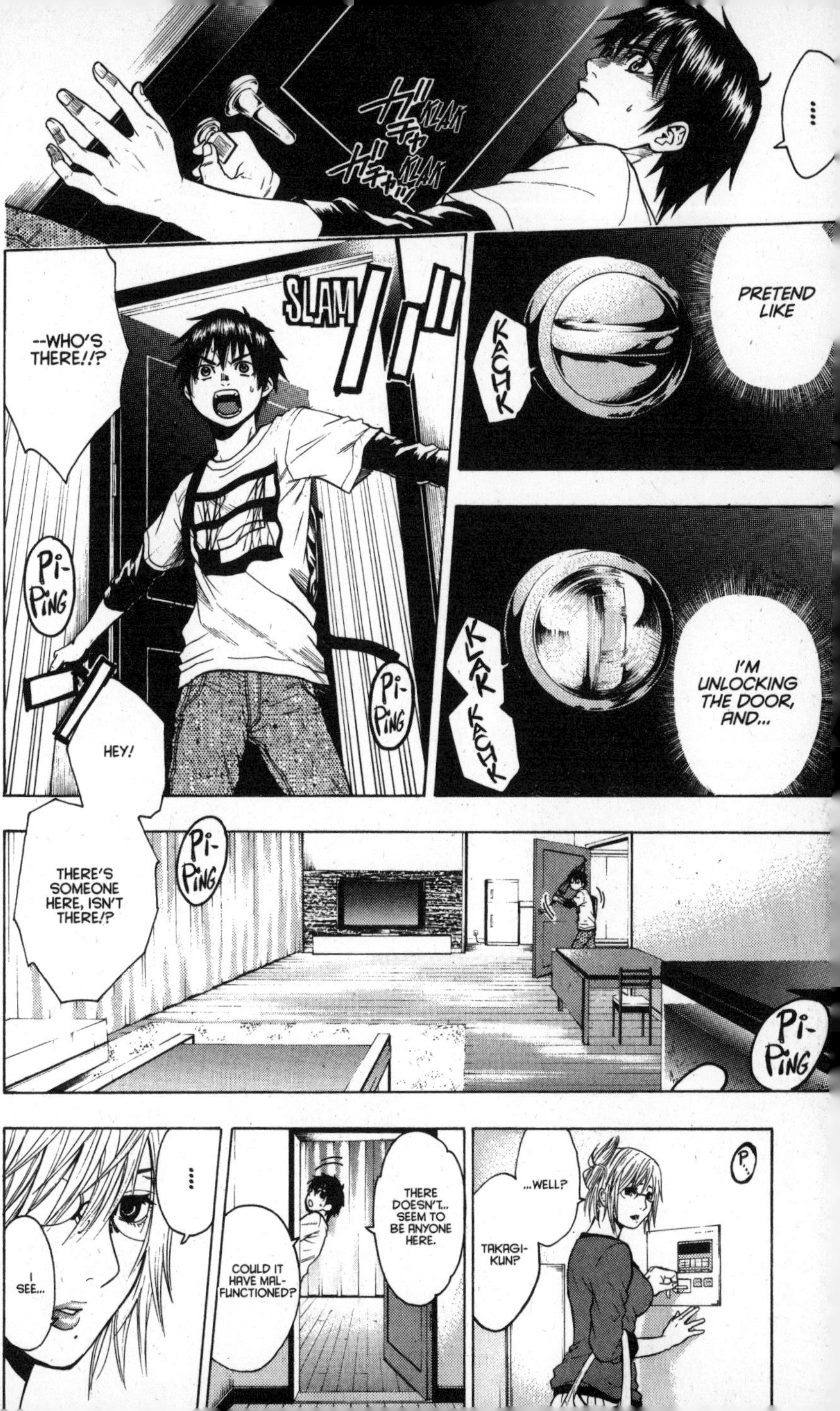
....
KLAK
KLAK
PRETEND LIKE
KACHK
I'M UNLOCKING THE DOOR, AND...
KLAK KACHK
SLAM
--WHO'S THERE!!?
Pi-PING
Pi-PING
HEY!
THERE'S SOMEONE HERE, ISN'T THERE!?
Pi-PING
Pi-PING
P...
...WELL?
TAKAGI-KUN?
THERE DOESN'T... SEEM TO BE ANYONE HERE.
COULD IT HAVE MAL-FUNCTIONED?
....
I SEE...

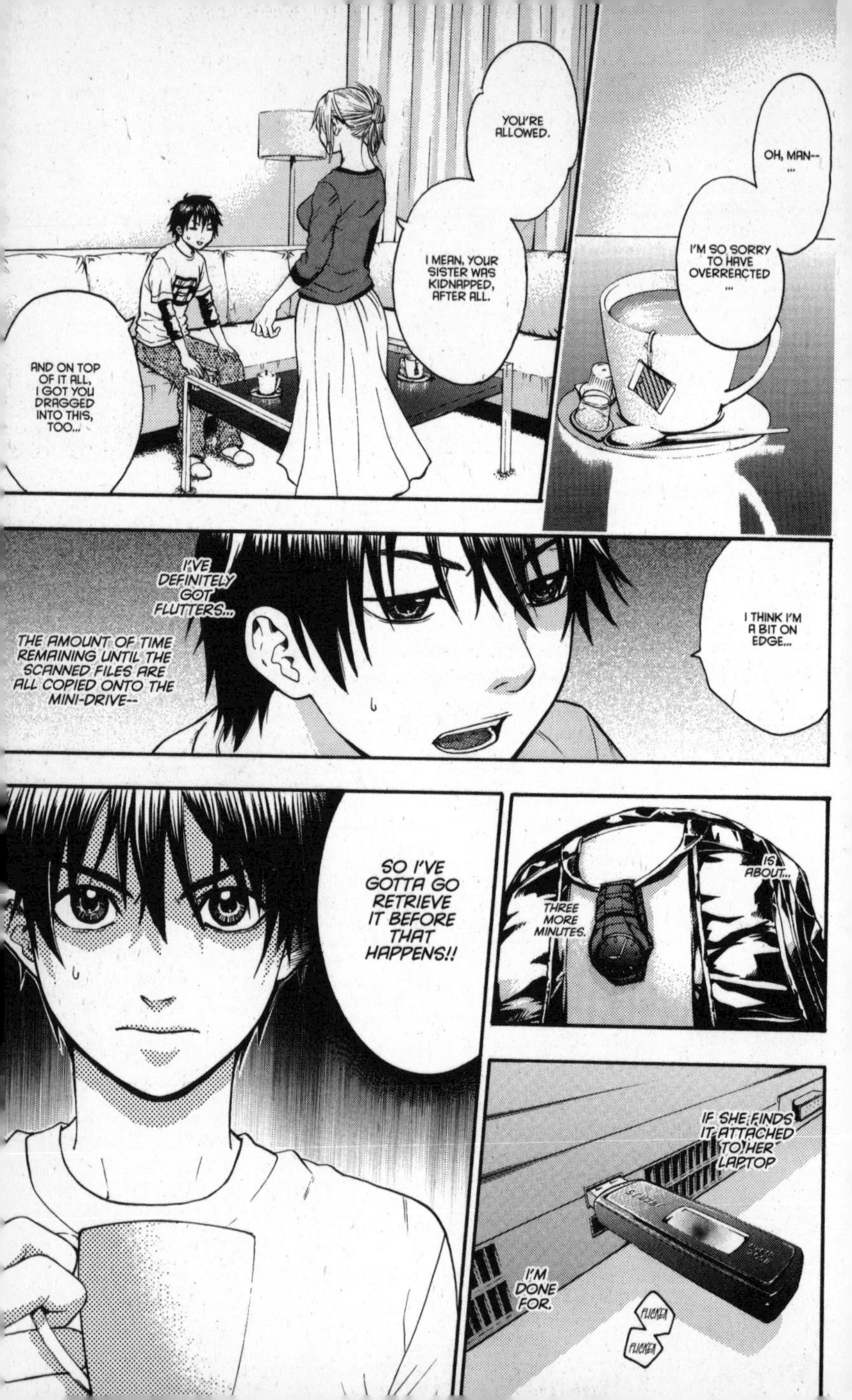
OH, MAN--...
I'M SO SORRY TO HAVE OVERREACTED ...
YOU'RE ALLOWED.
I MEAN, YOUR SISTER WAS KIDNAPPED, AFTER ALL.
AND ON TOP OF IT ALL, I GOT YOU DRAGGED INTO THIS, TOO...
I THINK I'M A BIT ON EDGE...
I'VE DEFINITELY GOT FLUTTERS...
THE AMOUNT OF TIME REMAINING UNTIL THE SCANNED FILES ARE ALL COPIED ONTO THE MINI-DRIVE--
IS ABOUT...
THREE MORE MINUTES.
IF SHE FINDS IT ATTACHED TO HER LAPTOP
I'M DONE FOR.
FLICKER
FLICKER
SO I'VE GOTTA GO RETRIEVE IT BEFORE THAT HAPPENS!!

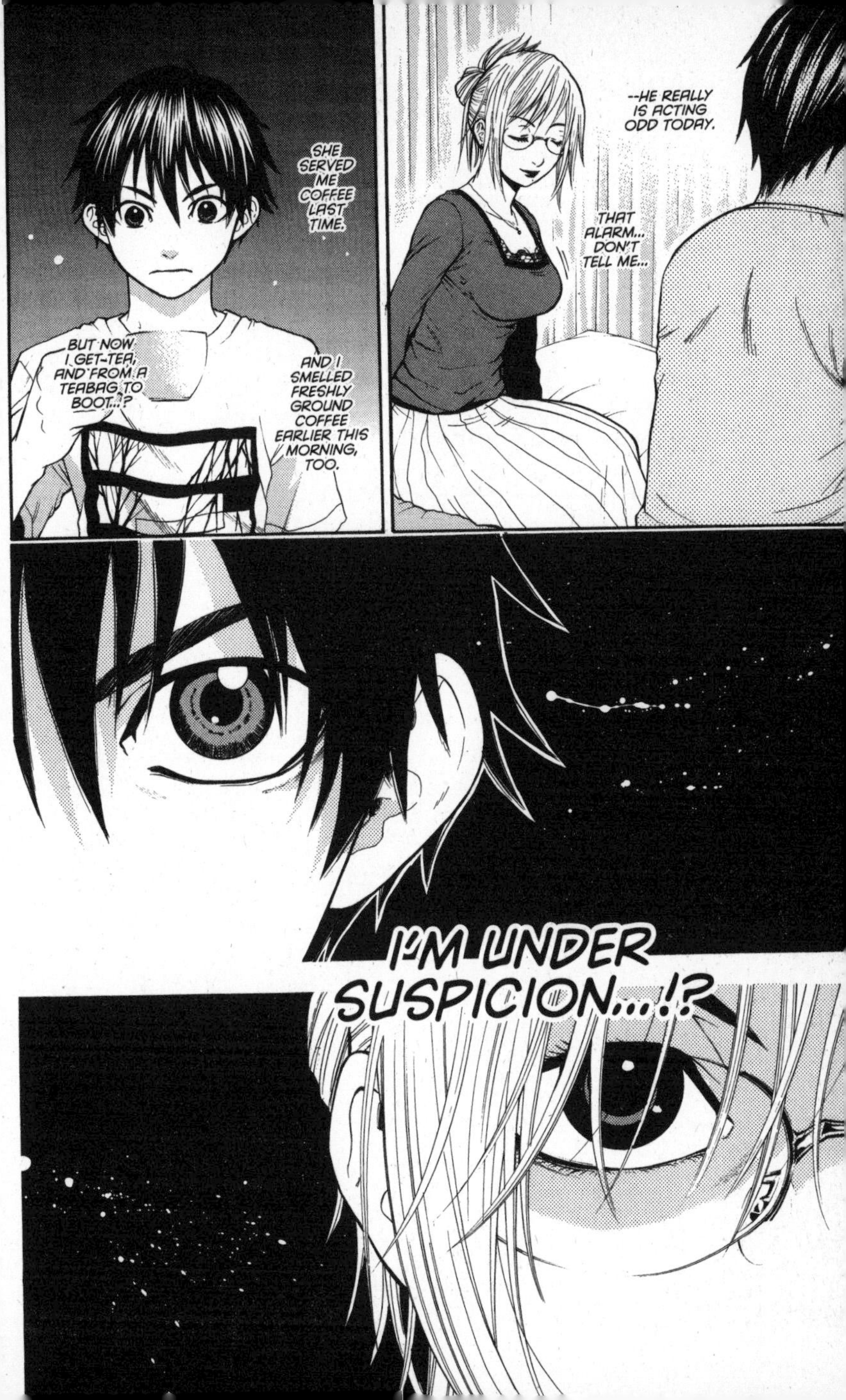
--HE REALLY IS ACTING ODD TODAY.
THAT ALARM... DON'T TELL ME...
SHE SERVED ME COFFEE LAST TIME.
AND I SMELLED FRESHLY GROUND COFFEE EARLIER THIS MORNING, TOO.
BUT NOW I GET TEA, AND FROM A TEABAG TO BOOT...?
I'M UNDER SUSPICION...!?

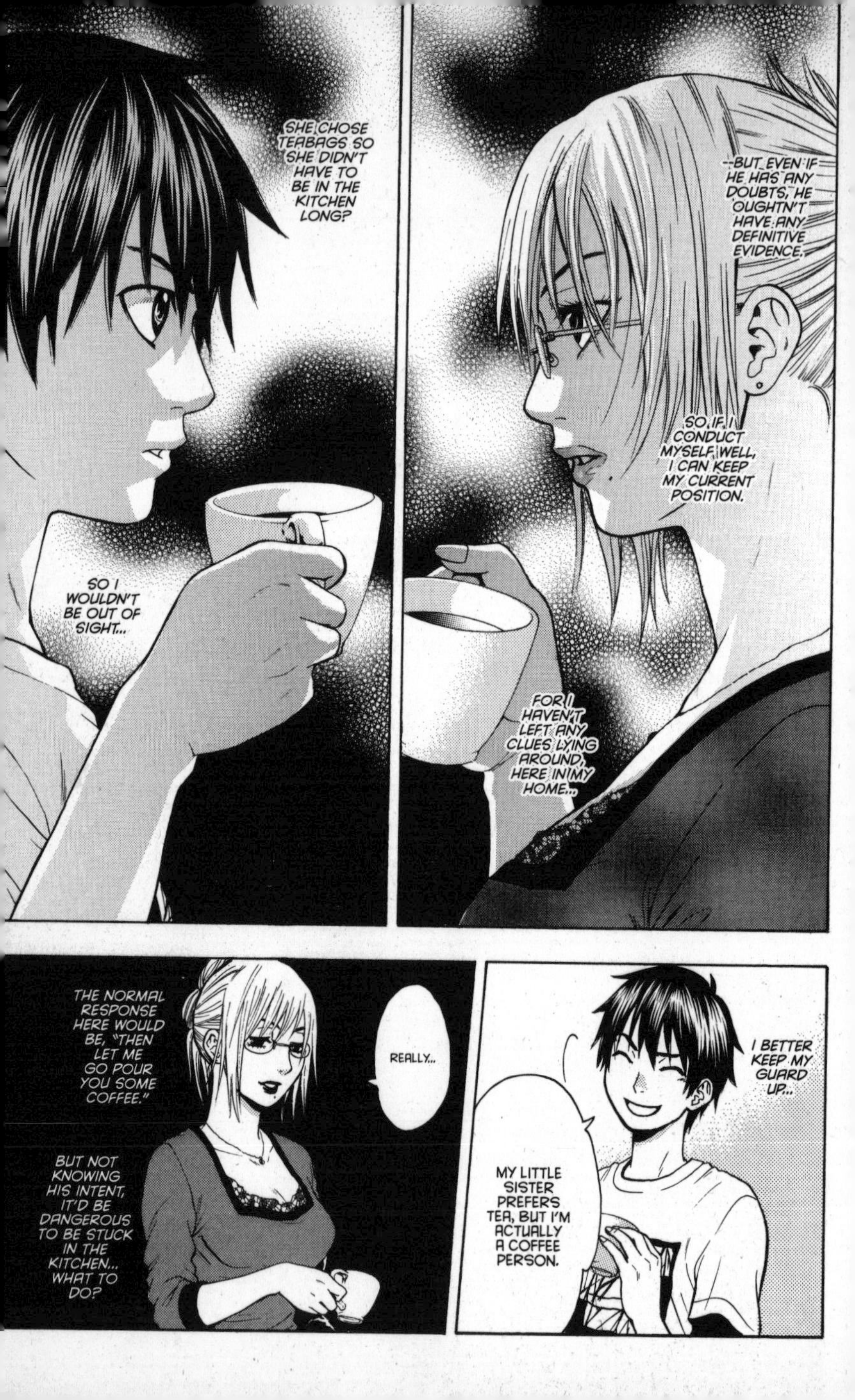
--BUT EVEN IF HE HAS ANY DOUBTS, HE OUGHTN'T HAVE ANY DEFINITIVE EVIDENCE.
SO, IF I CONDUCT MYSELF WELL, I CAN KEEP MY CURRENT POSITION.
FOR I HAVEN'T LEFT ANY CLUES LYING AROUND, HERE IN MY HOME...
SHE CHOSE TEABAGS SO SHE DIDN'T HAVE TO BE IN THE KITCHEN LONG?
SO I WOULDN'T BE OUT OF SIGHT...
I BETTER KEEP MY GUARD UP...
MY LITTLE SISTER PREFERS TEA, BUT I'M ACTUALLY A COFFEE PERSON.
REALLY...
THE NORMAL RESPONSE HERE WOULD BE, "THEN LET ME GO POUR YOU SOME COFFEE."
BUT NOT KNOWING HIS INTENT, IT'D BE DANGEROUS TO BE STUCK IN THE KITCHEN... WHAT TO DO?

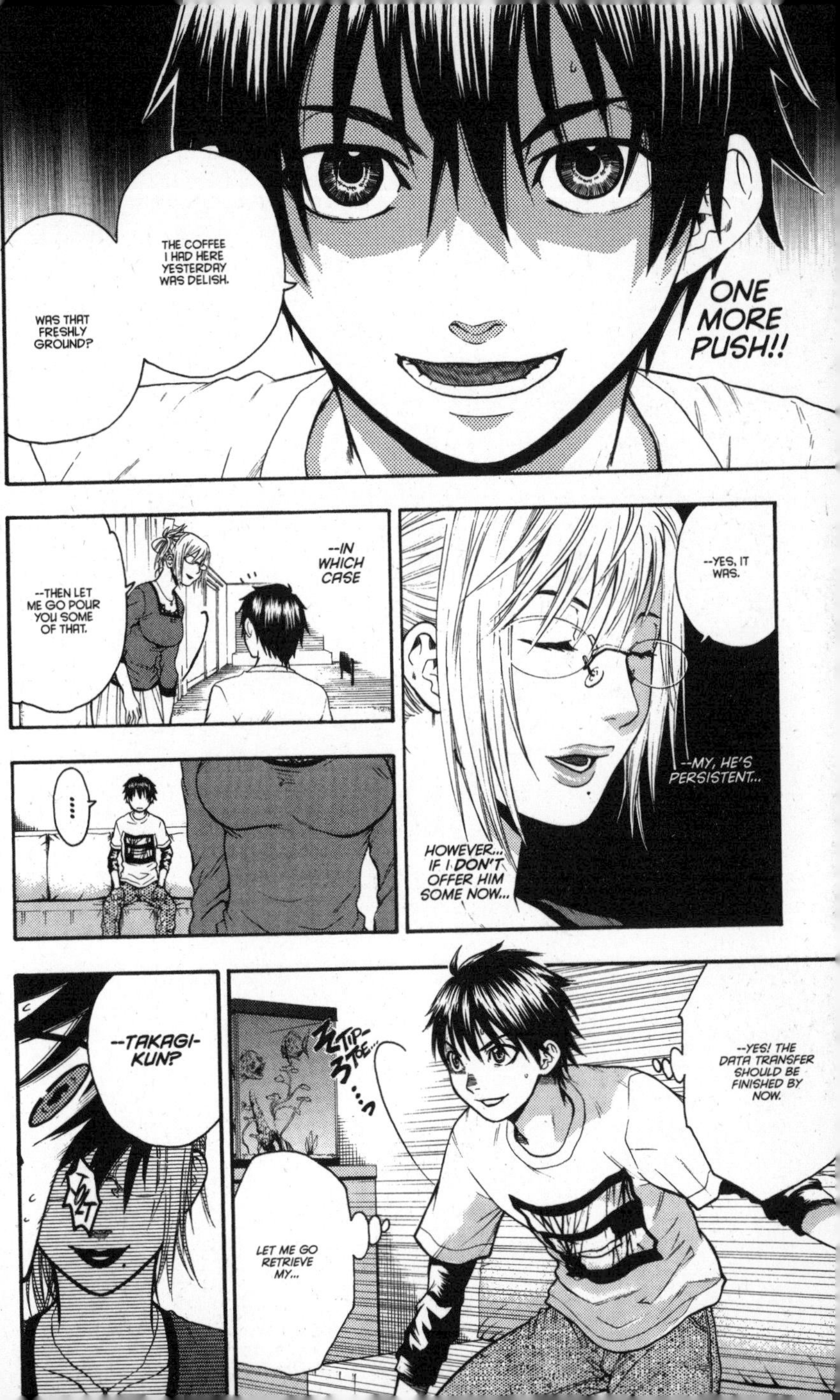
ONE MORE PUSH!!
THE COFFEE I HAD HERE YESTERDAY WAS DELISH.
WAS THAT FRESHLY GROUND?
--YES, IT WAS.
--MY, HE'S PERSISTENT...
HOWEVER... IF I DON'T OFFER HIM SOME NOW...
--IN WHICH CASE
--THEN LET ME GO POUR YOU SOME OF THAT.
....
--YES! THE DATA TRANSFER SHOULD BE FINISHED BY NOW.
TIP-TOE...
LET ME GO RETRIEVE MY...
--TAKAGI-KUN?
JOLT

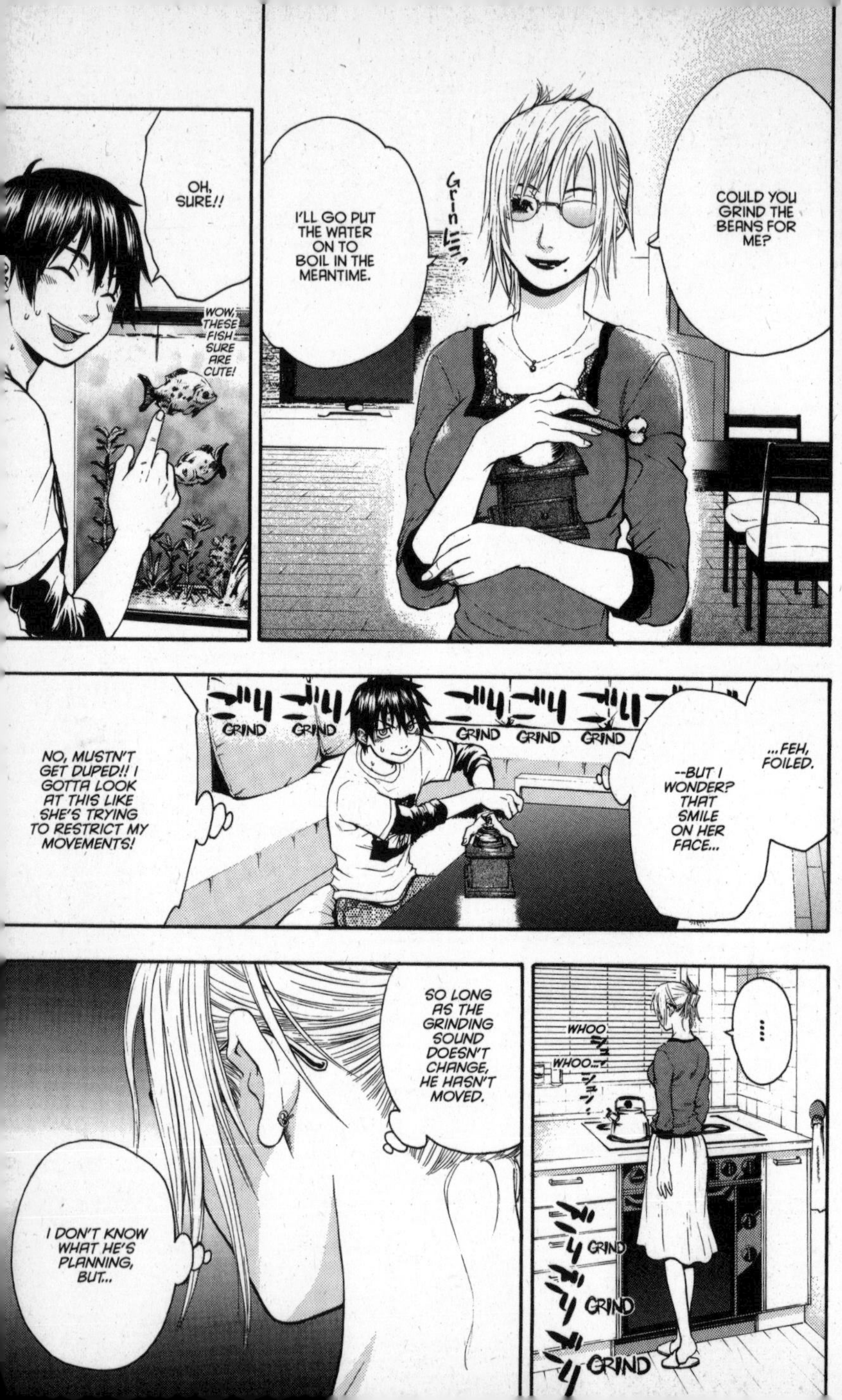

COULD YOU GRIND THE BEANS FOR ME?
Grin
I'LL GO PUT THE WATER ON TO BOIL IN THE MEANTIME.
OH, SURE!!
WOW, THESE FISH SURE ARE CUTE!
...FEH, FOILED.
--BUT I WONDER? THAT SMILE ON HER FACE...
GRIND GRIND GRIND GRIND GRIND
NO, MUSTN'T GET DUPED!! I GOTTA LOOK AT THIS LIKE SHE'S TRYING TO RESTRICT MY MOVEMENTS!
....
WHOO
WHOO...
GRIND
GRIND
GRIND
SO LONG AS THE GRINDING SOUND DOESN'T CHANGE, HE HASN'T MOVED.
I DON'T KNOW WHAT HE'S PLANNING, BUT...

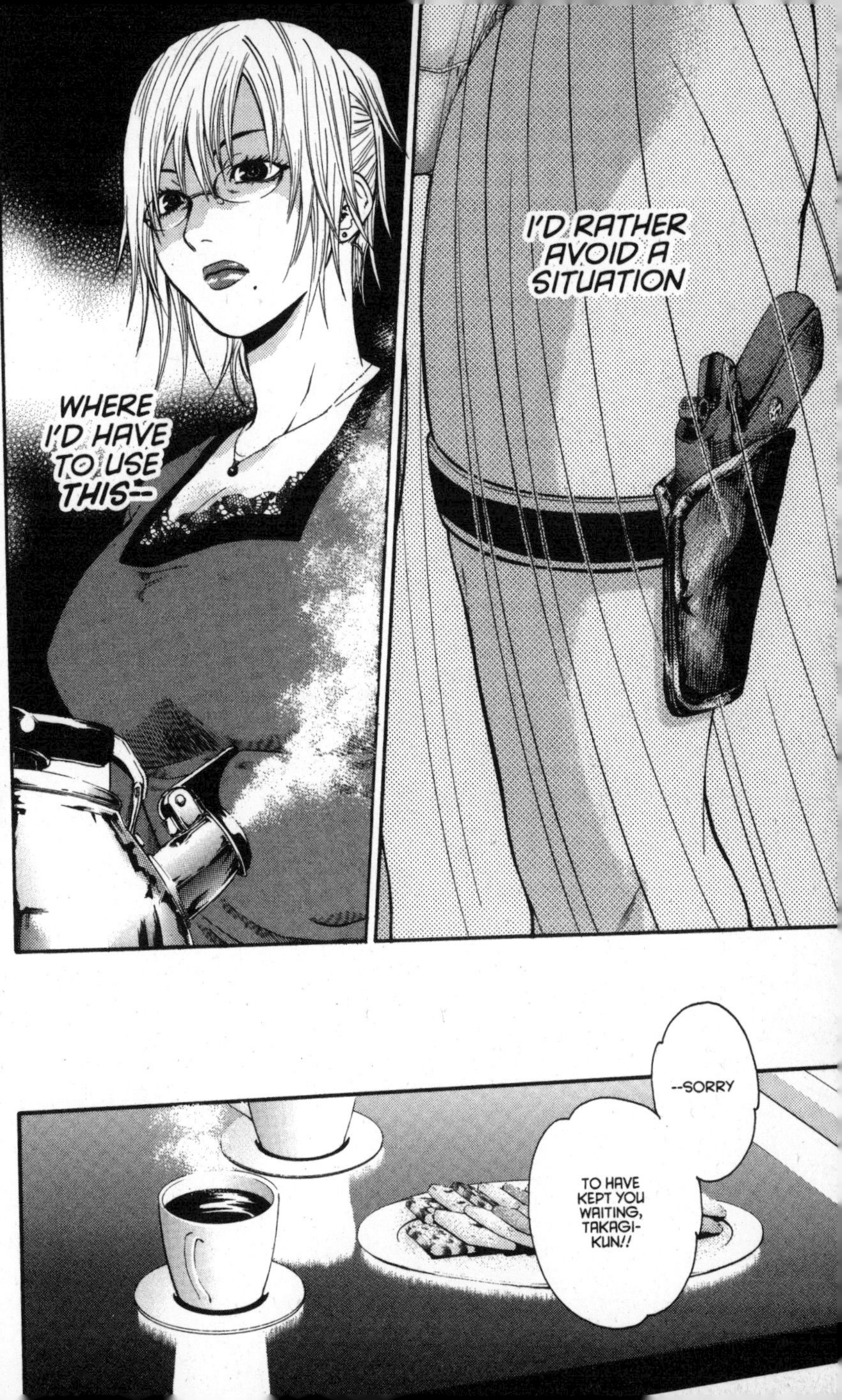
I'D RATHER AVOID A SITUATION
WHERE I'D HAVE TO USE THIS--
--SORRY
TO HAVE KEPT YOU WAITING, TAKAGI-KUN!!

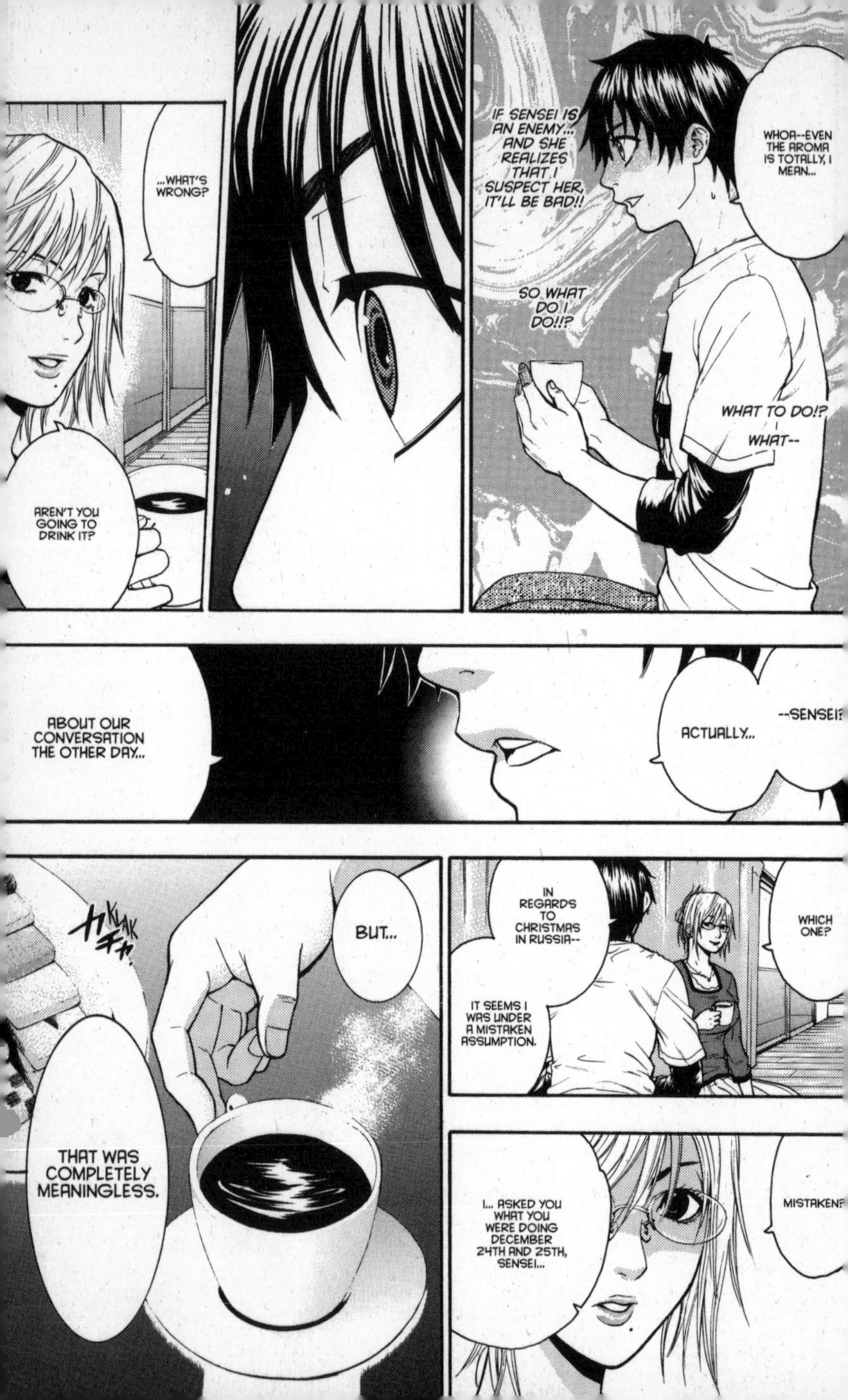
WHOA--EVEN THE AROMA IS TOTALLY, I MEAN...
WHAT--
WHAT TO DO!?
IF SENSEI IS AN ENEMY... AND SHE REALIZES THAT I SUSPECT HER, IT'LL BE BAD!!
SO WHAT DO I DO!!?
...WHAT'S WRONG?
AREN'T YOU GOING TO DRINK IT?
--SENSEI?
ACTUALLY...
ABOUT OUR CONVERSATION THE OTHER DAY...
WHICH ONE?
IN REGARDS TO CHRISTMAS IN RUSSIA--
IT SEEMS I WAS UNDER A MISTAKEN ASSUMPTION.
MISTAKEN?
I... ASKED YOU WHAT YOU WERE DOING DECEMBER 24TH AND 25TH, SENSEI...
KLAK
BUT...
THAT WAS COMPLETELY MEANINGLESS.

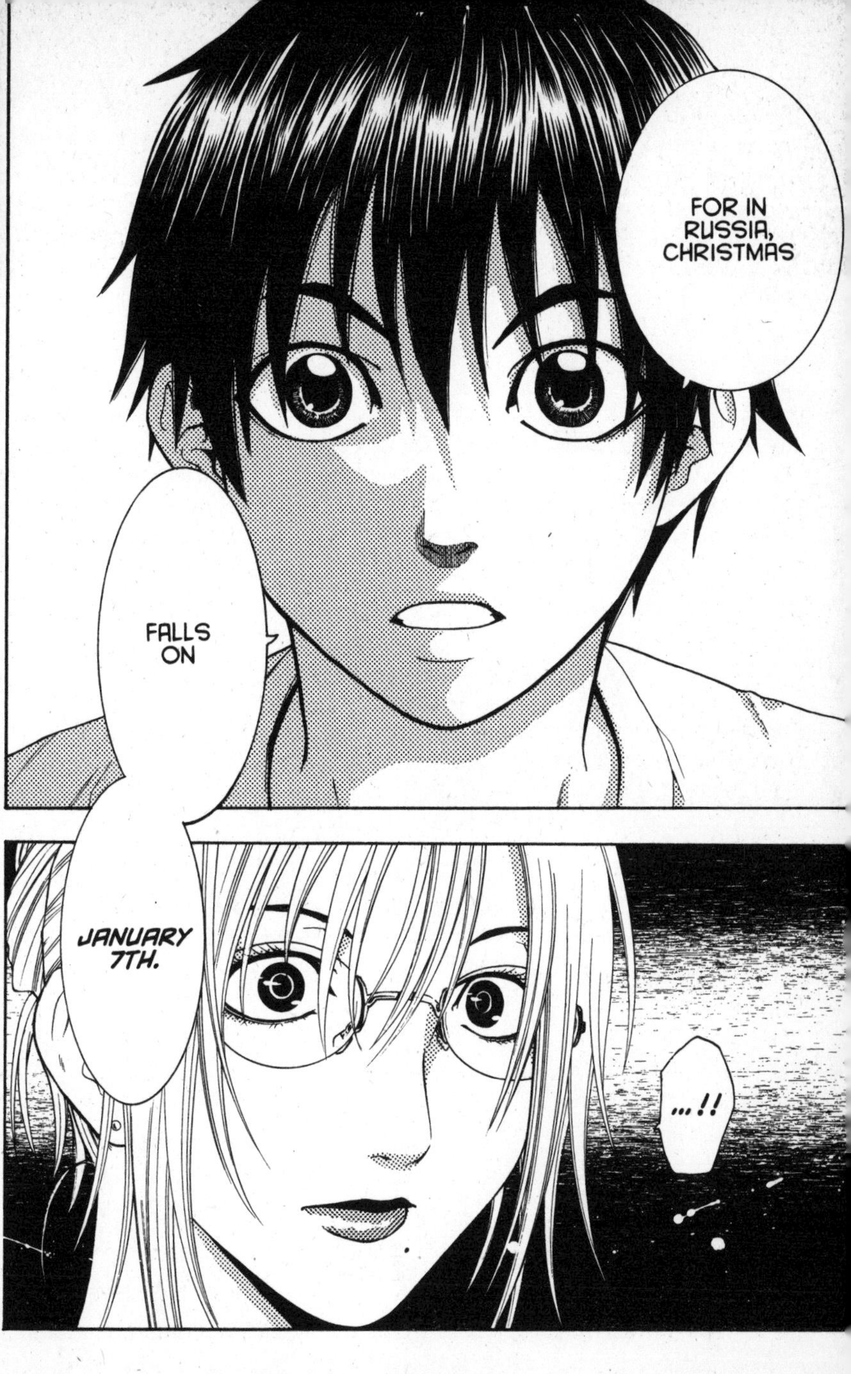
FOR IN RUSSIA, CHRISTMAS
FALLS ON
JANUARY 7TH.
...!!

BLOODY MONDAY

- GLOSSARY OF TERMS • LIST 5 -

Hard drive p9
A type of data storage device. Refers to the external memory built into laptops and various other types of computers. Often abbreviate HD (hard drive) or HDD (hard disk drive). Computers are also equippe with a separate main or internal memory, where only the most necessary items are saved and invoked from, and the hard drive is used for long-term storage.

Storage p10
A general term for any data storage device the records and preserv digital information. Examples include hard drives, floppy disks, MO (Magneto-Optical drives), CD-R, and magnetic tape. Many of these employ magnetization to record data, and even if electricity is not supplied, the data will not disappear.

OS p10
Software that manages the entire computing system, from input-output functions such as screen output and keyboard input to disk memory management, as well as supplying basic functions commor to many application software. Also called "basic software" in Japan.

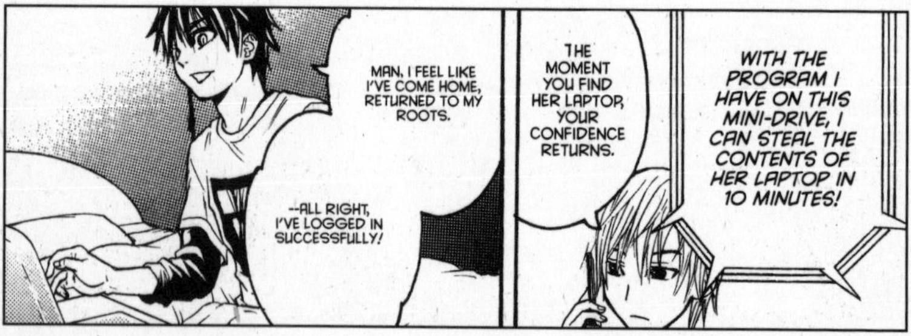
WITH THE PROGRAM I HAVE ON THIS MINI-DRIVE, I CAN STEAL THE CONTENTS OF HER LAPTOP IN 10 MINUTES!
THE MOMENT YOU FIND HER LAPTOP, YOUR CONFIDENCE RETURNS.
MAN, I FEEL LIKE I'VE COME HOME, RETURNED TO MY ROOTS.
--ALL RIGHT, I'VE LOGGED IN SUCCESSFULLY!

BLOODY MONDAY

- GLOSSARY OF TERMS • LIST 6 -

Sleep p12
A standby state in which electrical consumption is minimized. If a laptop is not used for a certain period of time, it cuts electricity to its screen and hard drive to conserve power. Sleep mode differs from a powered-off state, and operations can be resumed just by moving the mouse or touching the keyboard.

IP address p37
A unique numerical identifier assigned to each computer or other telecommunication equipment connected to a network, whether the internet or an internal company network. Networks such as the internet use a communications protocol known as the IP (Internet Protocol) to carry out transmissions. Thus, an IP address is like the address of a piece of telecommunication equipment within a network that operates using IP.

MAC address p37
The ID number of an Ethernet (the international standard for LAN) card. All Ethernet cards are assigned a unique number, via which data transmission between cards takes place.

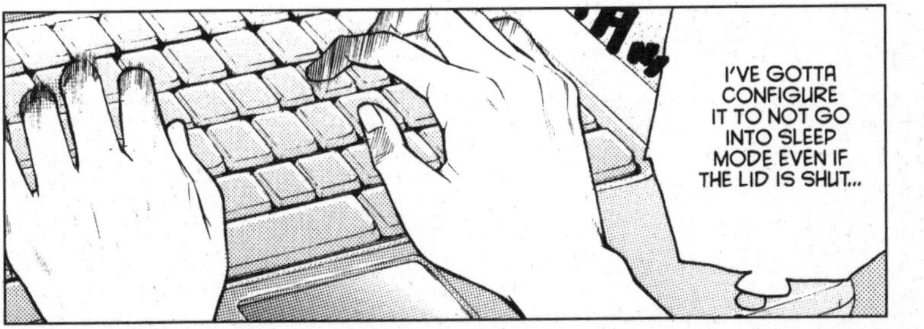
I'VE GOTTA CONFIGURE IT TO NOT GO INTO SLEEP MODE EVEN IF THE LID IS SHUT...

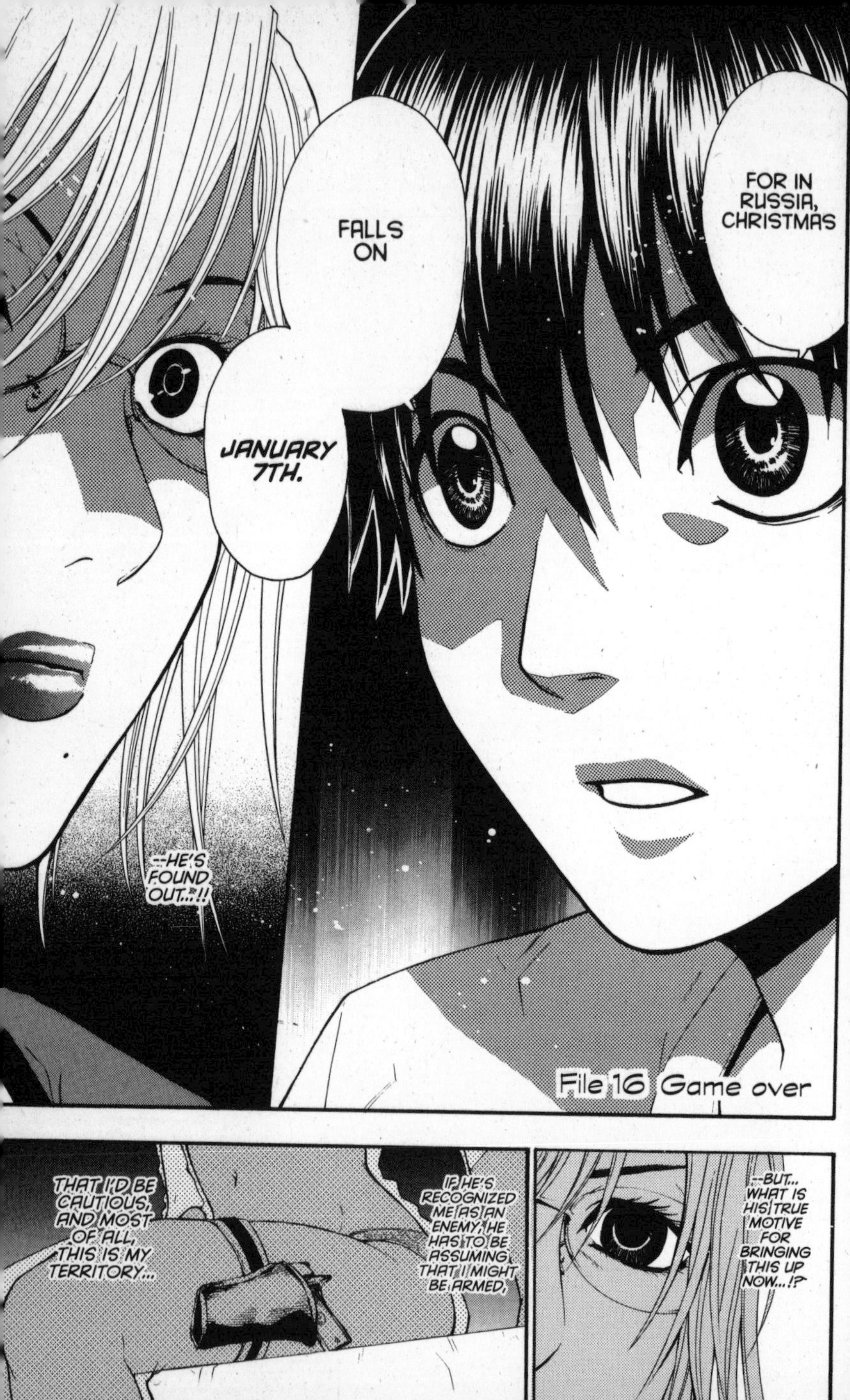
FOR IN RUSSIA, CHRISTMAS
FALLS ON
JANUARY 7TH.
--HE'S FOUND OUT...!!
File 16 Game over
--BUT... WHAT IS HIS TRUE MOTIVE FOR BRINGING THIS UP NOW...!?
IF HE'S RECOGNIZED ME AS AN ENEMY, HE HAS TO BE ASSUMING THAT I MIGHT BE ARMED,
THAT I'D BE CAUTIOUS, AND MOST OF ALL, THIS IS MY TERRITORY...

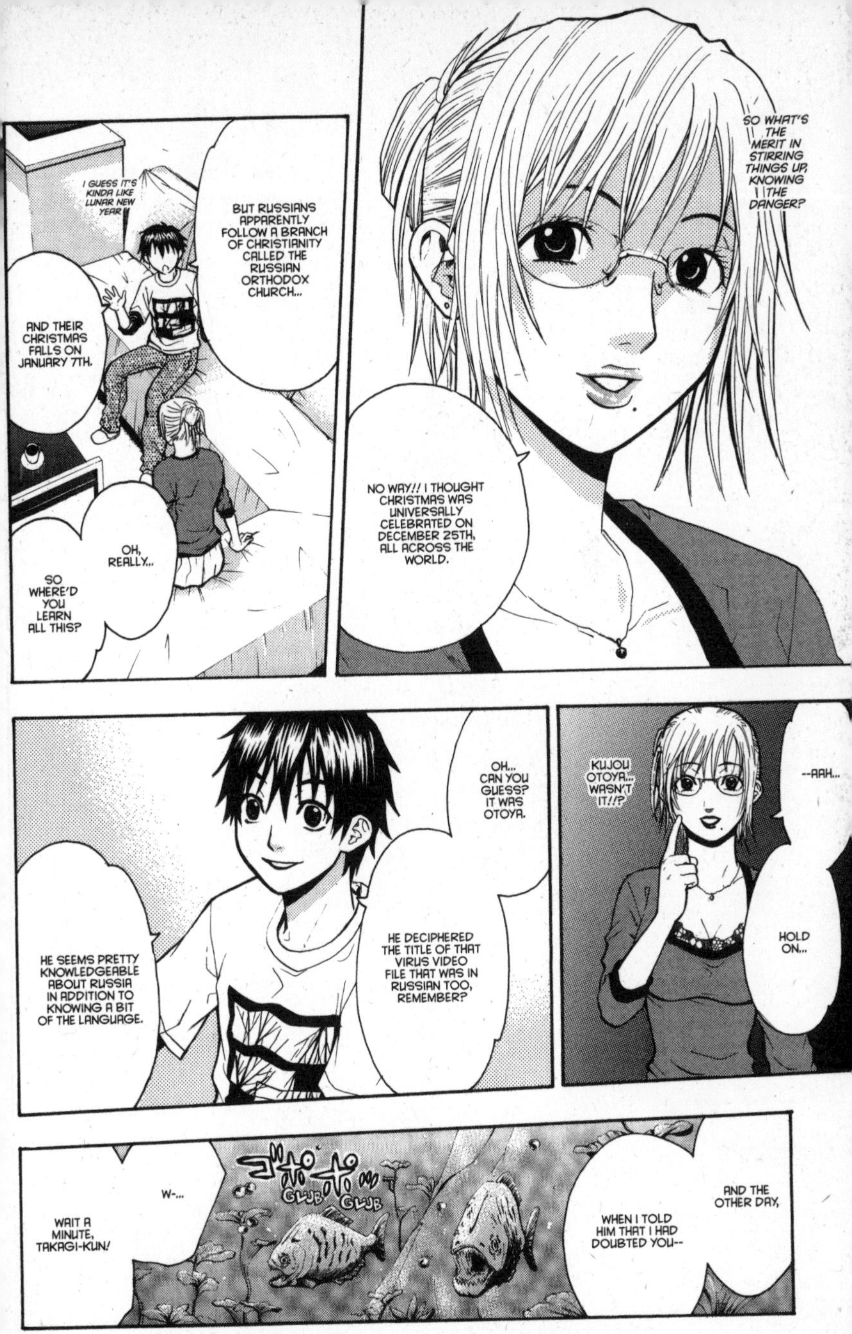
SO WHAT'S THE MERIT IN STIRRING THINGS UP, KNOWING THE DANGER?
NO WAY!! I THOUGHT CHRISTMAS WAS UNIVERSALLY CELEBRATED ON DECEMBER 25TH, ALL ACROSS THE WORLD.
BUT RUSSIANS APPARENTLY FOLLOW A BRANCH OF CHRISTIANITY CALLED THE RUSSIAN ORTHODOX CHURCH...
I GUESS IT'S KINDA LIKE LUNAR NEW YEAR
AND THEIR CHRISTMAS FALLS ON JANUARY 7TH.
OH, REALLY...
SO WHERE'D YOU LEARN ALL THIS?
--AAH...
KUJOU OTOYA... WASN'T IT!!?
HOLD ON...
OH... CAN YOU GUESS? IT WAS OTOYA.
HE DECIPHERED THE TITLE OF THAT VIRUS VIDEO FILE THAT WAS IN RUSSIAN TOO, REMEMBER?
HE SEEMS PRETTY KNOWLEDGEABLE ABOUT RUSSIA IN ADDITION TO KNOWING A BIT OF THE LANGUAGE.
AND THE OTHER DAY,
WHEN I TOLD HIM THAT I HAD DOUBTED YOU--
GLUB GLUB
W-...
WAIT A MINUTE, TAKAGI-KUN!

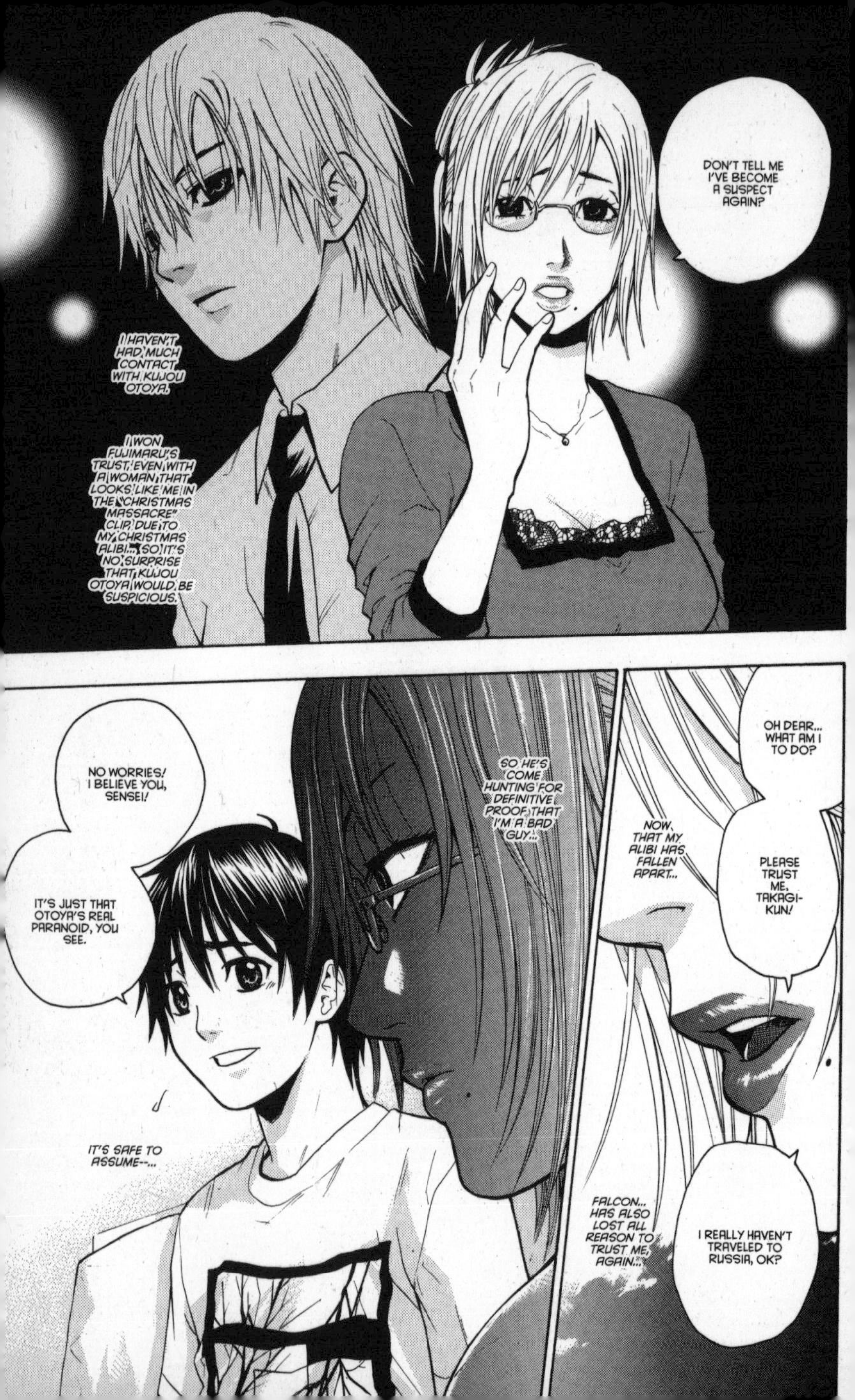
DON'T TELL ME I'VE BECOME A SUSPECT AGAIN?
I HAVEN'T HAD MUCH CONTACT WITH KUJOU OTOYA.
I WON FUJIMARU'S TRUST, EVEN WITH A WOMAN THAT LOOKS LIKE ME IN THE "CHRISTMAS MASSACRE" CLIP, DUE TO MY CHRISTMAS ALIBI... SO IT'S NO SURPRISE THAT KUJOU OTOYA WOULD BE SUSPICIOUS.
OH DEAR... WHAT AM I TO DO?
NOW, THAT MY ALIBI HAS FALLEN APART...
PLEASE TRUST ME, TAKAGI-KUN!
FALCON... HAS ALSO LOST ALL REASON TO TRUST ME, AGAIN...
I REALLY HAVEN'T TRAVELED TO RUSSIA, OK?
SO HE'S COME HUNTING FOR DEFINITIVE PROOF THAT I'M A BAD GUY...
NO WORRIES! I BELIEVE YOU, SENSEI!
IT'S JUST THAT OTOYA'S REAL PARANOID, YOU SEE.
IT'S SAFE TO ASSUME--...

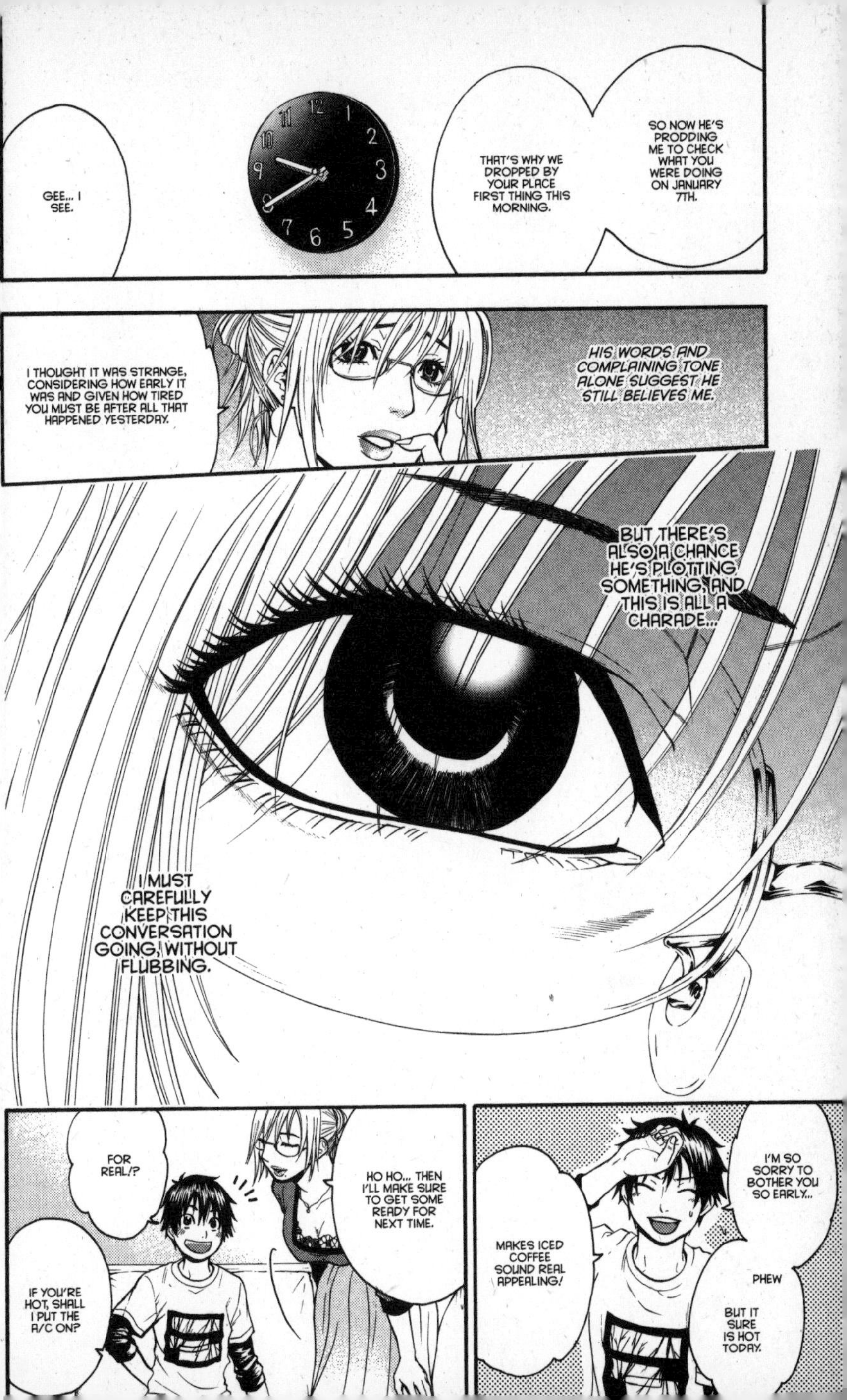
SO NOW HE'S PRODDING ME TO CHECK WHAT YOU WERE DOING ON JANUARY 7TH.
THAT'S WHY WE DROPPED BY YOUR PLACE FIRST THING THIS MORNING.
GEE... I SEE.
HIS WORDS AND COMPLAINING TONE ALONE SUGGEST HE STILL BELIEVES ME.
I THOUGHT IT WAS STRANGE, CONSIDERING HOW EARLY IT WAS AND GIVEN HOW TIRED YOU MUST BE AFTER ALL THAT HAPPENED YESTERDAY.
BUT THERE'S ALSO A CHANCE HE'S PLOTTING SOMETHING, AND THIS IS ALL A CHARADE...
I MUST CAREFULLY KEEP THIS CONVERSATION GOING, WITHOUT FLUBBING.
I'M SO SORRY TO BOTHER YOU SO EARLY...
PHEW
BUT IT SURE IS HOT TODAY.
MAKES ICED COFFEE SOUND REAL APPEALING!
HO HO... THEN I'LL MAKE SURE TO GET SOME READY FOR NEXT TIME.
FOR REAL!?
IF YOU'RE HOT, SHALL I PUT THE A/C ON?

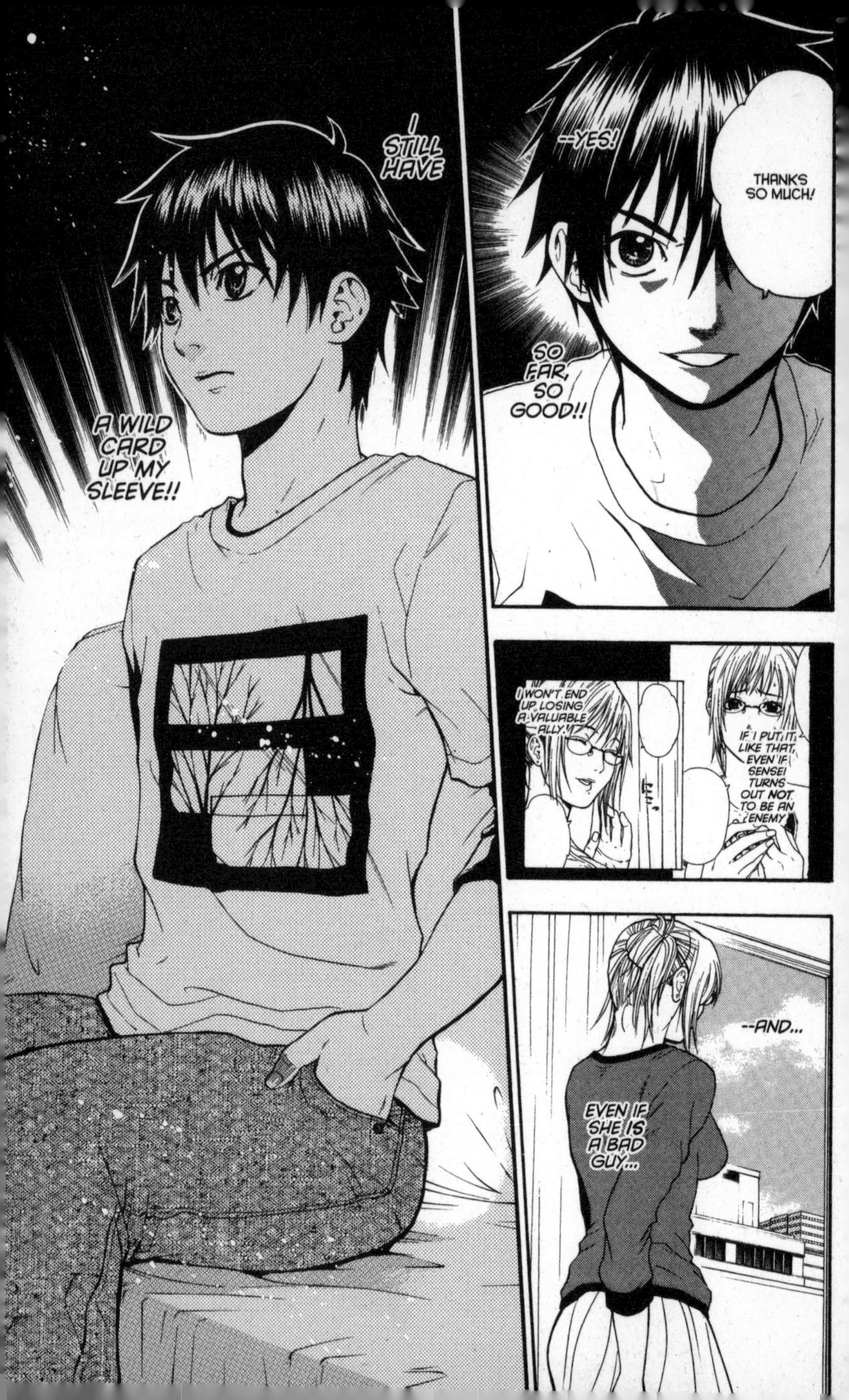
THANKS SO MUCH!
--YES!
SO FAR, SO GOOD!!
IF I PUT IT LIKE THAT, EVEN IF SENSEI TURNS OUT NOT TO BE AN ENEMY
I WON'T END UP LOSING A VALUABLE ALLY.
--AND...
EVEN IF SHE IS A BAD GUY...
I STILL HAVE
A WILD CARD UP MY SLEEVE!!

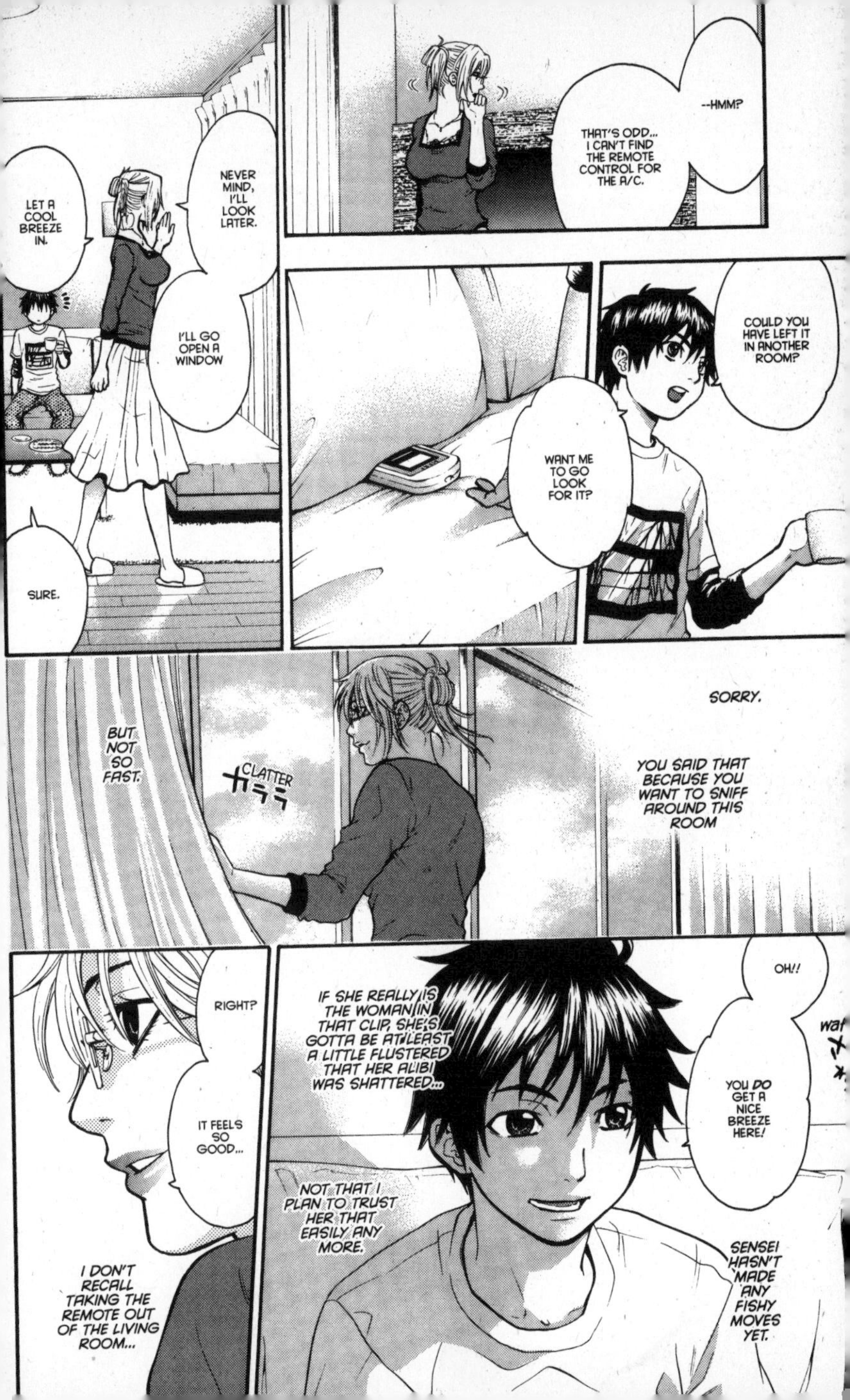
--HMM?
THAT'S ODD... I CAN'T FIND THE REMOTE CONTROL FOR THE A/C.
COULD YOU HAVE LEFT IT IN ANOTHER ROOM?
WANT ME TO GO LOOK FOR IT?
NEVER MIND, I'LL LOOK LATER.
LET A COOL BREEZE IN.
I'LL GO OPEN A WINDOW
SURE.
SORRY.
YOU SAID THAT BECAUSE YOU WANT TO SNIFF AROUND THIS ROOM
BUT NOT SO FAST.
CLATTER
OH!!
YOU *DO* GET A NICE BREEZE HERE!
SENSEI HASN'T MADE ANY FISHY MOVES YET.
IF SHE REALLY IS THE WOMAN IN THAT CLIP, SHE'S GOTTA BE AT LEAST A LITTLE FLUSTERED THAT HER ALIBI WAS SHATTERED...
NOT THAT I PLAN TO TRUST HER THAT EASILY ANY MORE.
RIGHT?
IT FEELS SO GOOD...
I DON'T RECALL TAKING THE REMOTE OUT OF THE LIVING ROOM...

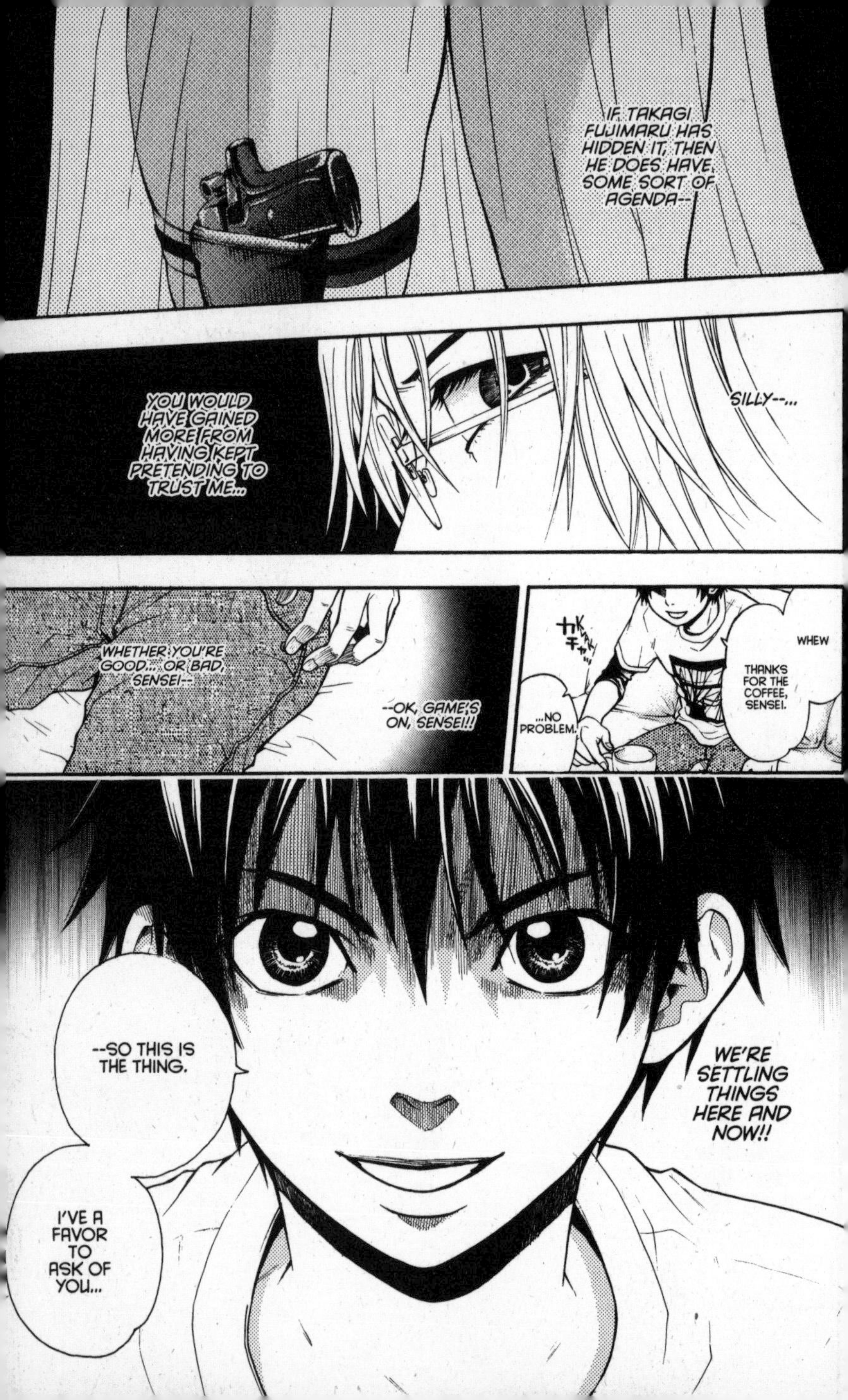
IF TAKAGI FUJIMARU HAS HIDDEN IT, THEN HE DOES HAVE SOME SORT OF AGENDA--
SILLY--...
YOU WOULD HAVE GAINED MORE FROM HAVING KEPT PRETENDING TO TRUST ME...
WHEW
THANKS FOR THE COFFEE, SENSEI.
KAK
...NO PROBLEM.
WHETHER YOU'RE GOOD... OR BAD, SENSEI--
--OK, GAME'S ON, SENSEI!!
WE'RE SETTLING THINGS HERE AND NOW!!
--SO THIS IS THE THING.
I'VE A FAVOR TO ASK OF YOU...

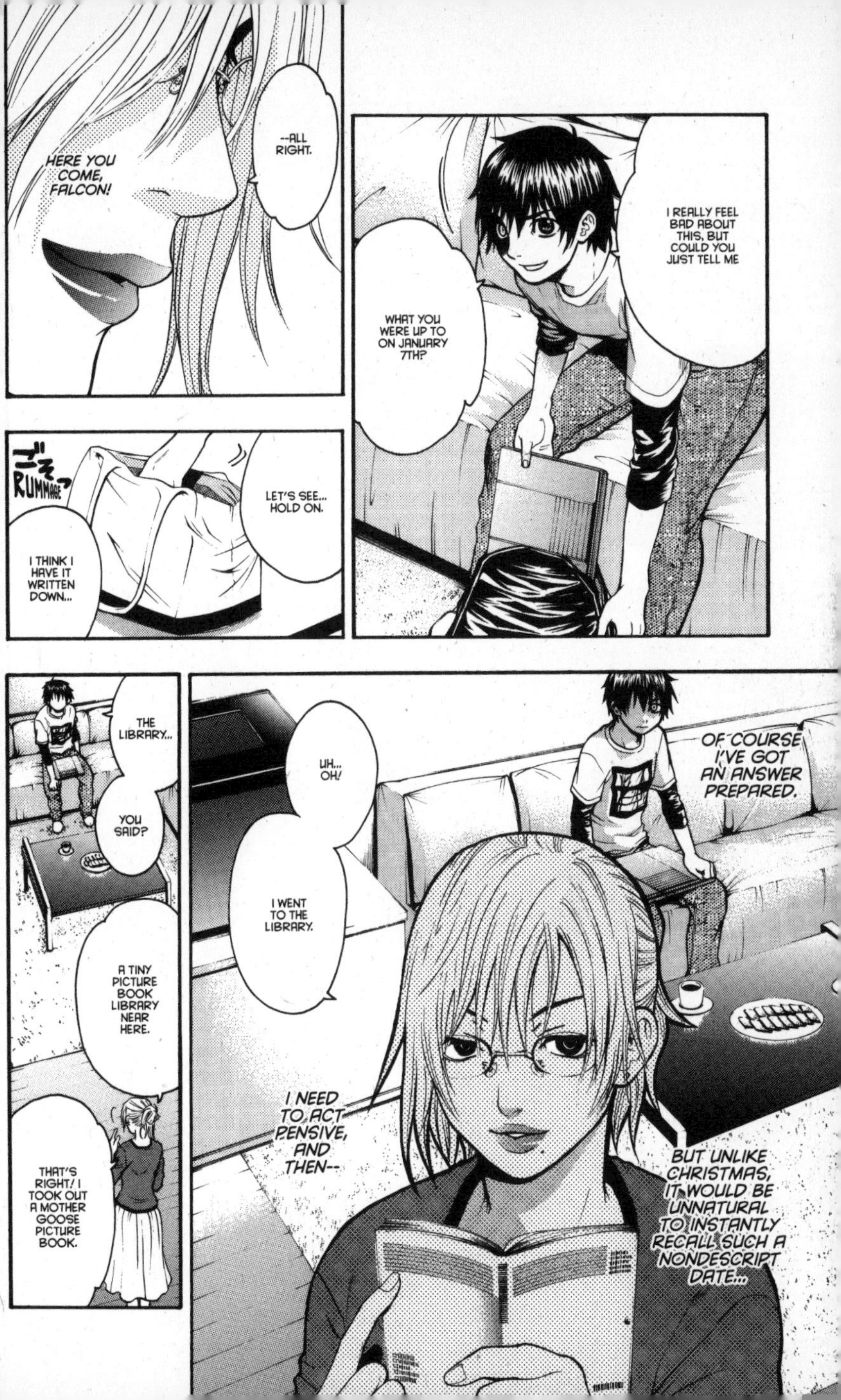

I REALLY FEEL BAD ABOUT THIS, BUT COULD YOU JUST TELL ME
WHAT YOU WERE UP TO ON JANUARY 7TH?
--ALL RIGHT.
HERE YOU COME, FALCON!
RUMMAGE
LET'S SEE... HOLD ON.
I THINK I HAVE IT WRITTEN DOWN...
OF COURSE I'VE GOT AN ANSWER PREPARED.
BUT UNLIKE CHRISTMAS, IT WOULD BE UNNATURAL TO INSTANTLY RECALL SUCH A NONDESCRIPT DATE...
I NEED TO ACT PENSIVE, AND THEN--
UH... OH!
I WENT TO THE LIBRARY.
THE LIBRARY...
YOU SAID?
A TINY PICTURE BOOK LIBRARY NEAR HERE.
THAT'S RIGHT! I TOOK OUT A MOTHER GOOSE PICTURE BOOK.

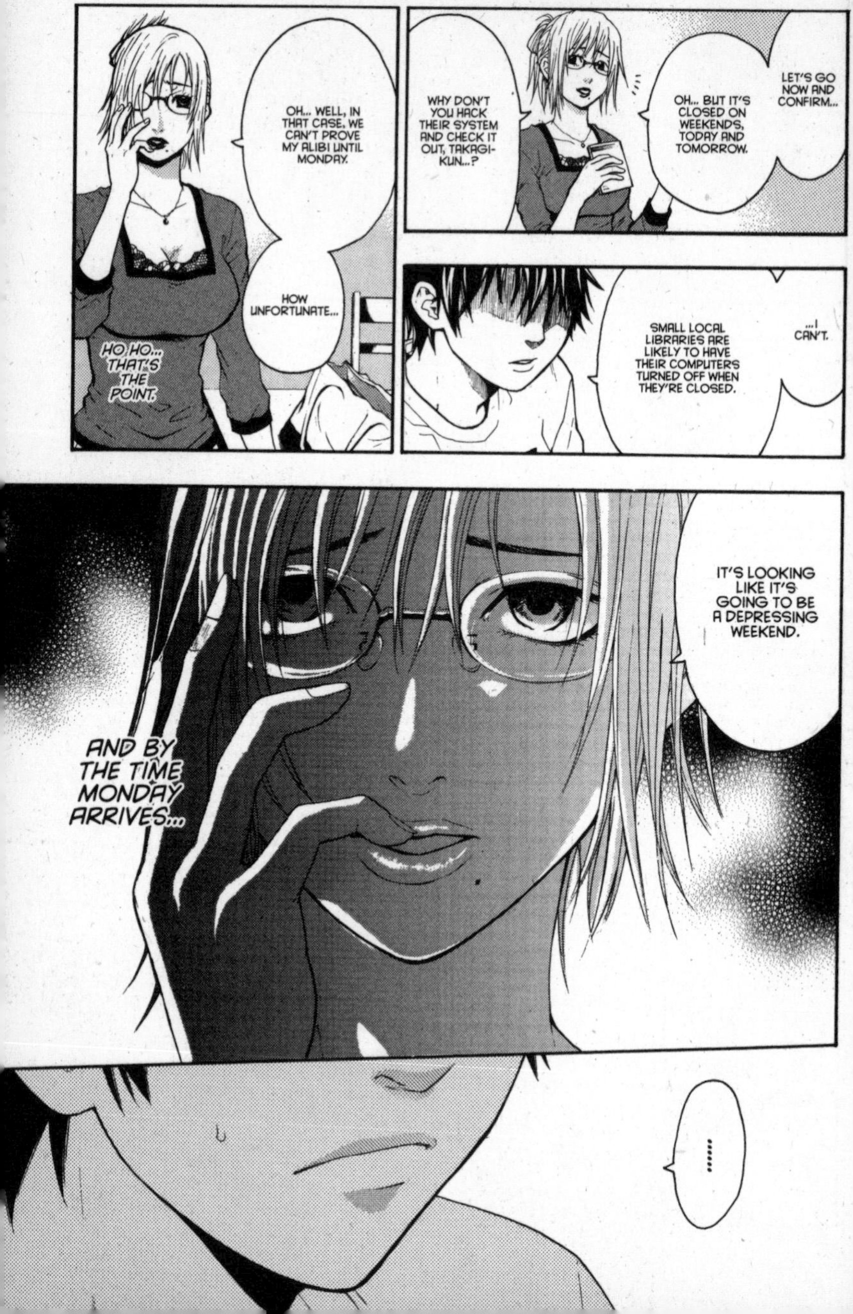
LET'S GO NOW AND CONFIRM...
OH... BUT IT'S CLOSED ON WEEKENDS, TODAY AND TOMORROW.
WHY DON'T YOU HACK THEIR SYSTEM AND CHECK IT OUT, TAKAGI-KUN...?
...I CAN'T.
SMALL LOCAL LIBRARIES ARE LIKELY TO HAVE THEIR COMPUTERS TURNED OFF WHEN THEY'RE CLOSED.
OH... WELL, IN THAT CASE, WE CAN'T PROVE MY ALIBI UNTIL MONDAY.
HOW UNFORTUNATE...
HO HO... THAT'S THE POINT.
IT'S LOOKING LIKE IT'S GOING TO BE A DEPRESSING WEEKEND.
AND BY THE TIME MONDAY ARRIVES...
......

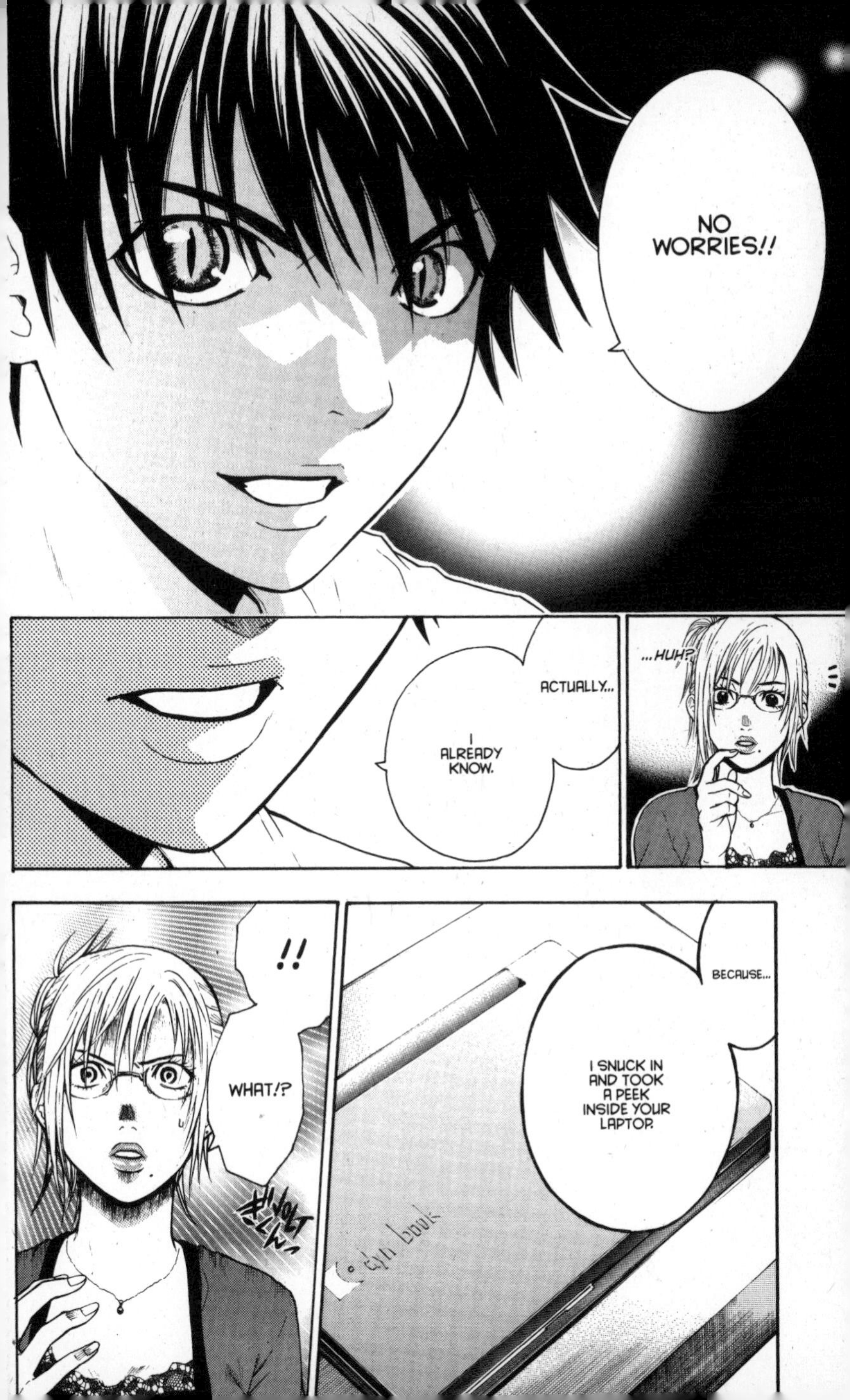
NO WORRIES!!
ACTUALLY...
I ALREADY KNOW.
...HUH?
!!
WHAT!?
BECAUSE...
I SNUCK IN AND TOOK A PEEK INSIDE YOUR LAPTOP.

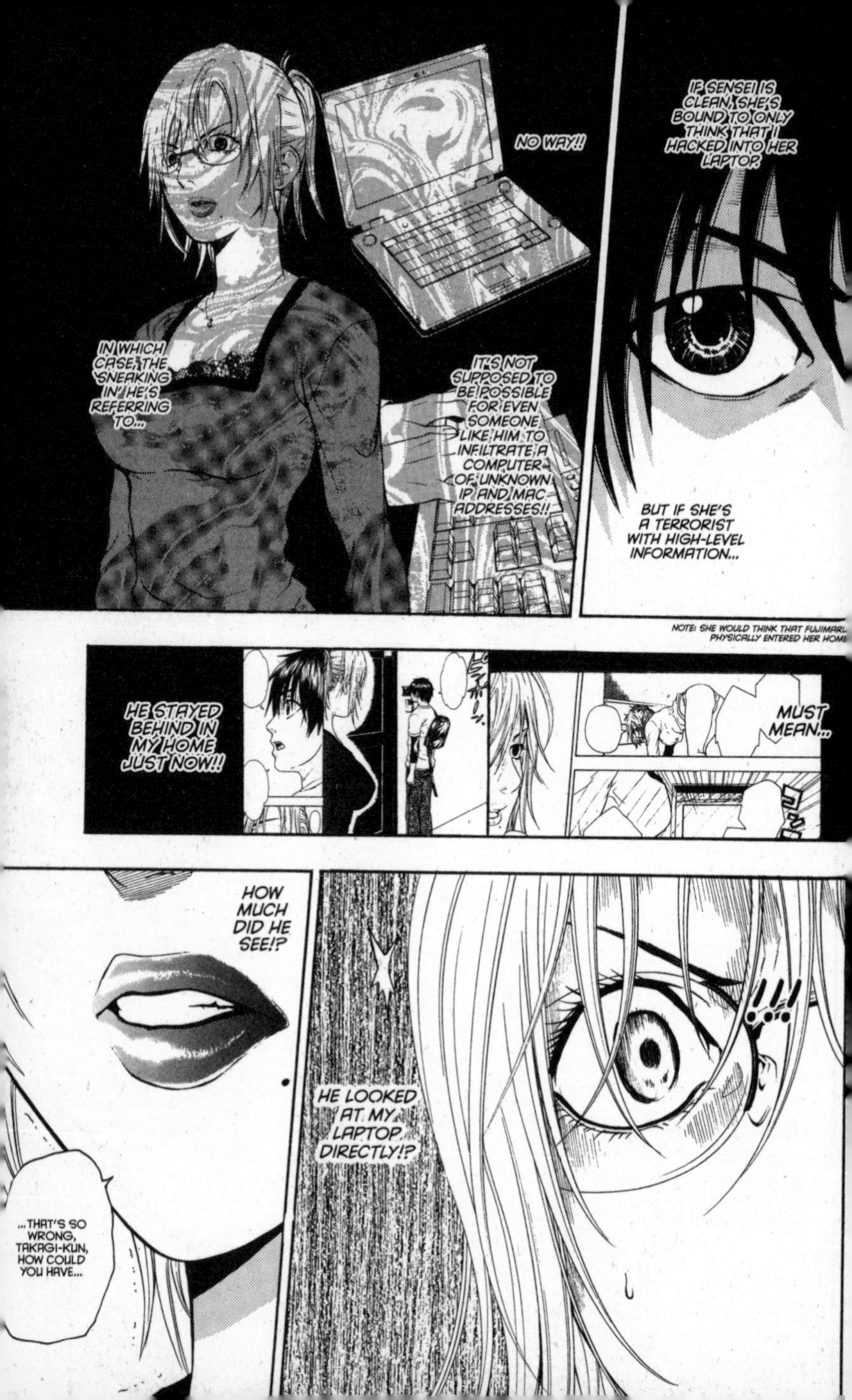
IF SENSEI IS CLEAN, SHE'S BOUND TO ONLY THINK THAT I HACKED INTO HER LAPTOP.
BUT IF SHE'S A TERRORIST WITH HIGH-LEVEL INFORMATION...
NO WAY!!
IT'S NOT SUPPOSED TO BE POSSIBLE FOR EVEN SOMEONE LIKE HIM TO INFILTRATE A COMPUTER OF UNKNOWN IP AND MAC ADDRESSES!!
IN WHICH CASE, THE 'SNEAKING IN' HE'S REFERRING TO...
NOTE: SHE WOULD THINK THAT FUJIMARU PHYSICALLY ENTERED HER HOME
MUST MEAN...
HE STAYED BEHIND IN MY HOME JUST NOW!!
HE LOOKED AT MY LAPTOP DIRECTLY!?
HOW MUCH DID HE SEE!?
...THAT'S SO WRONG, TAKAGI-KUN, HOW COULD YOU HAVE...

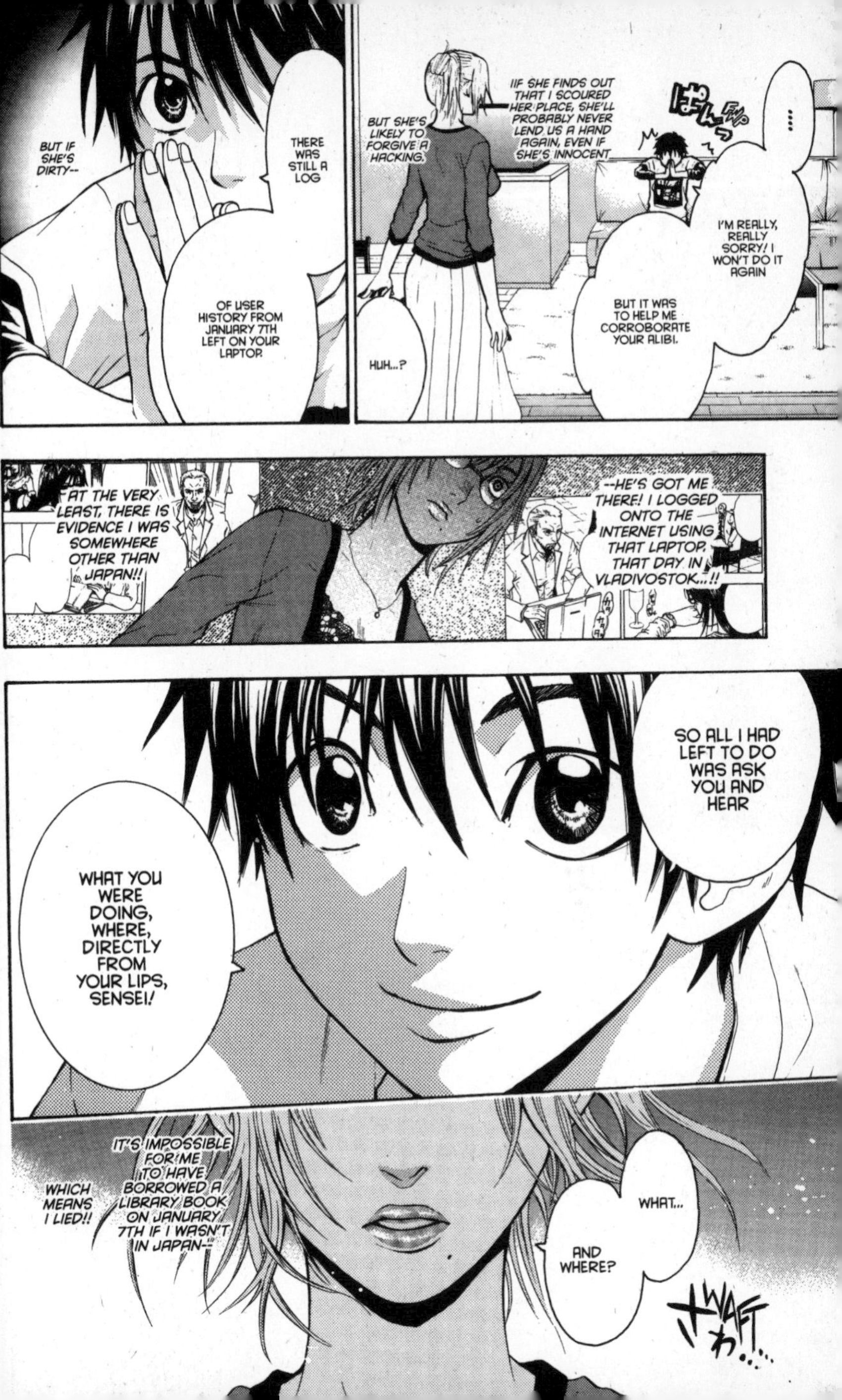
FWIP
....
I'M REALLY, REALLY SORRY! I WON'T DO IT AGAIN
BUT IT WAS TO HELP ME CORROBORATE YOUR ALIBI.
IIF SHE FINDS OUT THAT I SCOURED HER PLACE, SHE'LL PROBABLY NEVER LEND US A HAND AGAIN, EVEN IF SHE'S INNOCENT
BUT SHE'S LIKELY TO FORGIVE A HACKING.
HUH...?
THERE WAS STILL A LOG
OF USER HISTORY FROM JANUARY 7TH LEFT ON YOUR LAPTOP.
BUT IF SHE'S DIRTY--
--HE'S GOT ME THERE! I LOGGED ONTO THE INTERNET USING THAT LAPTOP, THAT DAY IN VLADIVOSTOK...!!
AT THE VERY LEAST, THERE IS EVIDENCE I WAS SOMEWHERE OTHER THAN JAPAN!!
SO ALL I HAD LEFT TO DO WAS ASK YOU AND HEAR
WHAT YOU WERE DOING, WHERE, DIRECTLY FROM YOUR LIPS, SENSEI!
WAFT
WHAT... AND WHERE?
IT'S IMPOSSIBLE FOR ME TO HAVE BORROWED A LIBRARY BOOK ON JANUARY 7TH IF I WASN'T IN JAPAN--
WHICH MEANS I LIED!!

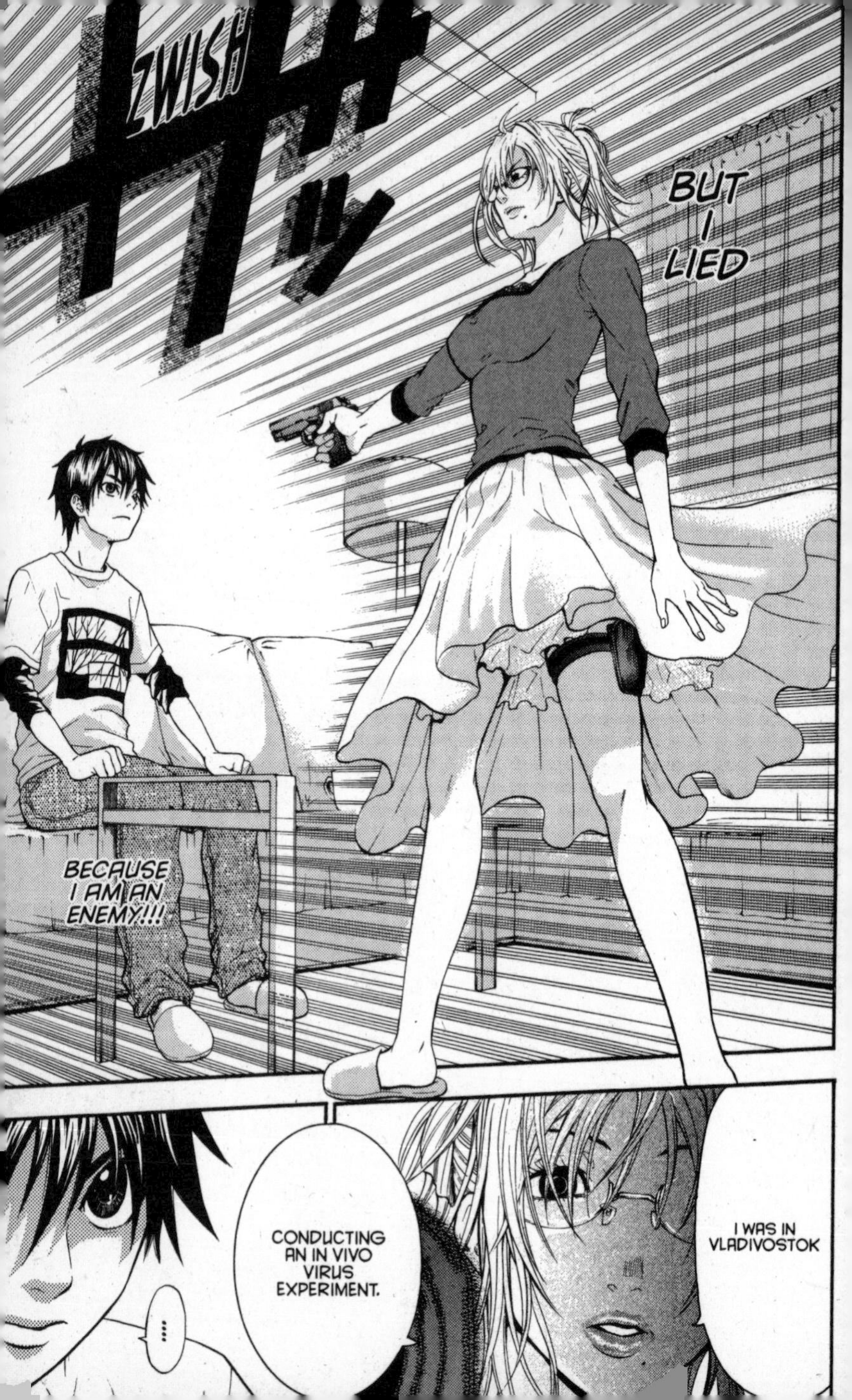
BUT I LIED
ZWISH
BECAUSE I AM AN ENEMY!!!
I WAS IN VLADIVOSTOK
CONDUCTING AN IN VIVO VIRUS EXPERIMENT.
....

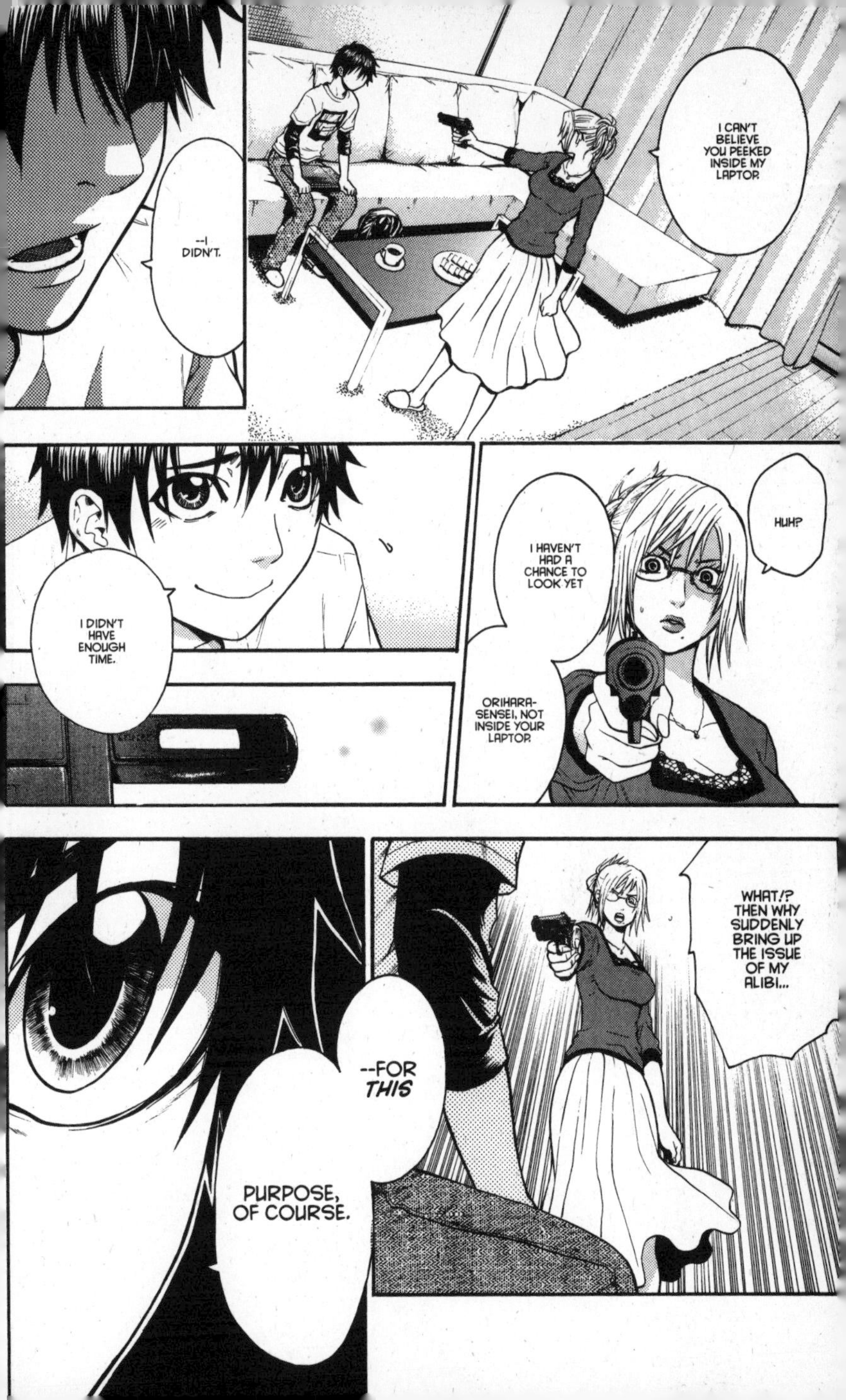
I CAN'T BELIEVE YOU PEEKED INSIDE MY LAPTOP.
--I DIDN'T.
HUH?
I HAVEN'T HAD A CHANCE TO LOOK YET
ORIHARA-SENSEI, NOT INSIDE YOUR LAPTOP.
I DIDN'T HAVE ENOUGH TIME.
WHAT!? THEN WHY SUDDENLY BRING UP THE ISSUE OF MY ALIBI...
--FOR *THIS*
PURPOSE, OF COURSE.

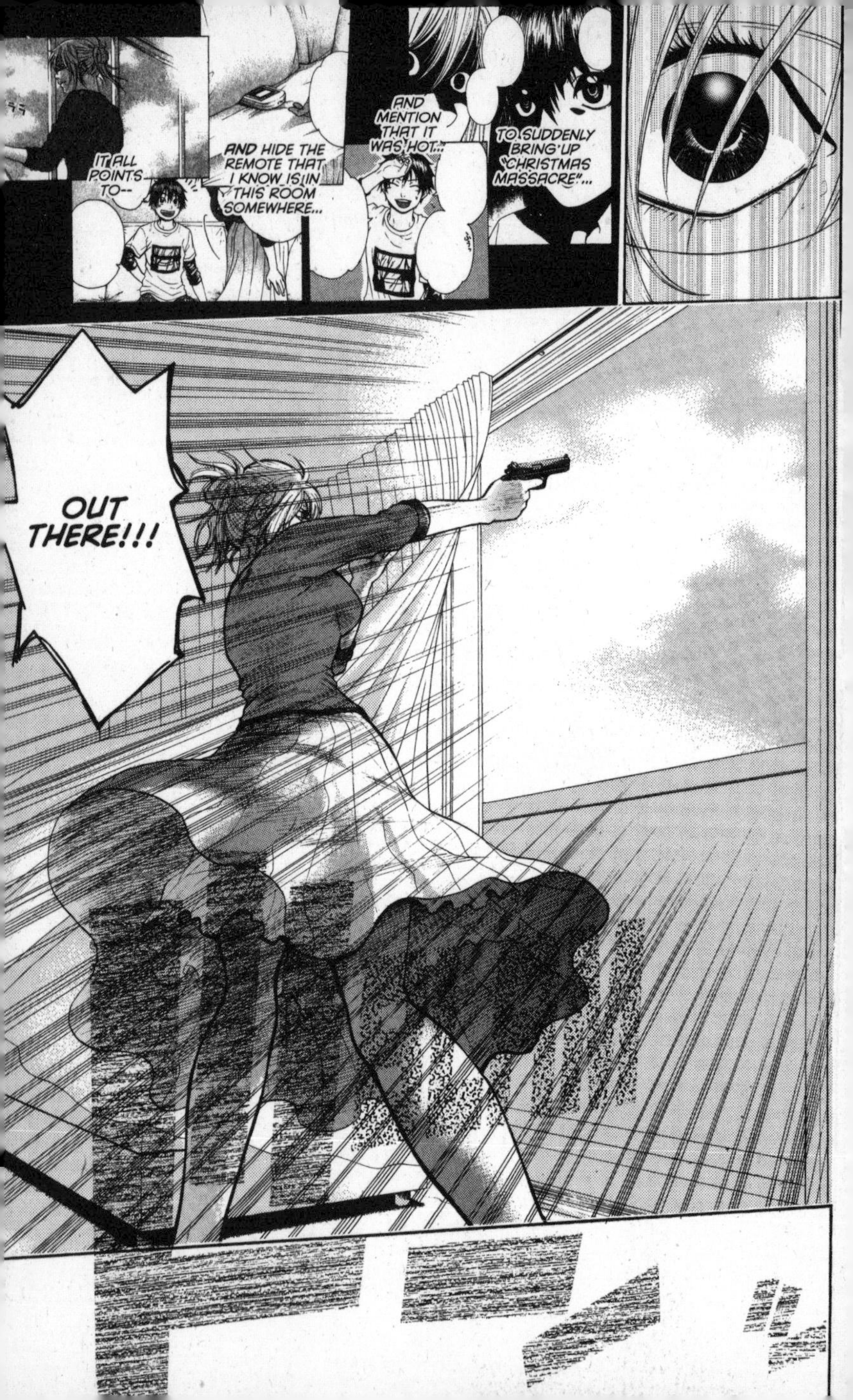
TO SUDDENLY BRING UP "CHRISTMAS MASSACRE"...
AND MENTION THAT IT WAS HOT...
AND HIDE THE REMOTE THAT I KNOW IS IN THIS ROOM SOMEWHERE...
IT ALL POINTS TO--
OUT THERE!!!

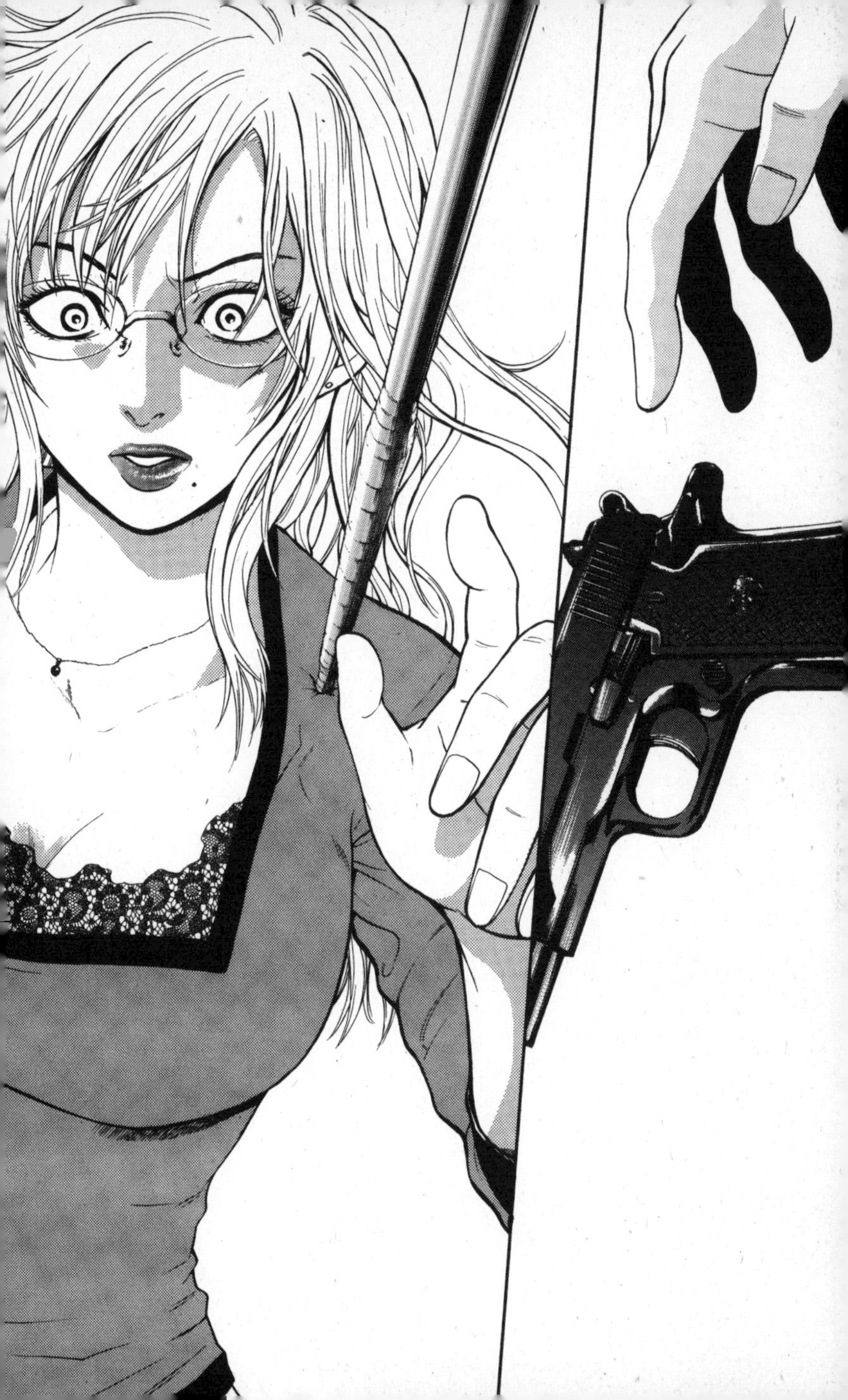

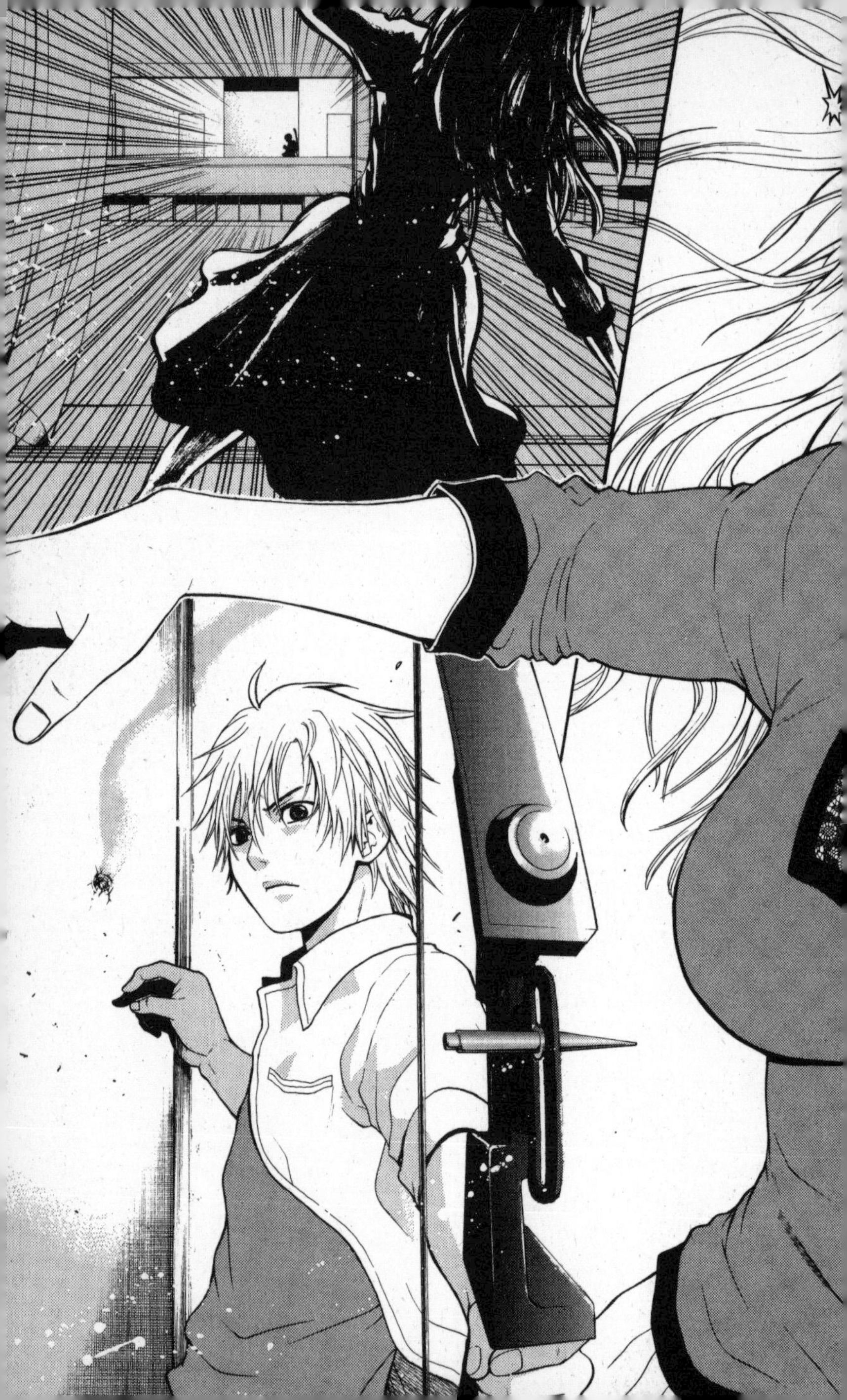

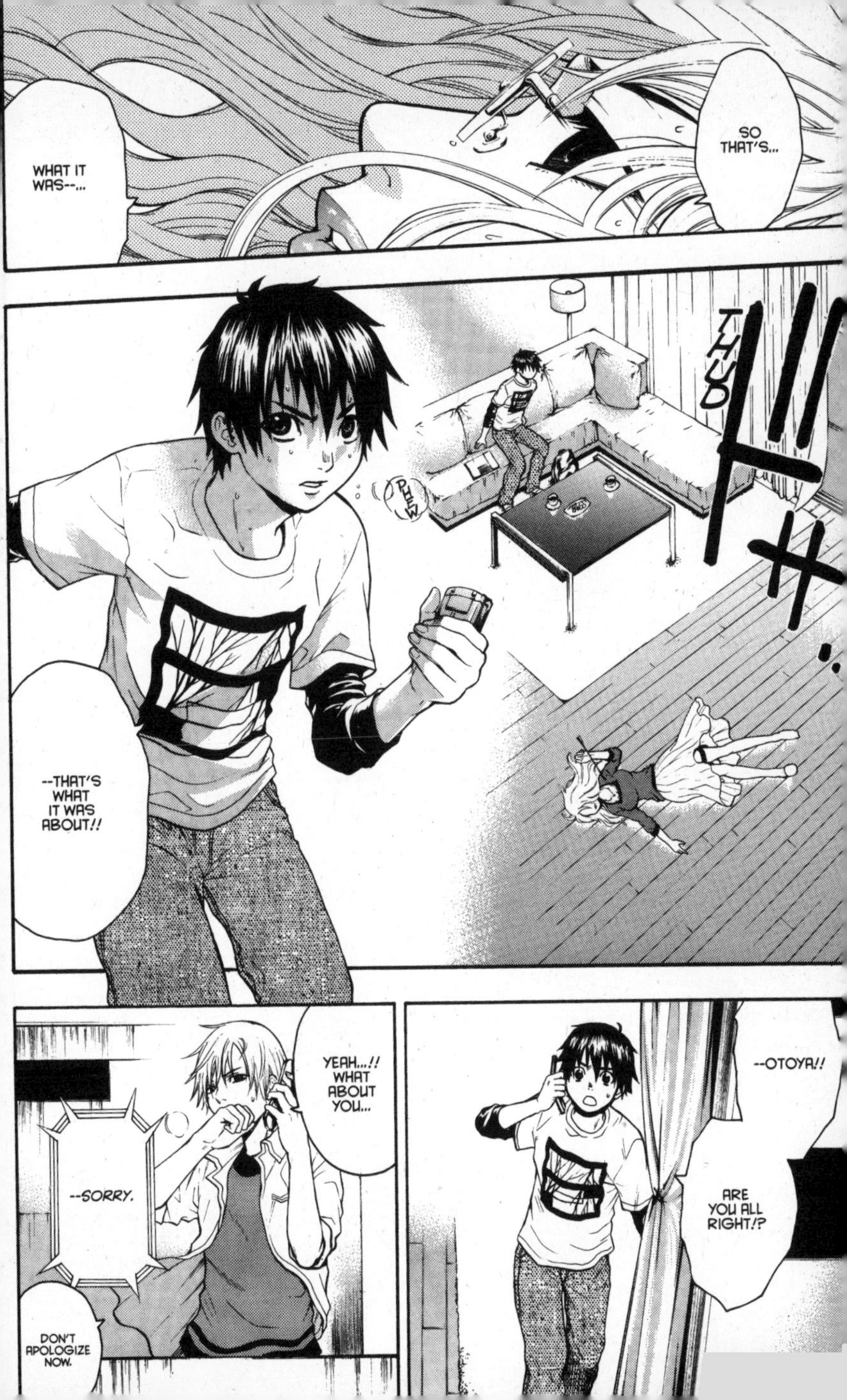
SO THAT'S...
WHAT IT WAS--...
THUD
PHEW
--THAT'S WHAT IT WAS ABOUT!!
--OTOYA!!
ARE YOU ALL RIGHT!?
YEAH...!! WHAT ABOUT YOU...
--SORRY.
DON'T APOLOGIZE NOW.

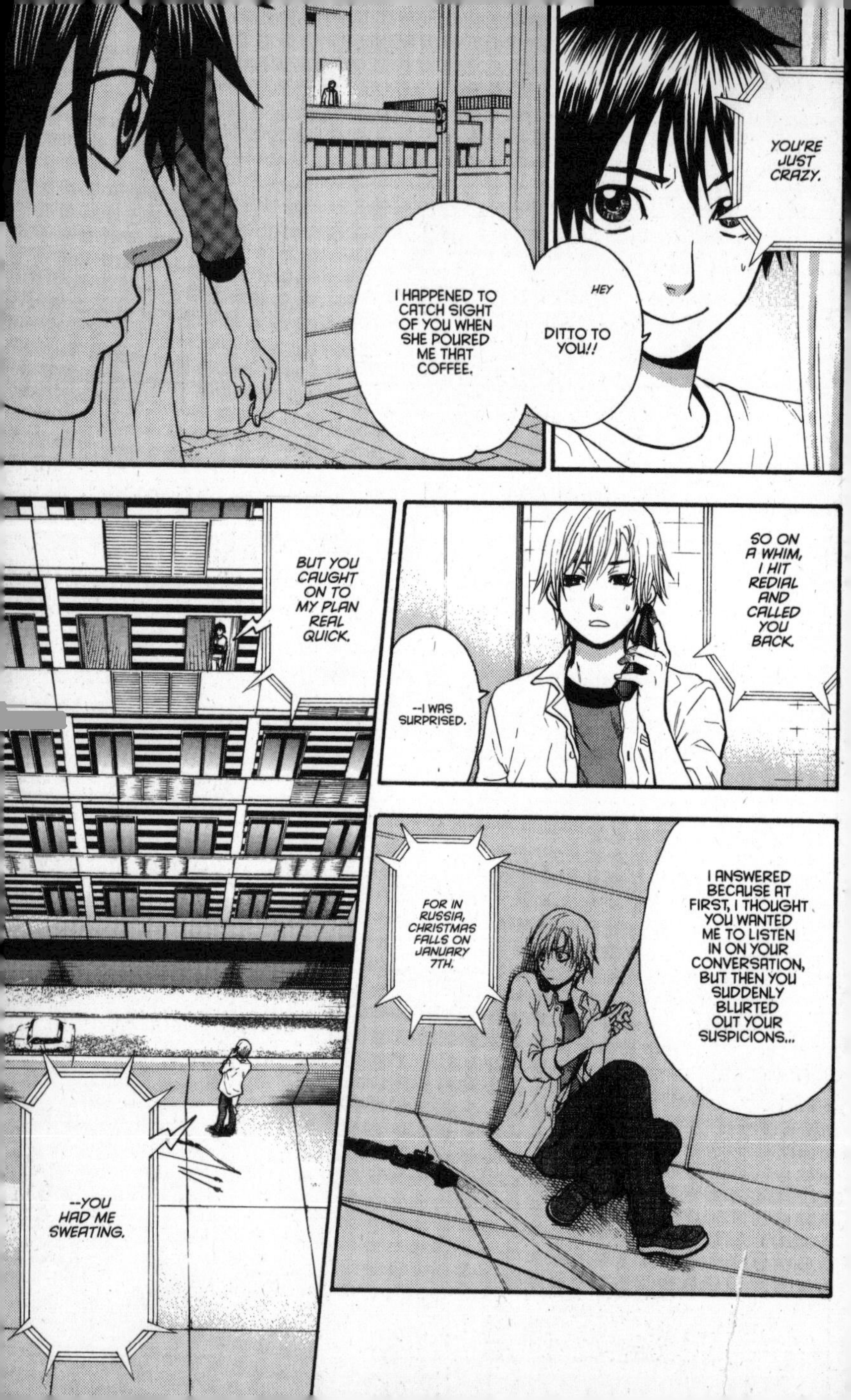
YOU'RE JUST CRAZY.
HEY
DITTO TO YOU!!
I HAPPENED TO CATCH SIGHT OF YOU WHEN SHE POURED ME THAT COFFEE.
SO ON A WHIM, I HIT REDIAL AND CALLED YOU BACK.
--I WAS SURPRISED.
I ANSWERED BECAUSE AT FIRST, I THOUGHT YOU WANTED ME TO LISTEN IN ON YOUR CONVERSATION, BUT THEN YOU SUDDENLY BLURTED OUT YOUR SUSPICIONS...
FOR IN RUSSIA, CHRISTMAS FALLS ON JANUARY 7TH.
BUT YOU CAUGHT ON TO MY PLAN REAL QUICK.
--YOU HAD ME SWEATING.

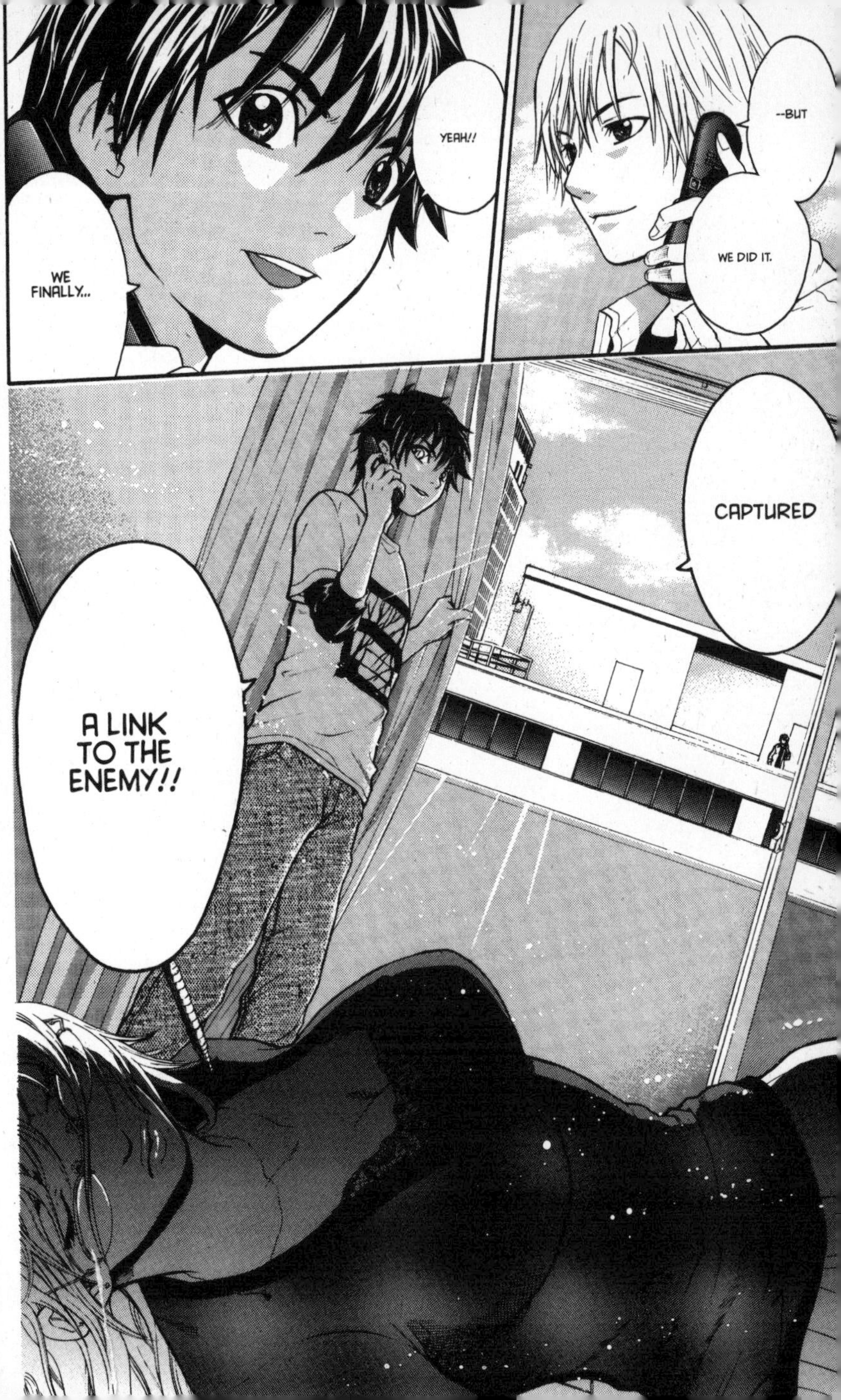
--BUT
WE DID IT.
YEAH!!
WE FINALLY...
CAPTURED
A LINK TO THE ENEMY!!

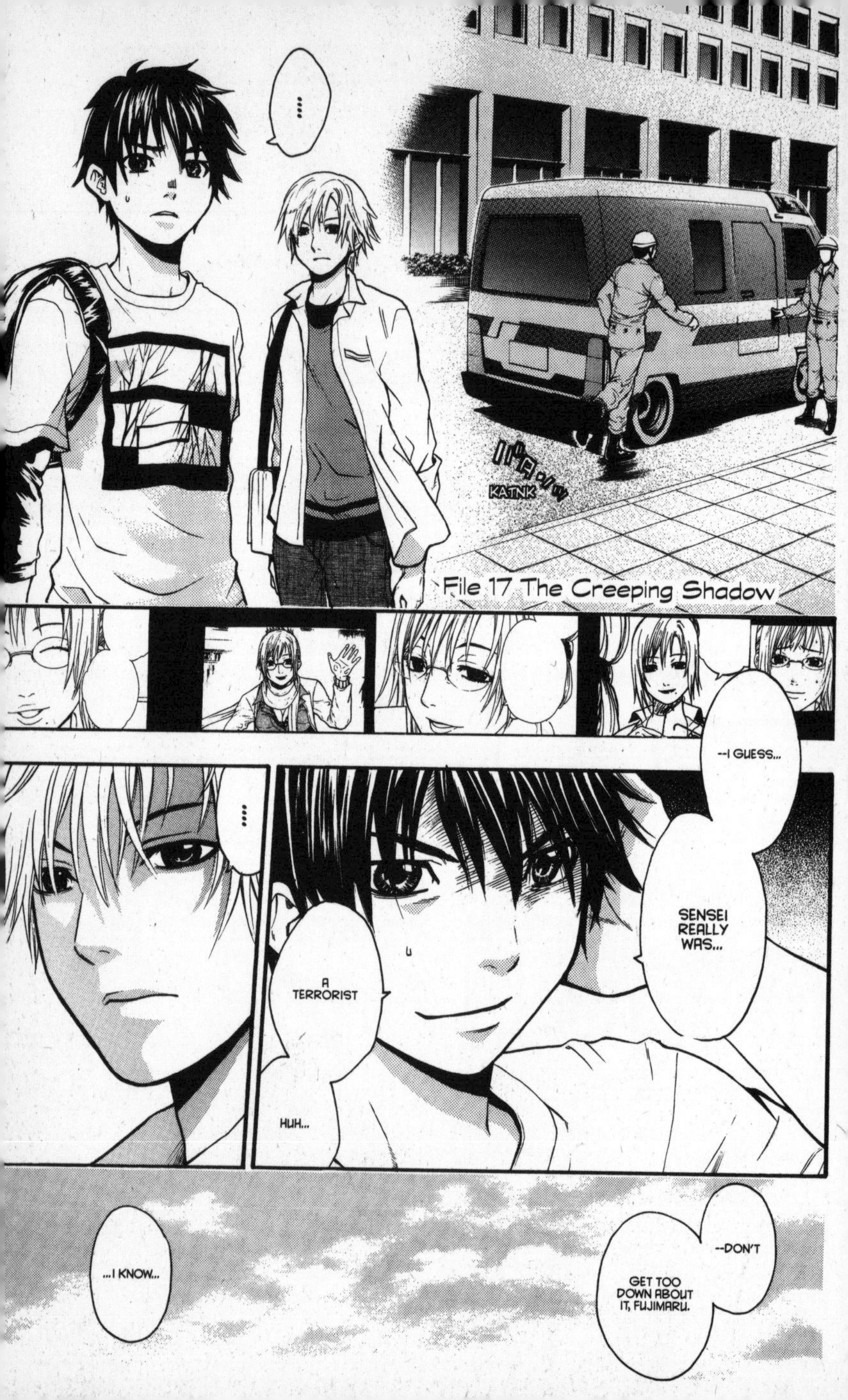
KATNK
....
File 17 The Creeping Shadow
--I GUESS...
SENSEI REALLY WAS...
A TERRORIST
HUH...
....
--DON'T GET TOO DOWN ABOUT IT, FUJIMARU.
...I KNOW...

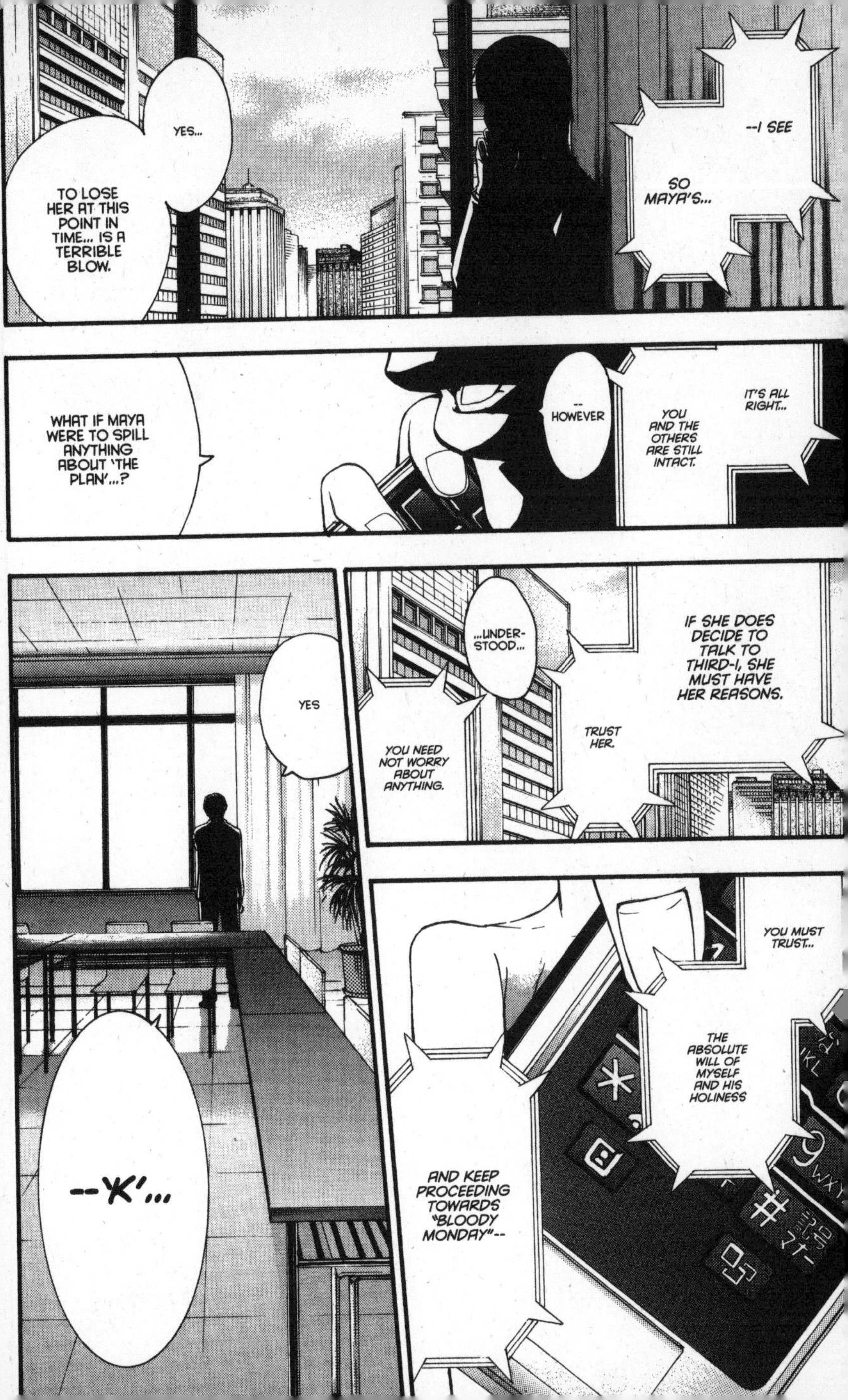
--I SEE
SO MAYA'S...
YES...
TO LOSE HER AT THIS POINT IN TIME... IS A TERRIBLE BLOW.
IT'S ALL RIGHT...
YOU AND THE OTHERS ARE STILL INTACT.
-- HOWEVER
WHAT IF MAYA WERE TO SPILL ANYTHING ABOUT 'THE PLAN'...?
IF SHE DOES DECIDE TO TALK TO THIRD-I, SHE MUST HAVE HER REASONS.
...UNDER-STOOD...
TRUST HER.
YOU NEED NOT WORRY ABOUT ANYTHING.
YOU MUST TRUST...
THE ABSOLUTE WILL OF MYSELF AND HIS HOLINESS
AND KEEP PROCEEDING TOWARDS "BLOODY MONDAY"--
YES
--'K'...

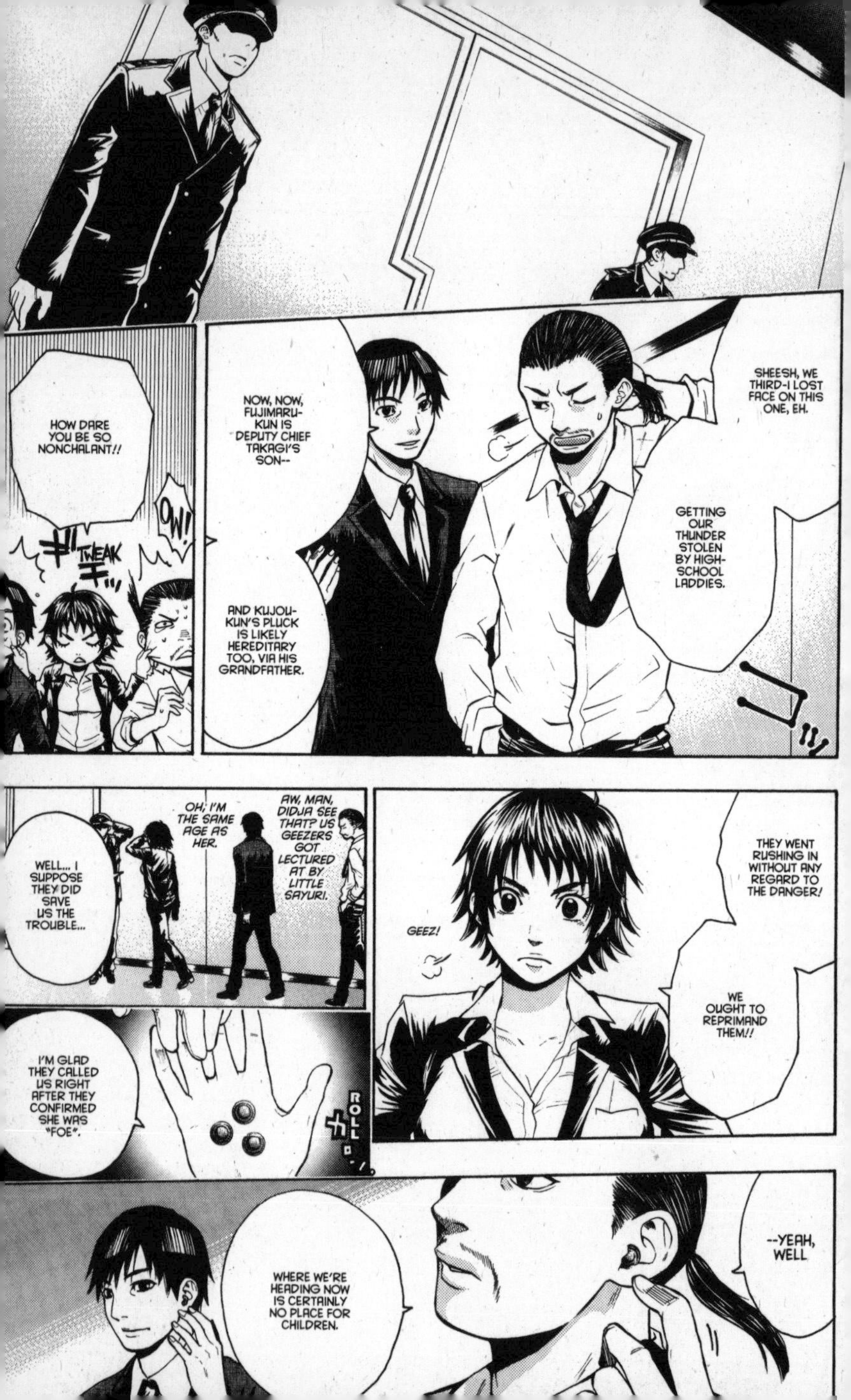
SHEESH, WE THIRD-I LOST FACE ON THIS ONE, EH.
GETTING OUR THUNDER STOLEN BY HIGH-SCHOOL LADDIES.
NOW, NOW, FUJIMARU-KUN IS DEPUTY CHIEF TAKAGI'S SON--
AND KUJOU-KUN'S PLUCK IS LIKELY HEREDITARY TOO, VIA HIS GRANDFATHER.
HOW DARE YOU BE SO NONCHALANT!!
OW!
TWEAK
THEY WENT RUSHING IN WITHOUT ANY REGARD TO THE DANGER!
GEEZ!
WE OUGHT TO REPRIMAND THEM!!
AW, MAN, DIDJA SEE THAT? US GEEZERS GOT LECTURED AT BY LITTLE SAYURI.
OH, I'M THE SAME AGE AS HER.
WELL... I SUPPOSE THEY DID SAVE US THE TROUBLE...
ROLL
I'M GLAD THEY CALLED US RIGHT AFTER THEY CONFIRMED SHE WAS "FOE".
--YEAH, WELL
WHERE WE'RE HEADING NOW IS CERTAINLY NO PLACE FOR CHILDREN.

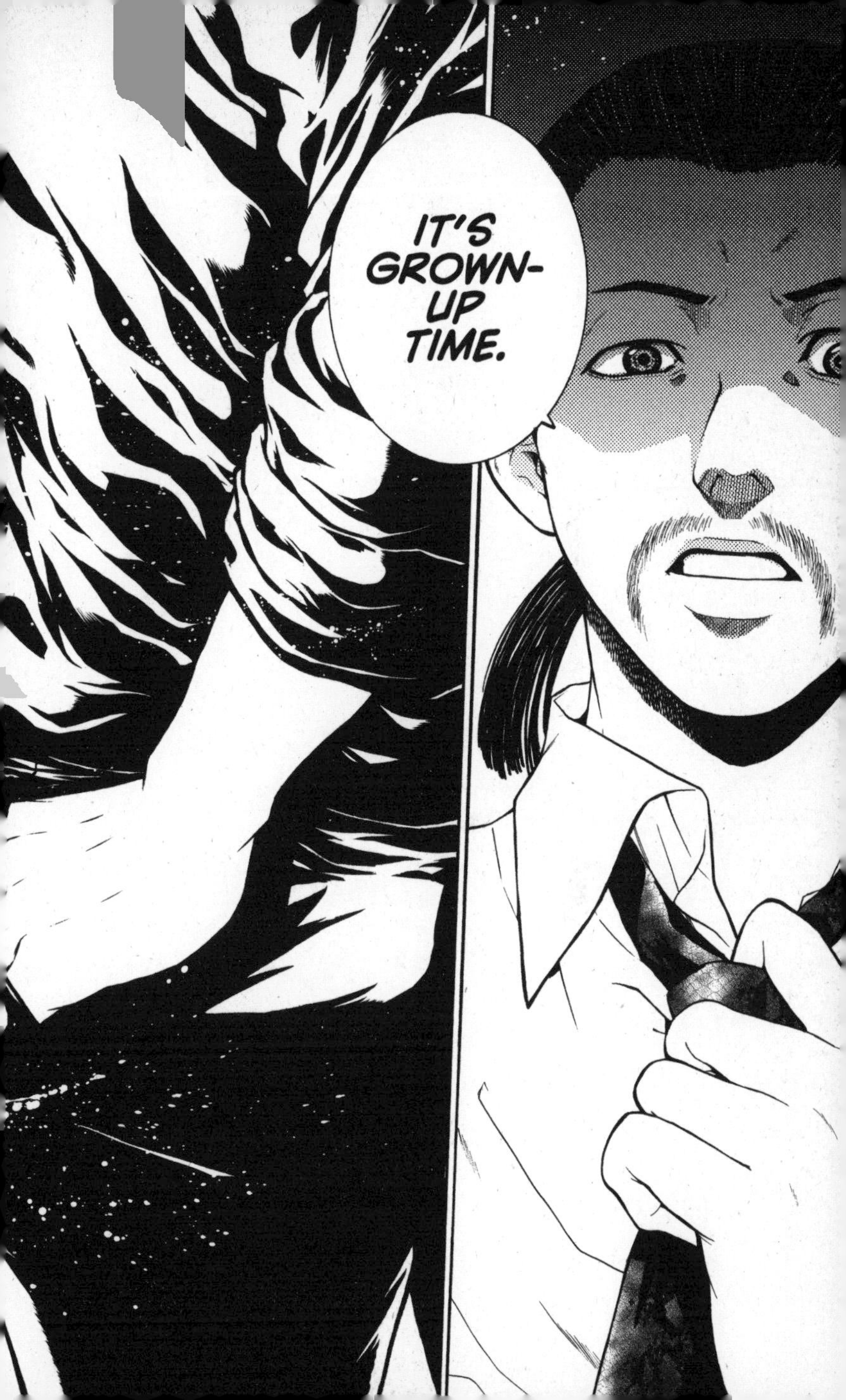
IT'S GROWN-UP TIME.

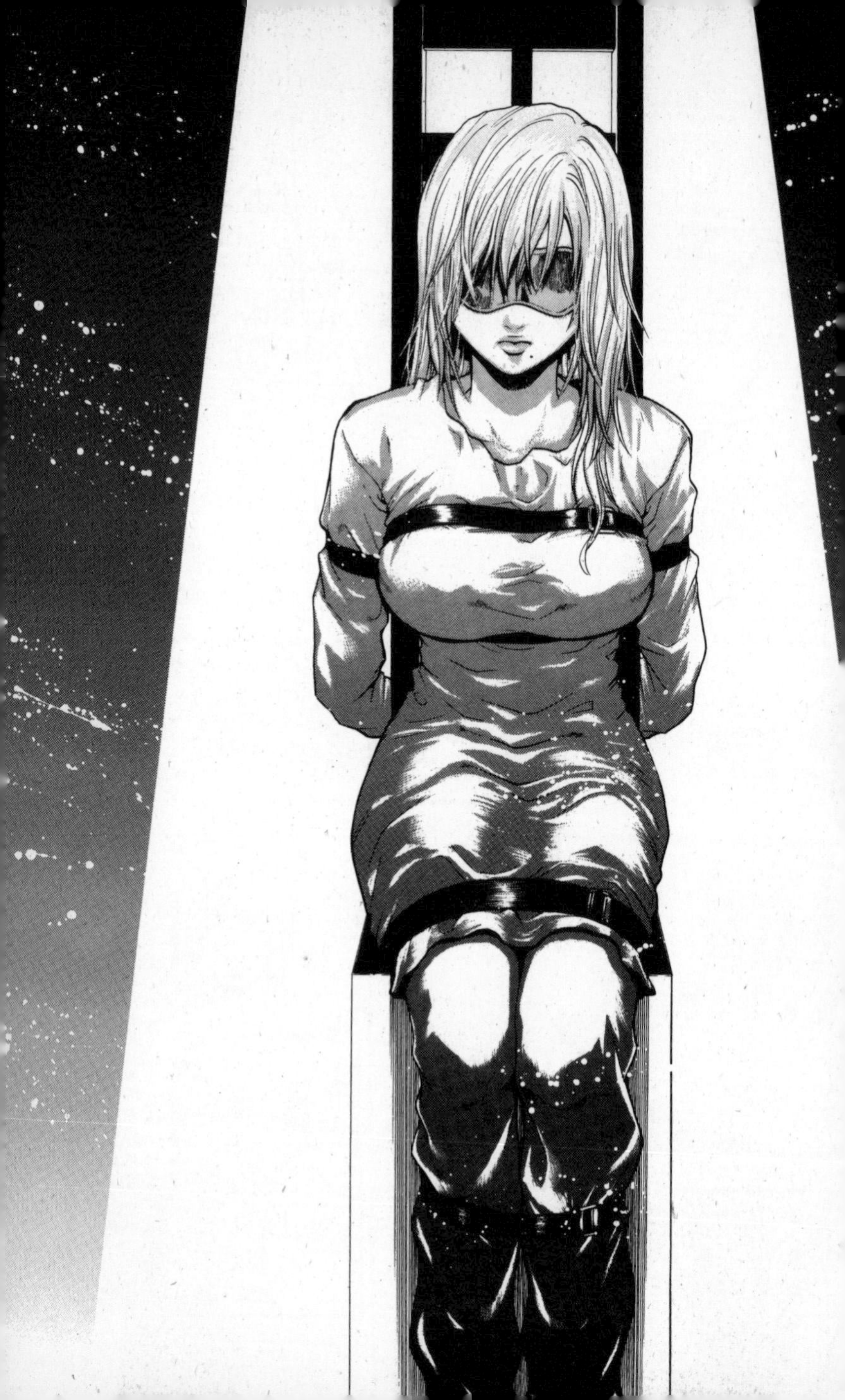

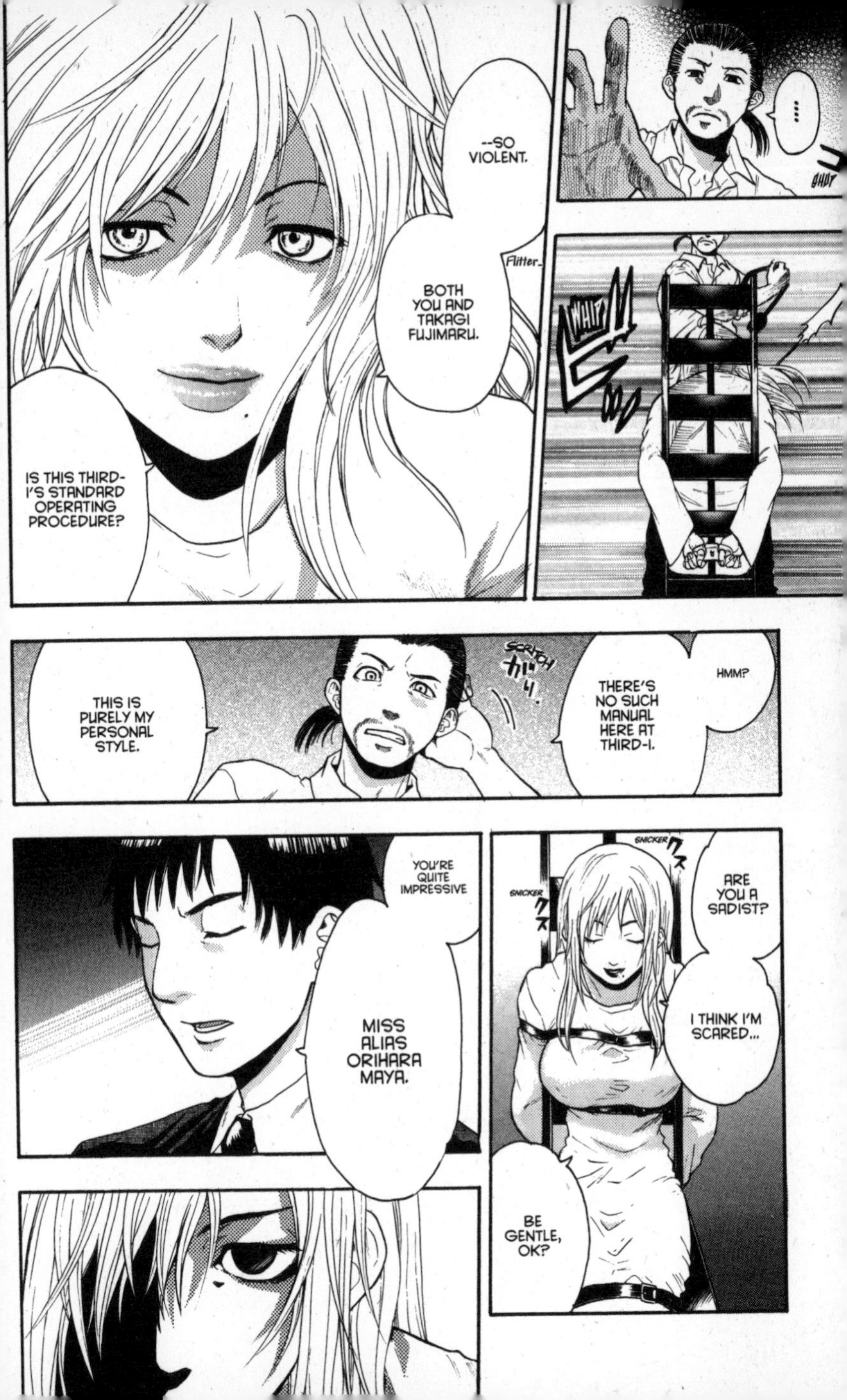
...
WHIP
Flitter
--SO VIOLENT.
BOTH YOU AND TAKAGI FUJIMARU.
IS THIS THIRD-I'S STANDARD OPERATING PROCEDURE?
HMM?
THERE'S NO SUCH MANUAL HERE AT THIRD-I.
SCRTCH
THIS IS PURELY MY PERSONAL STYLE.
SNICKER
SNICKER
ARE YOU A SADIST?
I THINK I'M SCARED...
BE GENTLE, OK?
YOU'RE QUITE IMPRESSIVE
MISS ALIAS ORIHARA MAYA.

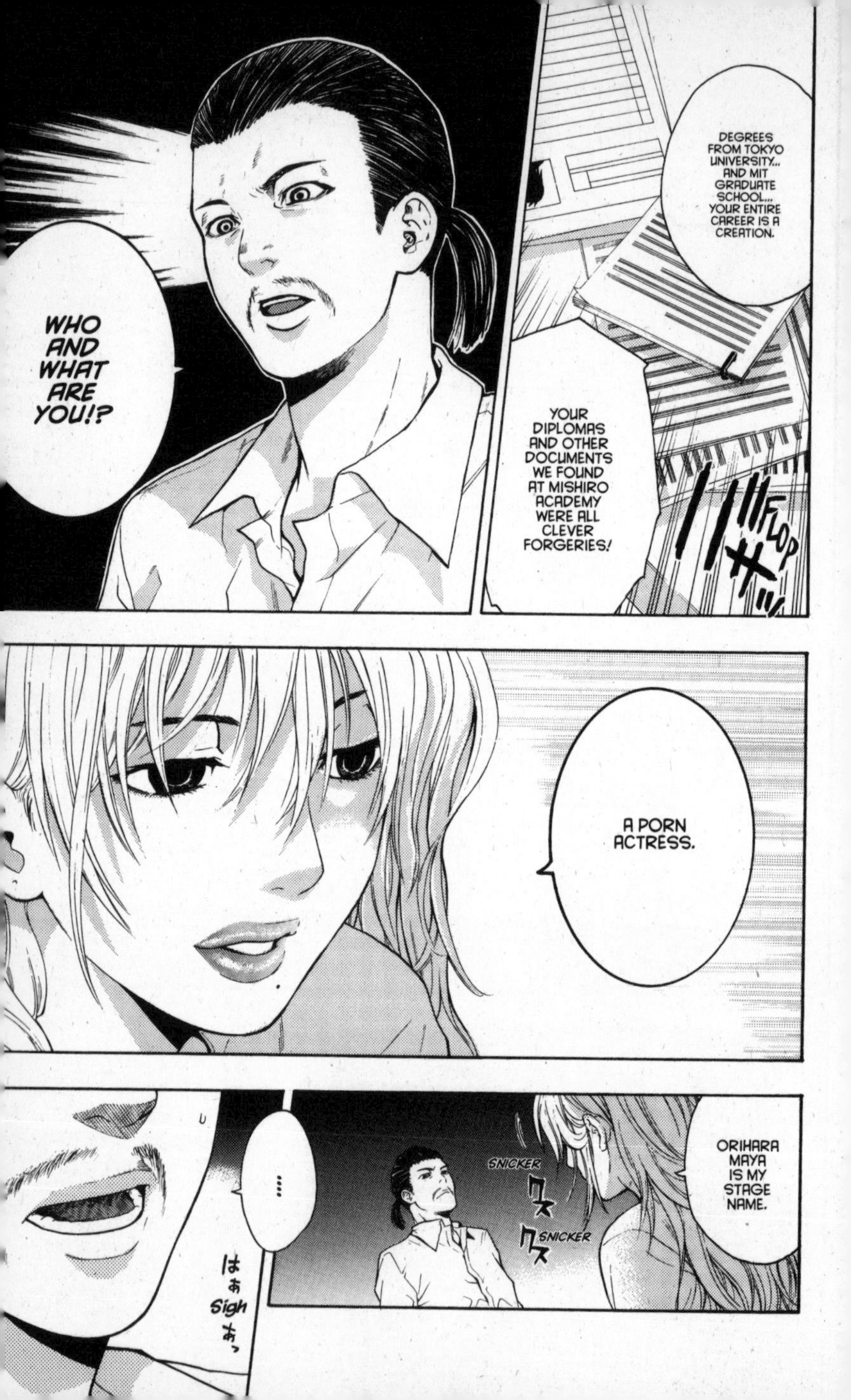
DEGREES FROM TOKYO UNIVERSITY... AND MIT GRADUATE SCHOOL... YOUR ENTIRE CAREER IS A CREATION.
YOUR DIPLOMAS AND OTHER DOCUMENTS WE FOUND AT MISHIRO ACADEMY WERE ALL CLEVER FORGERIES!
FLOP
WHO AND WHAT ARE YOU!?
A PORN ACTRESS.
ORIHARA MAYA IS MY STAGE NAME.
SNICKER
SNICKER
...
Sigh

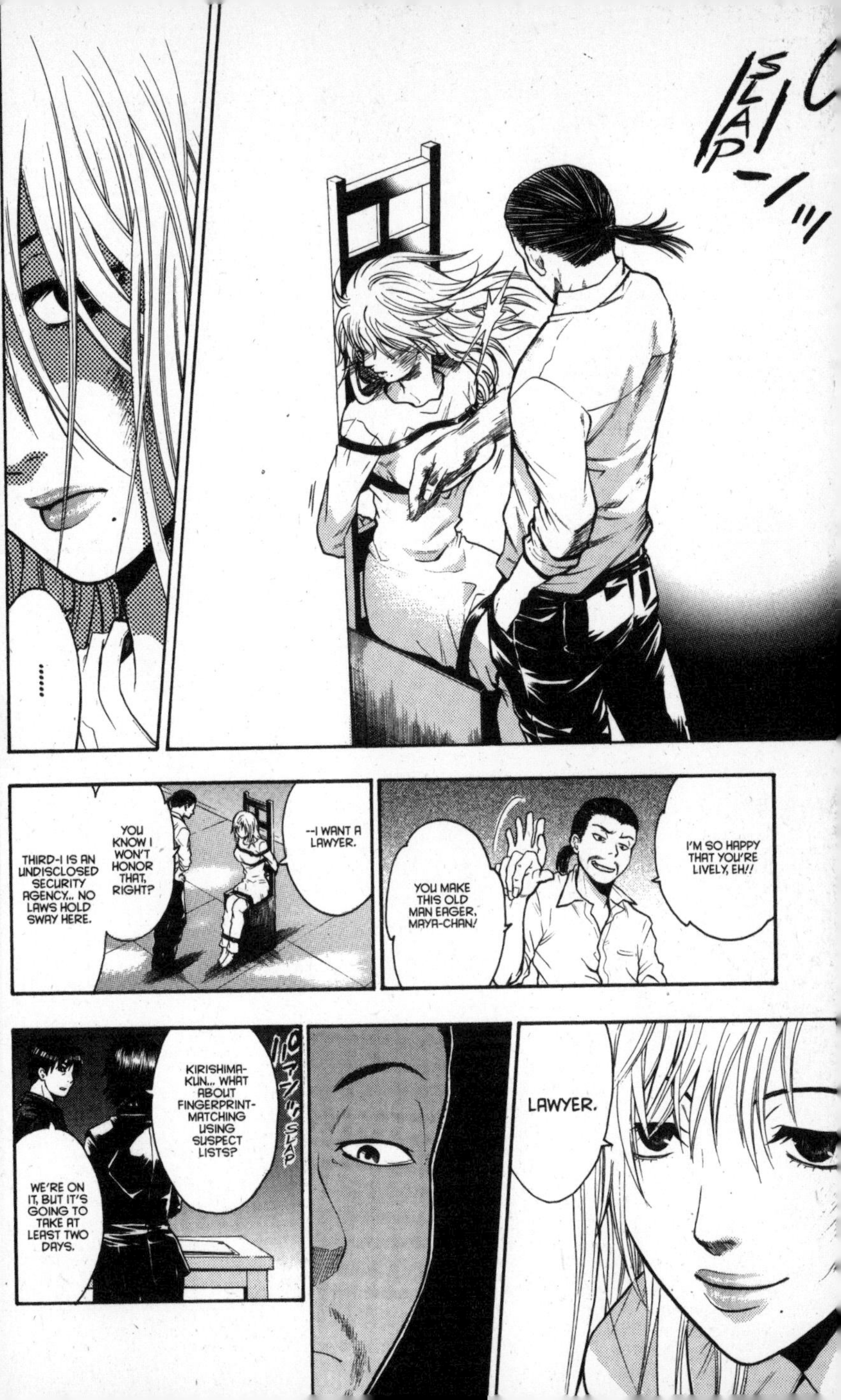
SLAP!!
......
I'M SO HAPPY THAT YOU'RE LIVELY, EH!!
YOU MAKE THIS OLD MAN EAGER, MAYA-CHAN!
--I WANT A LAWYER.
YOU KNOW I WON'T HONOR THAT, RIGHT?
THIRD-I IS AN UNDISCLOSED SECURITY AGENCY... NO LAWS HOLD SWAY HERE.
LAWYER.
SLAP
KIRISHIMA-KUN... WHAT ABOUT FINGERPRINT-MATCHING USING SUSPECT LISTS?
WE'RE ON IT, BUT IT'S GOING TO TAKE AT LEAST TWO DAYS.

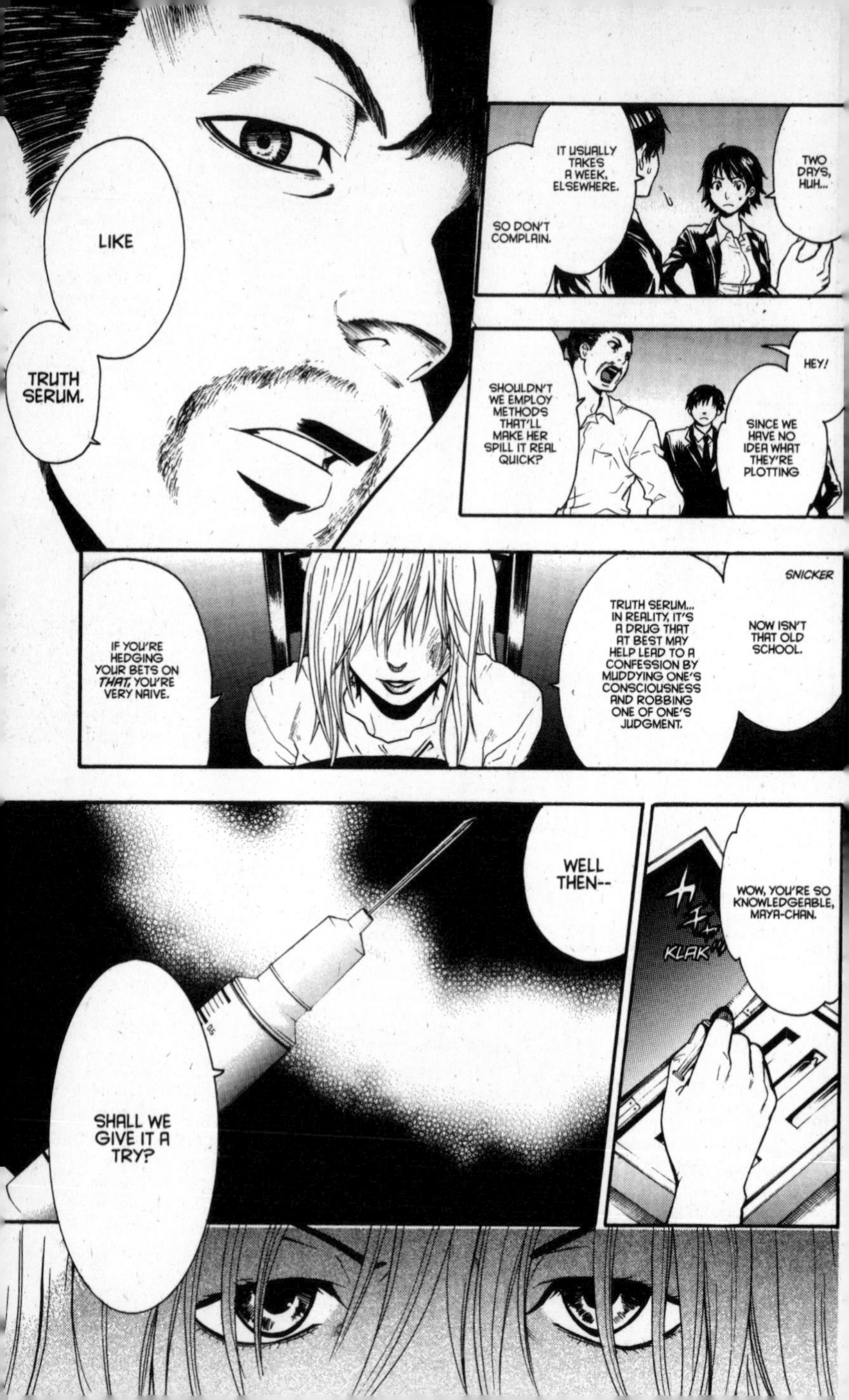

TWO DAYS, HUH...
IT USUALLY TAKES A WEEK, ELSEWHERE.
SO DON'T COMPLAIN.
HEY!
SINCE WE HAVE NO IDEA WHAT THEY'RE PLOTTING
SHOULDN'T WE EMPLOY METHODS THAT'LL MAKE HER SPILL IT REAL QUICK?
LIKE
TRUTH SERUM.
SNICKER
NOW ISN'T THAT OLD SCHOOL.
TRUTH SERUM... IN REALITY, IT'S A DRUG THAT AT BEST MAY HELP LEAD TO A CONFESSION BY MUDDYING ONE'S CONSCIOUSNESS AND ROBBING ONE OF ONE'S JUDGMENT.
IF YOU'RE HEDGING YOUR BETS ON *THAT,* YOU'RE VERY NAIVE.
WOW, YOU'RE SO KNOWLEDGEABLE, MAYA-CHAN.
KLAK
WELL THEN--
SHALL WE GIVE IT A TRY?

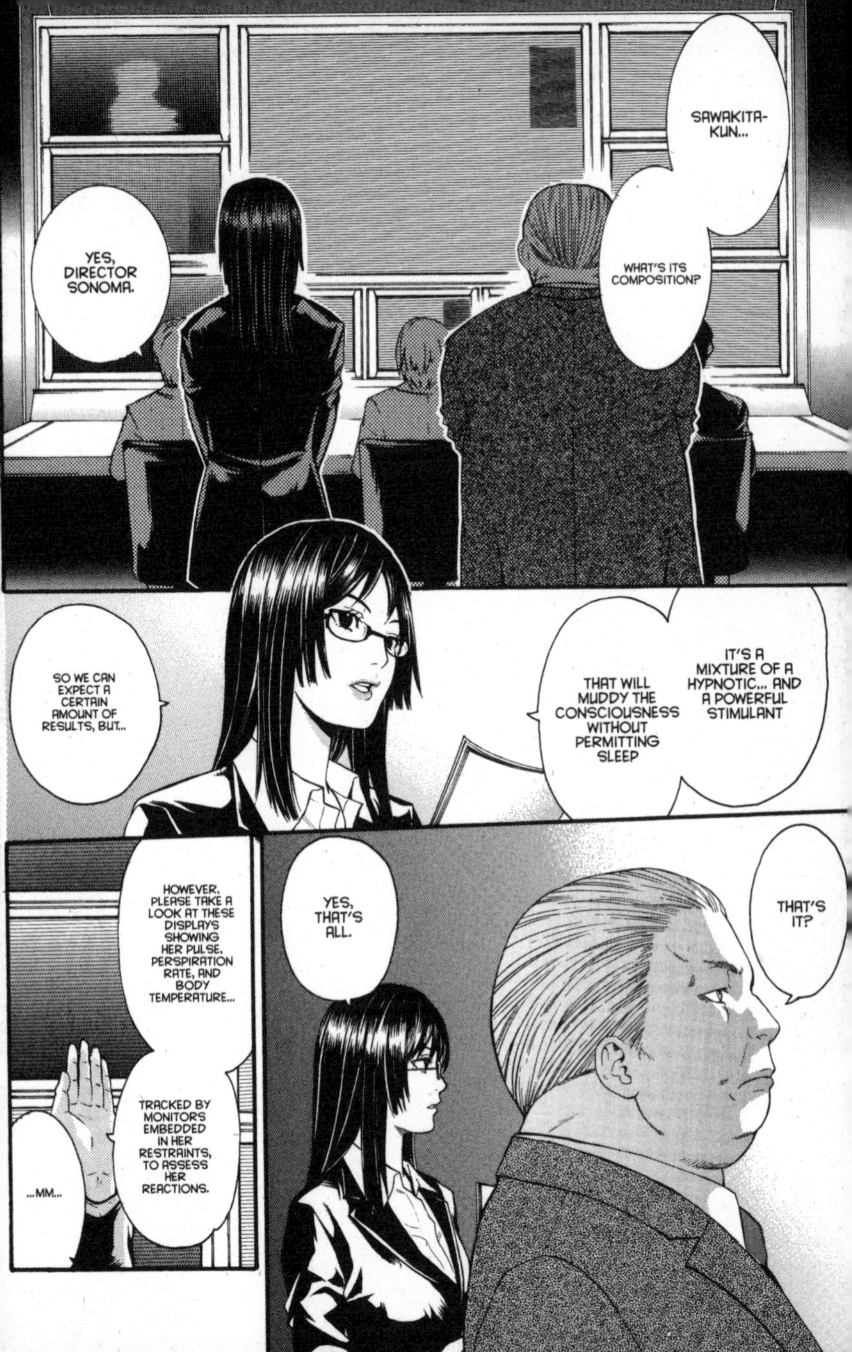
SAWAKITA-KUN...
WHAT'S ITS COMPOSITION?
YES, DIRECTOR SONOMA.
IT'S A MIXTURE OF A HYPNOTIC... AND A POWERFUL STIMULANT
THAT WILL MUDDY THE CONSCIOUSNESS WITHOUT PERMITTING SLEEP
SO WE CAN EXPECT A CERTAIN AMOUNT OF RESULTS, BUT...
THAT'S IT?
YES, THAT'S ALL.
HOWEVER, PLEASE TAKE A LOOK AT THESE DISPLAYS SHOWING HER PULSE, PERSPIRATION RATE, AND BODY TEMPERATURE...
TRACKED BY MONITORS EMBEDDED IN HER RESTRAINTS, TO ASSESS HER REACTIONS.
...MM...

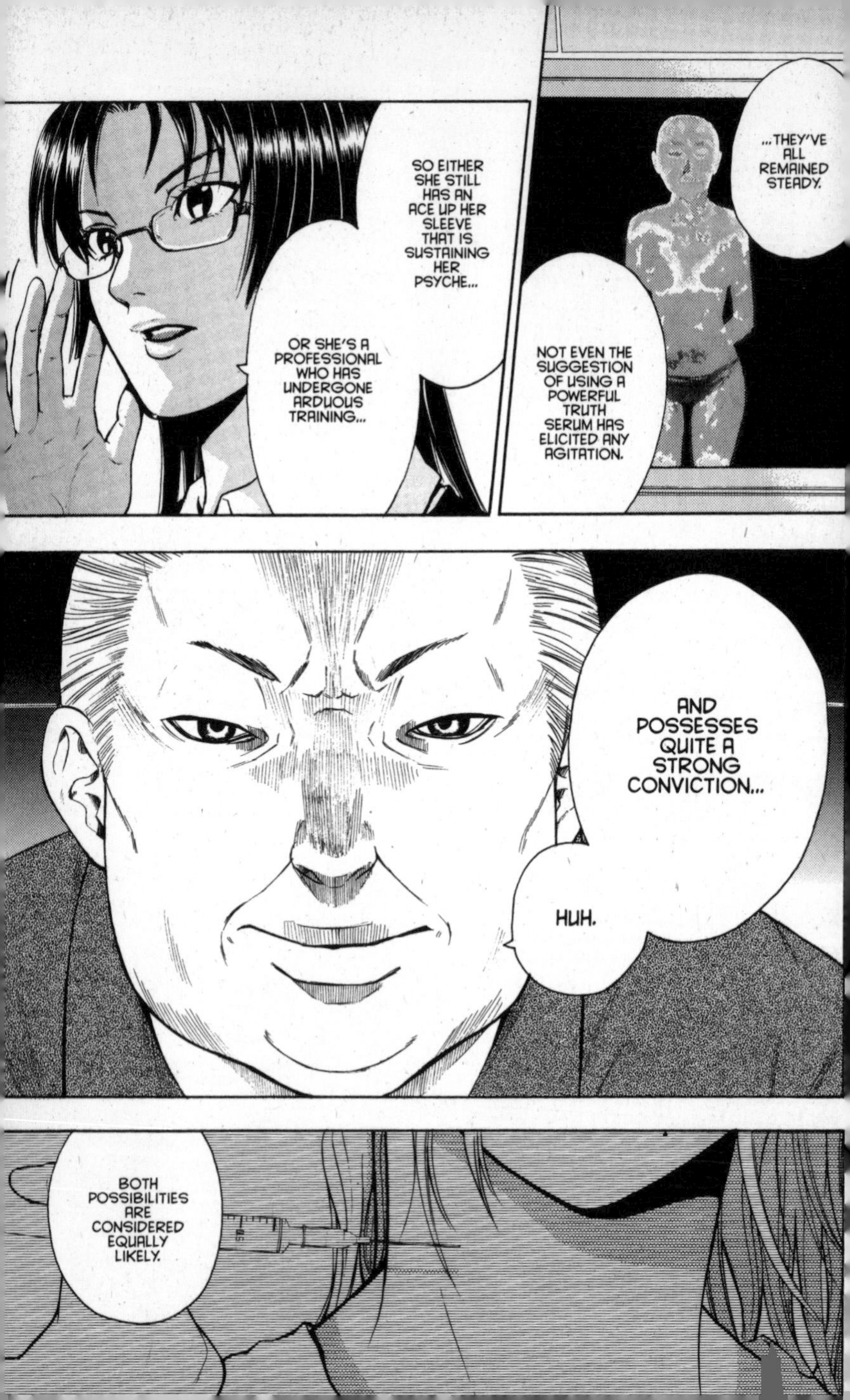
...THEY'VE ALL REMAINED STEADY.
NOT EVEN THE SUGGESTION OF USING A POWERFUL TRUTH SERUM HAS ELICITED ANY AGITATION.
SO EITHER SHE STILL HAS AN ACE UP HER SLEEVE THAT IS SUSTAINING HER PSYCHE...
OR SHE'S A PROFESSIONAL WHO HAS UNDERGONE ARDUOUS TRAINING...
AND POSSESSES QUITE A STRONG CONVICTION...
HUH.
BOTH POSSIBILITIES ARE CONSIDERED EQUALLY LIKELY.

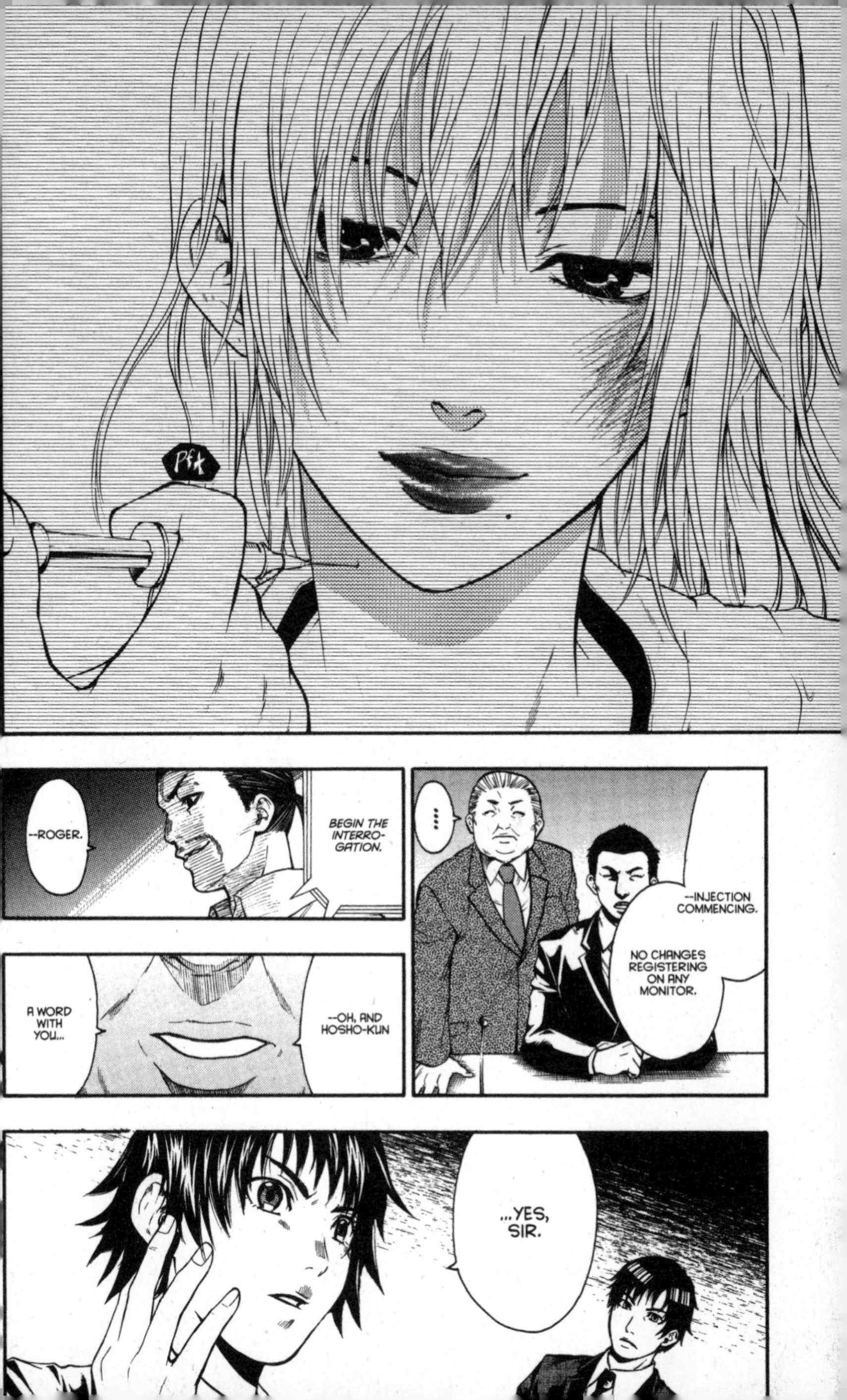

--INJECTION COMMENCING.
NO CHANGES REGISTERING ON ANY MONITOR.
....
BEGIN THE INTERRO-GATION.
--ROGER.
--OH, AND HOSHO-KUN
A WORD WITH YOU...
...YES, SIR.

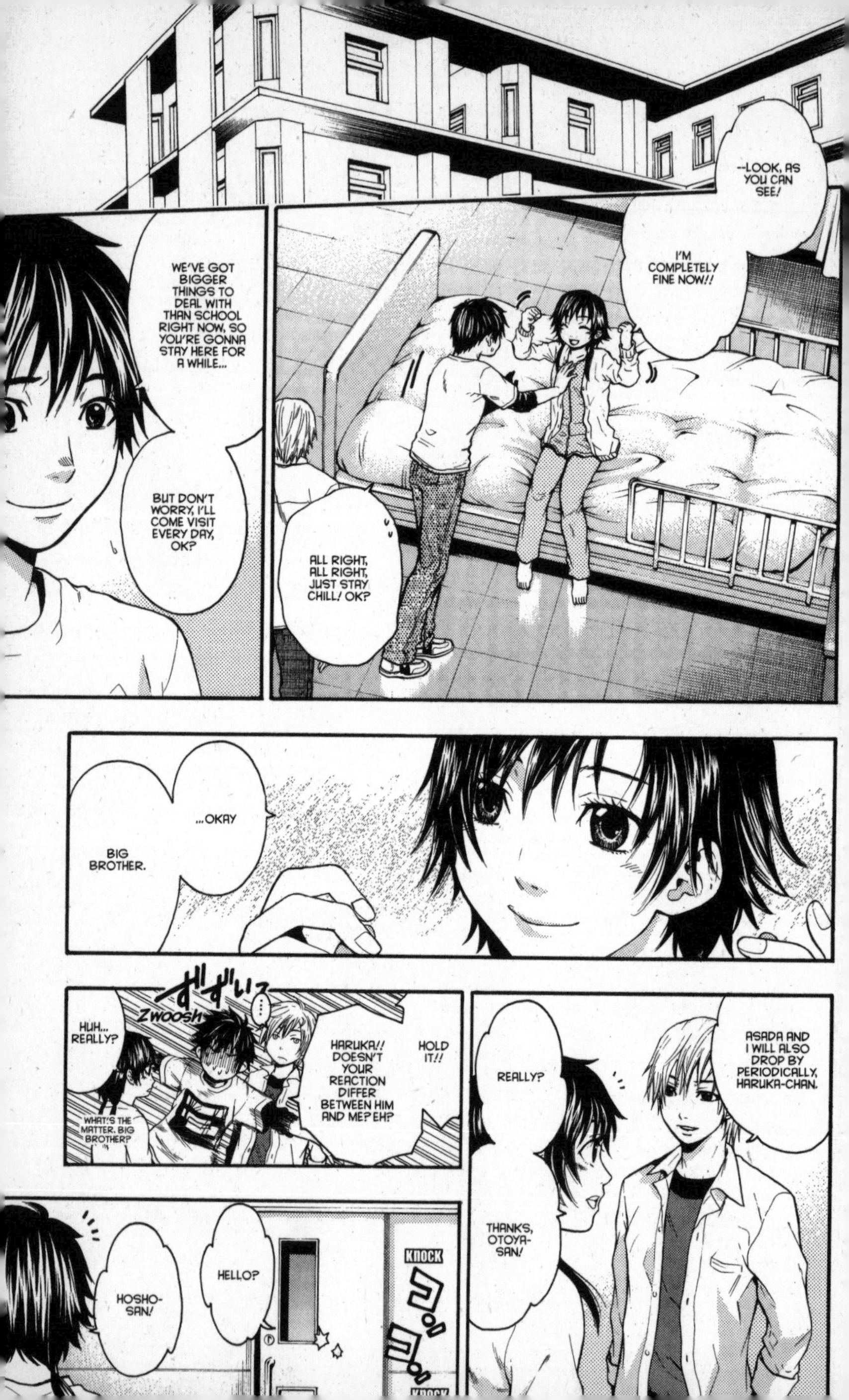
--LOOK, AS YOU CAN SEE!
I'M COMPLETELY FINE NOW!!
ALL RIGHT, ALL RIGHT, JUST STAY CHILL! OK?
WE'VE GOT BIGGER THINGS TO DEAL WITH THAN SCHOOL RIGHT NOW, SO YOU'RE GONNA STAY HERE FOR A WHILE...
BUT DON'T WORRY, I'LL COME VISIT EVERY DAY, OK?
...OKAY
BIG BROTHER.
ASADA AND I WILL ALSO DROP BY PERIODICALLY, HARUKA-CHAN.
REALLY?
THANKS, OTOYA-SAN!
ZWOOSH
HOLD IT!!
HARUKA!! DOESN'T YOUR REACTION DIFFER BETWEEN HIM AND ME? EH?
HUH... REALLY?
WHAT'S THE MATTER, BIG BROTHER?
KNOCK
HELLO?
HOSHO-SAN!

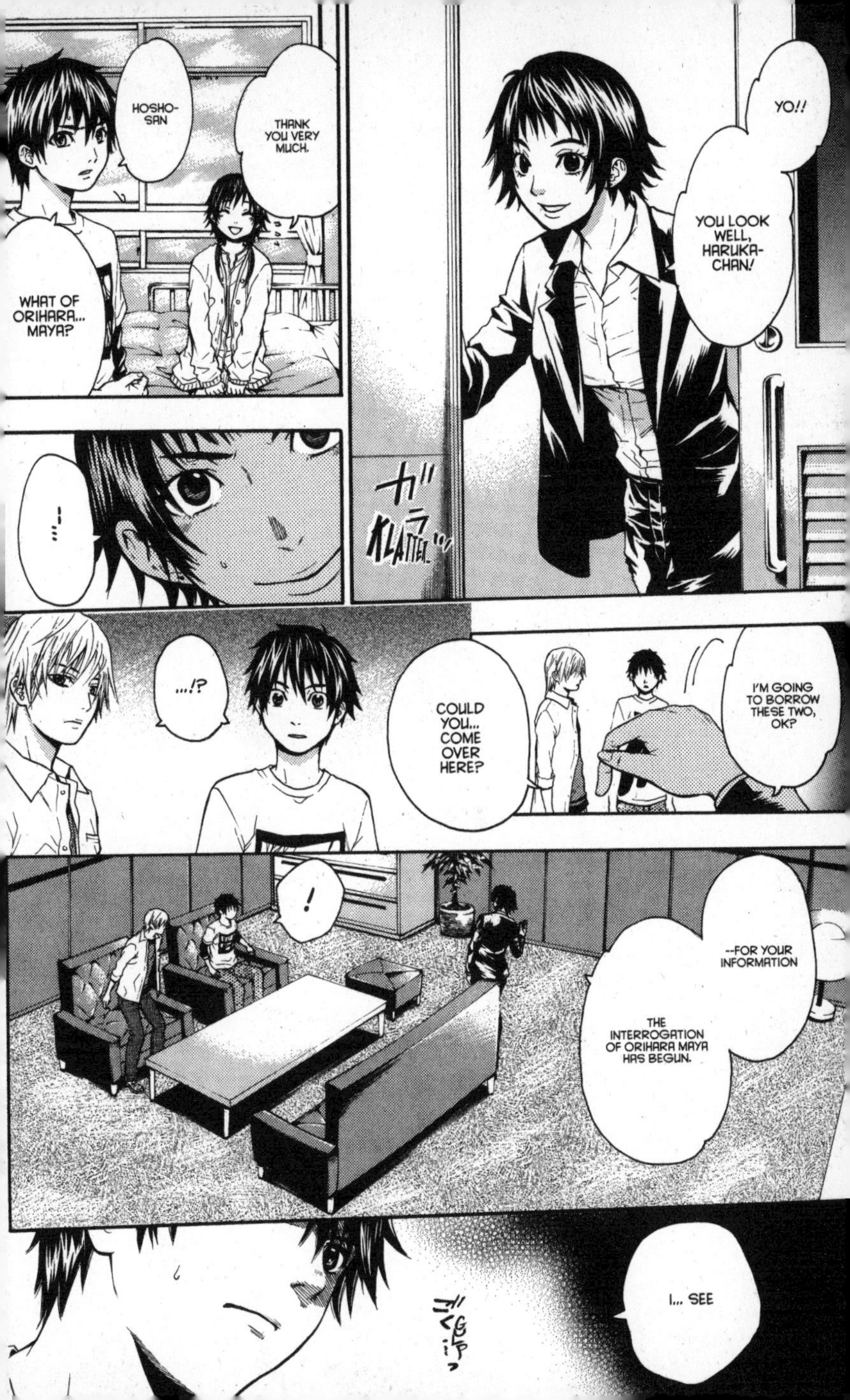
YO!!
YOU LOOK WELL, HARUKA-CHAN!
KLATTER
THANK YOU VERY MUCH.
HOSHO-SAN
WHAT OF ORIHARA... MAYA?
...!...
I'M GOING TO BORROW THESE TWO, OK?
COULD YOU... COME OVER HERE?
...!?
--FOR YOUR INFORMATION
THE INTERROGATION OF ORIHARA MAYA HAS BEGUN.
!
I... SEE
GULP

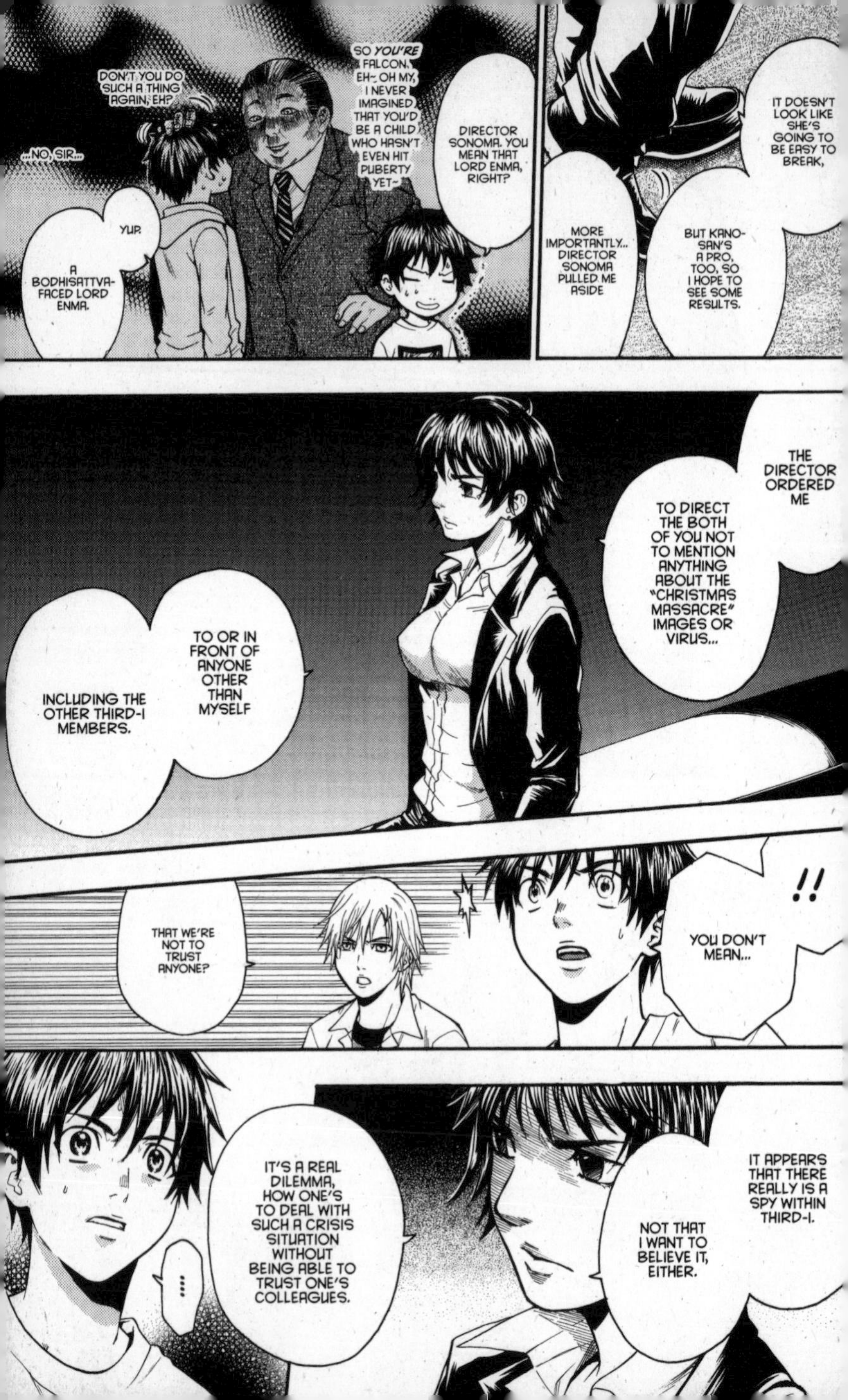
IT DOESN'T LOOK LIKE SHE'S GOING TO BE EASY TO BREAK,
BUT KANO-SAN'S A PRO, TOO, SO I HOPE TO SEE SOME RESULTS.
MORE IMPORTANTLY... DIRECTOR SONOMA PULLED ME ASIDE
DIRECTOR SONOMA. YOU MEAN THAT LORD ENMA, RIGHT?
SO *YOU'RE* FALCON, EH~ OH MY, I NEVER IMAGINED THAT YOU'D BE A CHILD WHO HASN'T EVEN HIT PUBERTY YET~
DON'T YOU DO SUCH A THING AGAIN, EH?
...NO, SIR...
YUP.
A BODHISATTVA-FACED LORD ENMA.
THE DIRECTOR ORDERED ME
TO DIRECT THE BOTH OF YOU NOT TO MENTION ANYTHING ABOUT THE "CHRISTMAS MASSACRE" IMAGES OR VIRUS...
TO OR IN FRONT OF ANYONE OTHER THAN MYSELF
INCLUDING THE OTHER THIRD-I MEMBERS.
!!
YOU DON'T MEAN...
THAT WE'RE NOT TO TRUST ANYONE?
IT APPEARS THAT THERE REALLY IS A SPY WITHIN THIRD-I.
NOT THAT I WANT TO BELIEVE IT, EITHER.
IT'S A REAL DILEMMA, HOW ONE'S TO DEAL WITH SUCH A CRISIS SITUATION WITHOUT BEING ABLE TO TRUST ONE'S COLLEAGUES.
....

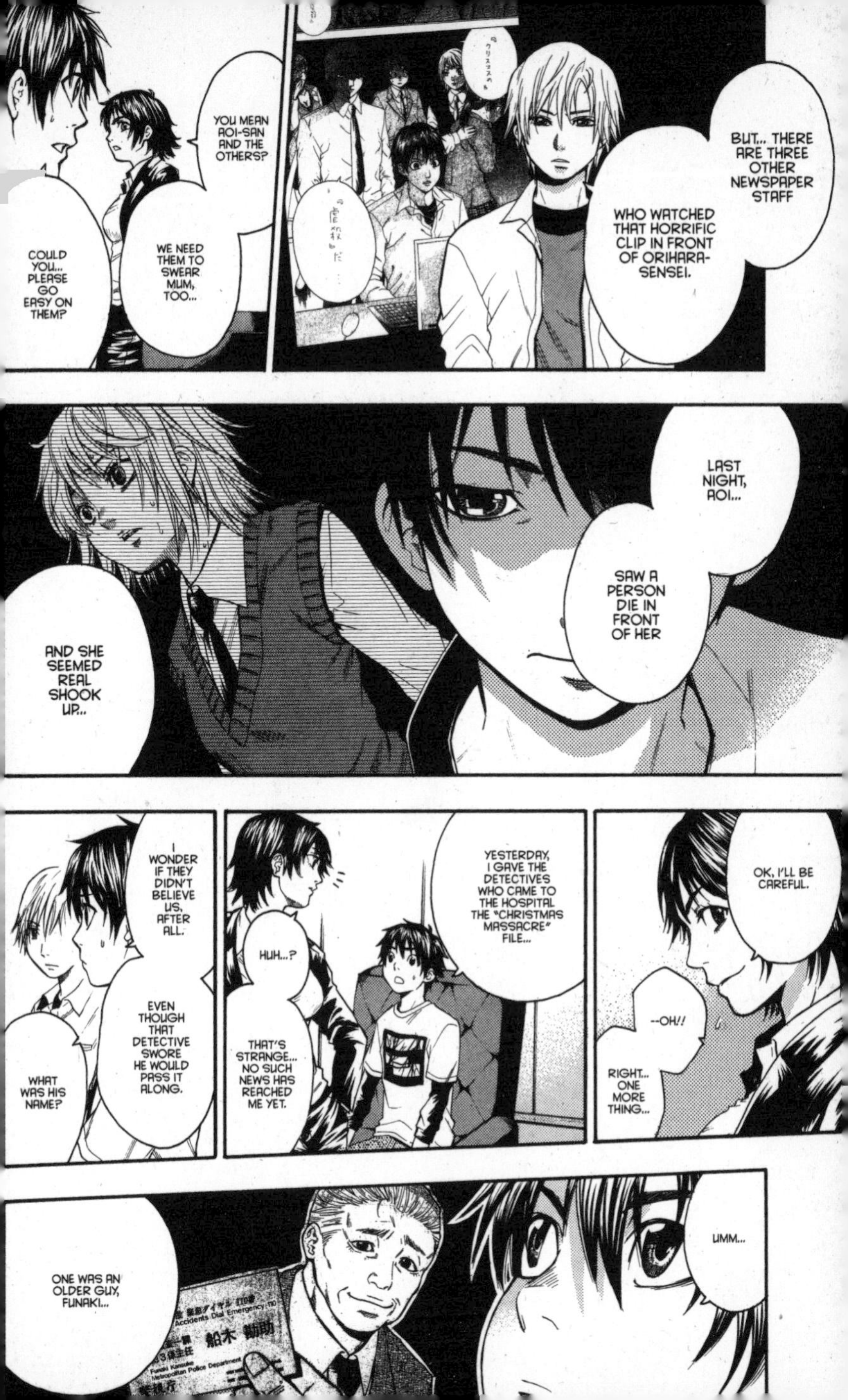
BUT... THERE ARE THREE OTHER NEWSPAPER STAFF
WHO WATCHED THAT HORRIFIC CLIP IN FRONT OF ORIHARA-SENSEI.
『クリスマスの』
『虐殺だ……』
YOU MEAN AOI-SAN AND THE OTHERS?
WE NEED THEM TO SWEAR MUM, TOO...
COULD YOU... PLEASE GO EASY ON THEM?
LAST NIGHT, AOI...
SAW A PERSON DIE IN FRONT OF HER
AND SHE SEEMED REAL SHOOK UP...
OK, I'LL BE CAREFUL.
--OH!!
RIGHT... ONE MORE THING...
YESTERDAY, I GAVE THE DETECTIVES WHO CAME TO THE HOSPITAL THE "CHRISTMAS MASSACRE" FILE...
HUH...?
THAT'S STRANGE... NO SUCH NEWS HAS REACHED ME YET.
I WONDER IF THEY DIDN'T BELIEVE US, AFTER ALL.
EVEN THOUGH THAT DETECTIVE SWORE HE WOULD PASS IT ALONG.
WHAT WAS HIS NAME?
UMM...
ONE WAS AN OLDER GUY, FUNAKI...

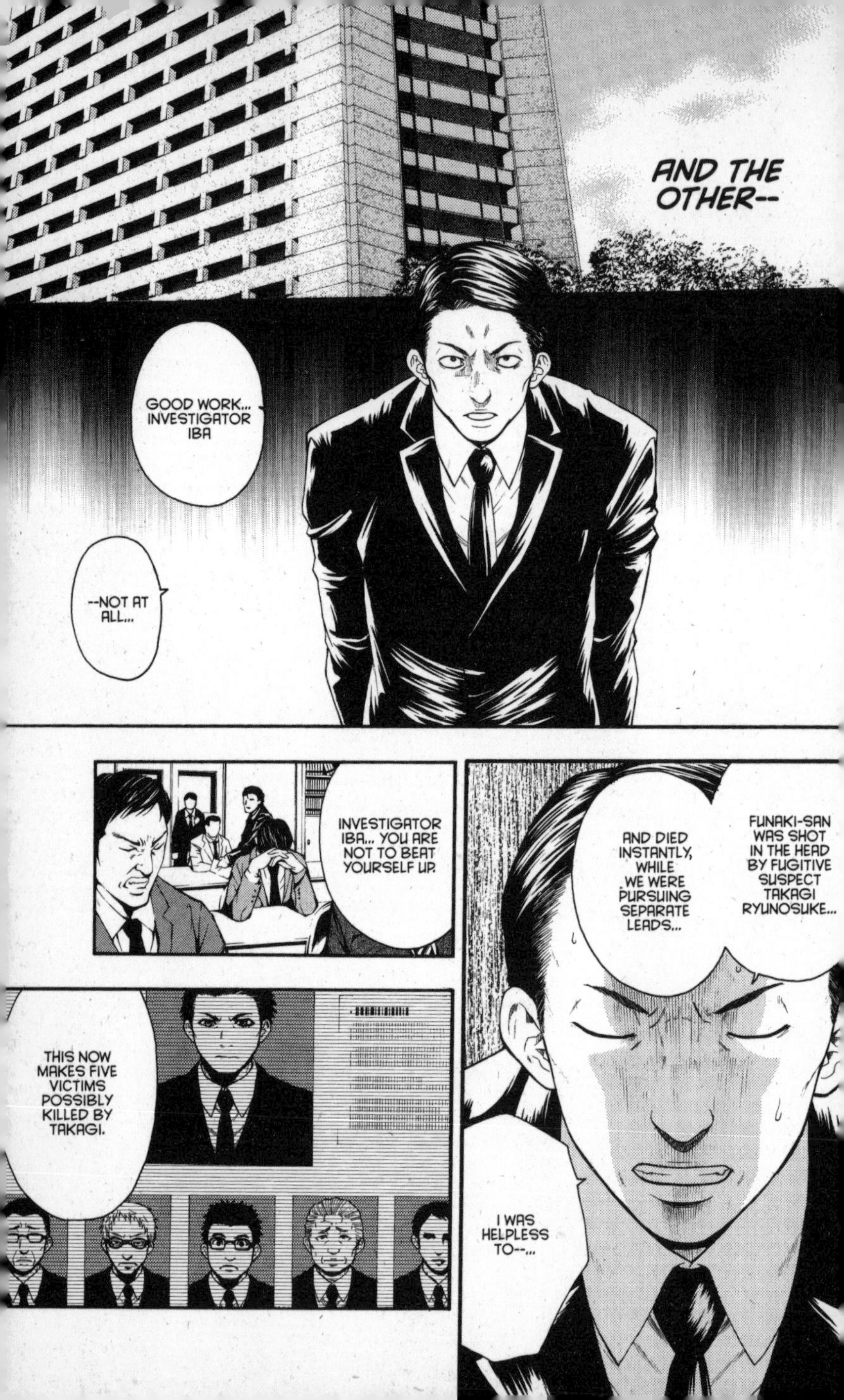
AND THE OTHER--
GOOD WORK... INVESTIGATOR IBA
--NOT AT ALL...
FUNAKI-SAN WAS SHOT IN THE HEAD BY FUGITIVE SUSPECT TAKAGI RYUNOSUKE...
AND DIED INSTANTLY, WHILE WE WERE PURSUING SEPARATE LEADS...
I WAS HELPLESS TO--...
INVESTIGATOR IBA... YOU ARE NOT TO BEAT YOURSELF UP.
THIS NOW MAKES FIVE VICTIMS POSSIBLY KILLED BY TAKAGI.

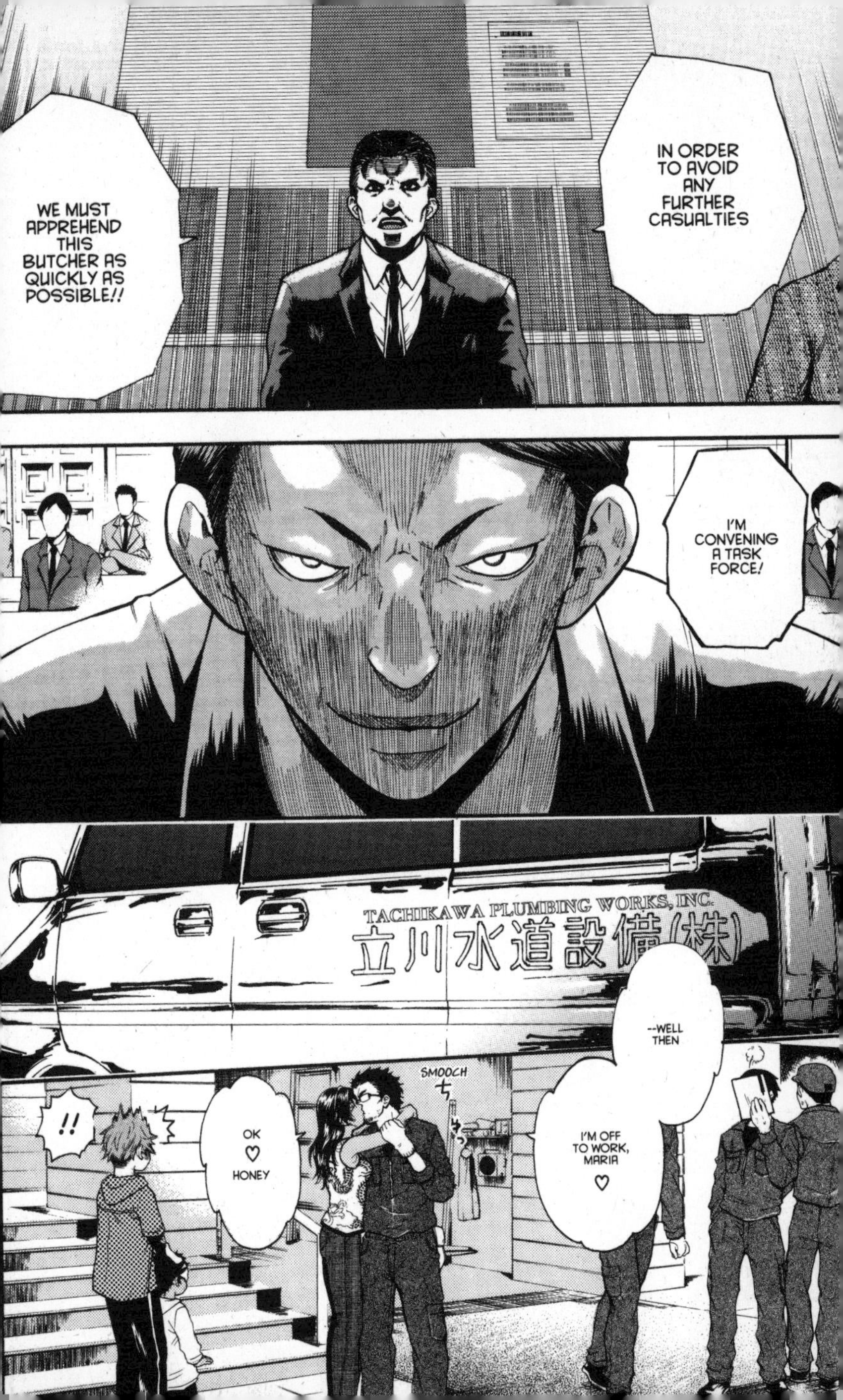
IN ORDER TO AVOID ANY FURTHER CASUALTIES
WE MUST APPREHEND THIS BUTCHER AS QUICKLY AS POSSIBLE!!
I'M CONVENING A TASK FORCE!
TACHIKAWA PLUMBING WORKS, INC.
立川水道設備(株)
--WELL THEN
I'M OFF TO WORK, MARIA ♡
SMOOCH
OK ♡ HONEY
!!

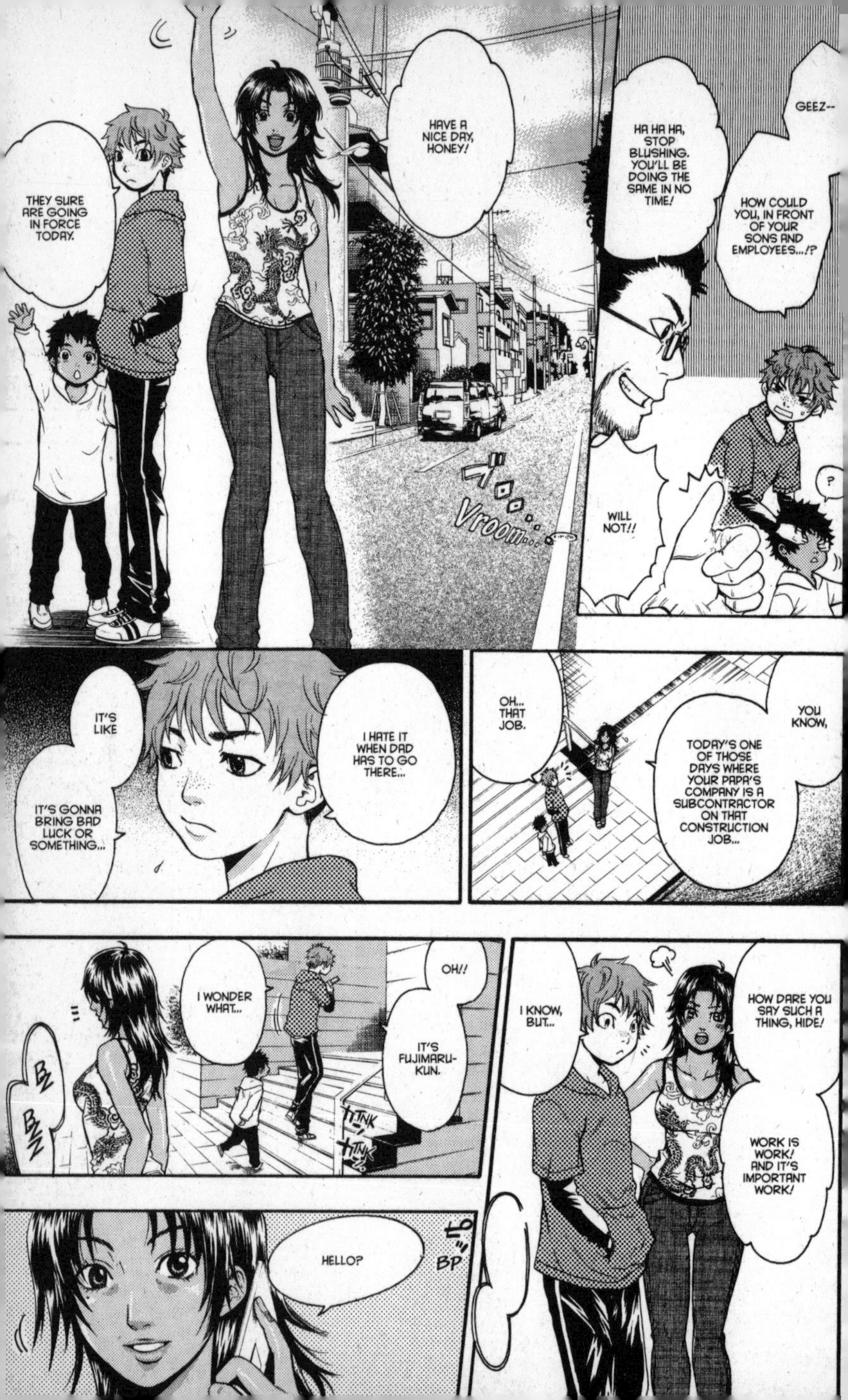
GEEZ--
HOW COULD YOU, IN FRONT OF YOUR SONS AND EMPLOYEES...!?
HA HA HA, STOP BLUSHING. YOU'LL BE DOING THE SAME IN NO TIME!
WILL NOT!!
?
HAVE A NICE DAY, HONEY!
THEY SURE ARE GOING IN FORCE TODAY.
Vroom...
YOU KNOW,
TODAY'S ONE OF THOSE DAYS WHERE YOUR PAPA'S COMPANY IS A SUBCONTRACTOR ON THAT CONSTRUCTION JOB...
OH... THAT JOB.
I HATE IT WHEN DAD HAS TO GO THERE...
IT'S LIKE
IT'S GONNA BRING BAD LUCK OR SOMETHING...
HOW DARE YOU SAY SUCH A THING, HIDE!
I KNOW, BUT...
WORK IS WORK! AND IT'S IMPORTANT WORK!
BP
OH!!
IT'S FUJIMARU-KUN.
I WONDER WHAT...
TI-TINK
TI-TINK
BZ
BZ
HELLO?

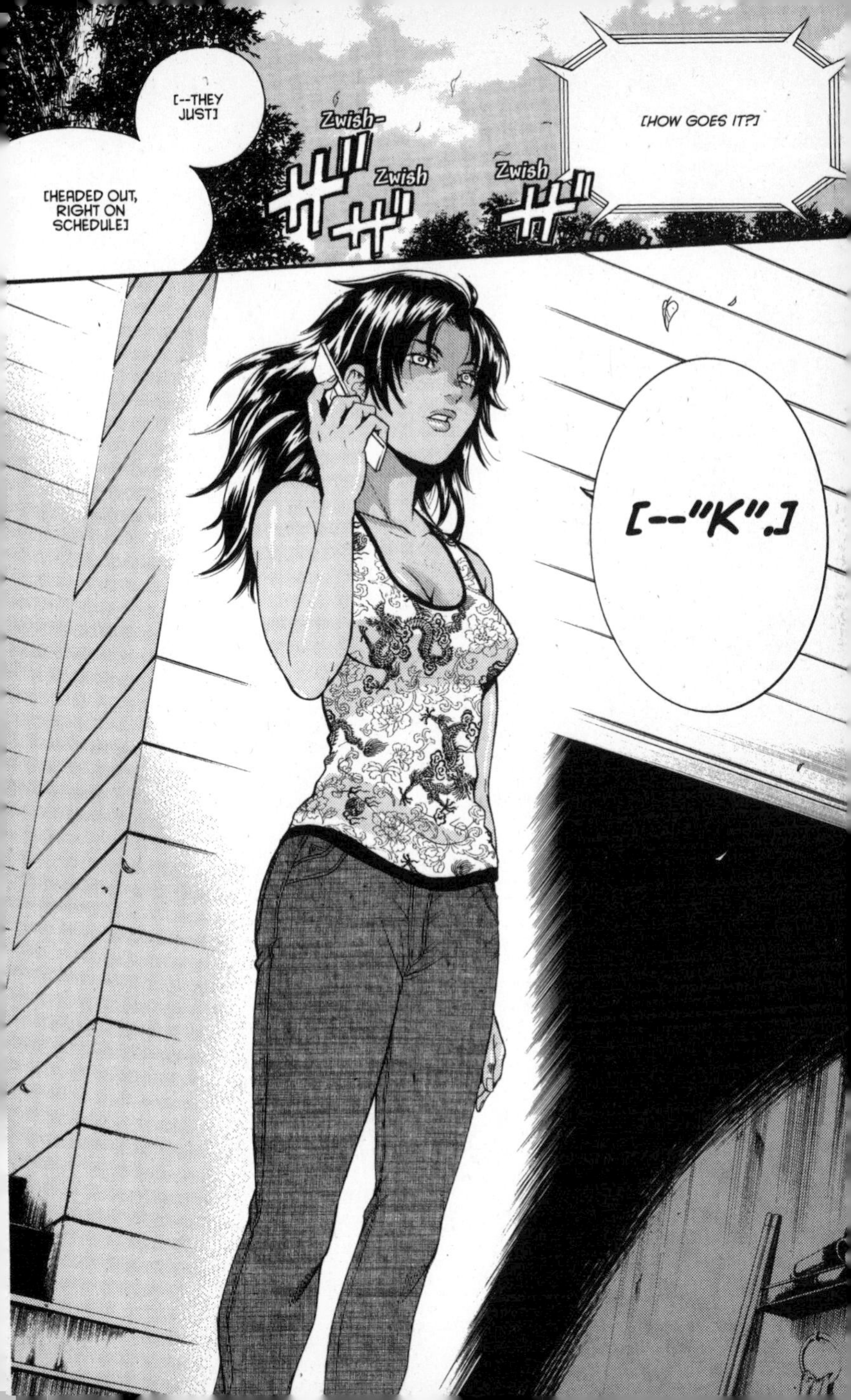
[HOW GOES IT?]
Zwish
Zwish
Zwish-
[--THEY JUST]
[HEADED OUT, RIGHT ON SCHEDULE]
[--"K".]

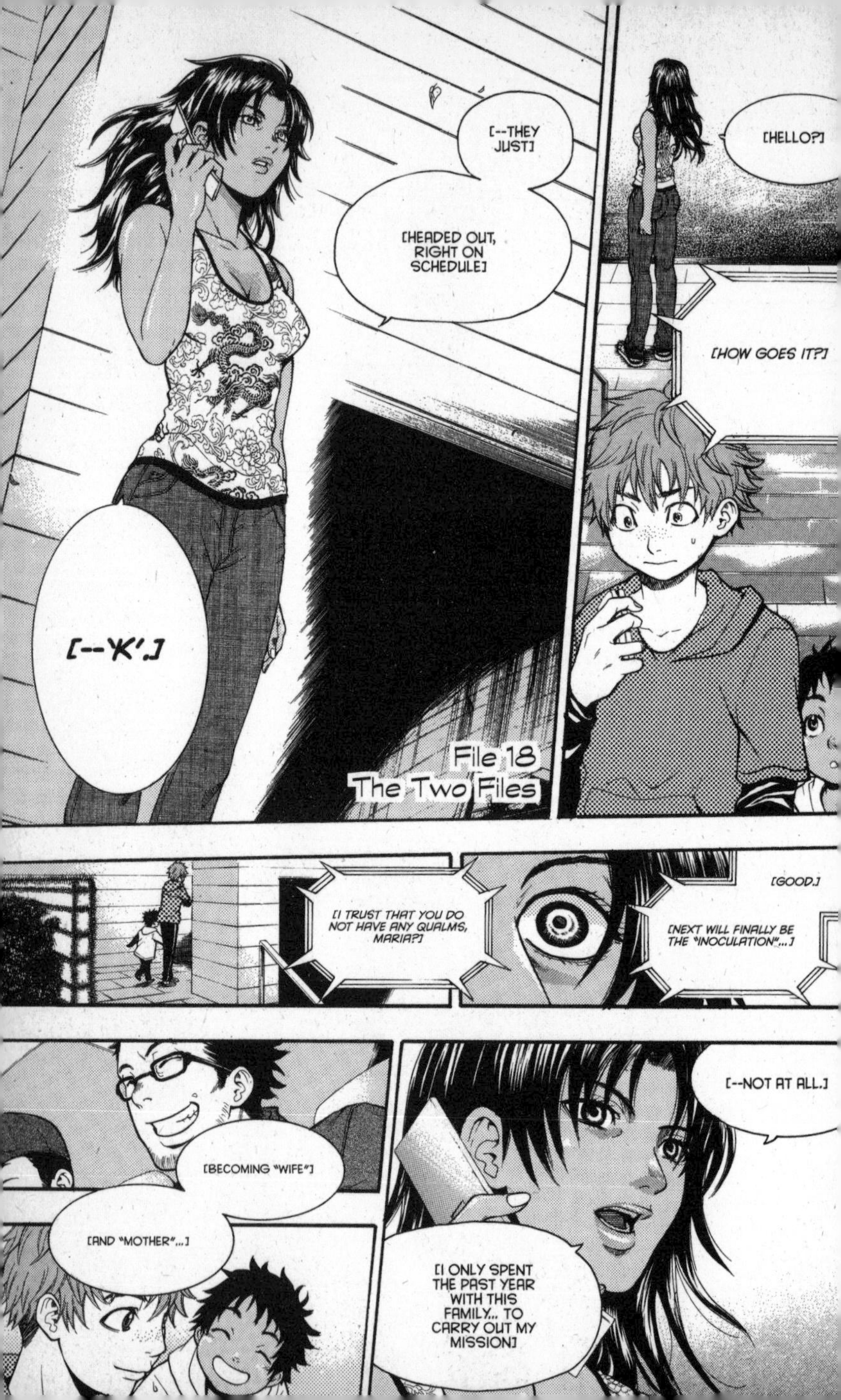
[HELLO?]
[HOW GOES IT?]
[--THEY JUST]
[HEADED OUT, RIGHT ON SCHEDULE]
[--'K'.]
File 18 The Two Files
[GOOD.]
[NEXT WILL FINALLY BE THE "INOCULATION"...]
[I TRUST THAT YOU DO NOT HAVE ANY QUALMS, MARIA?]
[--NOT AT ALL.]
[I ONLY SPENT THE PAST YEAR WITH THIS FAMILY... TO CARRY OUT MY MISSION]
[BECOMING "WIFE"]
[AND "MOTHER"...]

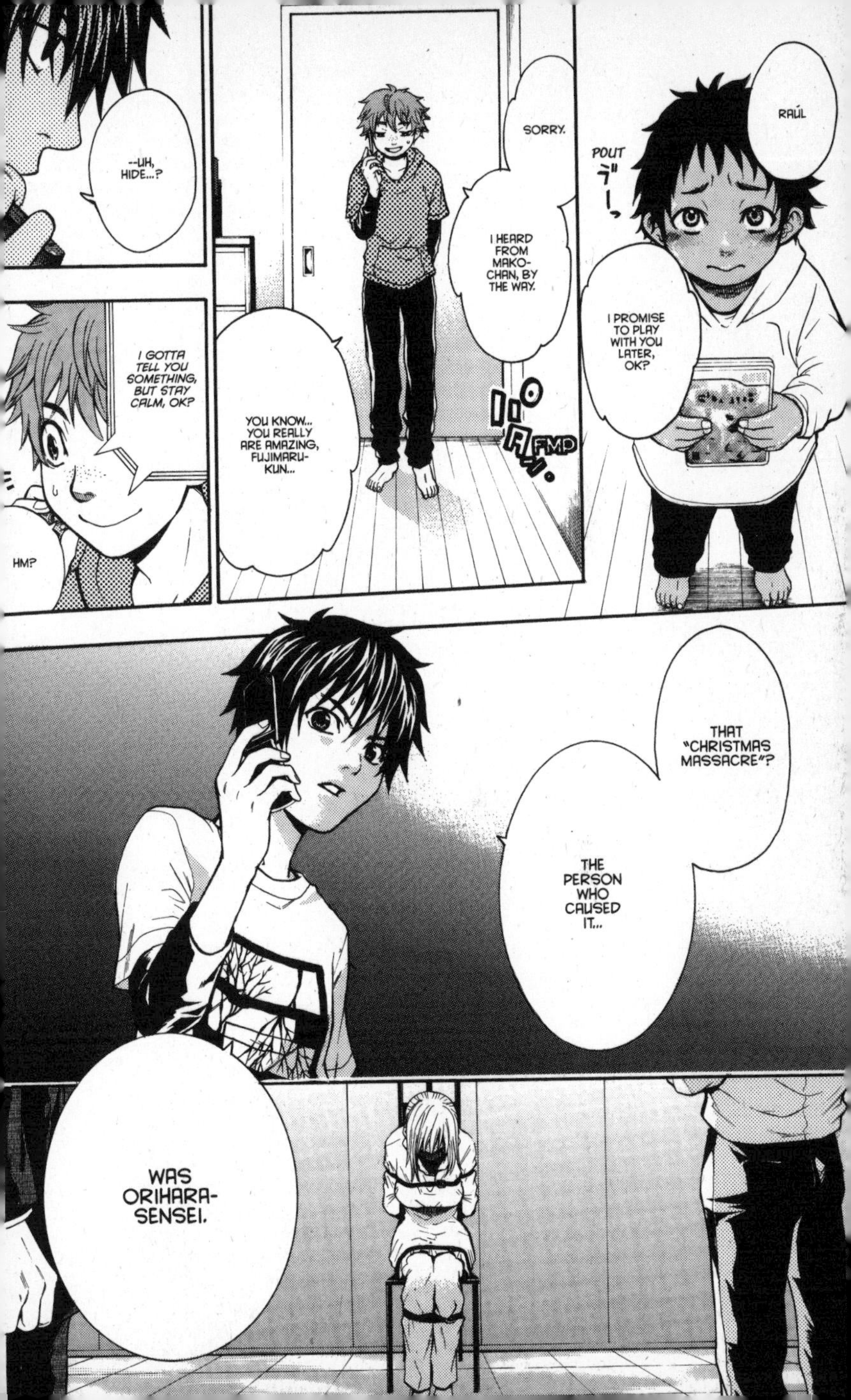
RAÚL
POUT
I PROMISE TO PLAY WITH YOU LATER, OK?
SORRY.
I HEARD FROM MAKO-CHAN, BY THE WAY.
YOU KNOW... YOU REALLY ARE AMAZING, FUJIMARU-KUN...
FMP
--UH, HIDE...?
I GOTTA TELL YOU SOMETHING, BUT STAY CALM, OK?
HM?
THAT "CHRISTMAS MASSACRE"?
THE PERSON WHO CAUSED IT...
WAS ORIHARA-SENSEI.

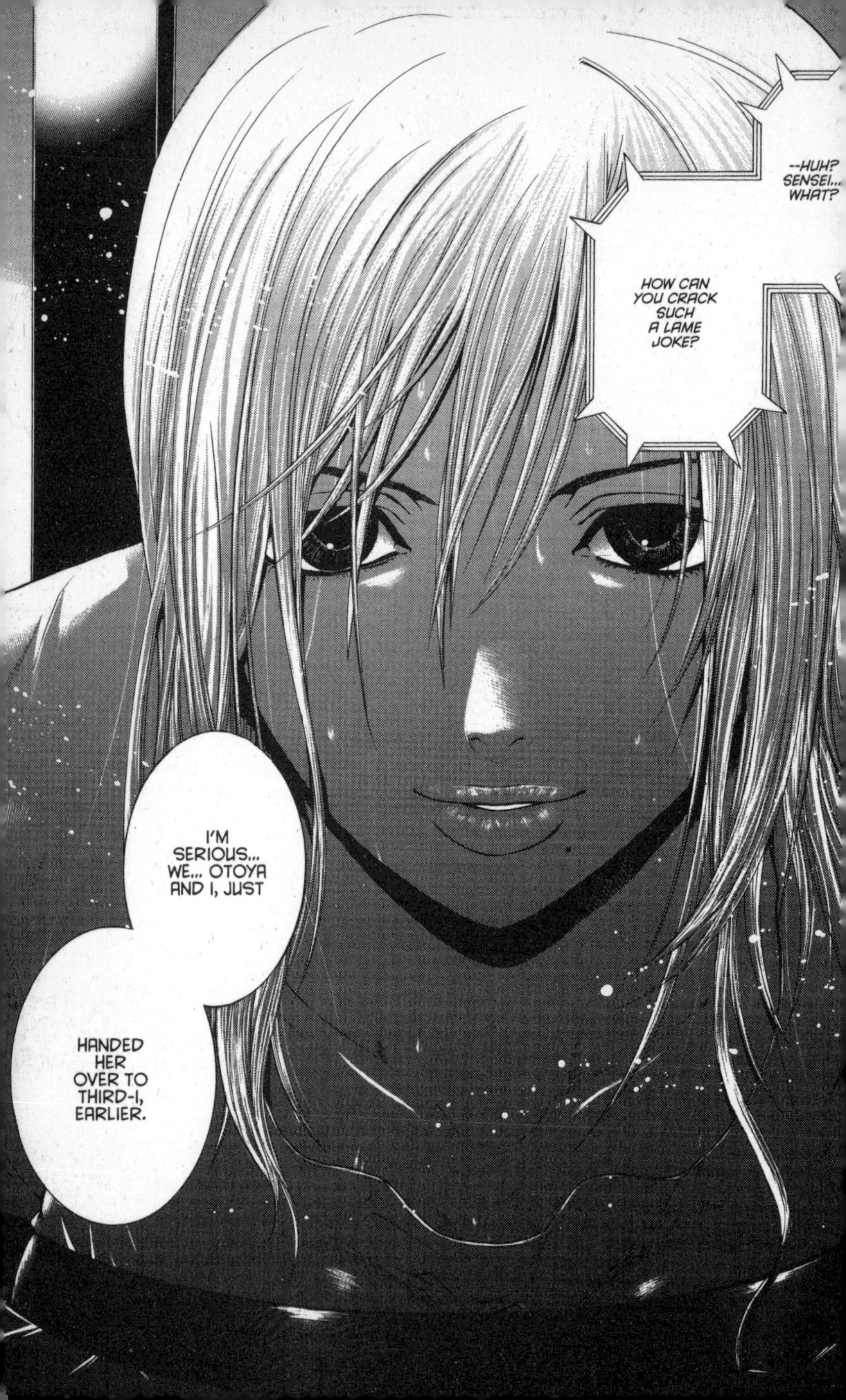
--HUH? SENSEI... WHAT?
HOW CAN YOU CRACK SUCH A LAME JOKE?
I'M SERIOUS... WE... OTOYA AND I, JUST
HANDED HER OVER TO THIRD-I, EARLIER.

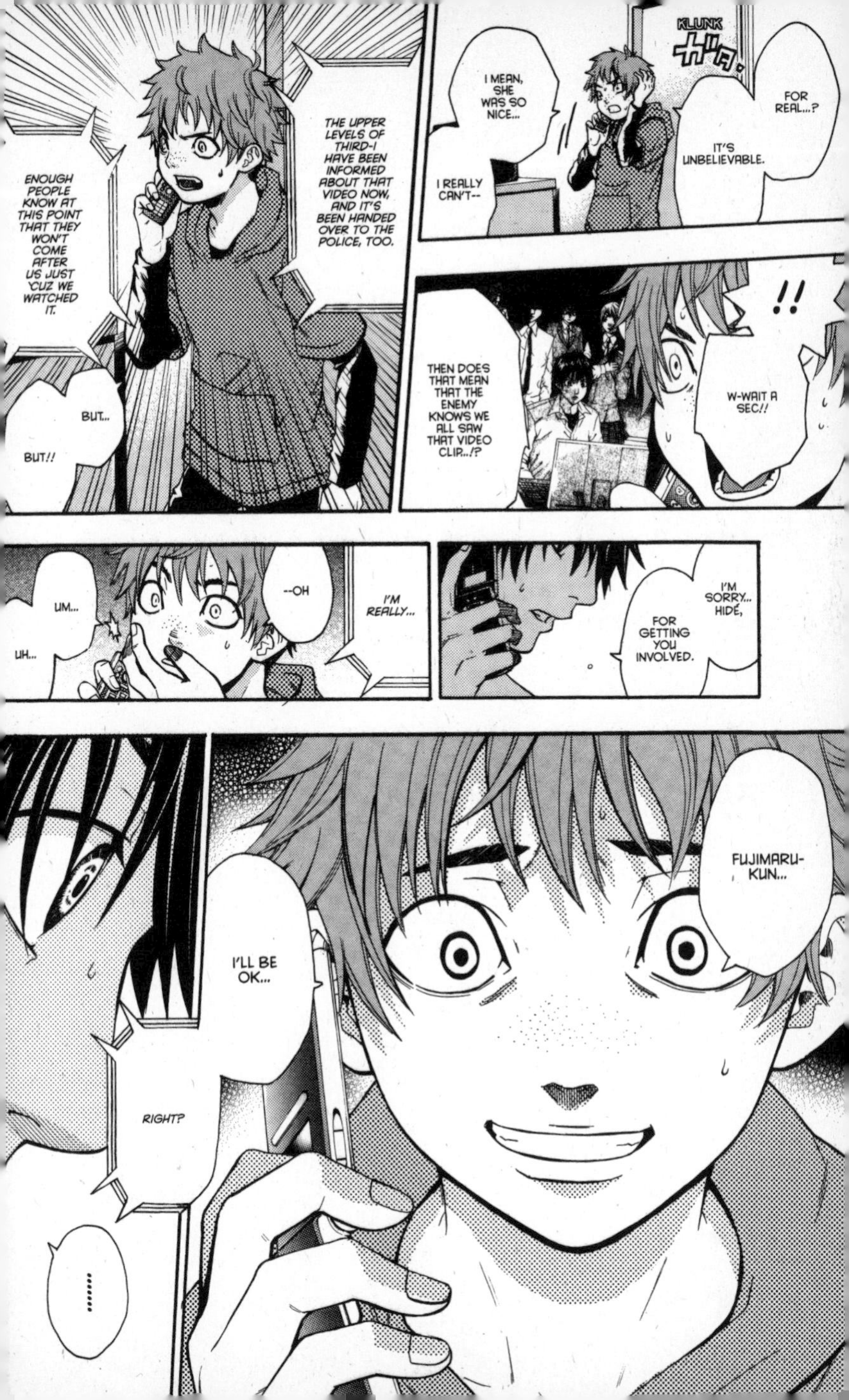
KLUNK
ガタ
FOR REAL...?
IT'S UNBELIEVABLE.
I MEAN, SHE WAS SO NICE...
I REALLY CAN'T--
!!
W-WAIT A SEC!!
THEN DOES THAT MEAN THAT THE ENEMY KNOWS WE ALL SAW THAT VIDEO CLIP...!?
THE UPPER LEVELS OF THIRD-I HAVE BEEN INFORMED ABOUT THAT VIDEO NOW, AND IT'S BEEN HANDED OVER TO THE POLICE, TOO.
ENOUGH PEOPLE KNOW AT THIS POINT THAT THEY WON'T COME AFTER US JUST 'CUZ WE WATCHED IT.
BUT...
BUT!!
I'M SORRY... HIDE,
FOR GETTING YOU INVOLVED.
I'M REALLY...
--OH
UM...
UH...
FUJIMARU-KUN...
I'LL BE OK...
RIGHT?
......

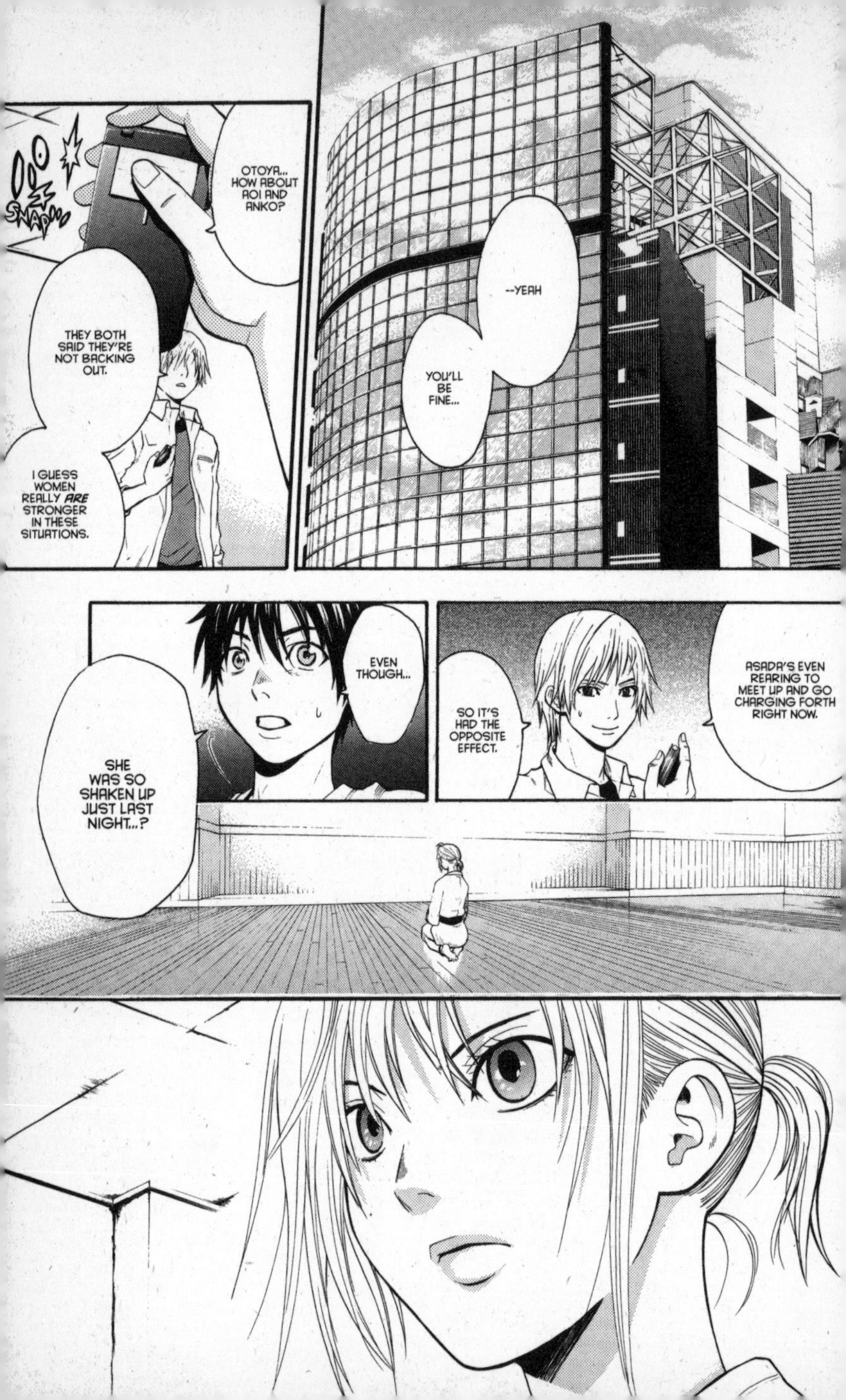
--YEAH
YOU'LL BE FINE...
SNAP
OTOYA... HOW ABOUT AOI AND ANKO?
THEY BOTH SAID THEY'RE NOT BACKING OUT.
I GUESS WOMEN REALLY *ARE* STRONGER IN THESE SITUATIONS.
ASADA'S EVEN REARING TO MEET UP AND GO CHARGING FORTH RIGHT NOW.
SO IT'S HAD THE OPPOSITE EFFECT.
EVEN THOUGH...
SHE WAS SO SHAKEN UP JUST LAST NIGHT...?

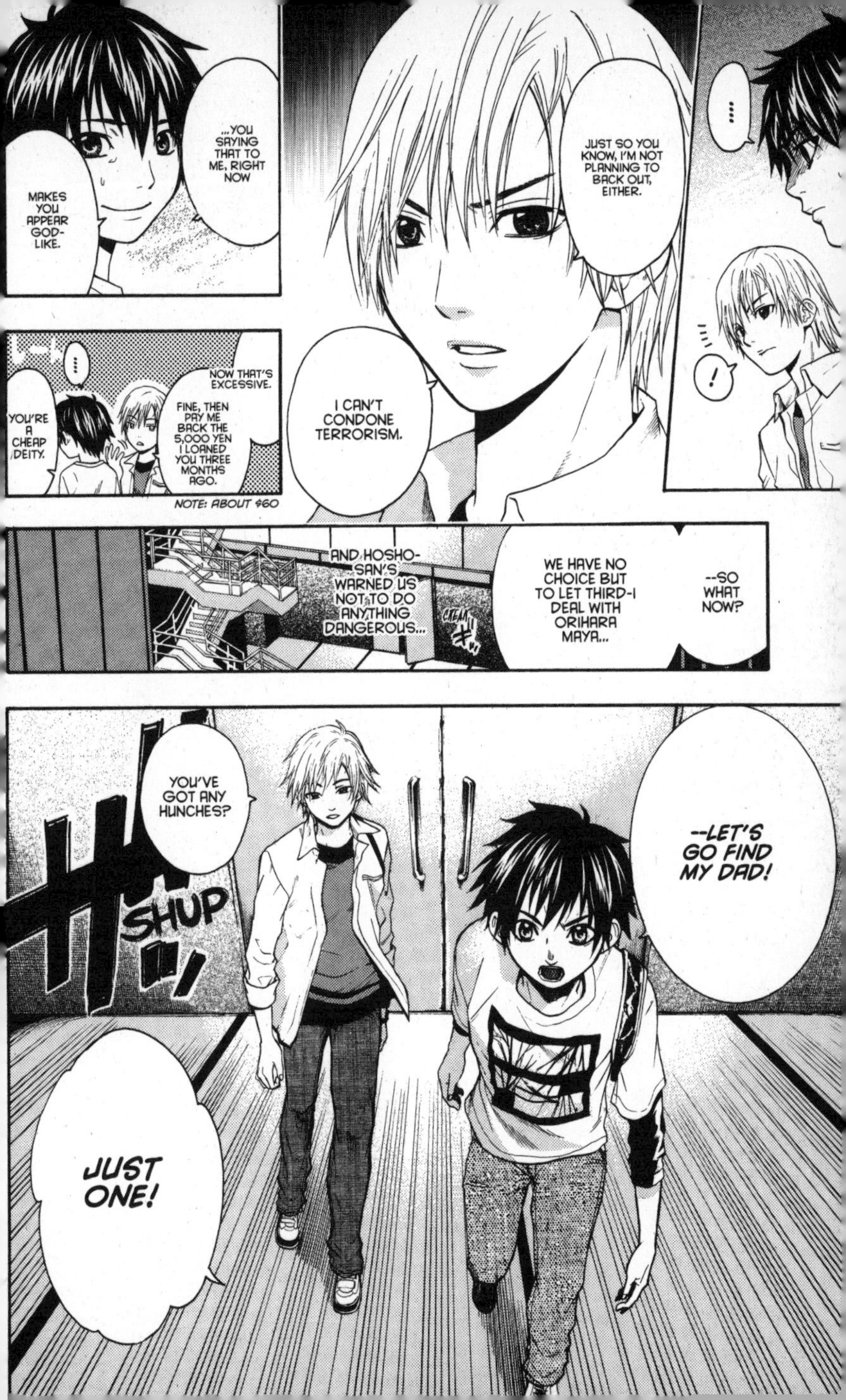
...
!
JUST SO YOU KNOW, I'M NOT PLANNING TO BACK OUT, EITHER.
I CAN'T CONDONE TERRORISM.
...YOU SAYING THAT TO ME, RIGHT NOW
MAKES YOU APPEAR GOD-LIKE.
...
NOW THAT'S EXCESSIVE.
FINE, THEN PAY ME BACK THE 5,000 YEN I LOANED YOU THREE MONTHS AGO.
YOU'RE A CHEAP DEITY.
NOTE: ABOUT $60
--SO WHAT NOW?
WE HAVE NO CHOICE BUT TO LET THIRD-I DEAL WITH ORIHARA MAYA...
AND HOSHO-SAN'S WARNED US NOT TO DO ANYTHING DANGEROUS...
--LET'S GO FIND MY DAD!
YOU'VE GOT ANY HUNCHES?
SHUP
JUST ONE!

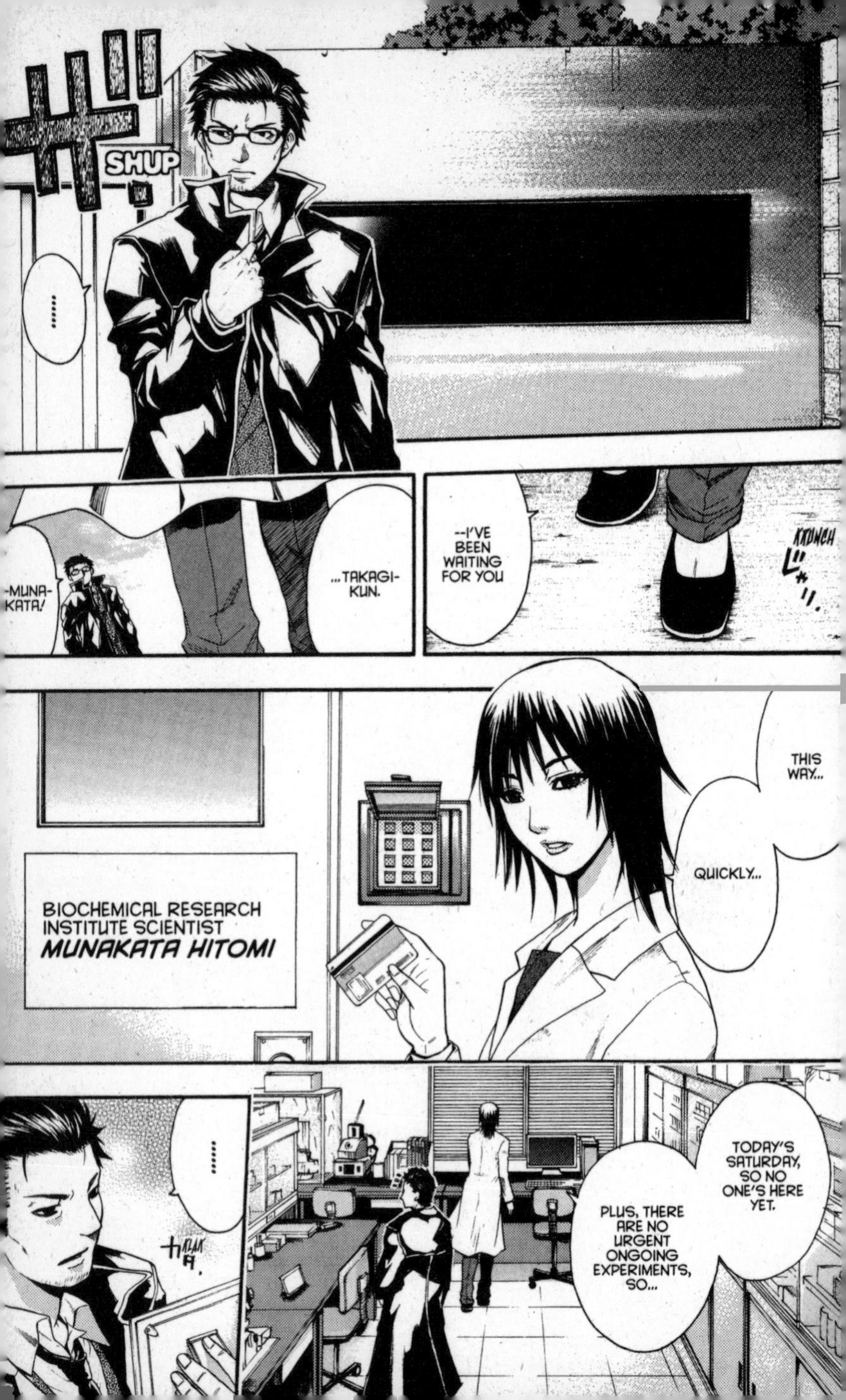
SHUP
......
KRUNCH
--I'VE BEEN WAITING FOR YOU
...TAKAGI-KUN.
-MUNA-KATA!
THIS WAY...
QUICKLY...
BIOCHEMICAL RESEARCH INSTITUTE SCIENTIST MUNAKATA HITOMI
TODAY'S SATURDAY, SO NO ONE'S HERE YET.
PLUS, THERE ARE NO URGENT ONGOING EXPERIMENTS, SO...
......

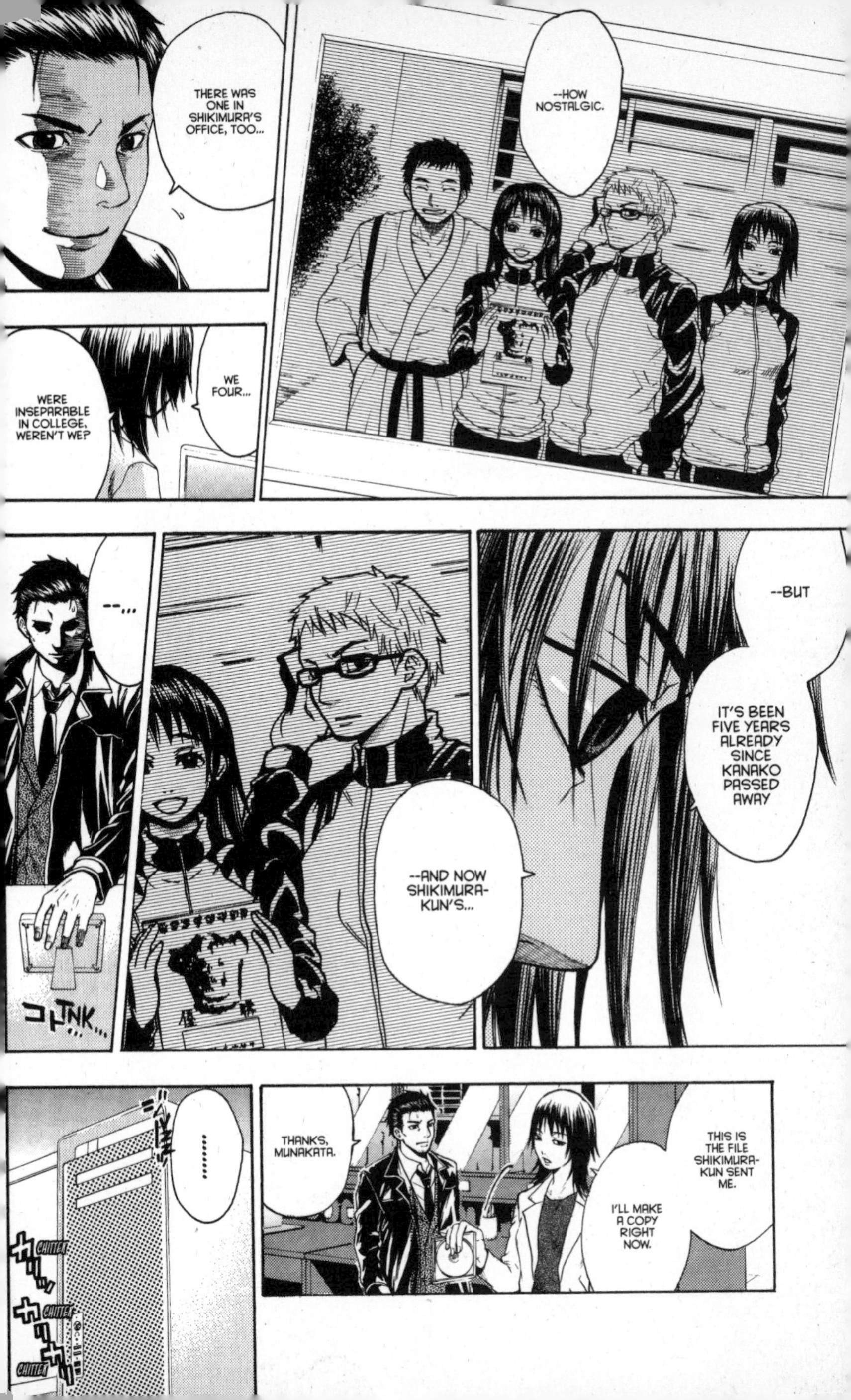
--HOW NOSTALGIC.
THERE WAS ONE IN SHIKIMURA'S OFFICE, TOO...
WE FOUR...
WERE INSEPARABLE IN COLLEGE, WEREN'T WE?
--BUT
IT'S BEEN FIVE YEARS ALREADY SINCE KANAKO PASSED AWAY
--AND NOW SHIKIMURA-KUN'S...
--...
TNK...
THIS IS THE FILE SHIKIMURA-KUN SENT ME.
I'LL MAKE A COPY RIGHT NOW.
THANKS, MUNAKATA.
....
CHITTEK
CHITTEK
CHITTEK

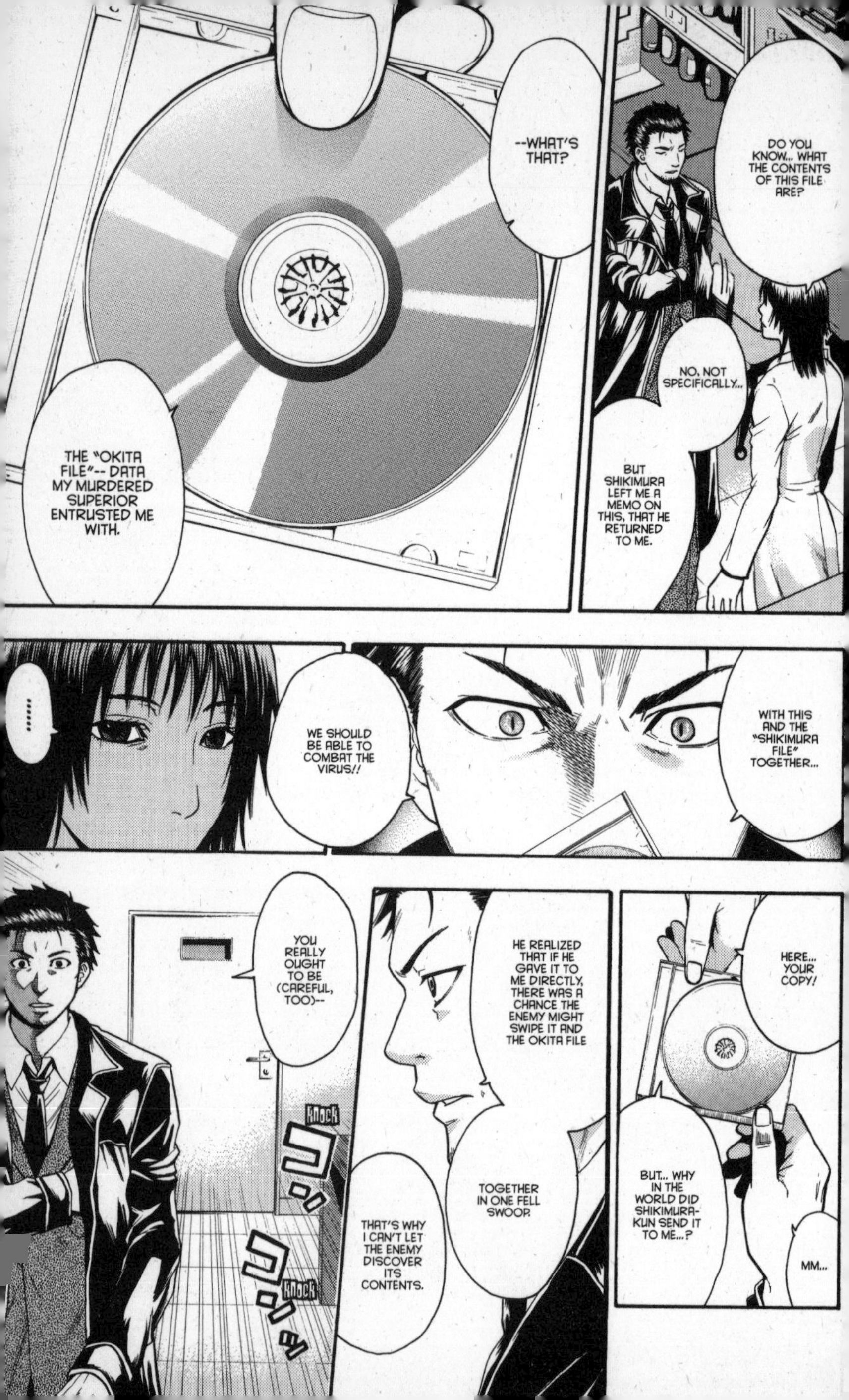
DO YOU KNOW... WHAT THE CONTENTS OF THIS FILE ARE?
NO, NOT SPECIFICALLY...
BUT SHIKIMURA LEFT ME A MEMO ON THIS, THAT HE RETURNED TO ME.
--WHAT'S THAT?
THE "OKITA FILE"-- DATA MY MURDERED SUPERIOR ENTRUSTED ME WITH.
WITH THIS AND THE "SHIKIMURA FILE" TOGETHER...
WE SHOULD BE ABLE TO COMBAT THE VIRUS!!
......
HERE... YOUR COPY!
BUT... WHY IN THE WORLD DID SHIKIMURA-KUN SEND IT TO ME...?
MM...
HE REALIZED THAT IF HE GAVE IT TO ME DIRECTLY, THERE WAS A CHANCE THE ENEMY MIGHT SWIPE IT AND THE OKITA FILE
TOGETHER IN ONE FELL SWOOP.
THAT'S WHY I CAN'T LET THE ENEMY DISCOVER ITS CONTENTS.
YOU REALLY OUGHT TO BE (CAREFUL, TOO)--
KNOCK
KNOCK

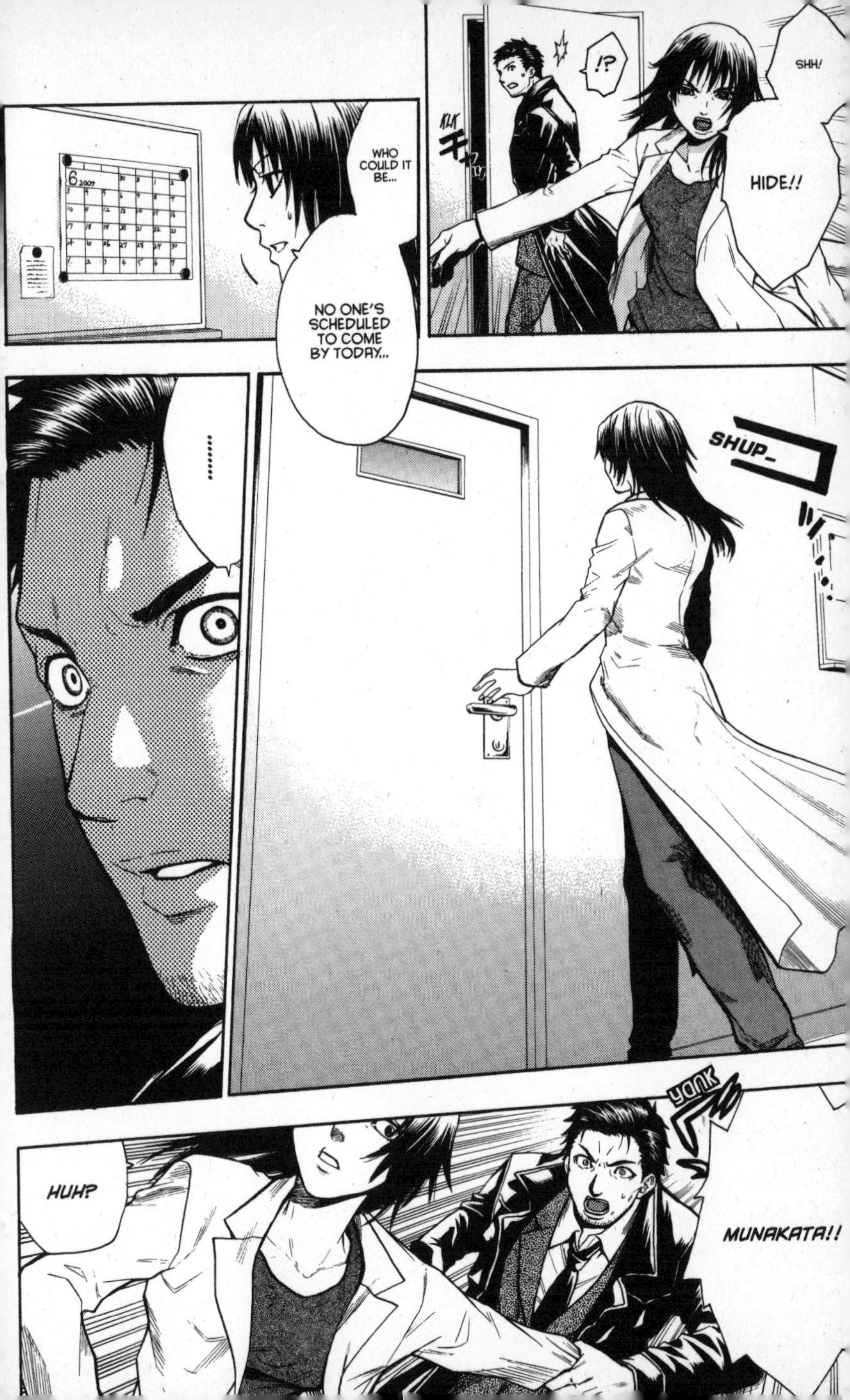
SHH!
HIDE!!
!?
KLIK
WHO COULD IT BE...
NO ONE'S SCHEDULED TO COME BY TODAY...
SHUP_
......
MUNAKATA!!
YANK
HUH?

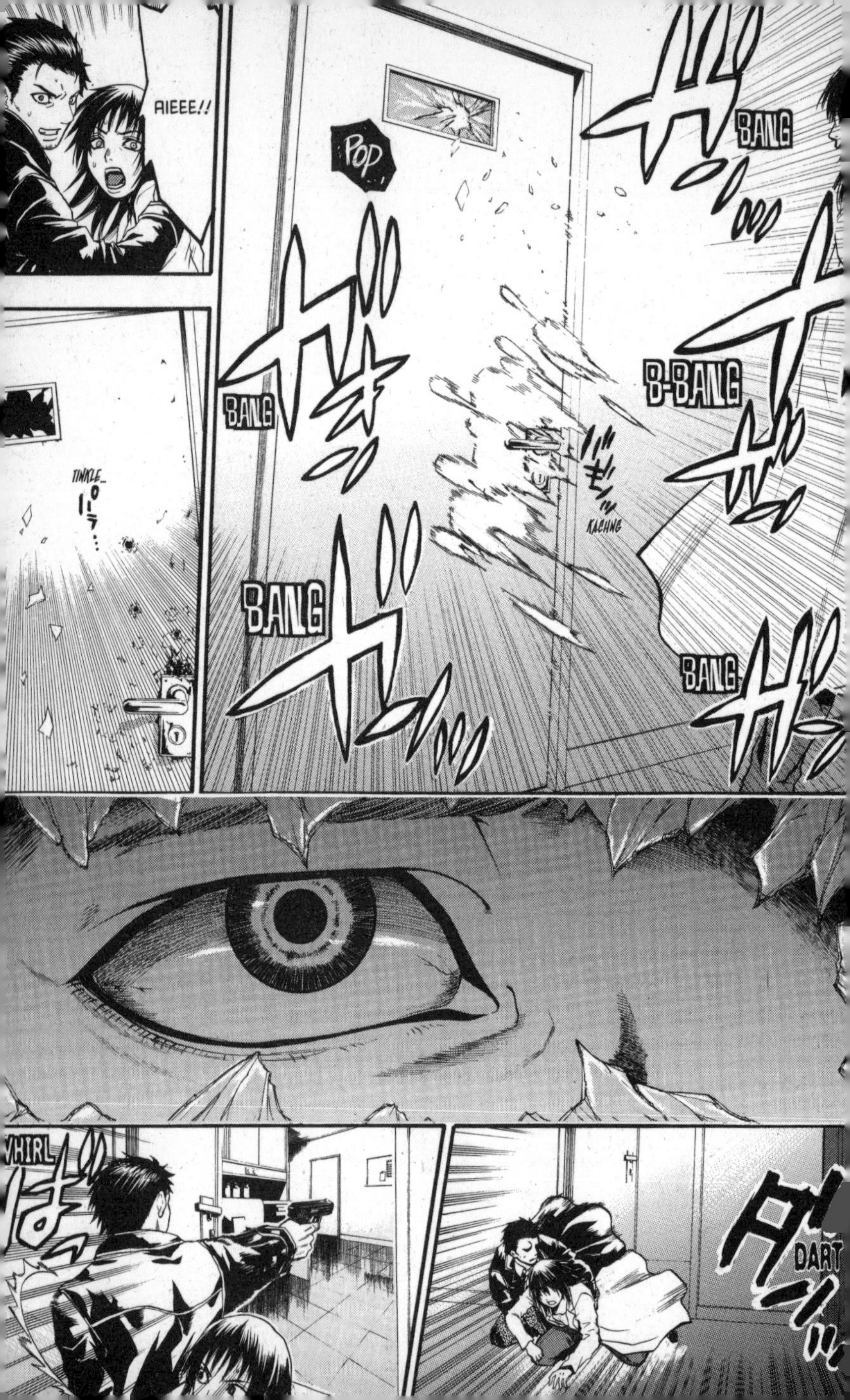
BANG
POP
B-BANG
BANG
KACHNG
BANG
BANG
AIEEE!!
TINKLE...
DART
WHIRL

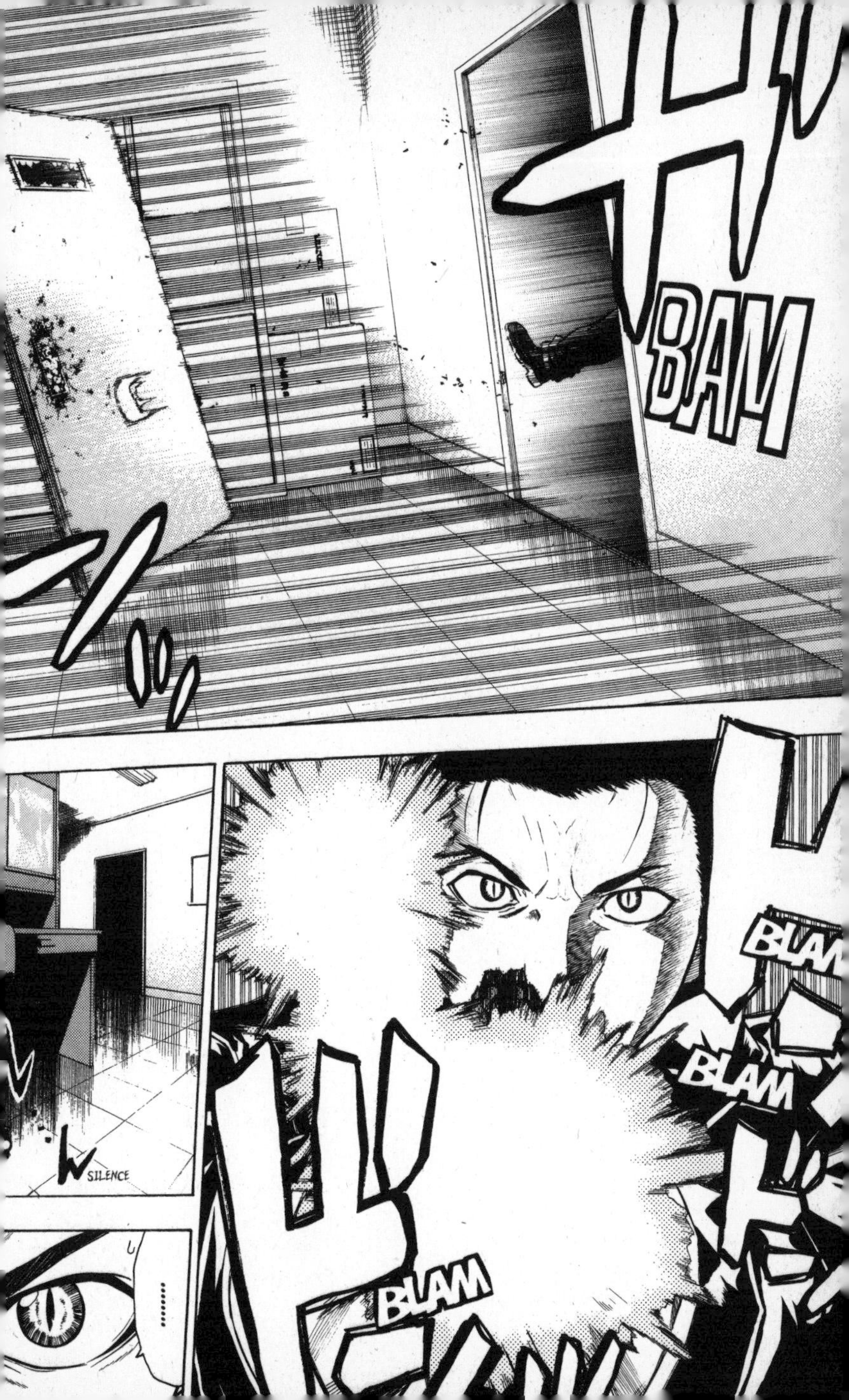
BAM
BLAM
BLAM
BLAM
SILENCE
......

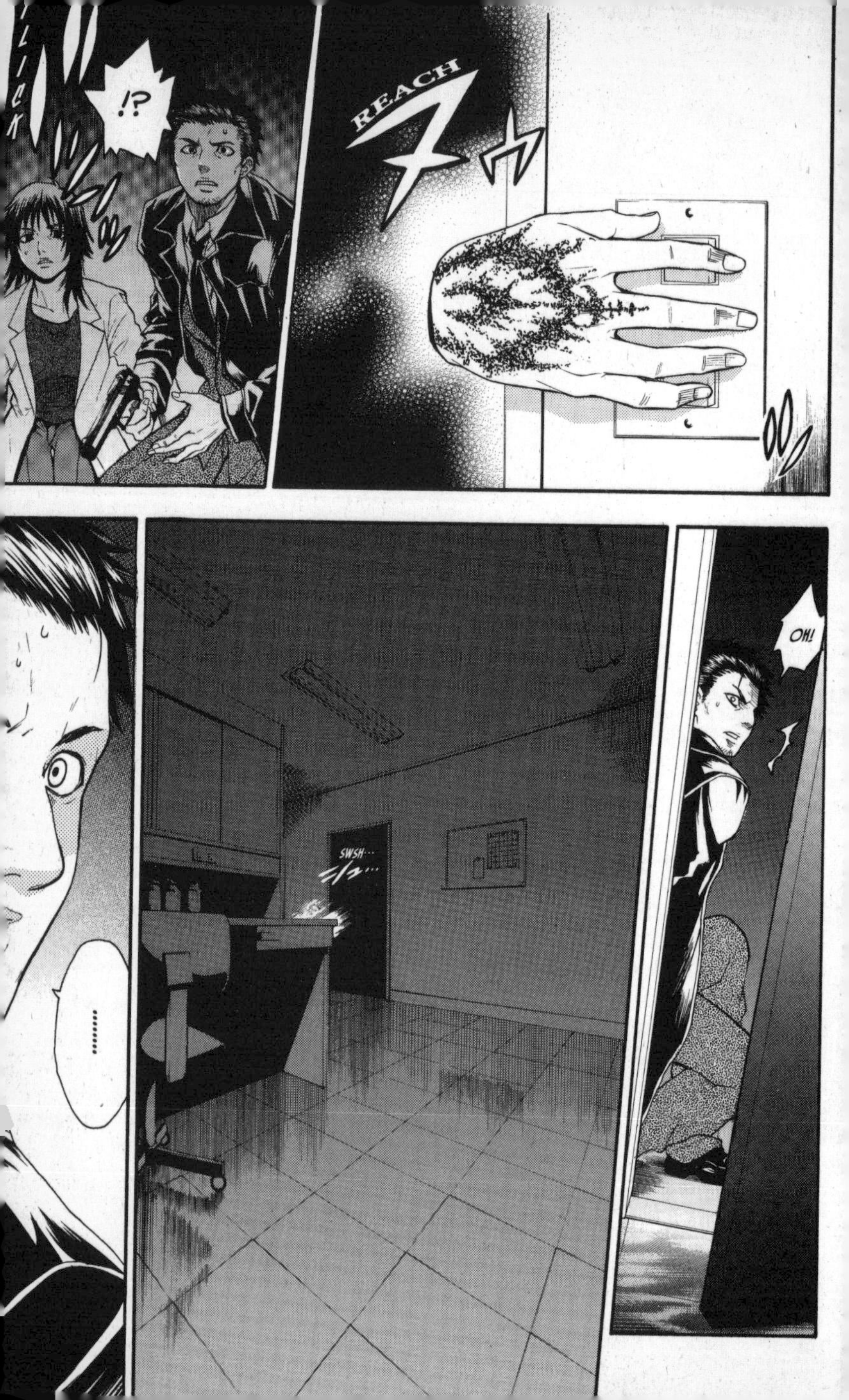
REACH
!?
OH!
SWSH...
......

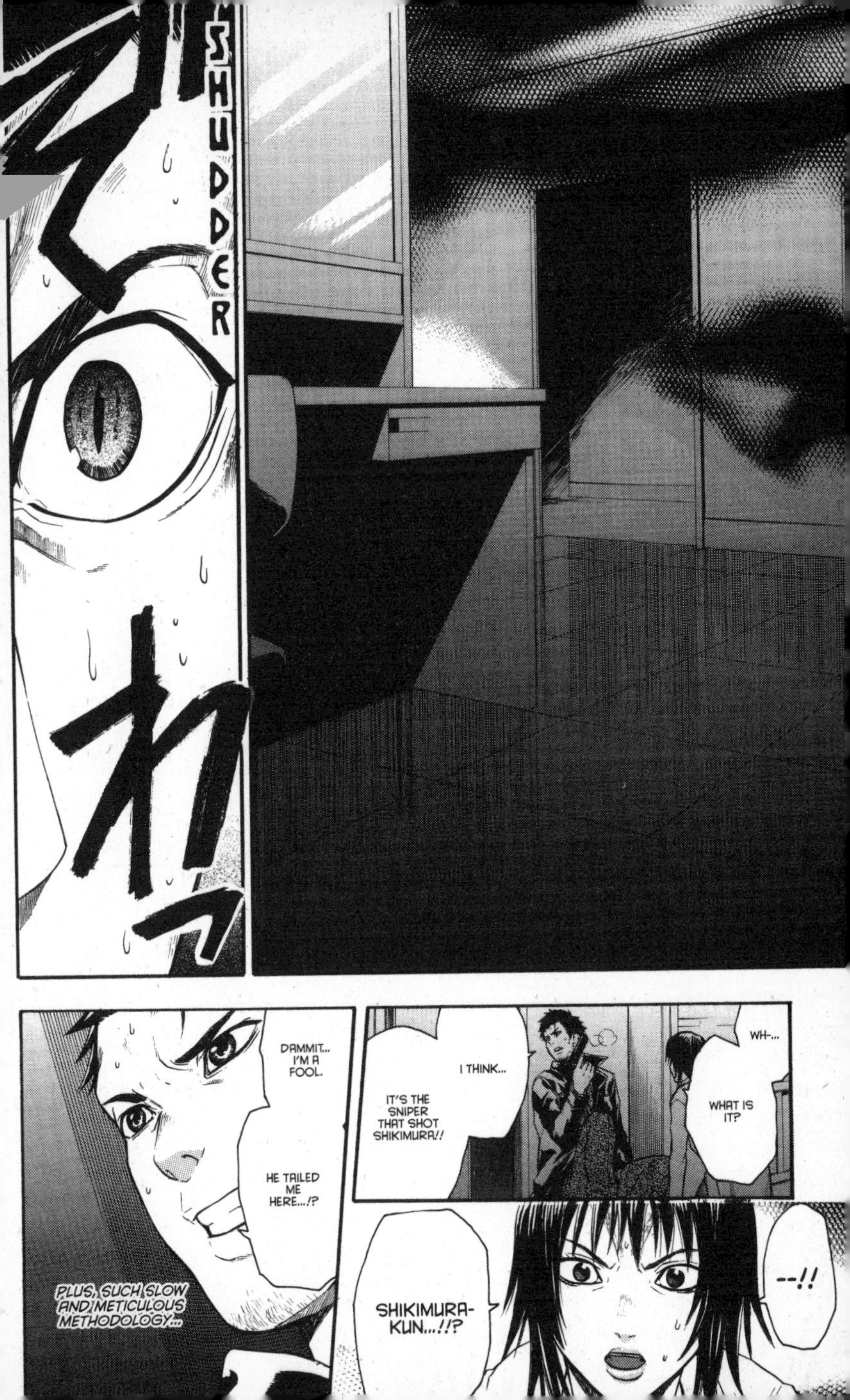
SHUDDER
WH-... WHAT IS IT?
I THINK...
IT'S THE SNIPER THAT SHOT SHIKIMURA!!
--!!
SHIKIMURA-KUN...!!?
DAMMIT... I'M A FOOL.
HE TAILED ME HERE...!?
PLUS, SUCH SLOW AND METICULOUS METHODOLOGY...

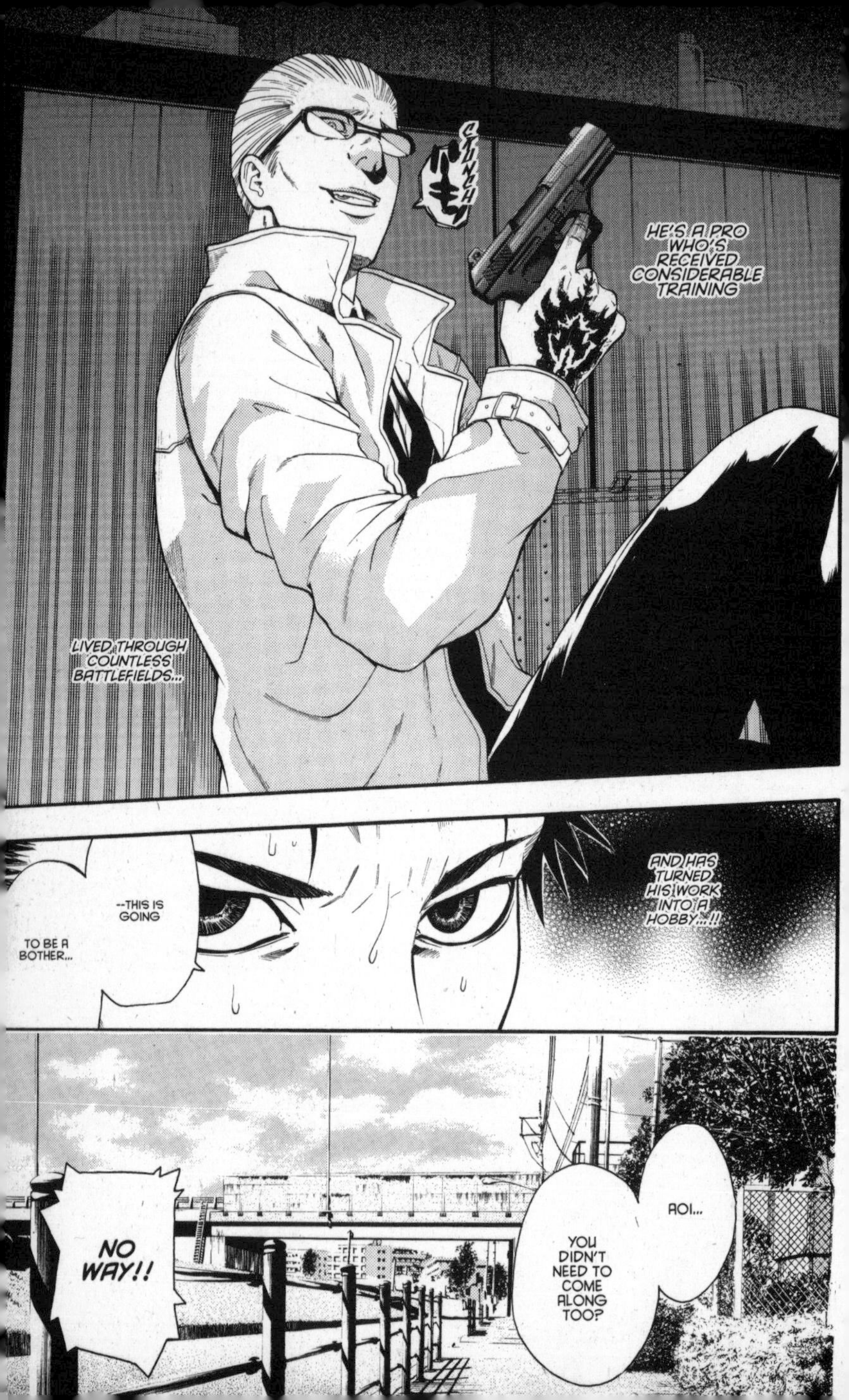
CHUNCH
HE'S A PRO WHO'S RECEIVED CONSIDERABLE TRAINING
LIVED THROUGH COUNTLESS BATTLEFIELDS...
AND HAS TURNED HIS WORK INTO A HOBBY...!!
--THIS IS GOING
TO BE A BOTHER...
AOI...
YOU DIDN'T NEED TO COME ALONG TOO?
NO WAY!!

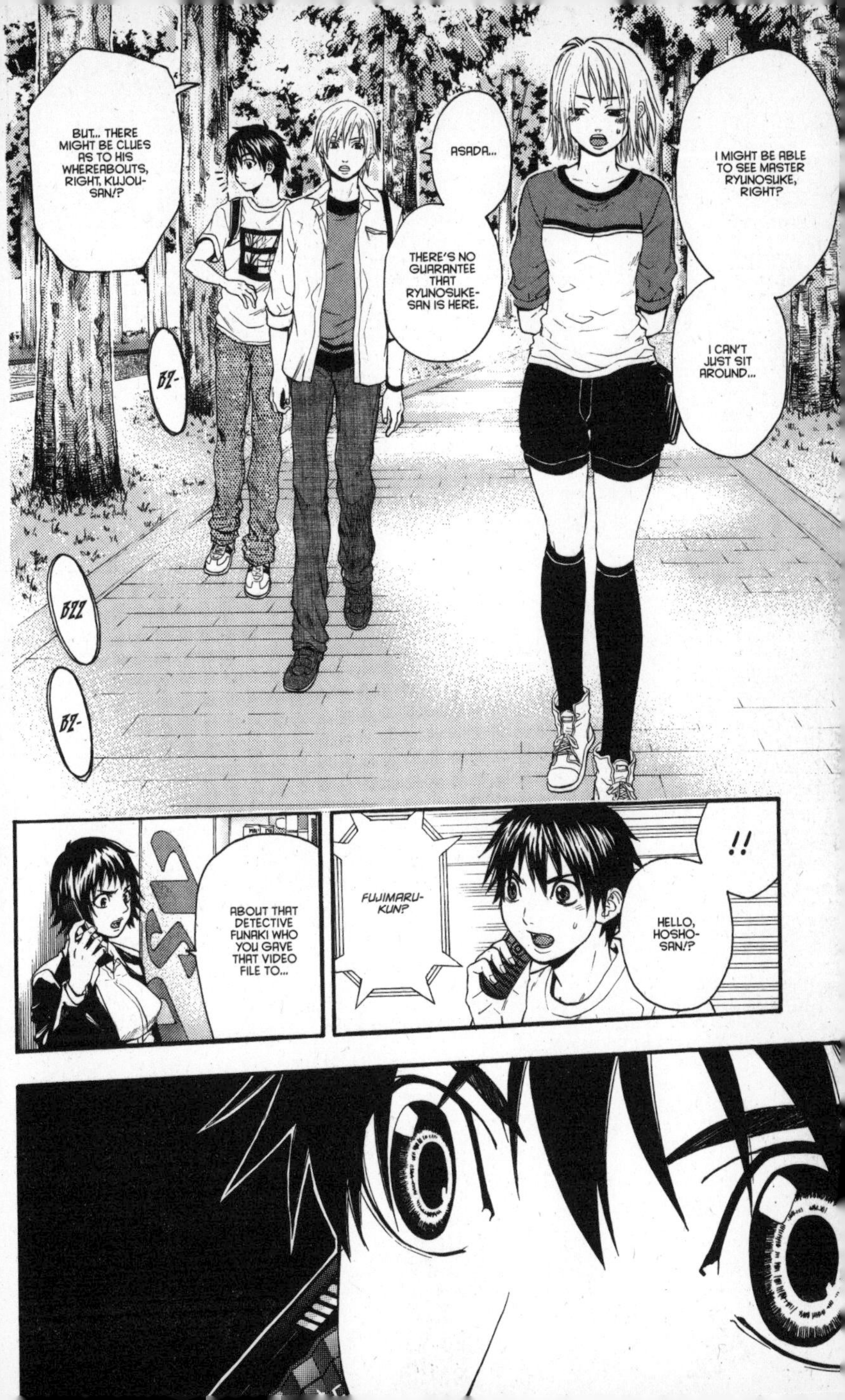
I MIGHT BE ABLE TO SEE MASTER RYUNOSUKE, RIGHT?
I CAN'T JUST SIT AROUND...
ASADA...
THERE'S NO GUARANTEE THAT RYUNOSUKE-SAN IS HERE.
BUT... THERE MIGHT BE CLUES AS TO HIS WHEREABOUTS, RIGHT, KUJOU-SAN!?
BZ-
BZZ
BZ-
!!
HELLO, HOSHO-SAN!?
FUJIMARU-KUN?
ABOUT THAT DETECTIVE FUNAKI WHO YOU GAVE THAT VIDEO FILE TO...

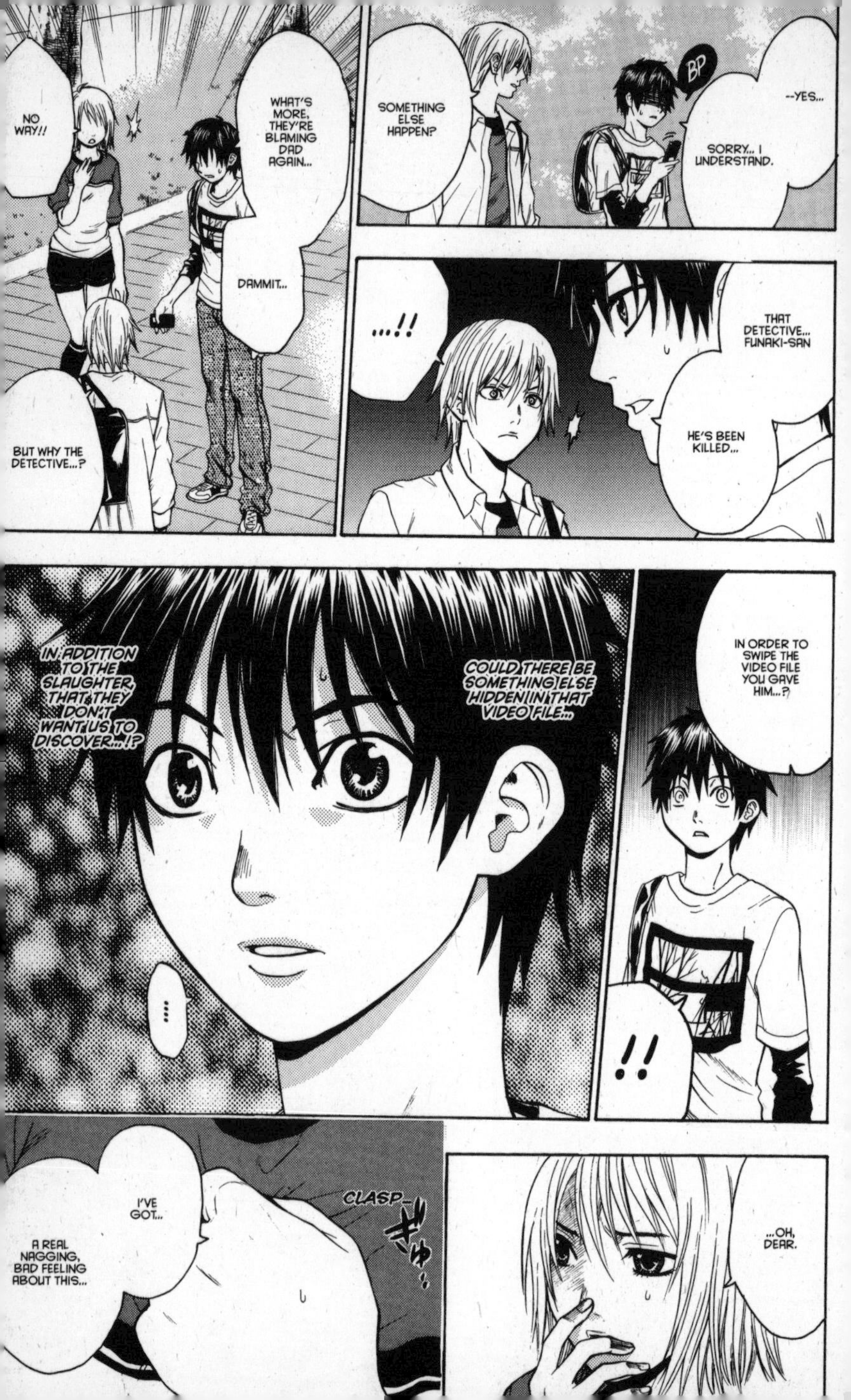
--YES...
SORRY... I UNDERSTAND.
SOMETHING ELSE HAPPEN?
THAT DETECTIVE... FUNAKI-SAN
HE'S BEEN KILLED...
...!!
WHAT'S MORE, THEY'RE BLAMING DAD AGAIN...
NO WAY!!
DAMMIT...
BUT WHY THE DETECTIVE...?
IN ORDER TO SWIPE THE VIDEO FILE YOU GAVE HIM...?
!!
COULD THERE BE SOMETHING ELSE HIDDEN IN THAT VIDEO FILE...
IN ADDITION TO THE SLAUGHTER, THAT THEY DON'T WANT US TO DISCOVER...!?
...
...OH, DEAR.
CLASP
I'VE GOT...
A REAL NAGGING, BAD FEELING ABOUT THIS...

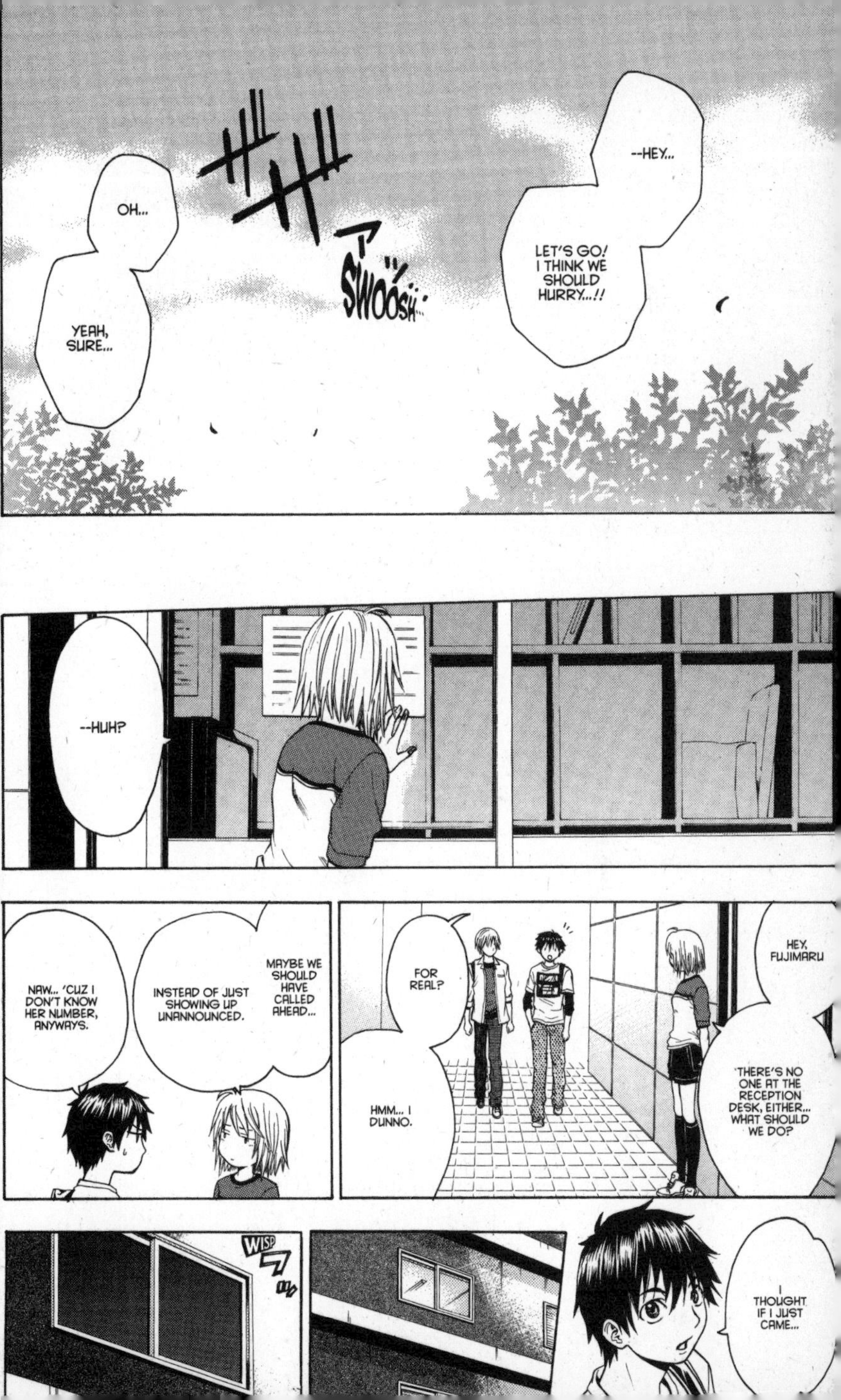
--HEY...
LET'S GO! I THINK WE SHOULD HURRY...!!
SWOOSH...
OH...
YEAH, SURE...
--HUH?
HEY, FUJIMARU
'THERE'S NO ONE AT THE RECEPTION DESK, EITHER... WHAT SHOULD WE DO?
FOR REAL?
HMM... I DUNNO.
MAYBE WE SHOULD HAVE CALLED AHEAD...
INSTEAD OF JUST SHOWING UP UNANNOUNCED.
NAW... 'CUZ I DON'T KNOW HER NUMBER, ANYWAYS.
I THOUGHT IF I JUST CAME...
WISP

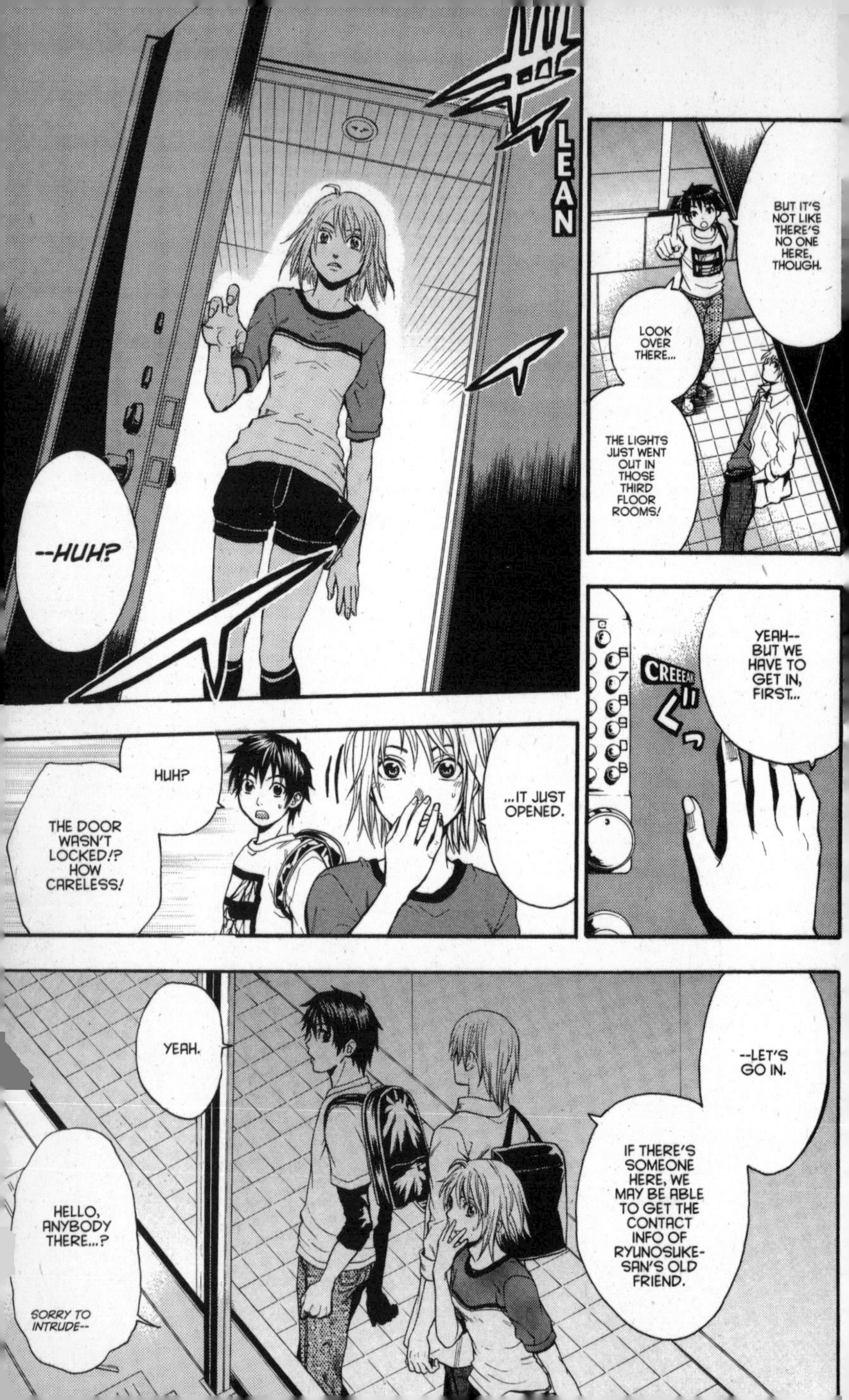

BUT IT'S NOT LIKE THERE'S NO ONE HERE, THOUGH.
LOOK OVER THERE...
THE LIGHTS JUST WENT OUT IN THOSE THIRD FLOOR ROOMS!
YEAH-- BUT WE HAVE TO GET IN, FIRST...
CREEEAK
LEAN
--HUH?
...IT JUST OPENED.
HUH?
THE DOOR WASN'T LOCKED!? HOW CARELESS!
--LET'S GO IN.
IF THERE'S SOMEONE HERE, WE MAY BE ABLE TO GET THE CONTACT INFO OF RYUNOSUKE-SAN'S OLD FRIEND.
YEAH.
HELLO, ANYBODY THERE...?
SORRY TO INTRUDE--

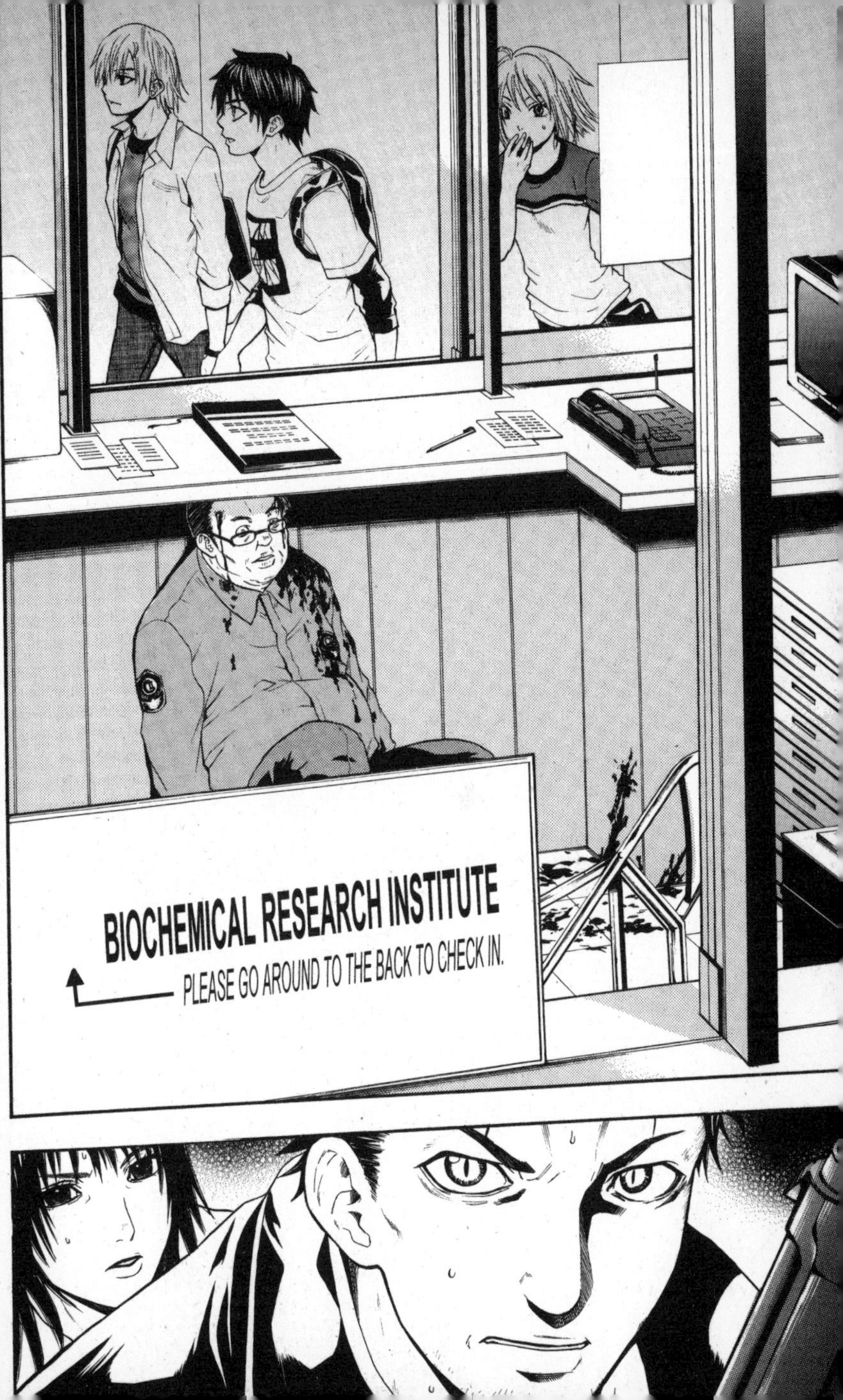
BIOCHEMICAL RESEARCH INSTITUTE
PLEASE GO AROUND TO THE BACK TO CHECK IN.

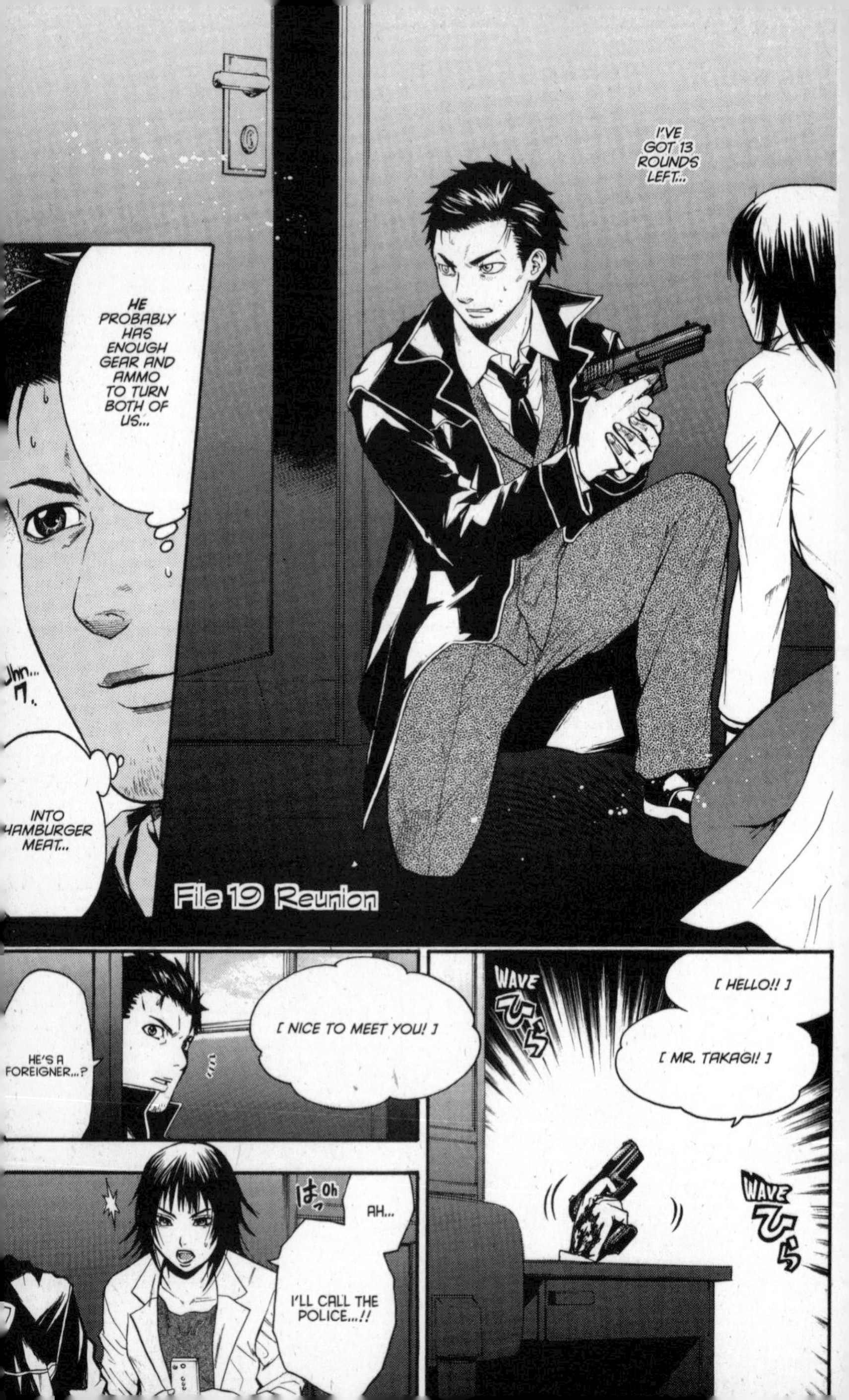
I'VE GOT 13 ROUNDS LEFT...
HE PROBABLY HAS ENOUGH GEAR AND AMMO TO TURN BOTH OF US...
Uhn...
INTO HAMBURGER MEAT...
File 19 Reunion
WAVE ひら
[HELLO!!]
[MR. TAKAGI!]
WAVE ひら
[NICE TO MEET YOU!]
HE'S A FOREIGNER...?
はっ Oh
AH...
I'LL CALL THE POLICE...!!

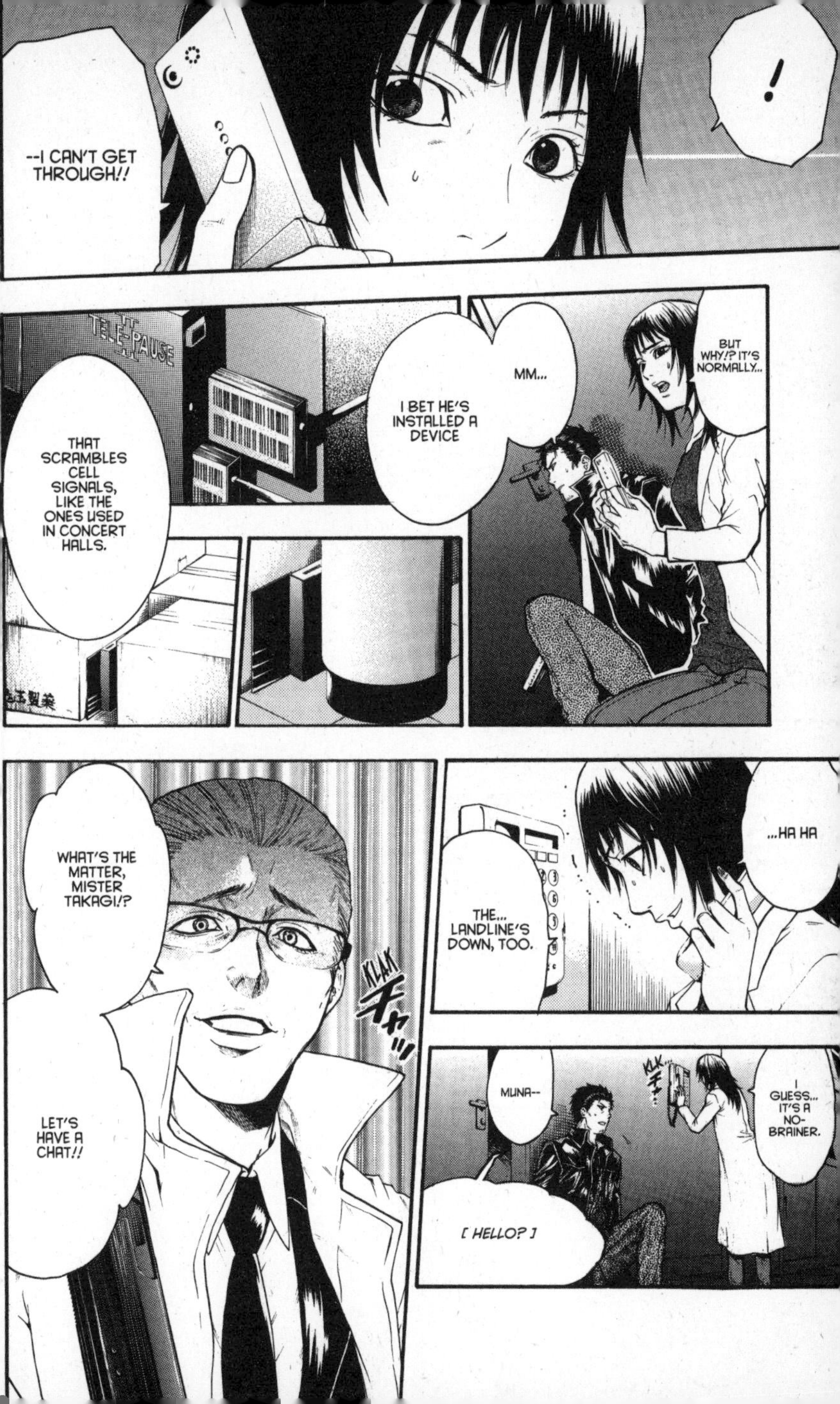
!
--I CAN'T GET THROUGH!!
BUT WHY!? IT'S NORMALLY...
TELE-PAUSE
MM...
I BET HE'S INSTALLED A DEVICE
THAT SCRAMBLES CELL SIGNALS, LIKE THE ONES USED IN CONCERT HALLS.
...HA HA
THE... LANDLINE'S DOWN, TOO.
I GUESS... IT'S A NO-BRAINER.
KLK
MUNA--
[HELLO?]
WHAT'S THE MATTER, MISTER TAKAGI!?
KLAK
LET'S HAVE A CHAT!!

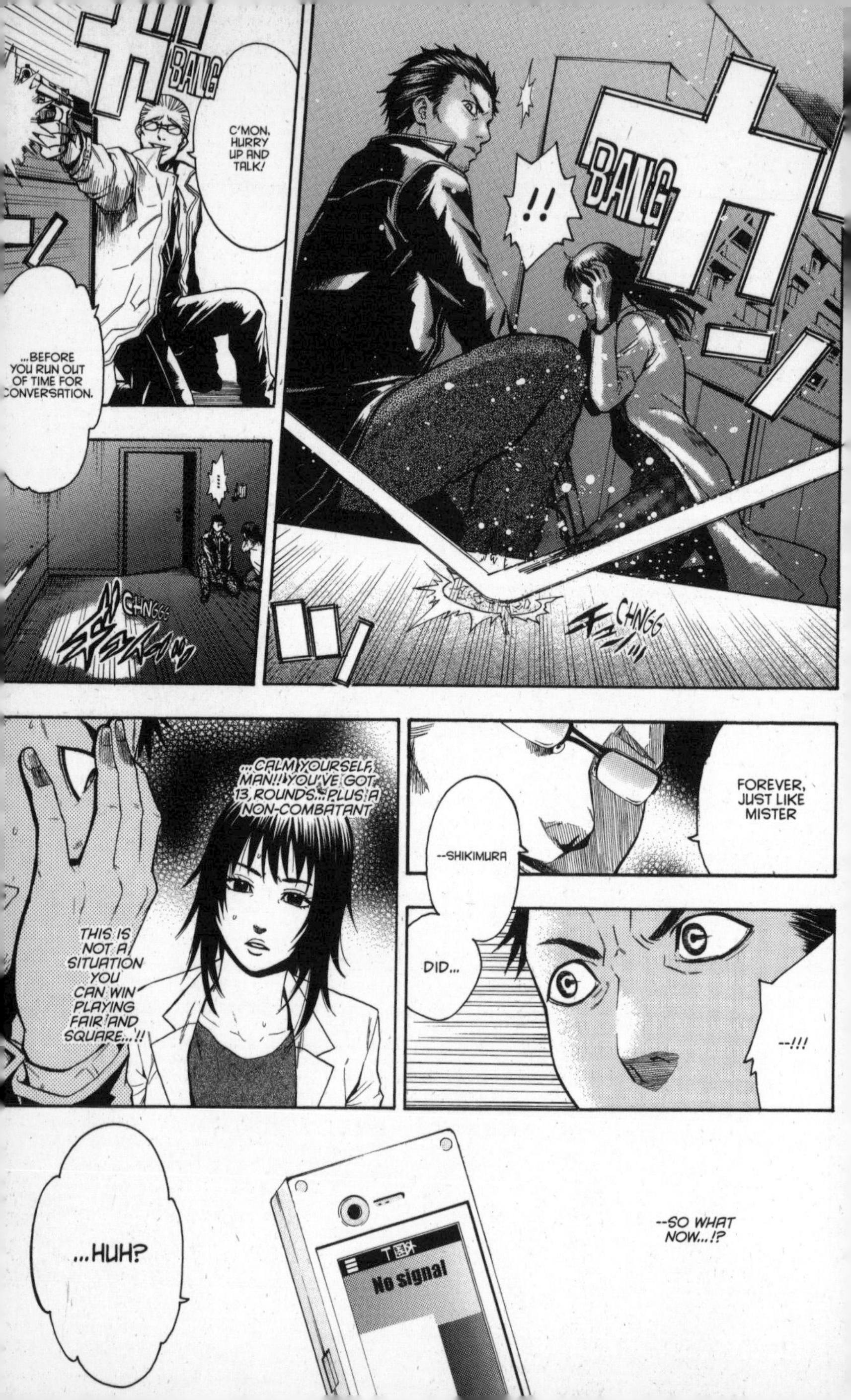
BANG
!!
CHNGG
BANG
C'MON, HURRY UP AND TALK!
...BEFORE YOU RUN OUT OF TIME FOR CONVERSATION.
...!
CHNGGG
FOREVER, JUST LIKE MISTER
--SHIKIMURA
DID...
--!!!
...CALM YOURSELF, MAN!! YOU'VE GOT 13 ROUNDS... PLUS A NON-COMBATANT
THIS IS NOT A SITUATION YOU CAN WIN PLAYING FAIR AND SQUARE...!!
--SO WHAT NOW...!?
No signal
...HUH?

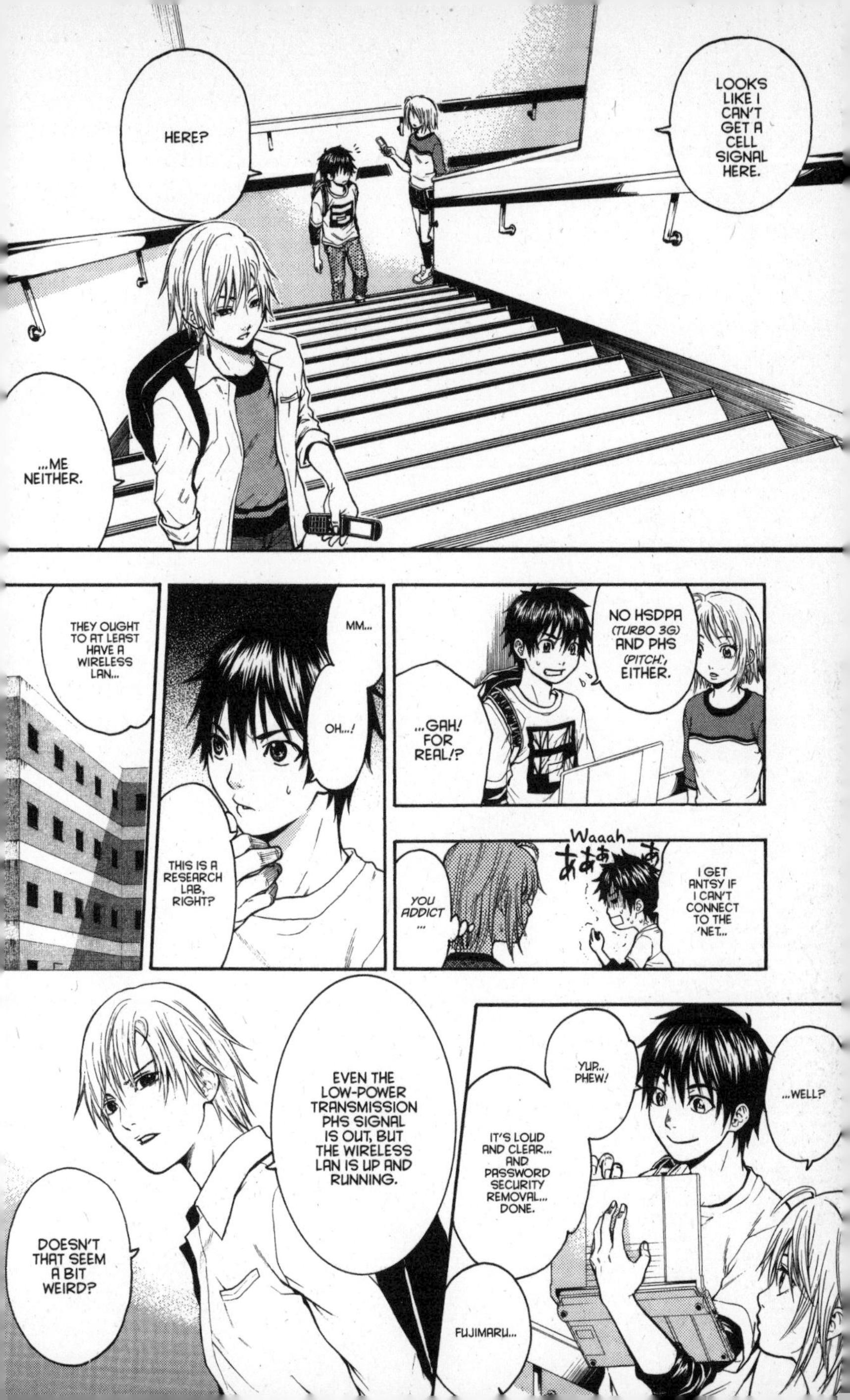
LOOKS LIKE I CAN'T GET A CELL SIGNAL HERE.
HERE?
...ME NEITHER.
NO HSDPA (TURBO 3G) AND PHS (PITCH), EITHER.
...GAH! FOR REAL!?
I GET ANTSY IF I CAN'T CONNECT TO THE 'NET...
Waaah
YOU ADDICT...
MM...
OH...!
THIS IS A RESEARCH LAB, RIGHT?
THEY OUGHT TO AT LEAST HAVE A WIRELESS LAN...
...WELL?
YUP... PHEW!
IT'S LOUD AND CLEAR... AND PASSWORD SECURITY REMOVAL... DONE.
FUJIMARU...
EVEN THE LOW-POWER TRANSMISSION PHS SIGNAL IS OUT, BUT THE WIRELESS LAN IS UP AND RUNNING.
DOESN'T THAT SEEM A BIT WEIRD?

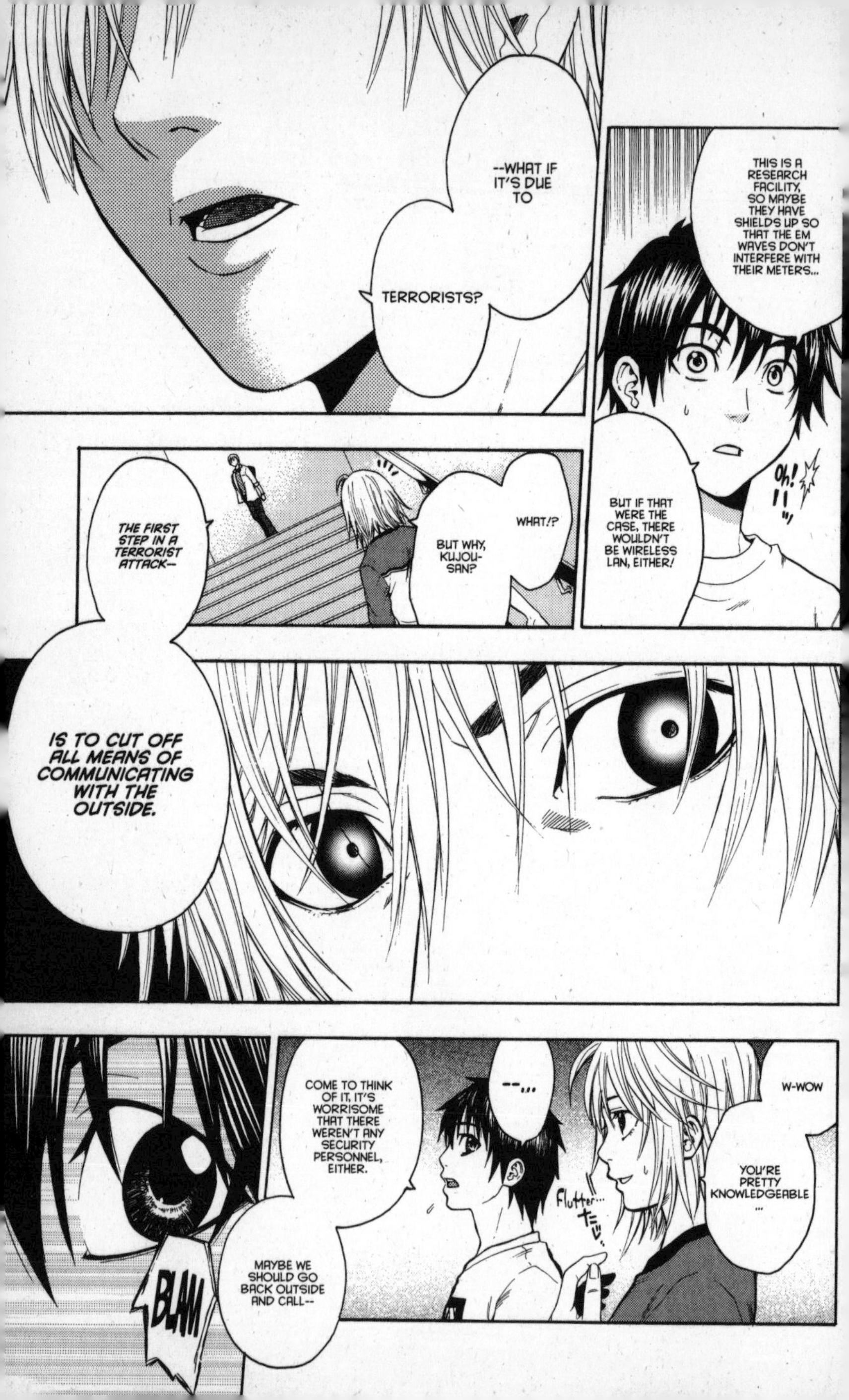
THIS IS A RESEARCH FACILITY, SO MAYBE THEY HAVE SHIELDS UP SO THAT THE EM WAVES DON'T INTERFERE WITH THEIR METERS...
Oh!!!
BUT IF THAT WERE THE CASE, THERE WOULDN'T BE WIRELESS LAN, EITHER!
--WHAT IF IT'S DUE TO
TERRORISTS?
WHAT!?
BUT WHY, KUJOU-SAN?
THE FIRST STEP IN A TERRORIST ATTACK--
IS TO CUT OFF ALL MEANS OF COMMUNICATING WITH THE OUTSIDE.
W-WOW
YOU'RE PRETTY KNOWLEDGEABLE ...
--...
COME TO THINK OF IT, IT'S WORRISOME THAT THERE WEREN'T ANY SECURITY PERSONNEL, EITHER.
Flutter...
MAYBE WE SHOULD GO BACK OUTSIDE AND CALL--
BLAM

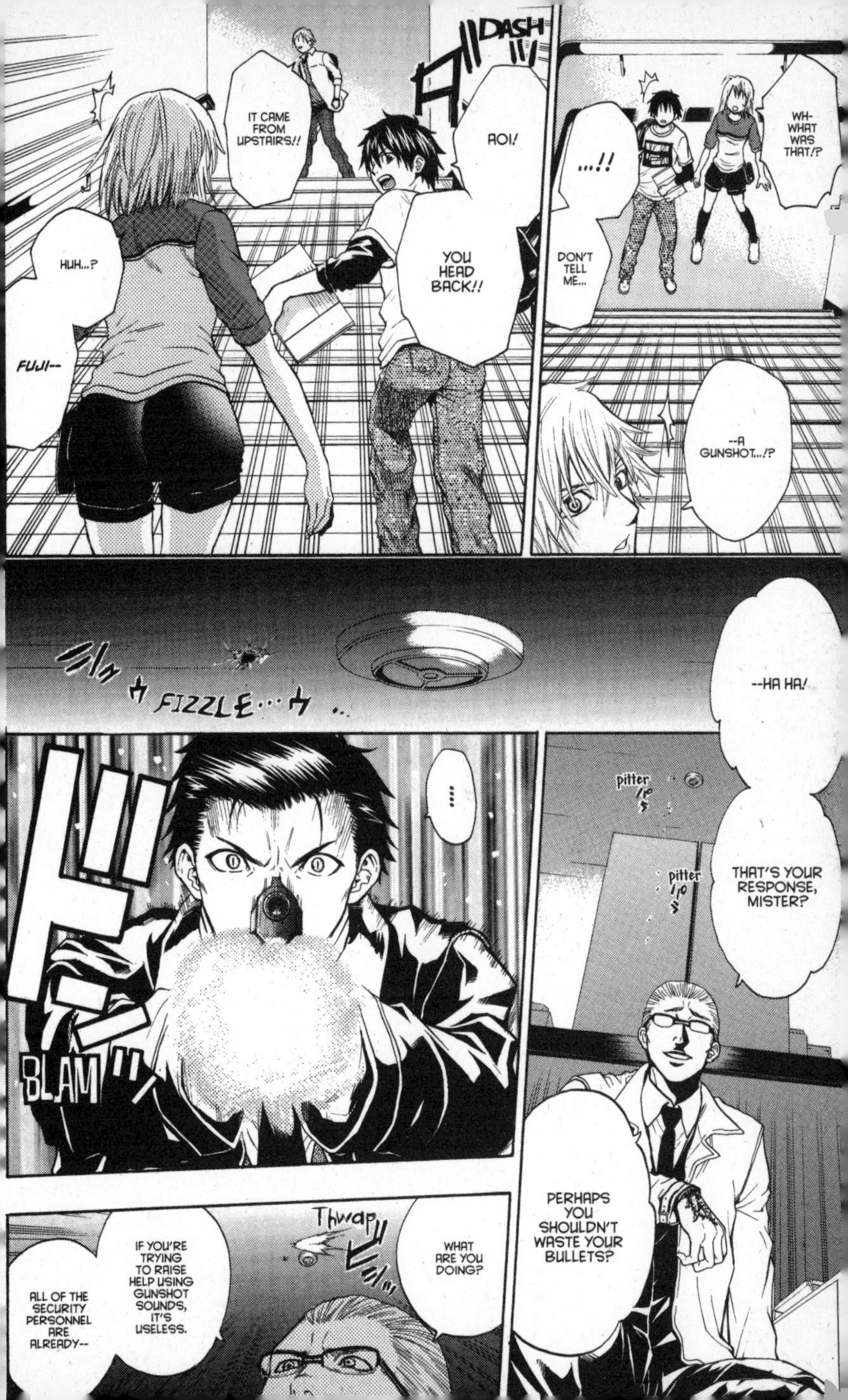
WH-WHAT WAS THAT!?
...!!
DON'T TELL ME...
--A GUNSHOT...!?
DASH
AOI!
IT CAME FROM UPSTAIRS!!
YOU HEAD BACK!!
HUH...?
FUJI--
--HA HA!
FIZZLE...
THAT'S YOUR RESPONSE, MISTER?
pitter
pitter
PERHAPS YOU SHOULDN'T WASTE YOUR BULLETS?
....
BLAM
WHAT ARE YOU DOING?
Thwap
IF YOU'RE TRYING TO RAISE HELP USING GUNSHOT SOUNDS, IT'S USELESS.
ALL OF THE SECURITY PERSONNEL ARE ALREADY--

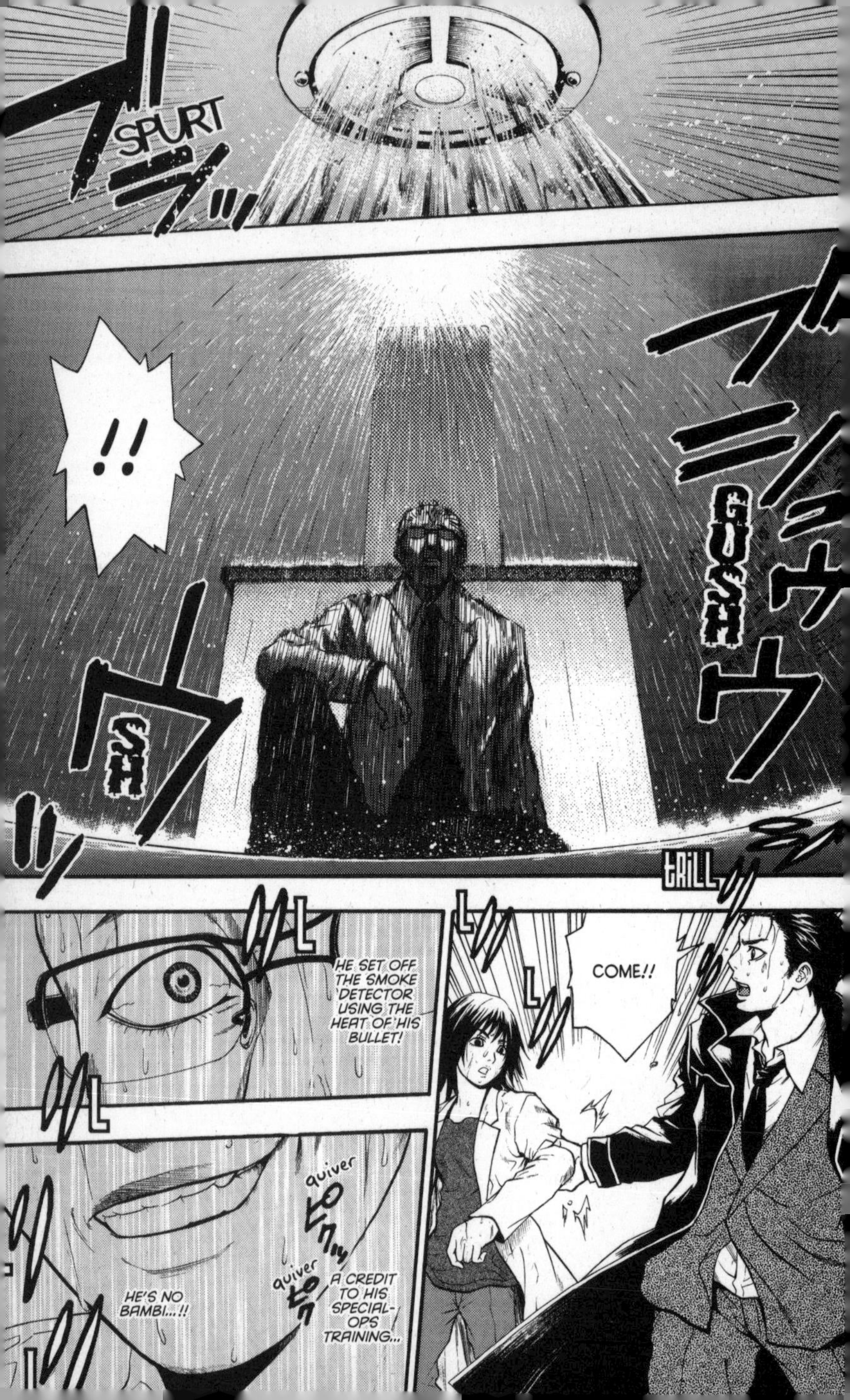
SPURT
GUSH
!!
SH
TRILL
COME!!
HE SET OFF THE SMOKE DETECTOR USING THE HEAT OF HIS BULLET!
quiver
quiver
A CREDIT TO HIS SPECIAL-OPS TRAINING...
HE'S NO BAMBI...!!

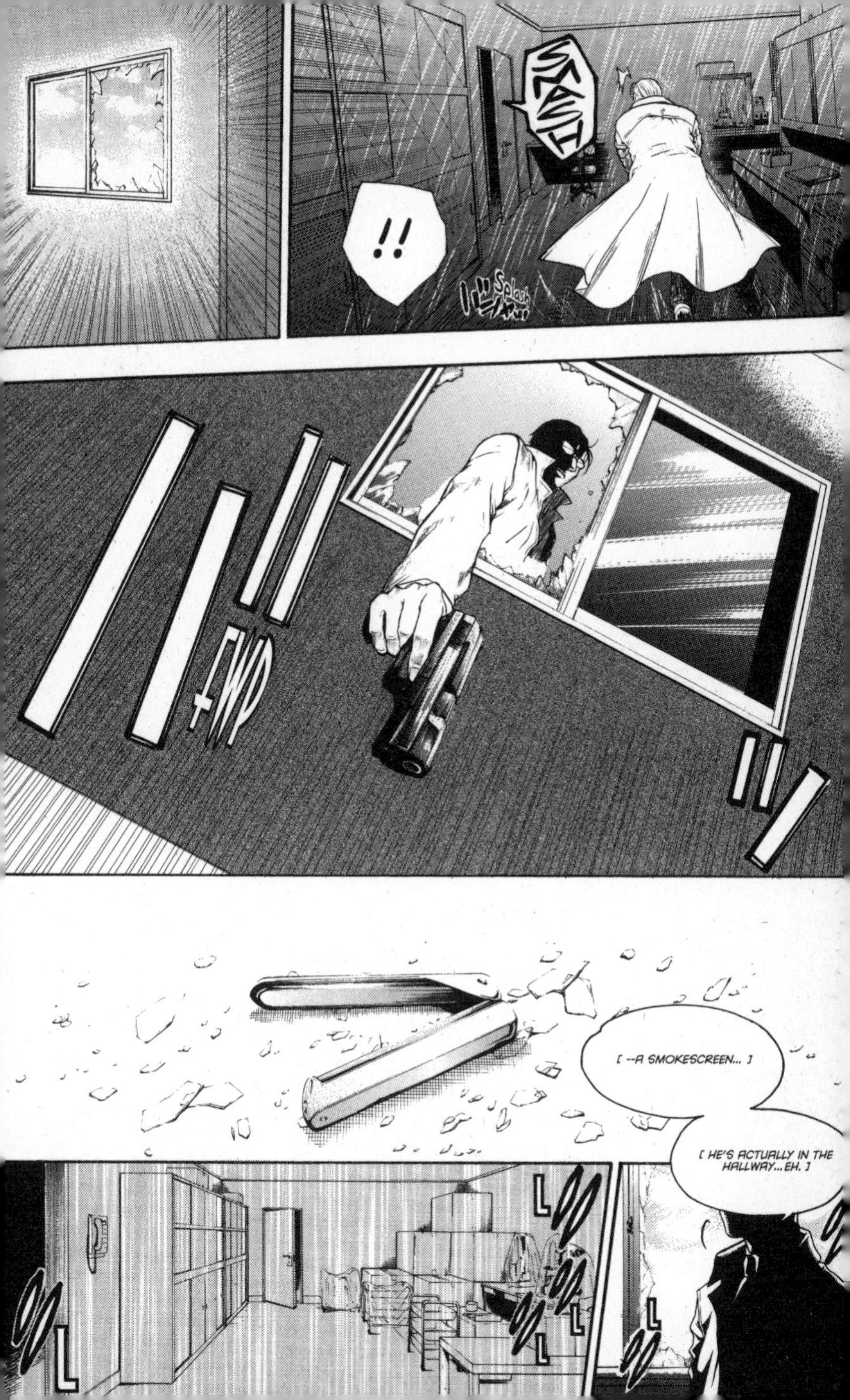
SMASH
!!
Splash
[--A SMOKESCREEN...]
[HE'S ACTUALLY IN THE HALLWAY...EH.]

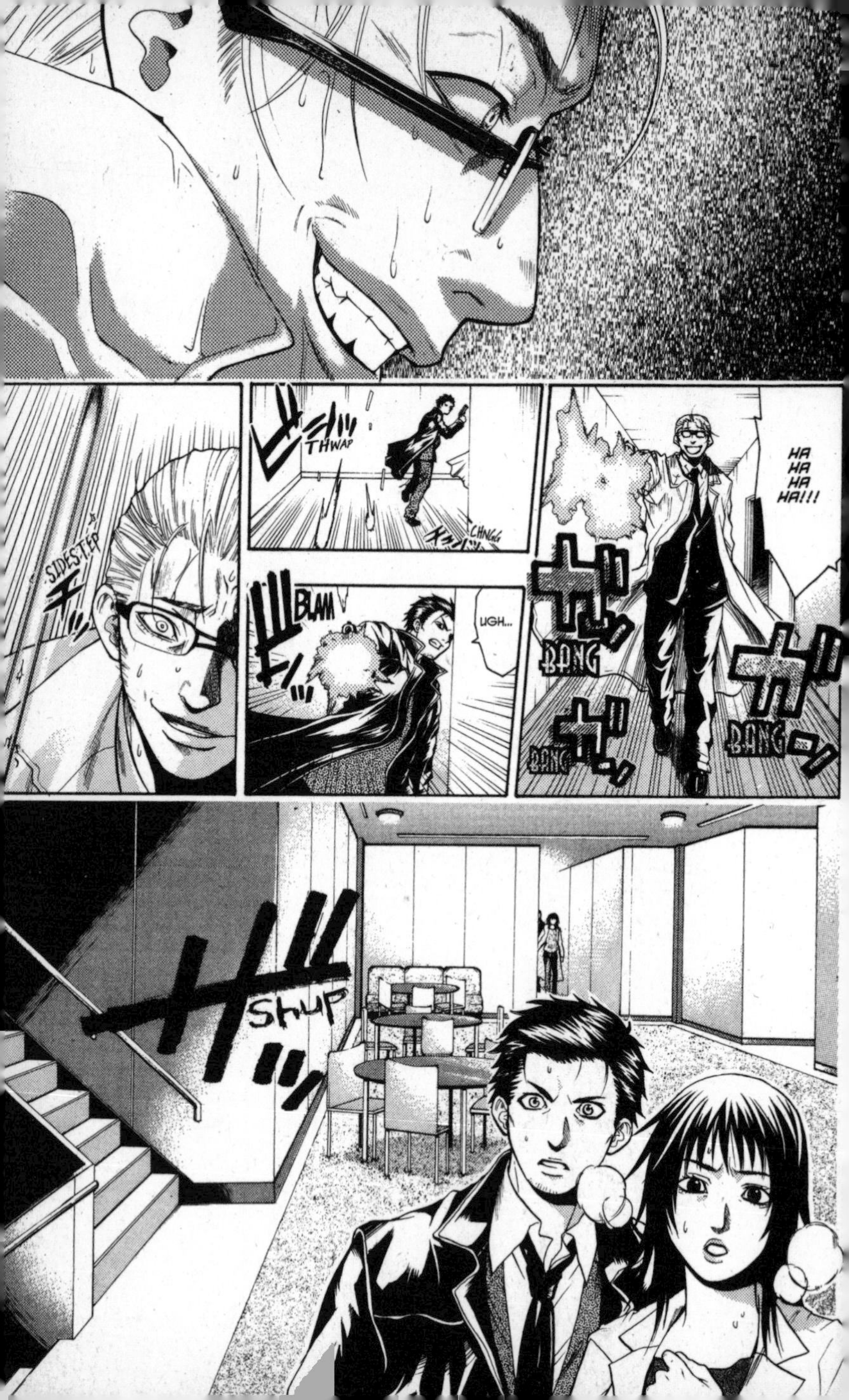
HA HA HA HA!!!
BANG
BANG
BANG
THWAP
CHNGG
BLAM
UGH...
SIDESTEP
Shup

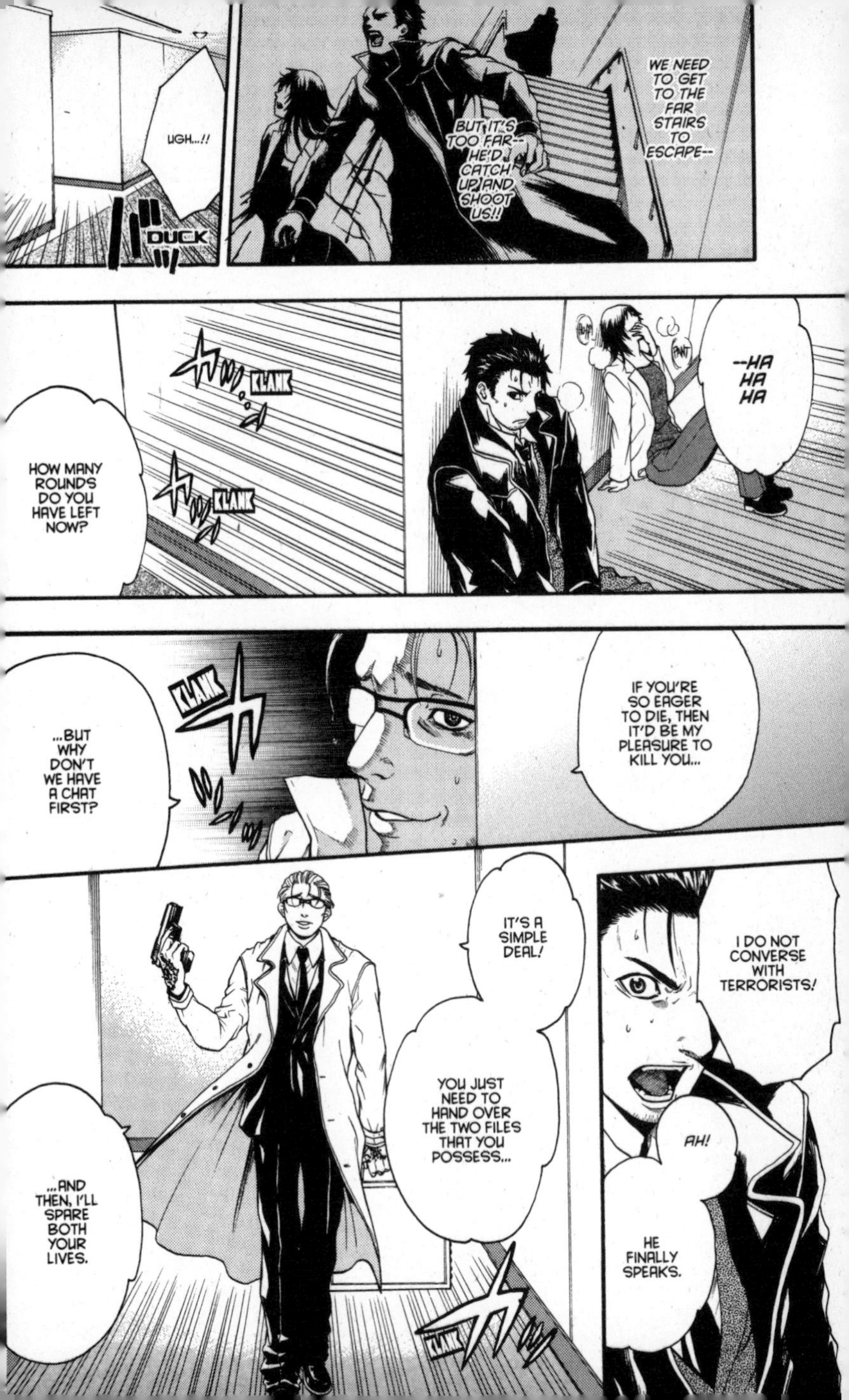
WE NEED TO GET TO THE FAR STAIRS TO ESCAPE--
BUT IT'S TOO FAR-- HE'D CATCH UP AND SHOOT US!!
UGH...!!
DUCK
--HA HA HA
HAH
PANT
KLANK
KLANK
HOW MANY ROUNDS DO YOU HAVE LEFT NOW?
IF YOU'RE SO EAGER TO DIE, THEN IT'D BE MY PLEASURE TO KILL YOU...
KLANK
...BUT WHY DON'T WE HAVE A CHAT FIRST?
I DO NOT CONVERSE WITH TERRORISTS!
AH!
HE FINALLY SPEAKS.
IT'S A SIMPLE DEAL!
YOU JUST NEED TO HAND OVER THE TWO FILES THAT YOU POSSESS...
KLANK
...AND THEN, I'LL SPARE BOTH YOUR LIVES.

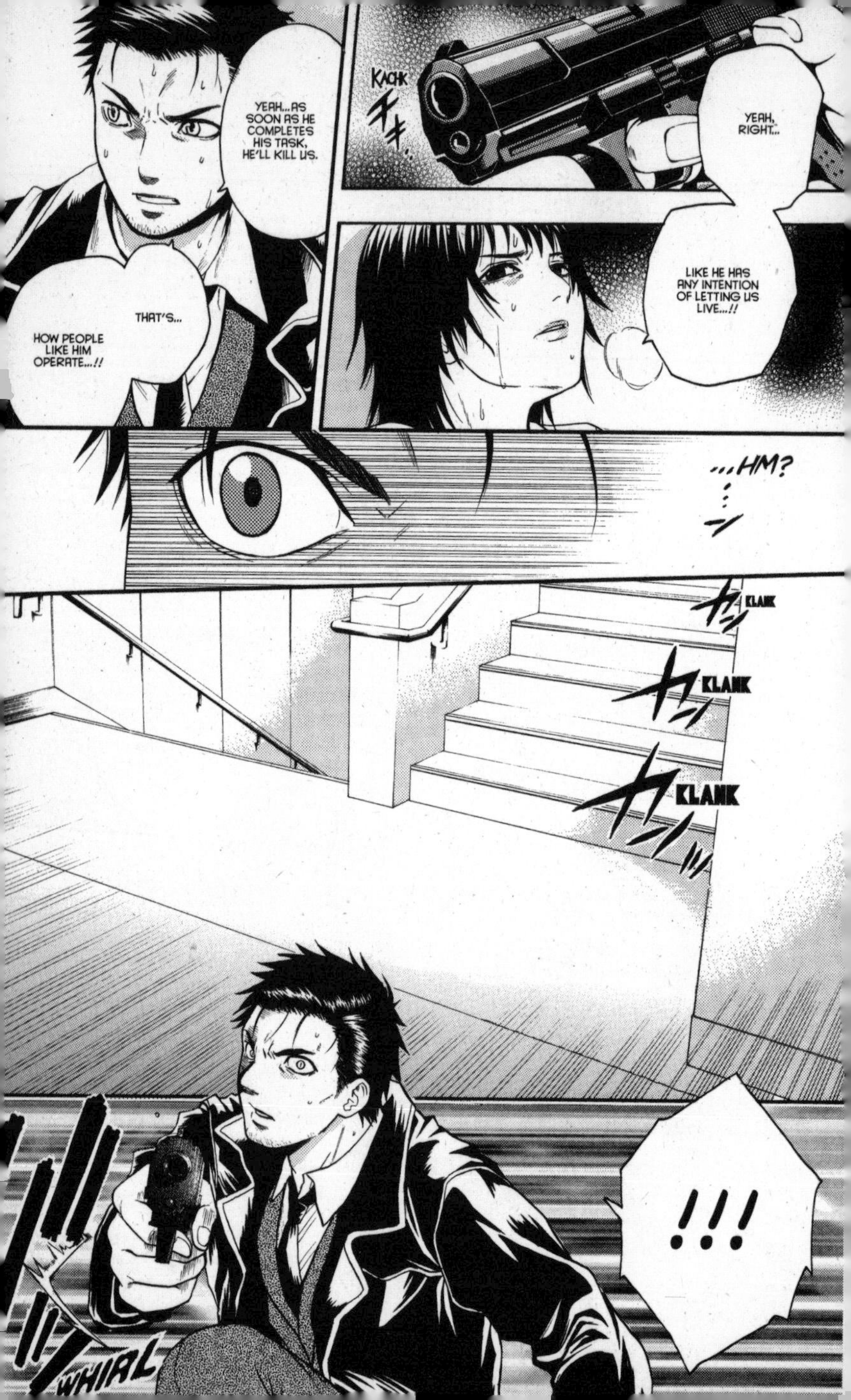

YEAH, RIGHT...
KACHK
LIKE HE HAS ANY INTENTION OF LETTING US LIVE...!!
YEAH...AS SOON AS HE COMPLETES HIS TASK, HE'LL KILL US.
THAT'S...
HOW PEOPLE LIKE HIM OPERATE...!!
...HM?
KLANK
KLANK
KLANK
!!!
WHIRL

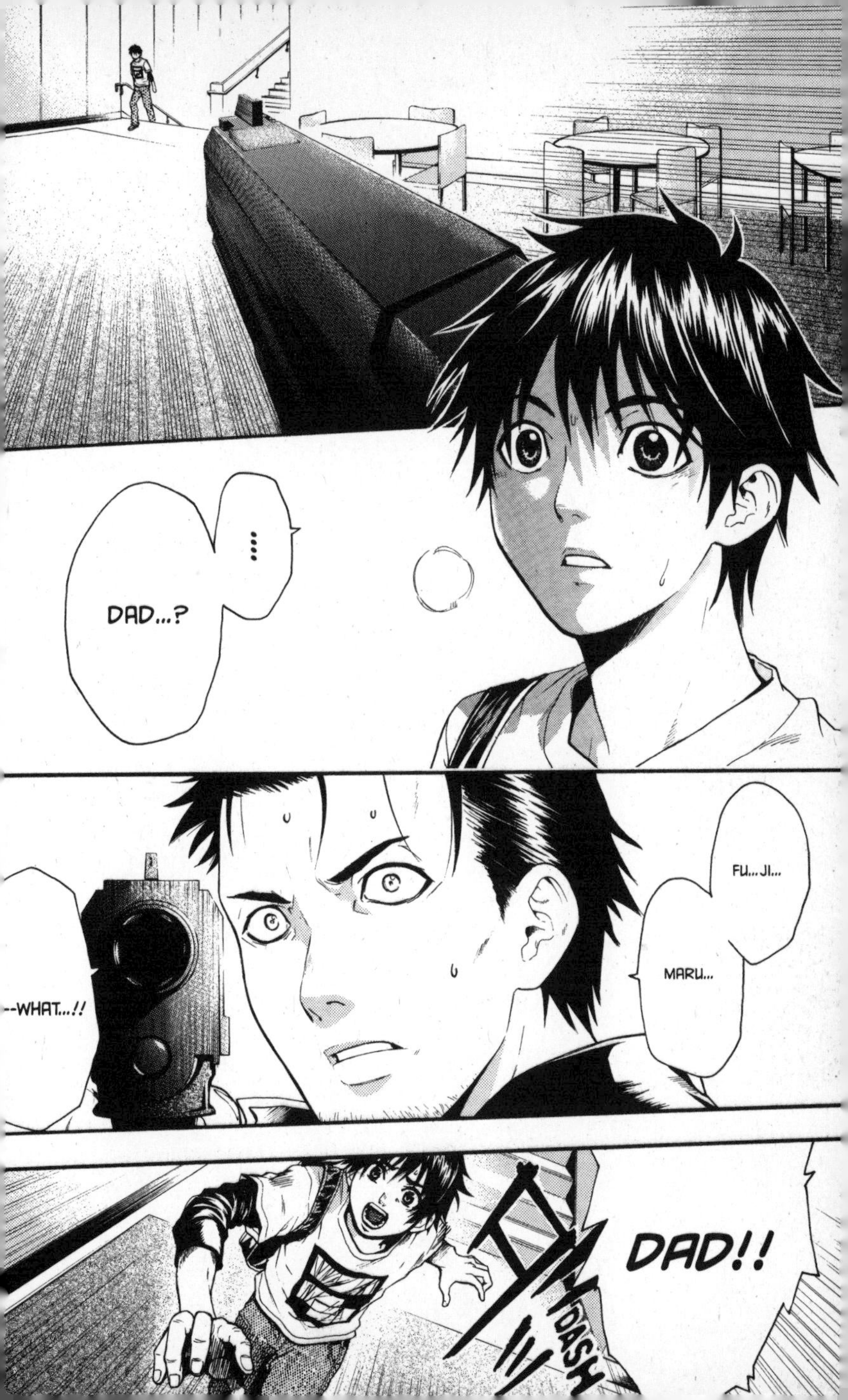
...
DAD...?
FU... JI...
MARU...
--WHAT...!!
DAD!!
DASH

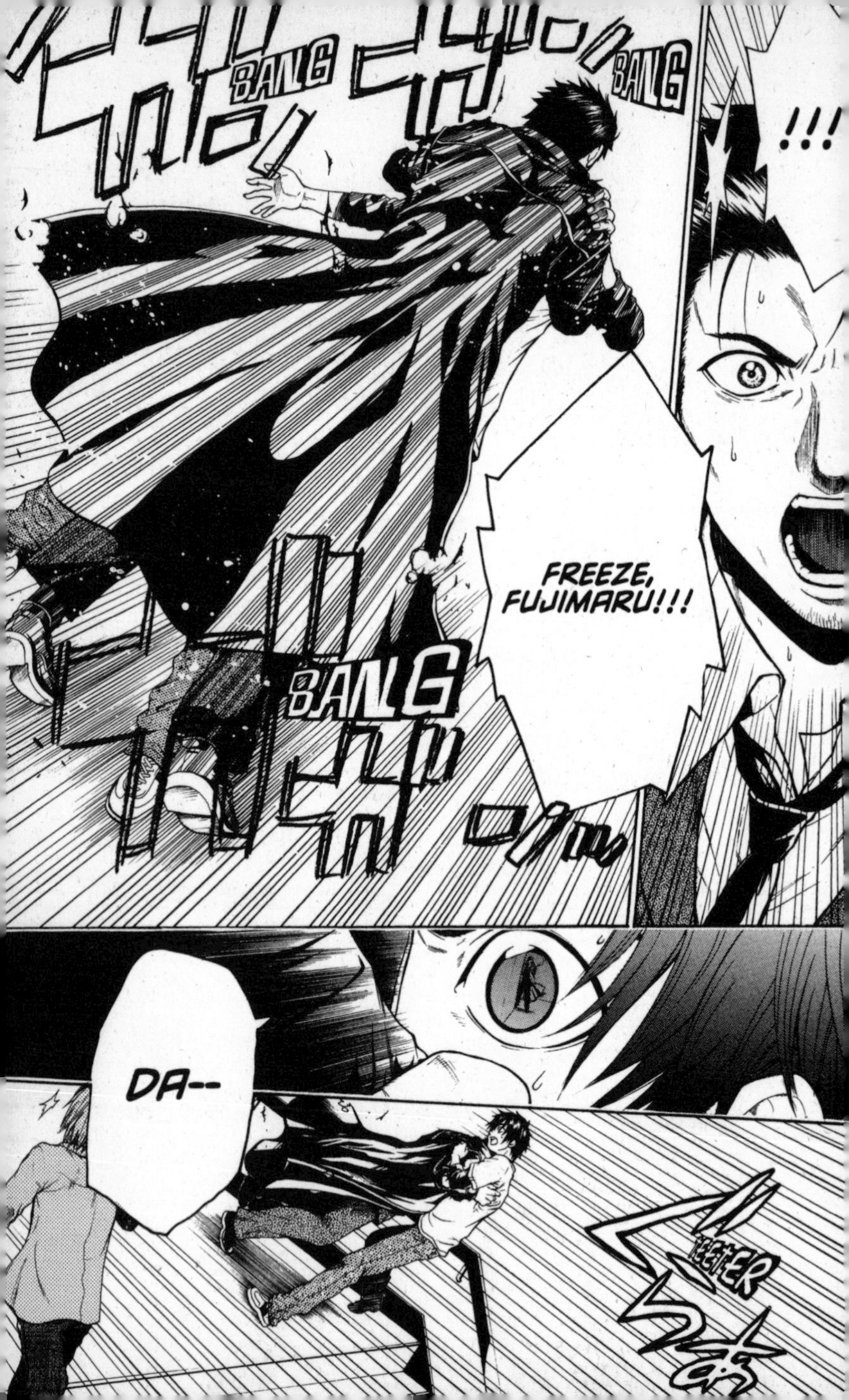
BANG
!!!
BANG
FREEZE, FUJIMARU!!!
BANG
DA--
TEETER

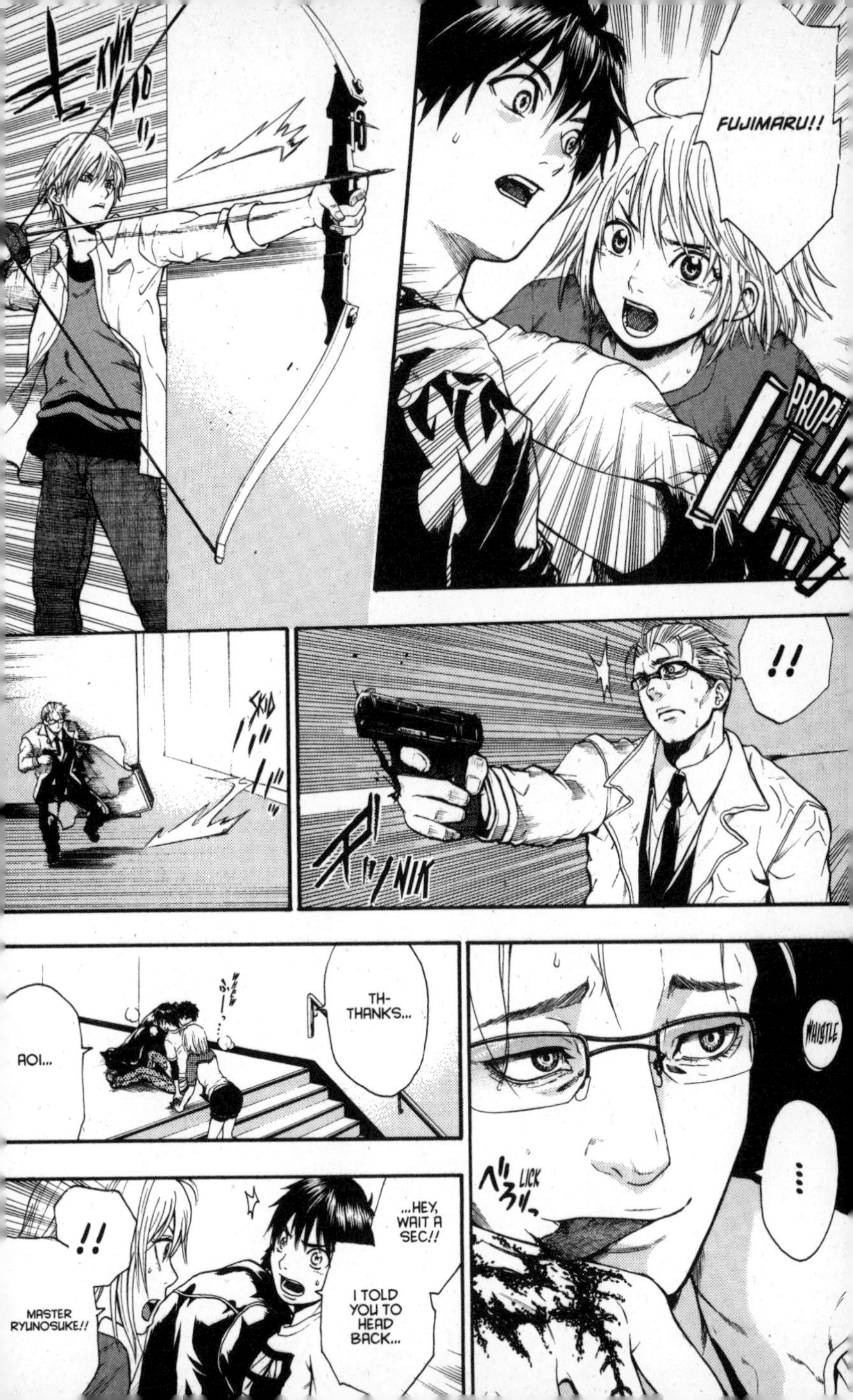
FUJIMARU!!
PROP
KWIK
TO
!!
NIK
SKID
WHISTLE
....
LICK
TH- THANKS...
AOI...
...HEY, WAIT A SEC!!
I TOLD YOU TO HEAD BACK...
!!
MASTER RYUNOSUKE!!

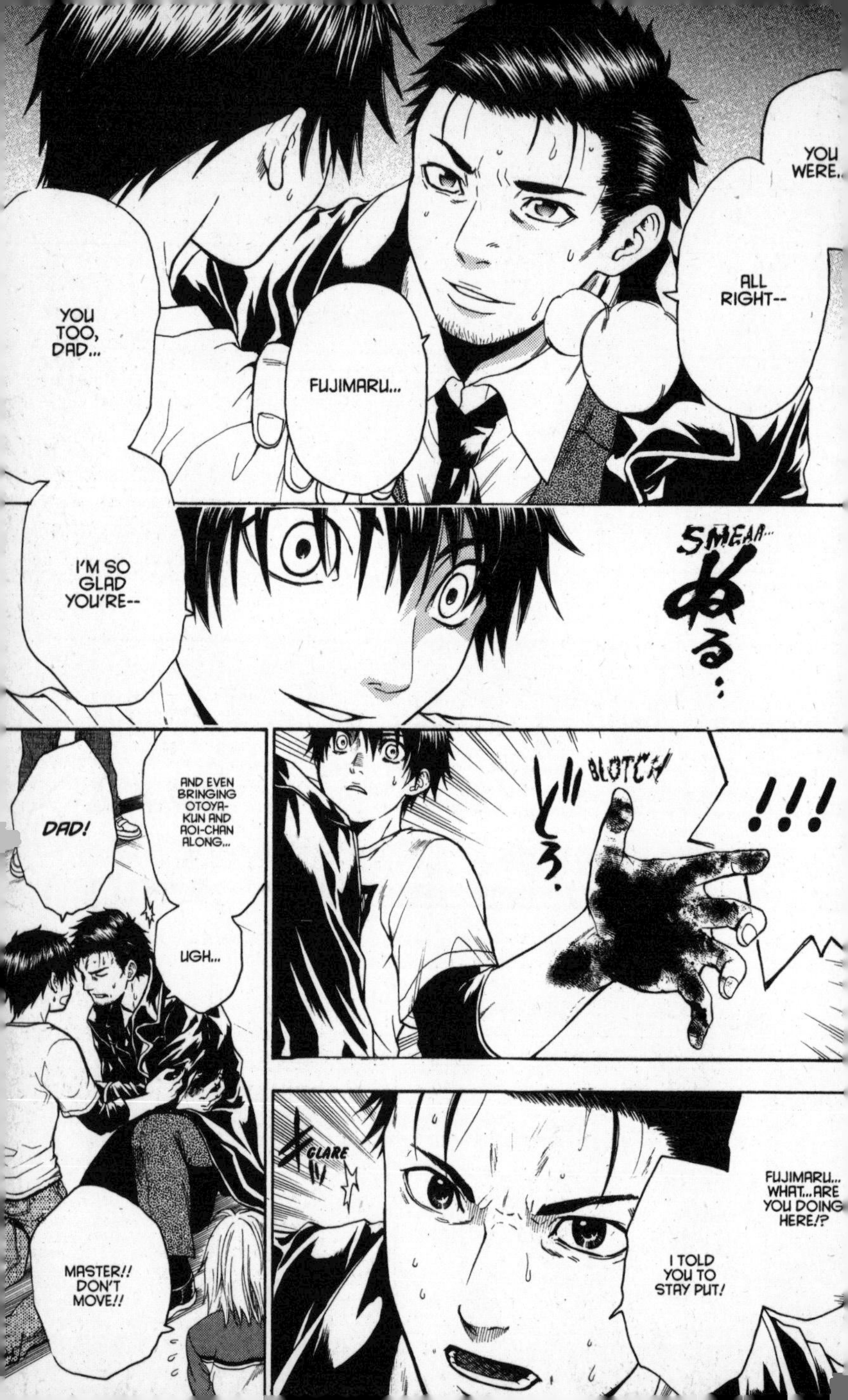
YOU WERE..
ALL RIGHT--
FUJIMARU...
YOU TOO, DAD...
SMEAR...
ぬる…
I'M SO GLAD YOU'RE--
!!!
BLOTCH
どろ…
FUJIMARU... WHAT...ARE YOU DOING HERE!?
I TOLD YOU TO STAY PUT!
GLARE
AND EVEN BRINGING OTOYA-KUN AND AOI-CHAN ALONG...
DAD!
UGH...
MASTER!! DON'T MOVE!!

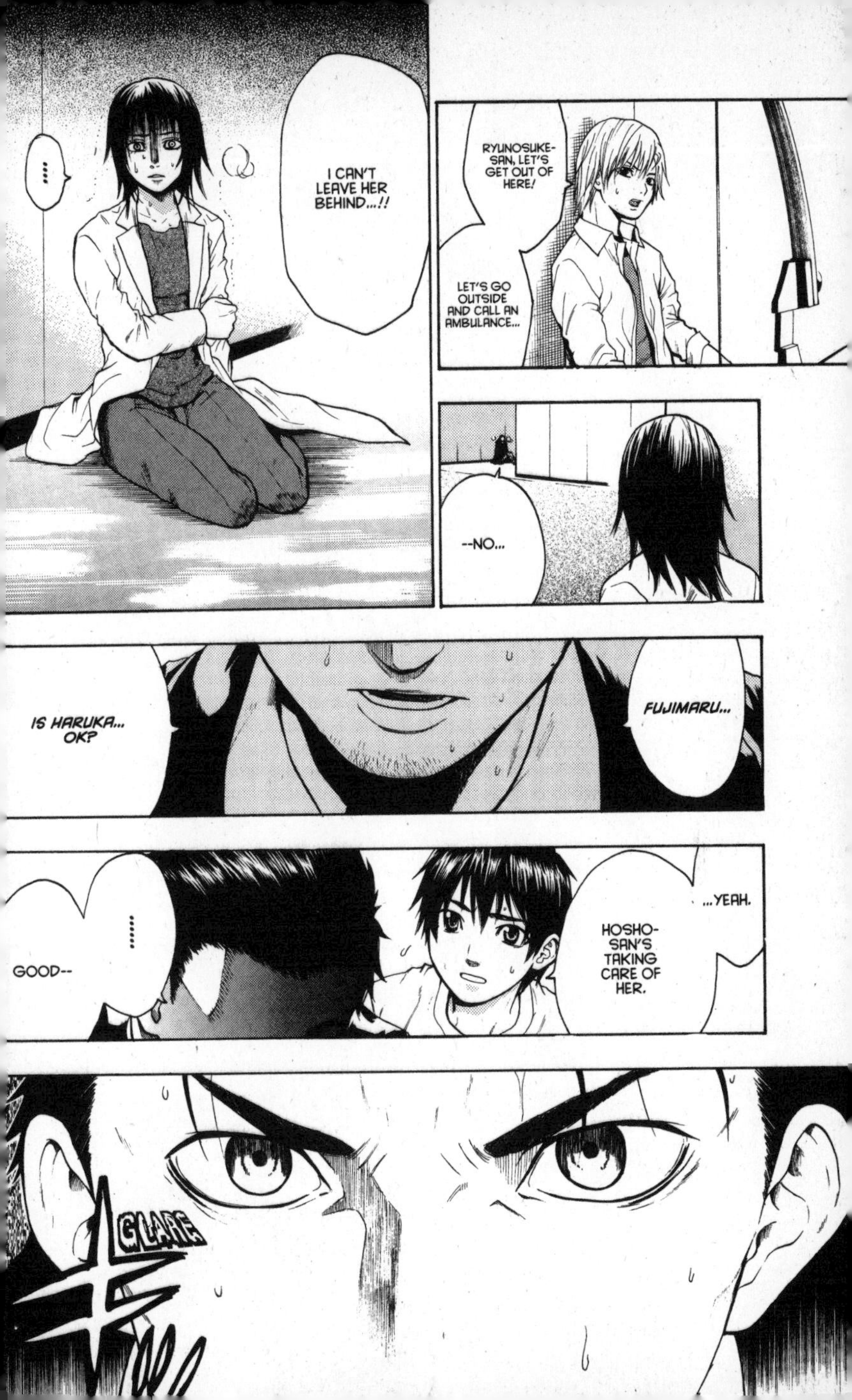
RYUNOSUKE-SAN, LET'S GET OUT OF HERE!
LET'S GO OUTSIDE AND CALL AN AMBULANCE...
--NO...
I CAN'T LEAVE HER BEHIND...!!
....
FUJIMARU...
IS HARUKA... OK?
...YEAH.
HOSHO-SAN'S TAKING CARE OF HER.
......
GOOD--
GLARE

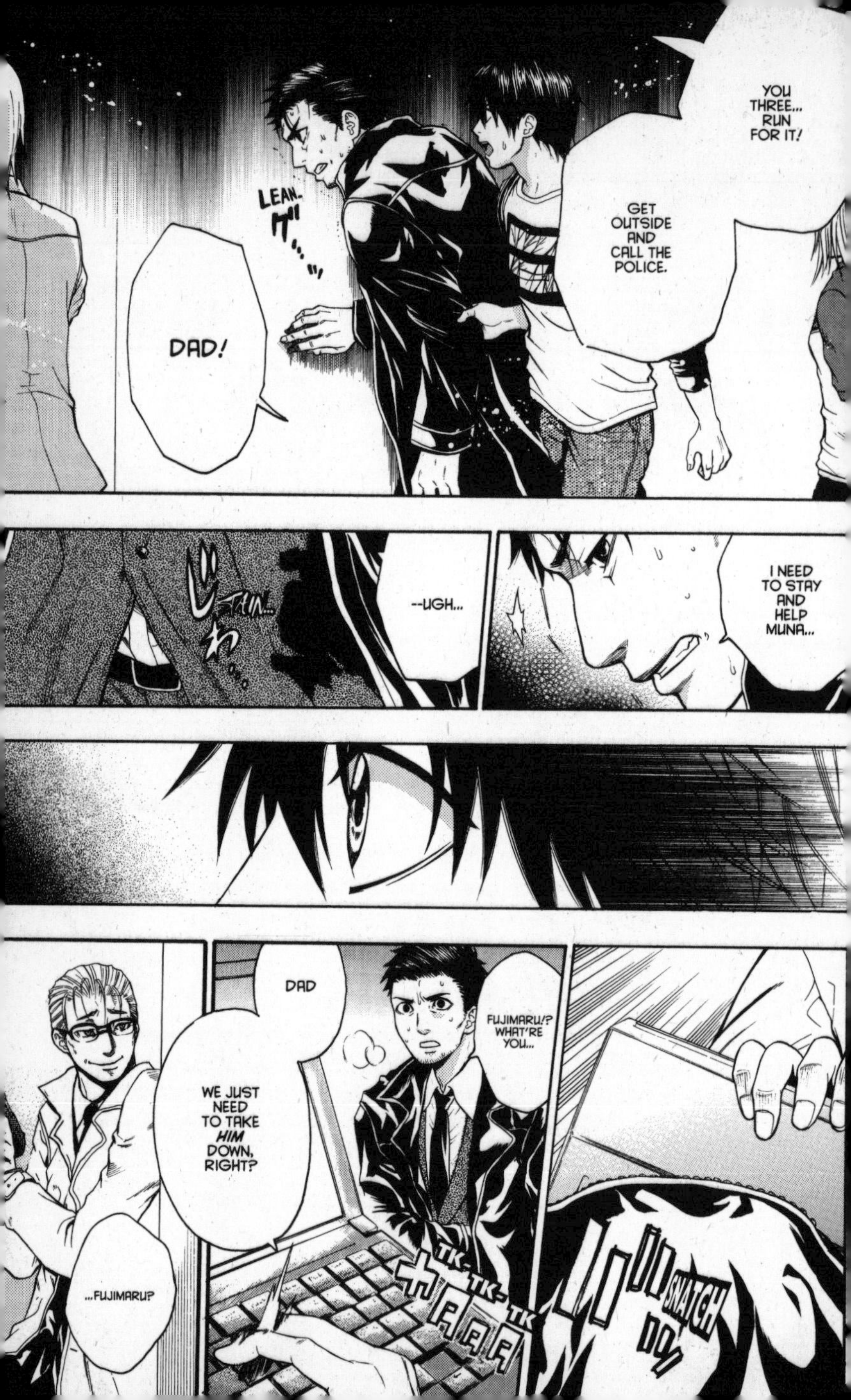
YOU THREE... RUN FOR IT!
GET OUTSIDE AND CALL THE POLICE.
LEAN-
DAD!
I NEED TO STAY AND HELP MUNA...
--UGH...
STAIN...
SNATCH
FUJIMARU!? WHAT'RE YOU...
DAD
WE JUST NEED TO TAKE *HIM* DOWN, RIGHT?
TK-TK-TK
...FUJIMARU?

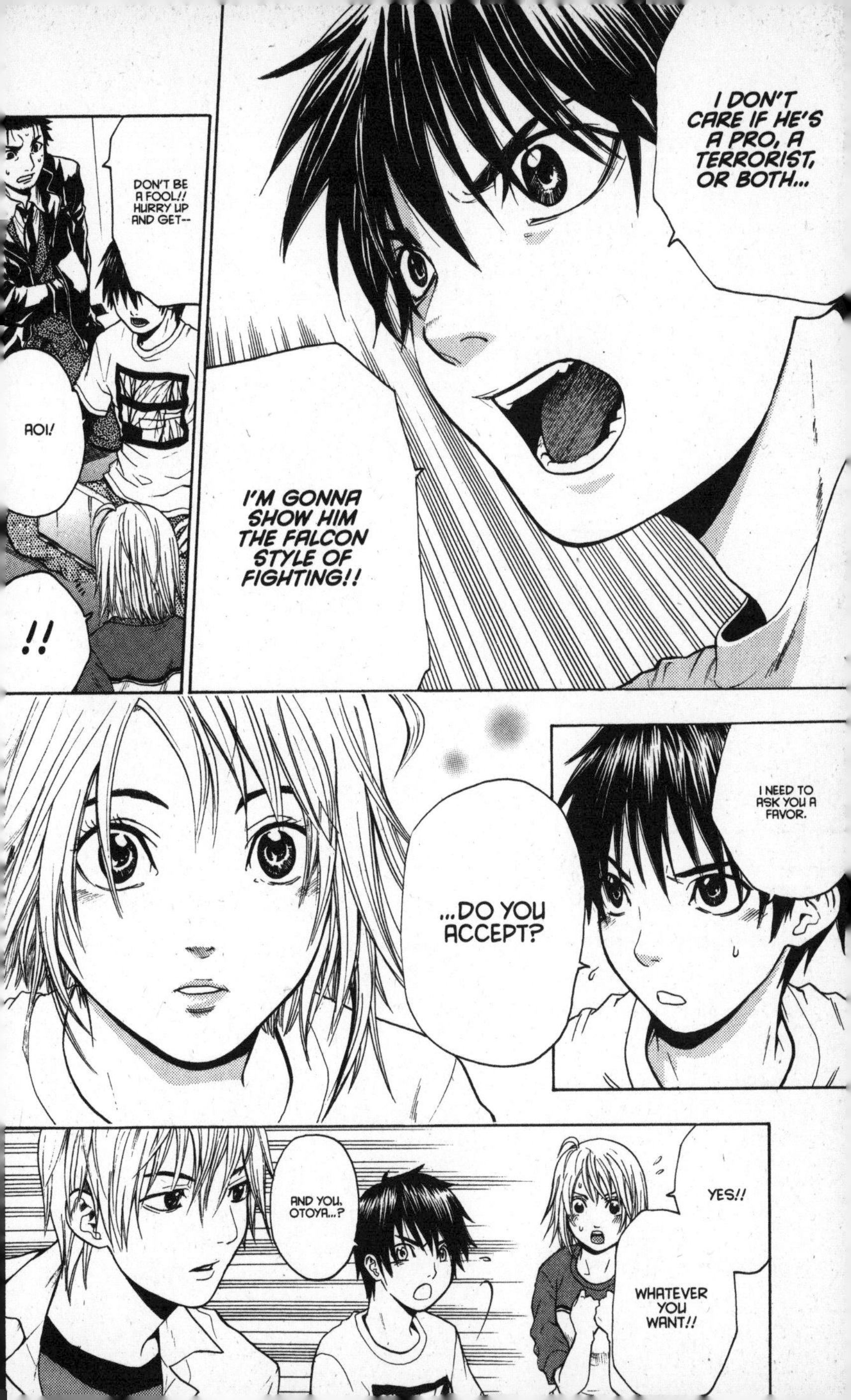
I DON'T CARE IF HE'S A PRO, A TERRORIST, OR BOTH...
I'M GONNA SHOW HIM THE FALCON STYLE OF FIGHTING!!
DON'T BE A FOOL!! HURRY UP AND GET--
AOI!
!!
I NEED TO ASK YOU A FAVOR.
...DO YOU ACCEPT?
YES!!
WHATEVER YOU WANT!!
AND YOU, OTOYA...?

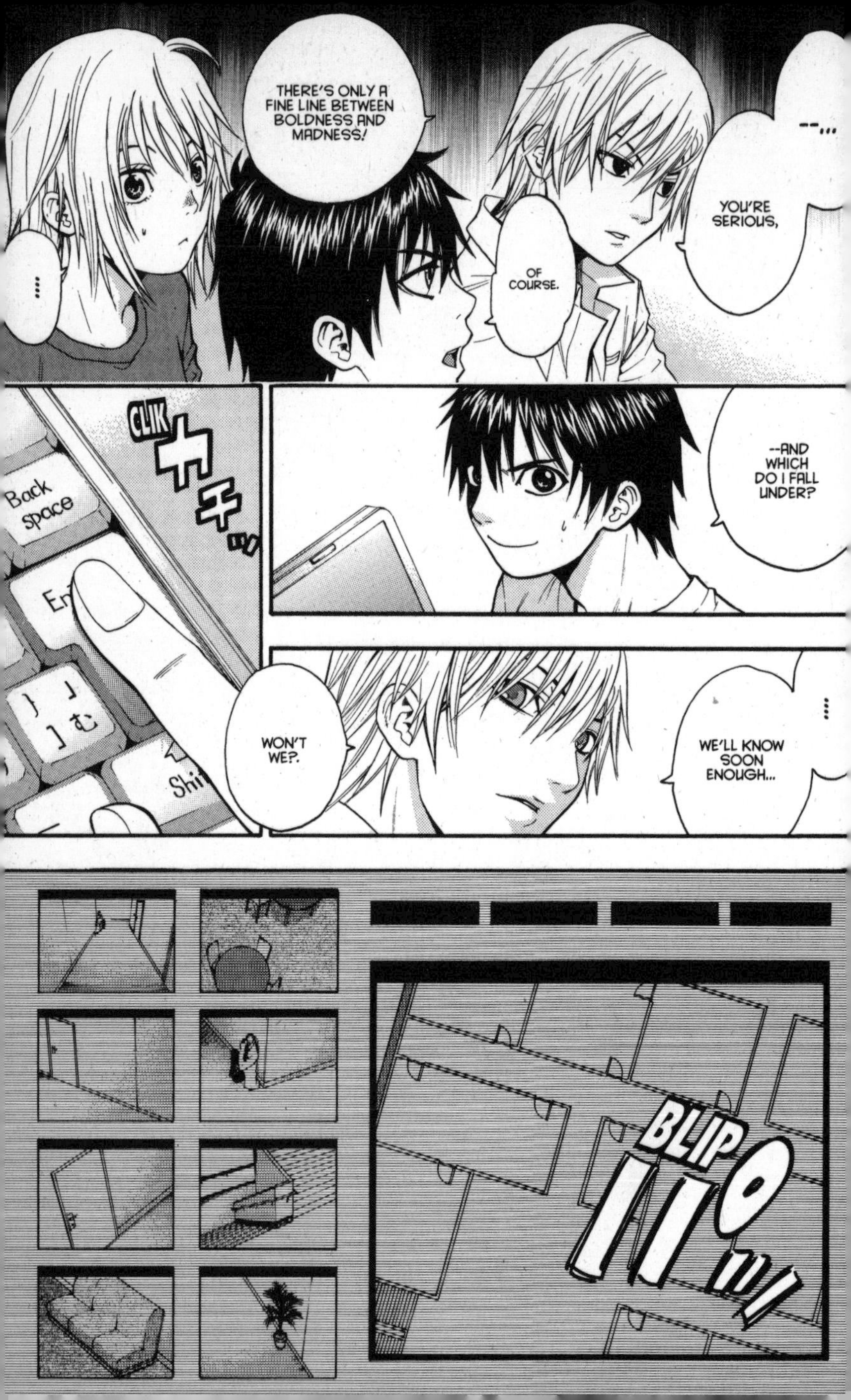
--...
YOU'RE SERIOUS,
OF COURSE.
THERE'S ONLY A FINE LINE BETWEEN BOLDNESS AND MADNESS!
....
--AND WHICH DO I FALL UNDER?
....
WE'LL KNOW SOON ENOUGH...
WON'T WE?.
CLIK
Back space
BLIP

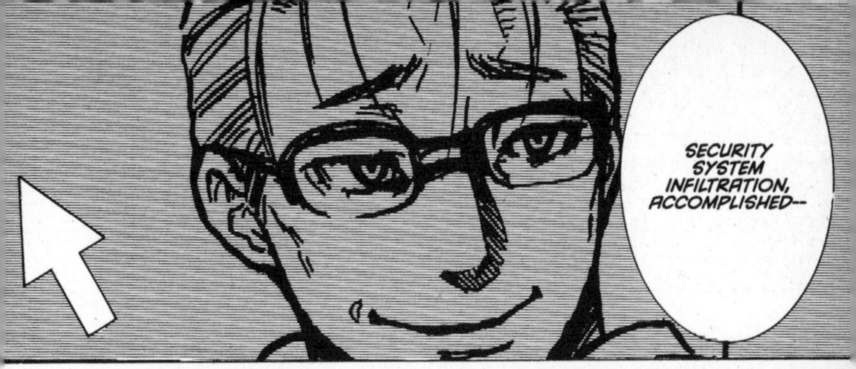
SECURITY SYSTEM INFILTRATION, ACCOMPLISHED--
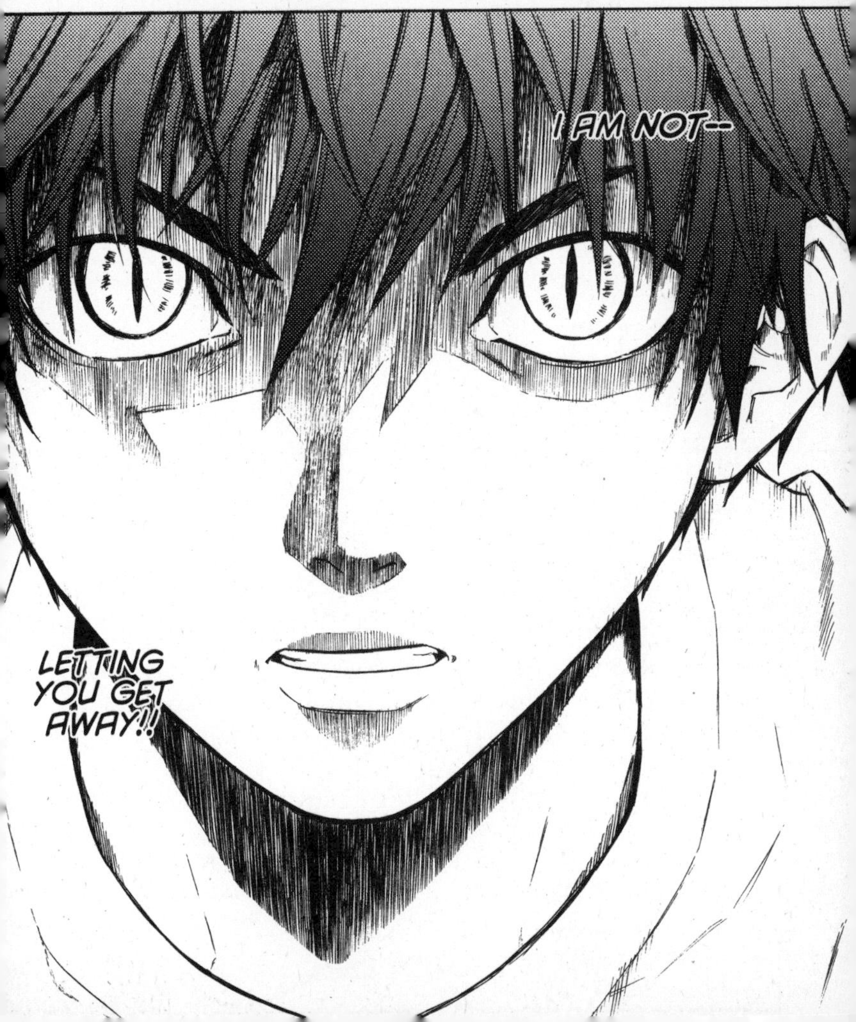
I AM NOT--
LETTING YOU GET AWAY!!

BLOODY MONDAY
- GLOSSARY OF TERMS · LIST 7 -

[Translator's note: HSDPA stands for "High-Speed Downlink Packet Access". It is also known as turbo 3G, 3.5G, and 3G+]

A protocol that increases the data transmission speed of third generation (3G) mobile telecommunications network standard W-DMA (Wideband Code Division Multiple Access).

Infrared Sensor p111
Infrared light possesses the characteristic of being emitted at a range of wavelengths corresponding to the temperature of an object. Infrared sensors are devices that pick up beams of designated bandwidths within the infrared spectrum, convert the received emission into an electrical signal, and extract data from it.

Bluetooth p127
A type of short-range wireless-transmission technology. It allows wireless transfer of data and sound between devices, such as cellular phones, laptops, and PDAs, without the need for cables. Unlike infrared light, Bluetooth can still be used even if physical obstacles are in the way.

IP Phone p152
A telephone service where telephone calls are made over an IP (Internet Protocol) network. The hardware converts voice data into digital data, partitions that data into packets, and transmits the packets to the call destination via an IP network, thereby enabling voice communication.

NO HSDPA
(TURBO 3G)
AND PHS
(PITCH),
EITHER.

BLOODY MONDAY

- GLOSSARY OF TERMS • LIST 8 -

Skype p152
A voice communication software application that utilizes P2P(Peer -to-Peer: see Volume 1,Page 131,as well as translation notes) technology. Users can engage in voice communication by installing the relevant software and connecting a microphone to their laptop.

MAST p158
[Translator's Note: MAST is short for "Military Anti-Shock Trousers". Also known as "Pneumatic Anti-Shock Garments" or PASG, the author originally used the term "shock pants" in the text.]

A medical device applied to patients in a state of hemorrhagic shock. It serves the function of increasing blood pressure by applying physical pressure to the lower half of the body and rerouting blood from the legs to the heart and brain, in addition to stabilizing any lower-body fractures.

U.S. Department of Defense (Pentagon) p170
One of America’ s central government agencies. It is the supreme military administrative body that oversees the U.S. Army, Navy, and Air Force. Its metonym "Pentagon" originated from the fact that its headquarters is located in a pentagon-shaped building.

Antiviral Drugs p181
Medications used to treat viral diseases. As opposed to vaccines, which prevent infection by building up the body's defenses before exposure, anti-viral drugs can stop virus replication inside the body even after infection has occurred.

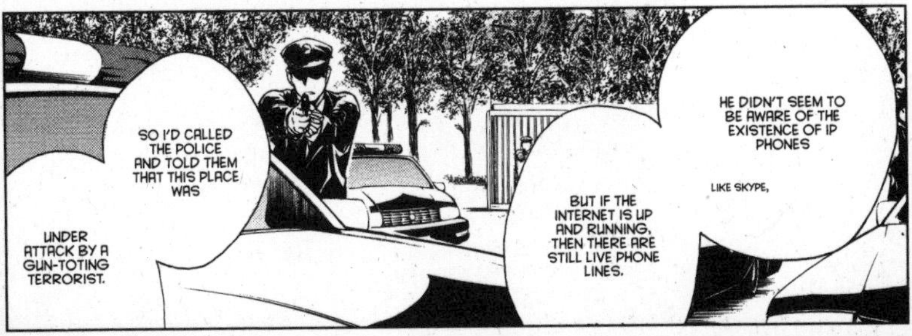
HE DIDN'T SEEM TO BE AWARE OF THE EXISTENCE OF IP PHONES
LIKE SKYPE,
BUT IF THE INTERNET IS UP AND RUNNING, THEN THERE ARE STILL LIVE PHONE LINES.
SO I'D CALLED THE POLICE AND TOLD THEM THAT THIS PLACE WAS
UNDER ATTACK BY A GUN-TOTING TERRORIST.

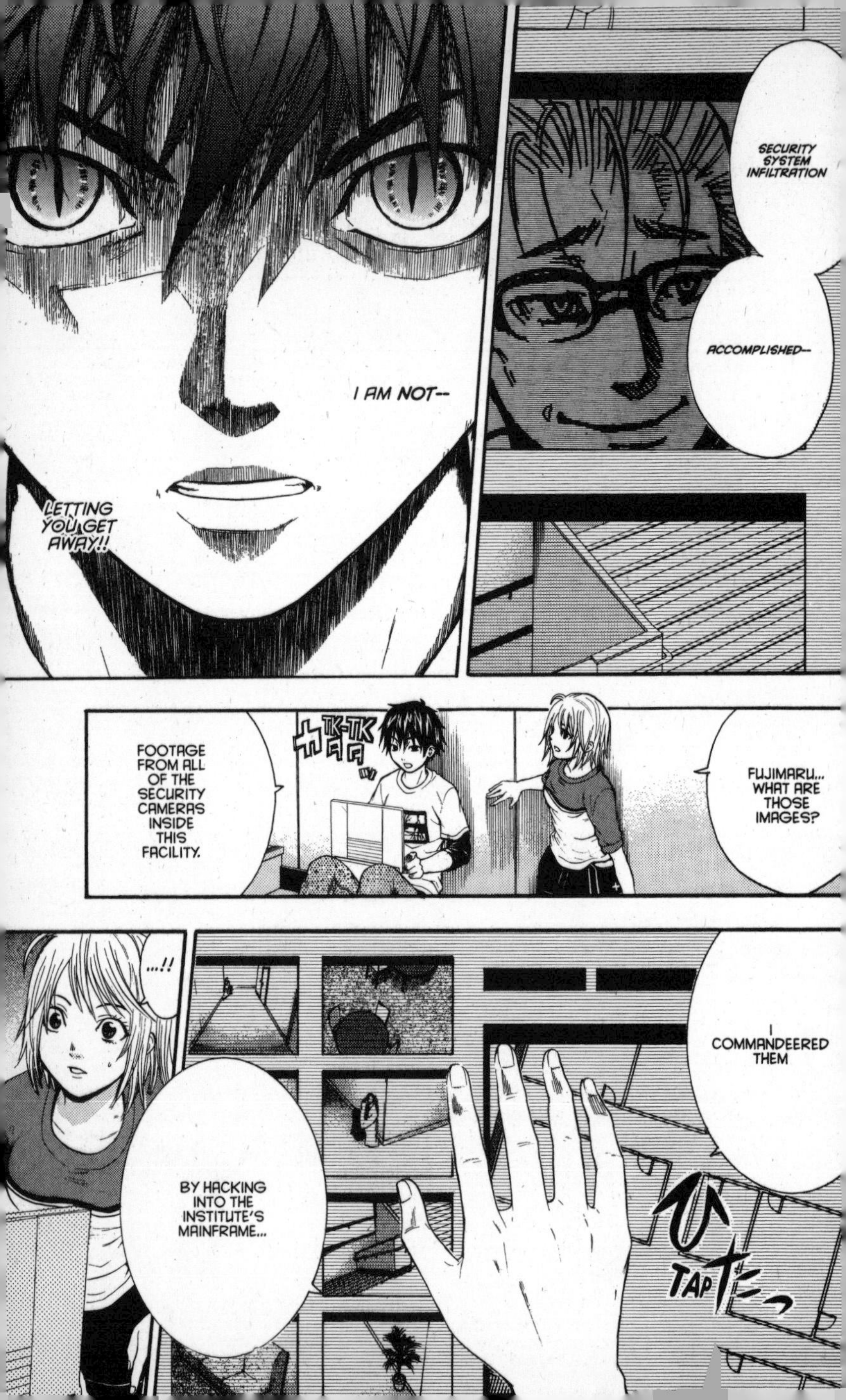
SECURITY SYSTEM INFILTRATION
ACCOMPLISHED--
I AM NOT--
LETTING YOU GET AWAY!!
FUJIMARU... WHAT ARE THOSE IMAGES?
TK-TK
FOOTAGE FROM ALL OF THE SECURITY CAMERAS INSIDE THIS FACILITY.
I COMMANDEERED THEM
TAP
BY HACKING INTO THE INSTITUTE'S MAINFRAME...
...!!

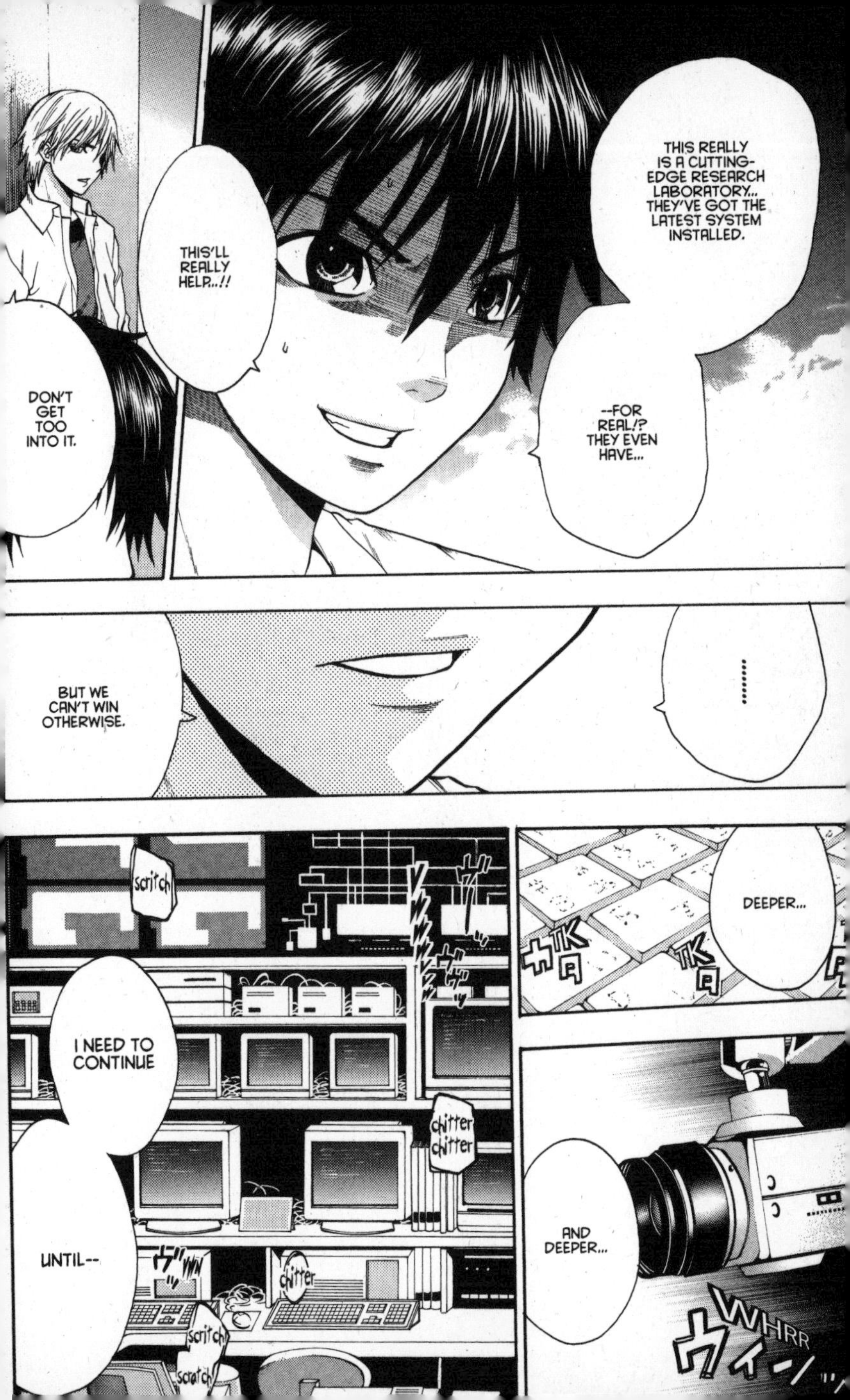
THIS REALLY IS A CUTTING-EDGE RESEARCH LABORATORY... THEY'VE GOT THE LATEST SYSTEM INSTALLED.
--FOR REAL!? THEY EVEN HAVE...
THIS'LL REALLY HELP...!!
DON'T GET TOO INTO IT.
......
BUT WE CAN'T WIN OTHERWISE.
DEEPER...
TK
TK
AND DEEPER...
WHRR
ウィーン
scritch
I NEED TO CONTINUE
chitter chitter
UNTIL--
chitter
scritch
scratch

File 20 The Battle in the Dark

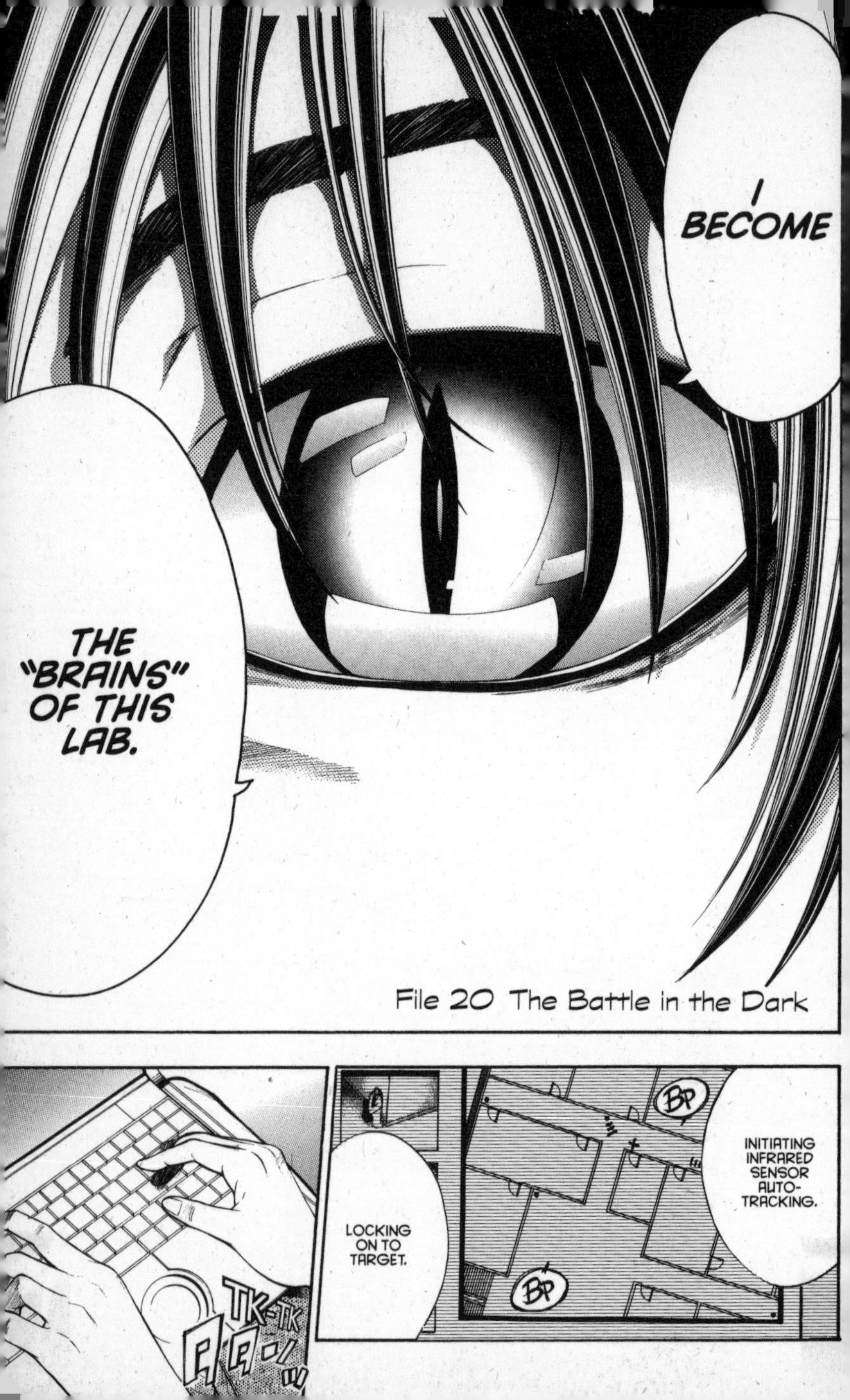
I BECOME
THE "BRAINS" OF THIS LAB.
BP
INITIATING INFRARED SENSOR AUTO-TRACKING.
LOCKING ON TO TARGET.
BP
TK-TK

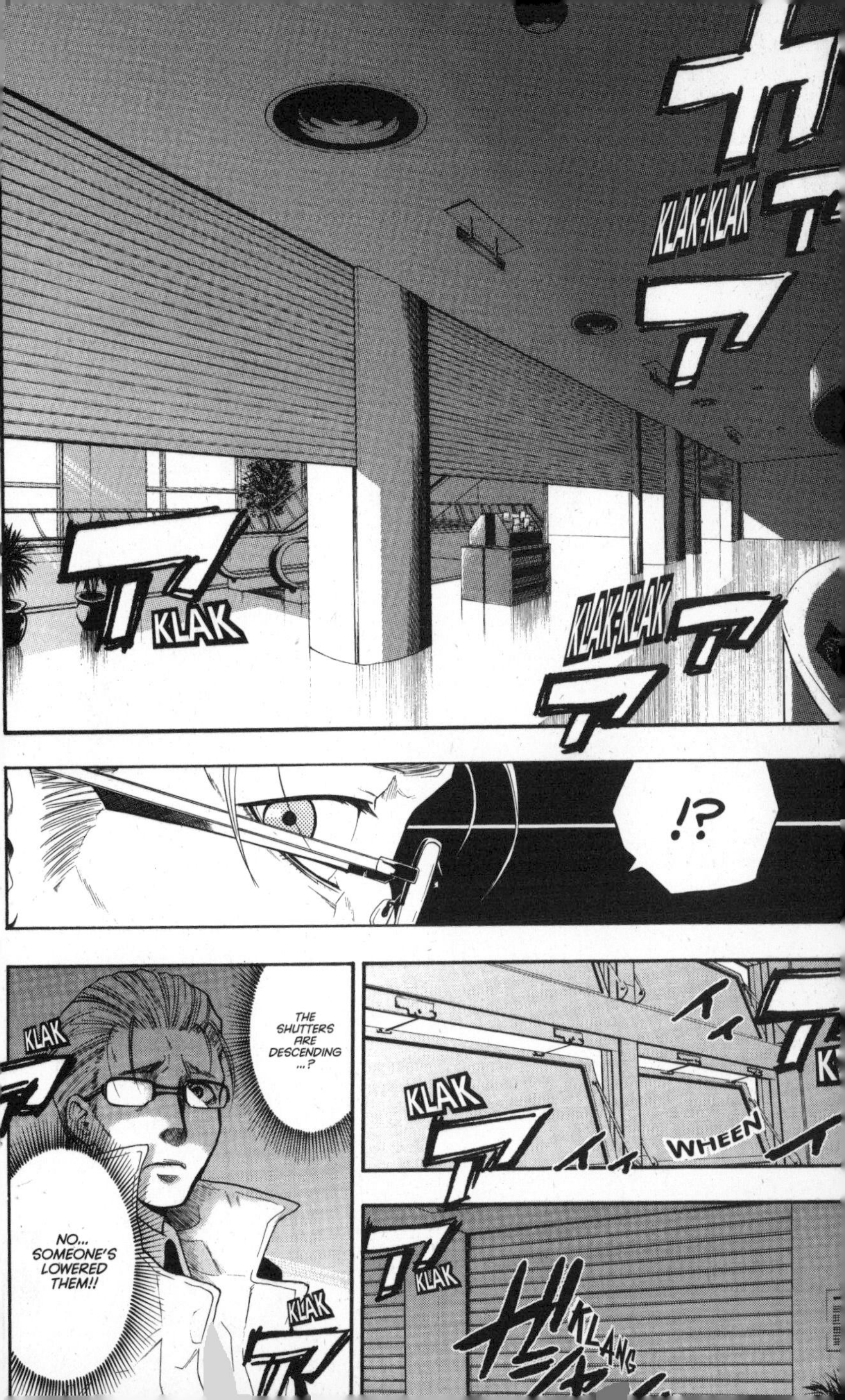
KLAK-KLAK
KLAK-KLAK
KLAK
!?
WHEEN
KLAK
KLANG
KLAK
THE SHUTTERS ARE DESCENDING ...?
KLAK
NO... SOMEONE'S LOWERED THEM!!
KLAK

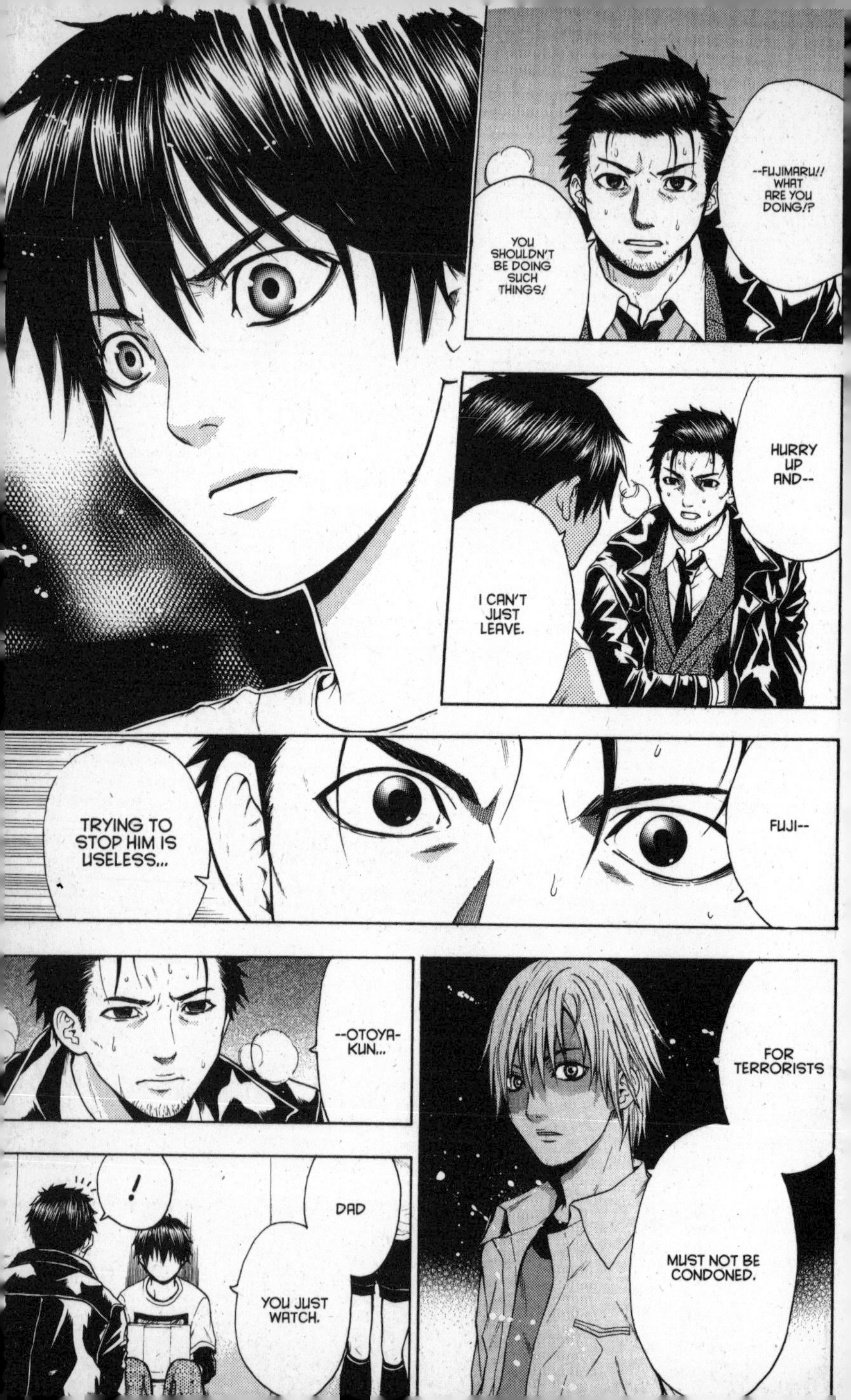
--FUJIMARU!! WHAT ARE YOU DOING!?
YOU SHOULDN'T BE DOING SUCH THINGS!
HURRY UP AND--
I CAN'T JUST LEAVE.
FUJI--
TRYING TO STOP HIM IS USELESS...
FOR TERRORISTS
MUST NOT BE CONDONED.
--OTOYA-KUN...
!
DAD
YOU JUST WATCH.

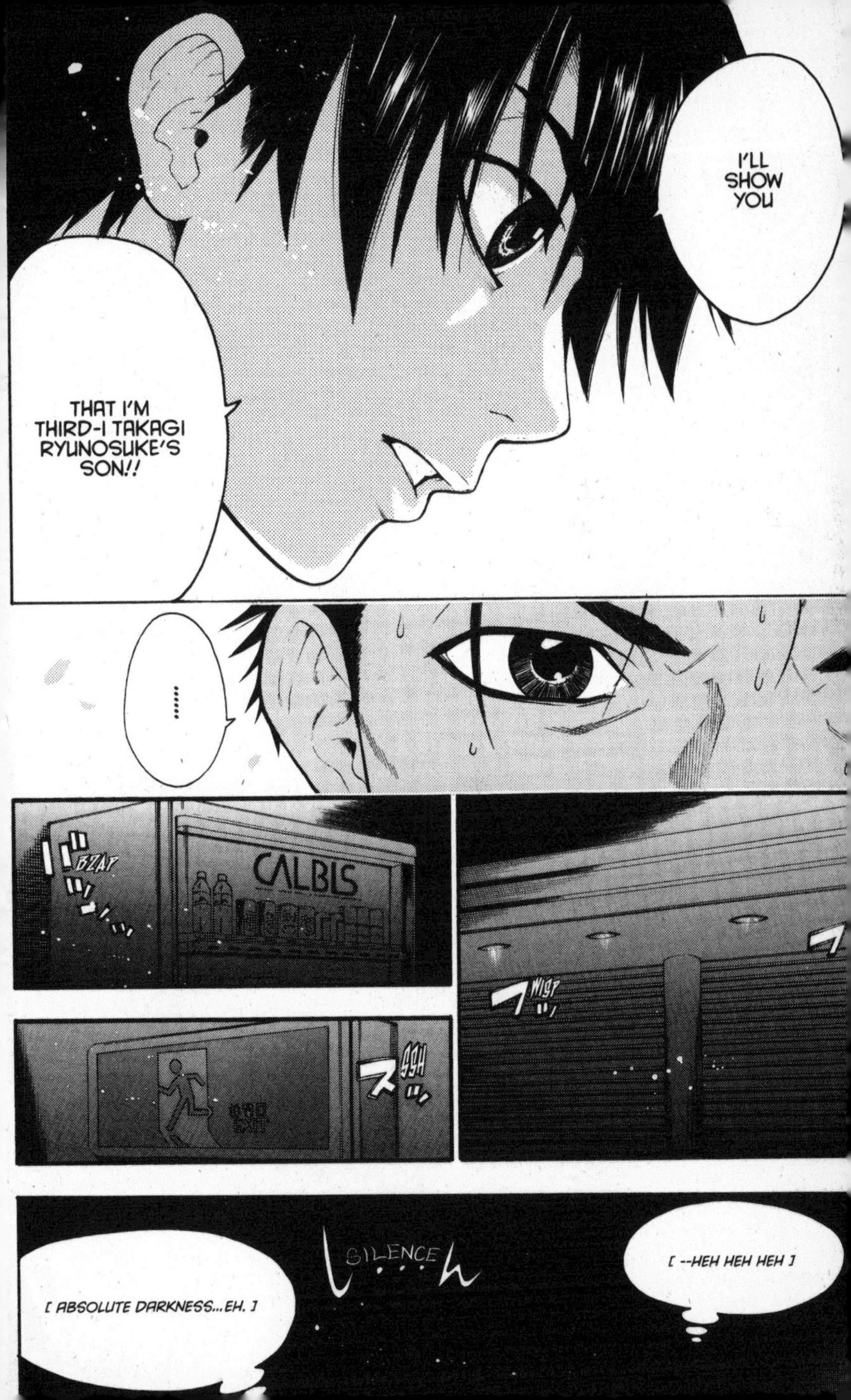
I'LL SHOW YOU
THAT I'M THIRD-I TAKAGI RYUNOSUKE'S SON!!
......
WISP
BZAP
SSH
SILENCE
[--HEH HEH HEH]
[ABSOLUTE DARKNESS...EH.]

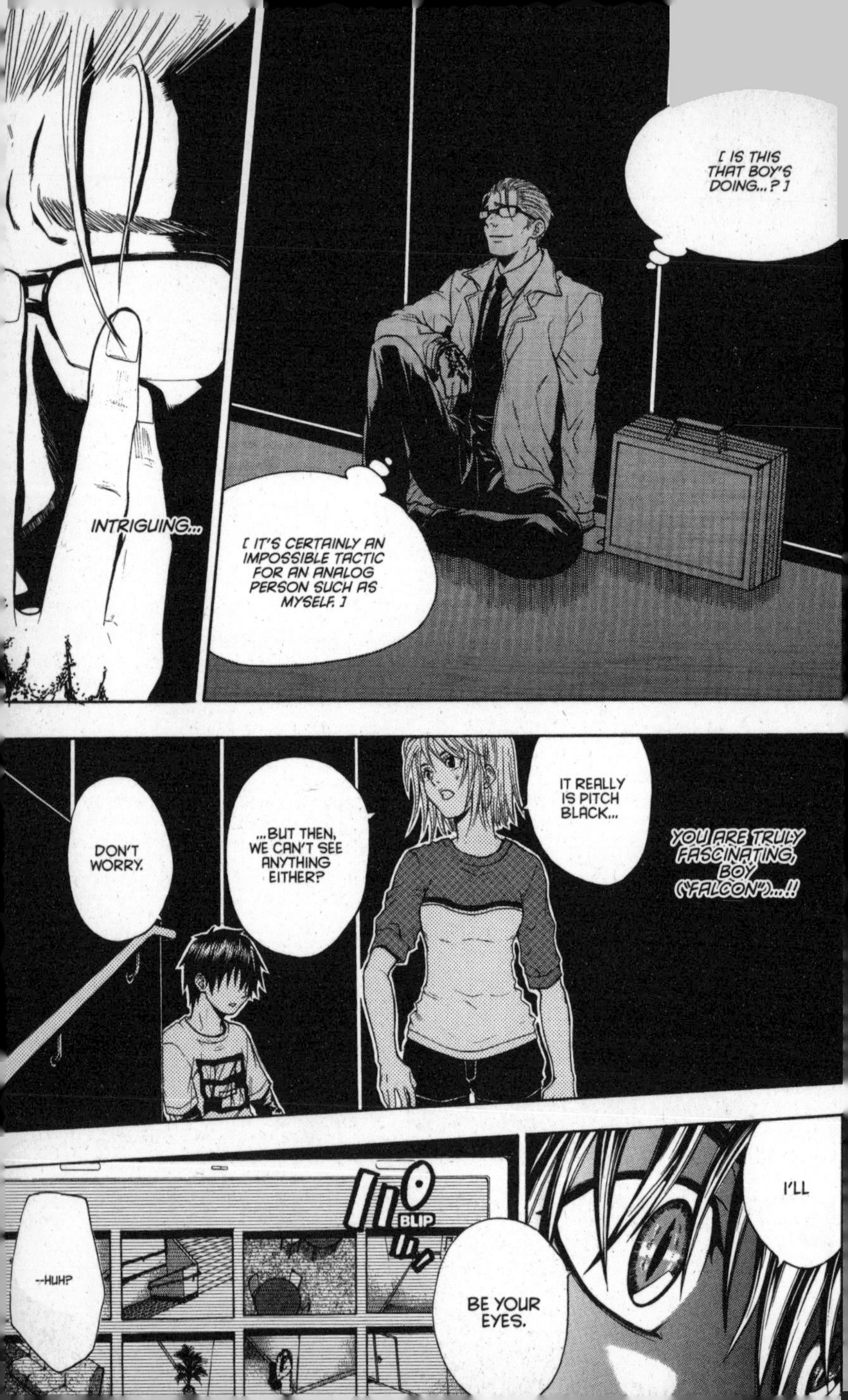
[IS THIS THAT BOY'S DOING...?]
[IT'S CERTAINLY AN IMPOSSIBLE TACTIC FOR AN ANALOG PERSON SUCH AS MYSELF.]
INTRIGUING...
YOU ARE TRULY FASCINATING, BOY ("FALCON")...!!
IT REALLY IS PITCH BLACK...
...BUT THEN, WE CAN'T SEE ANYTHING EITHER?
DON'T WORRY.
I'LL
BE YOUR EYES.
BLIP
--HUH?

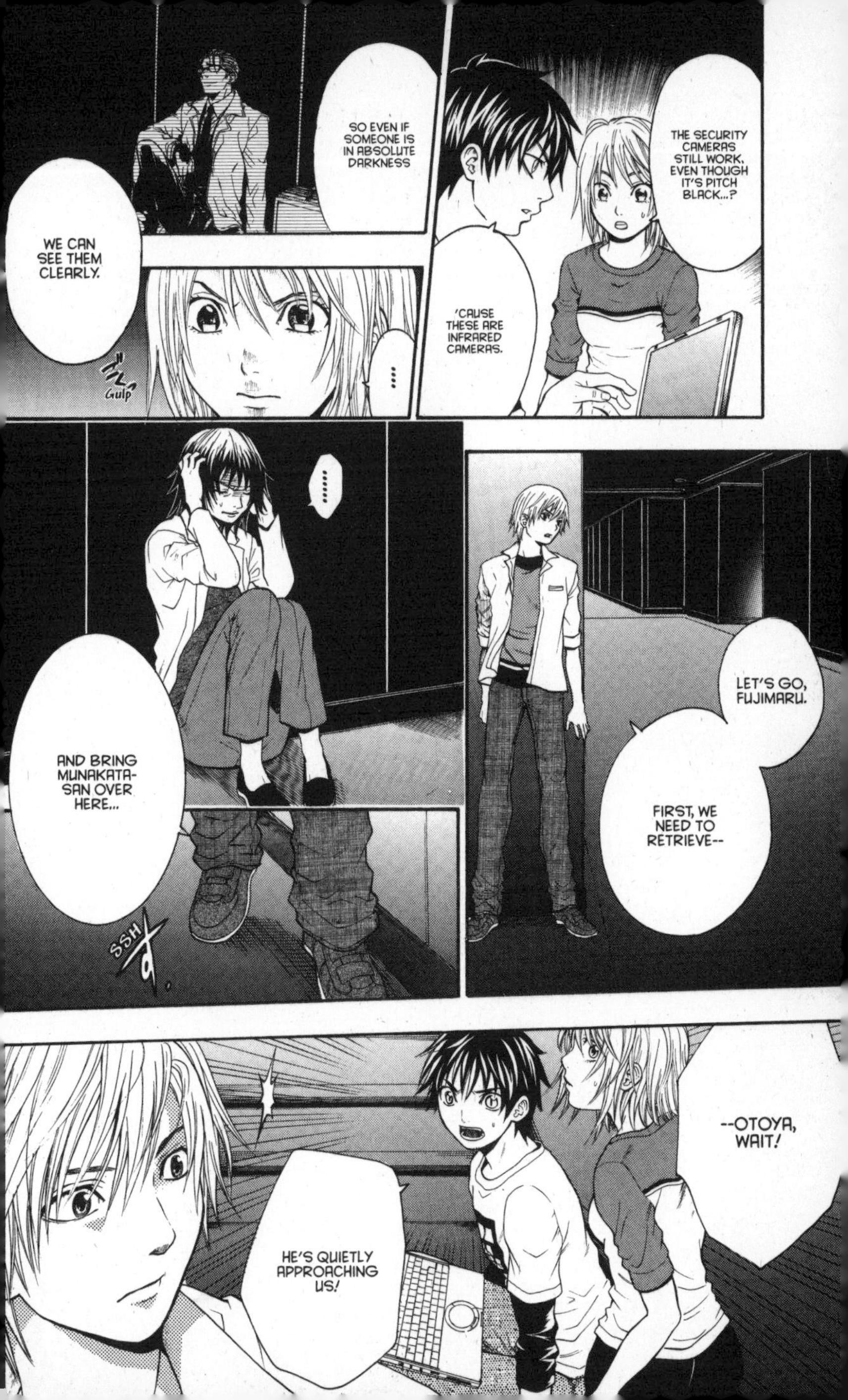
THE SECURITY CAMERAS STILL WORK, EVEN THOUGH IT'S PITCH BLACK...?
'CAUSE THESE ARE INFRARED CAMERAS.
SO EVEN IF SOMEONE IS IN ABSOLUTE DARKNESS
WE CAN SEE THEM CLEARLY.
.....
Gulp
LET'S GO, FUJIMARU.
FIRST, WE NEED TO RETRIEVE--
......
AND BRING MUNAKATA-SAN OVER HERE...
SSH
--OTOYA, WAIT!
HE'S QUIETLY APPROACHING US!

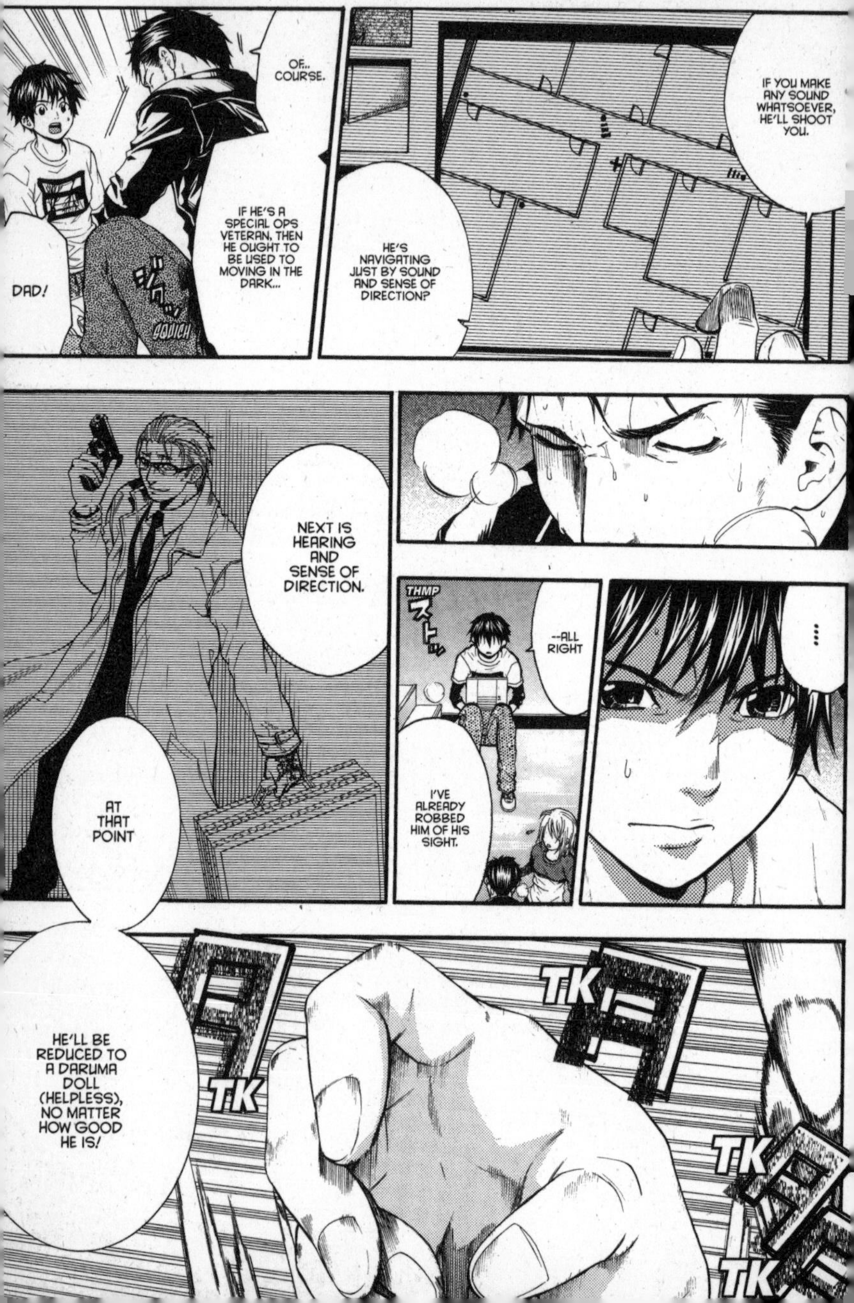
IF YOU MAKE ANY SOUND WHATSOEVER, HE'LL SHOOT YOU.
HE'S NAVIGATING JUST BY SOUND AND SENSE OF DIRECTION?
OF.. COURSE.
IF HE'S A SPECIAL OPS VETERAN, THEN HE OUGHT TO BE USED TO MOVING IN THE DARK...
SQUICH
DAD!
...
THMP
--ALL RIGHT
I'VE ALREADY ROBBED HIM OF HIS SIGHT.
NEXT IS HEARING AND SENSE OF DIRECTION.
AT THAT POINT
TK
TK
TK
HE'LL BE REDUCED TO A DARUMA DOLL (HELPLESS), NO MATTER HOW GOOD HE IS!
TK

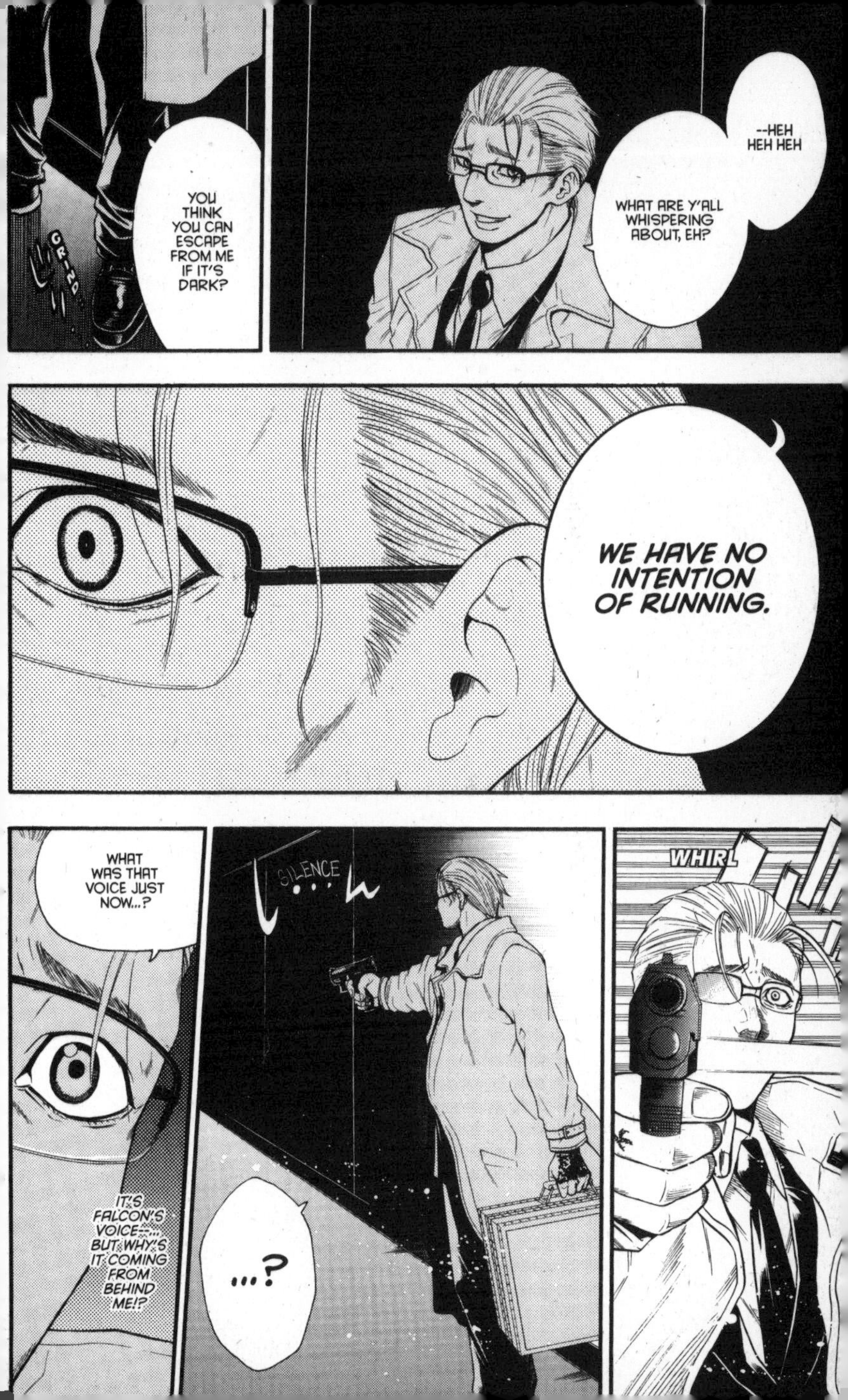
--HEH HEH HEH
WHAT ARE Y'ALL WHISPERING ABOUT, EH?
YOU THINK YOU CAN ESCAPE FROM ME IF IT'S DARK?
GRIND
WE HAVE NO INTENTION OF RUNNING.
WHIRL
SILENCE
...?
WHAT WAS THAT VOICE JUST NOW...?
IT'S FALCON'S VOICE--... BUT WHY'S IT COMING FROM BEHIND ME!?

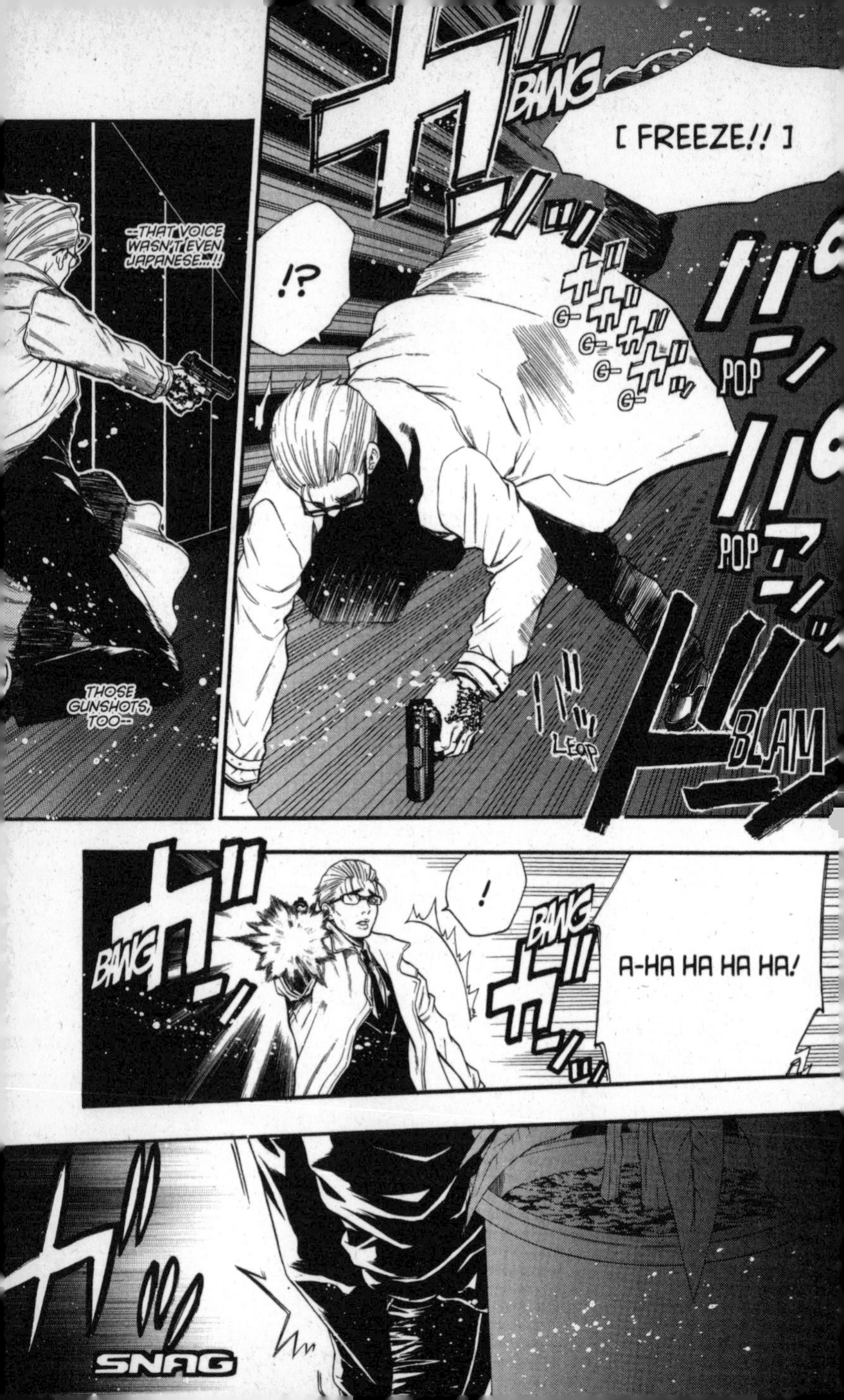
BANG
[FREEZE!!]
!?
POP
POP
LEAP
BLAM
--THAT VOICE WASN'T EVEN JAPANESE...!!
THOSE GUNSHOTS, TOO--
A-HA HA HA HA!
BANG
!
BANG
SNAG

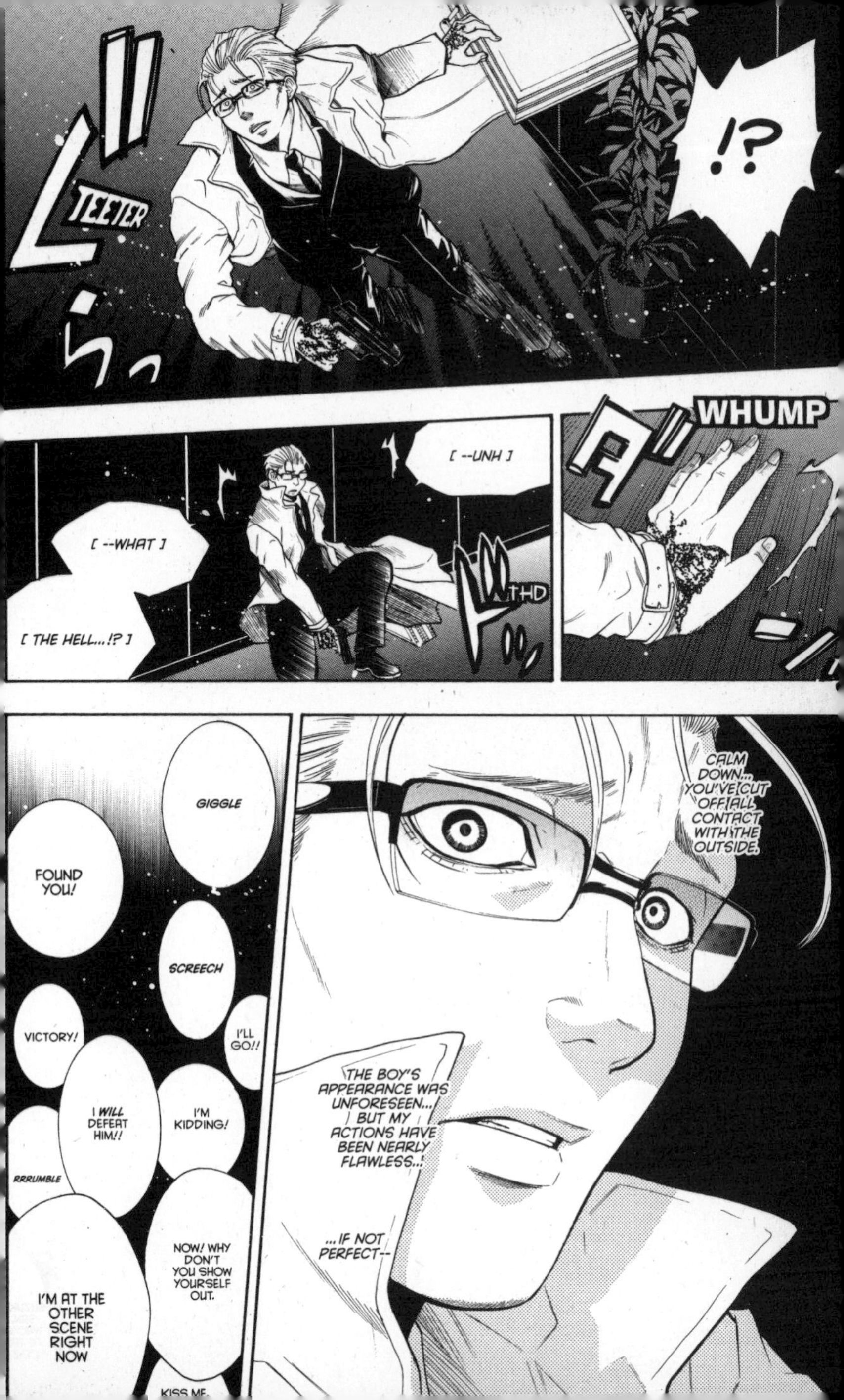

!?
TEETER
WHUMP
[--UNH]
THD
[--WHAT]
[THE HELL...!?]
CALM DOWN... YOU'VE CUT OFF ALL CONTACT WITH THE OUTSIDE.
THE BOY'S APPEARANCE WAS UNFORESEEN... BUT MY ACTIONS HAVE BEEN NEARLY FLAWLESS...!
...IF NOT PERFECT--
GIGGLE
FOUND YOU!
SCREECH
I'LL GO!!
VICTORY!
I'M KIDDING!
I *WILL* DEFEAT HIM!!
RRRUMBLE
NOW! WHY DON'T YOU SHOW YOURSELF OUT.
I'M AT THE OTHER SCENE RIGHT NOW
KISS ME.

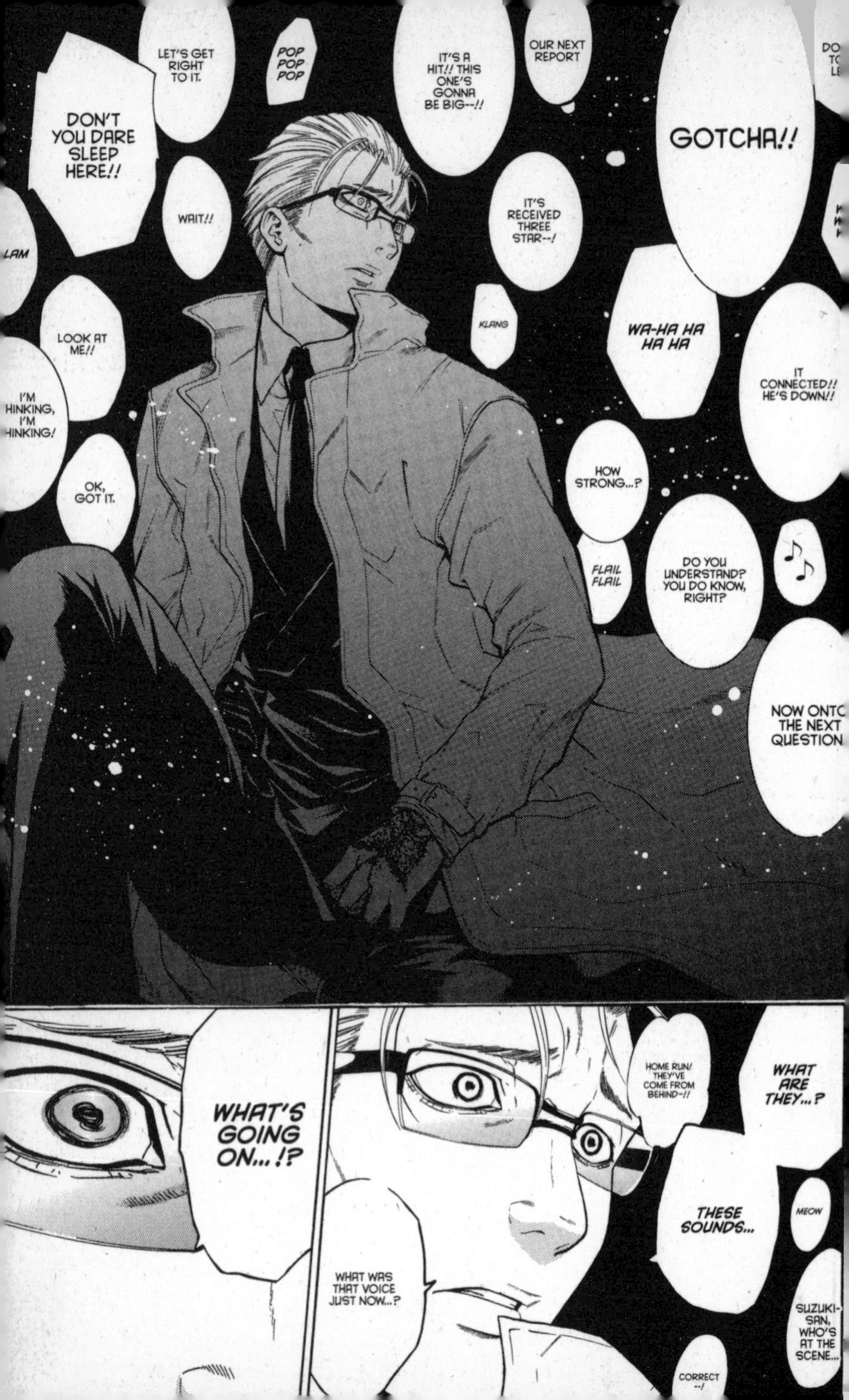
GOTCHA!!
OUR NEXT REPORT
IT'S A HIT!! THIS ONE'S GONNA BE BIG--!!
POP POP POP
LET'S GET RIGHT TO IT.
DON'T YOU DARE SLEEP HERE!!
IT CONNECTED!! HE'S DOWN!!
WA-HA HA HA HA
IT'S RECEIVED THREE STAR--!
KLANG
WAIT!!
LOOK AT ME!!
NOW ONTO THE NEXT QUESTION
♪♪
DO YOU UNDERSTAND? YOU DO KNOW, RIGHT?
HOW STRONG...?
FLAIL FLAIL
OK, GOT IT.
WHAT ARE THEY...?
HOME RUN! THEY'VE COME FROM BEHIND--!!
MEOW
THESE SOUNDS...
SUZUKI-SAN, WHO'S AT THE SCENE...
CORRECT--!
WHAT WAS THAT VOICE JUST NOW...?
WHAT'S GOING ON...!?

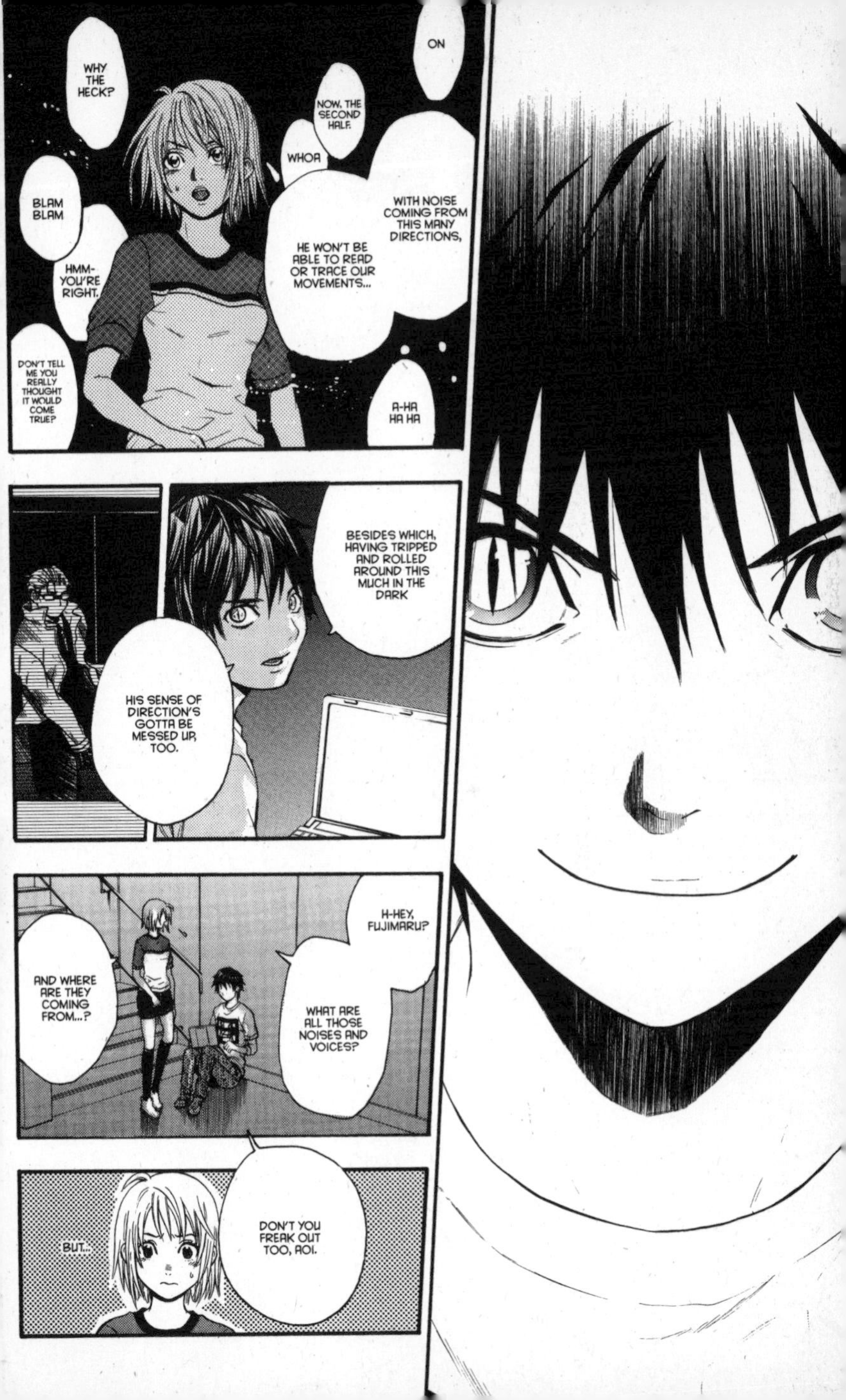
ON
NOW, THE SECOND HALF.
WHOA
WITH NOISE COMING FROM THIS MANY DIRECTIONS,
HE WON'T BE ABLE TO READ OR TRACE OUR MOVEMENTS...
WHY THE HECK?
BLAM BLAM
HMM- YOU'RE RIGHT.
A-HA HA HA
DON'T TELL ME YOU REALLY THOUGHT IT WOULD COME TRUE?
BESIDES WHICH, HAVING TRIPPED AND ROLLED AROUND THIS MUCH IN THE DARK
HIS SENSE OF DIRECTION'S GOTTA BE MESSED UP, TOO.
H-HEY, FUJIMARU?
WHAT ARE ALL THOSE NOISES AND VOICES?
AND WHERE ARE THEY COMING FROM...?
DON'T YOU FREAK OUT TOO, AOI.
BUT...

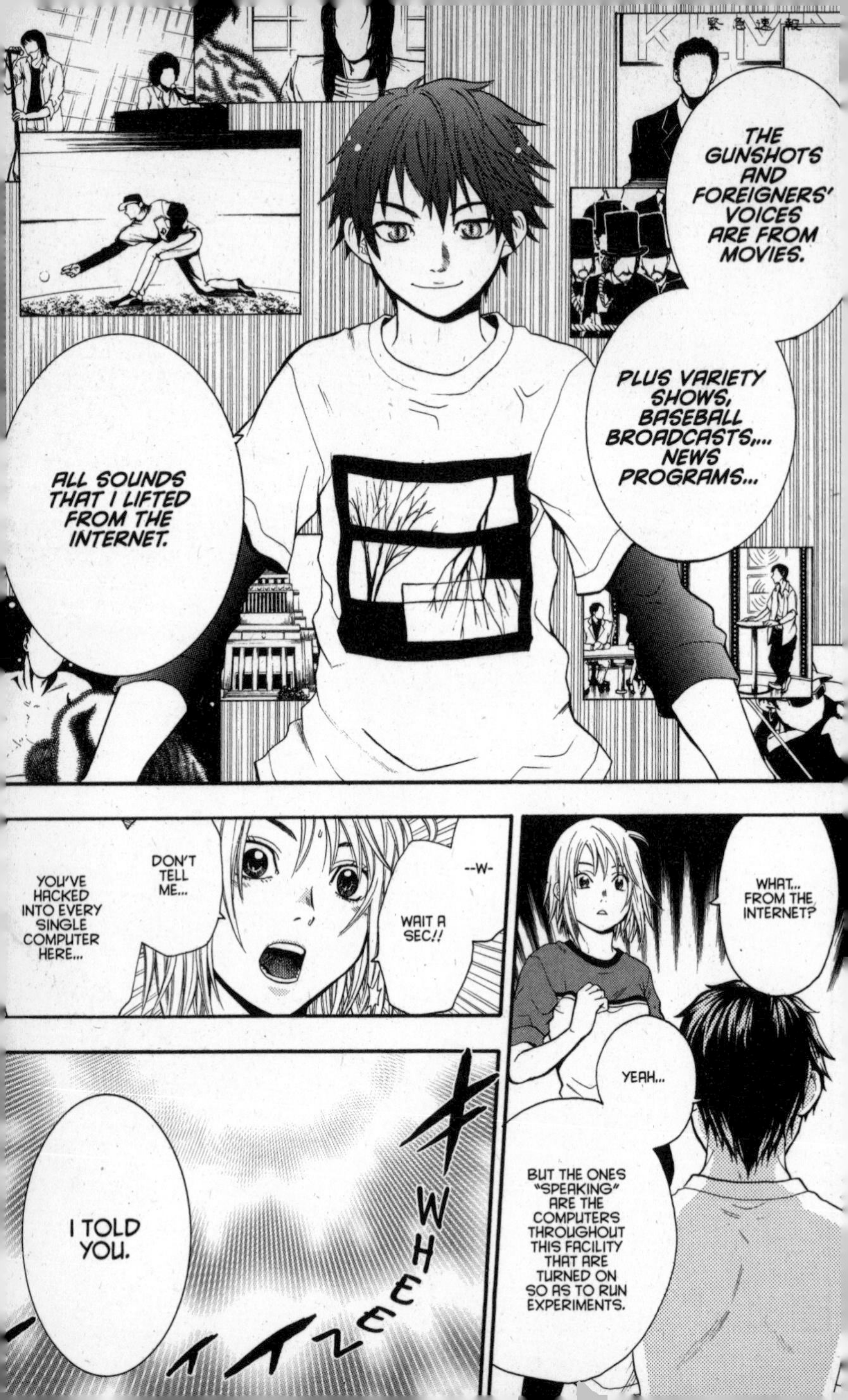
THE GUNSHOTS AND FOREIGNERS' VOICES ARE FROM MOVIES.
PLUS VARIETY SHOWS, BASEBALL BROADCASTS,... NEWS PROGRAMS...
ALL SOUNDS THAT I LIFTED FROM THE INTERNET.
WHAT... FROM THE INTERNET?
YEAH...
BUT THE ONES "SPEAKING" ARE THE COMPUTERS THROUGHOUT THIS FACILITY THAT ARE TURNED ON SO AS TO RUN EXPERIMENTS.
--W-
WAIT A SEC!!
DON'T TELL ME...
YOU'VE HACKED INTO EVERY SINGLE COMPUTER HERE...
WHEEZE
I TOLD YOU.

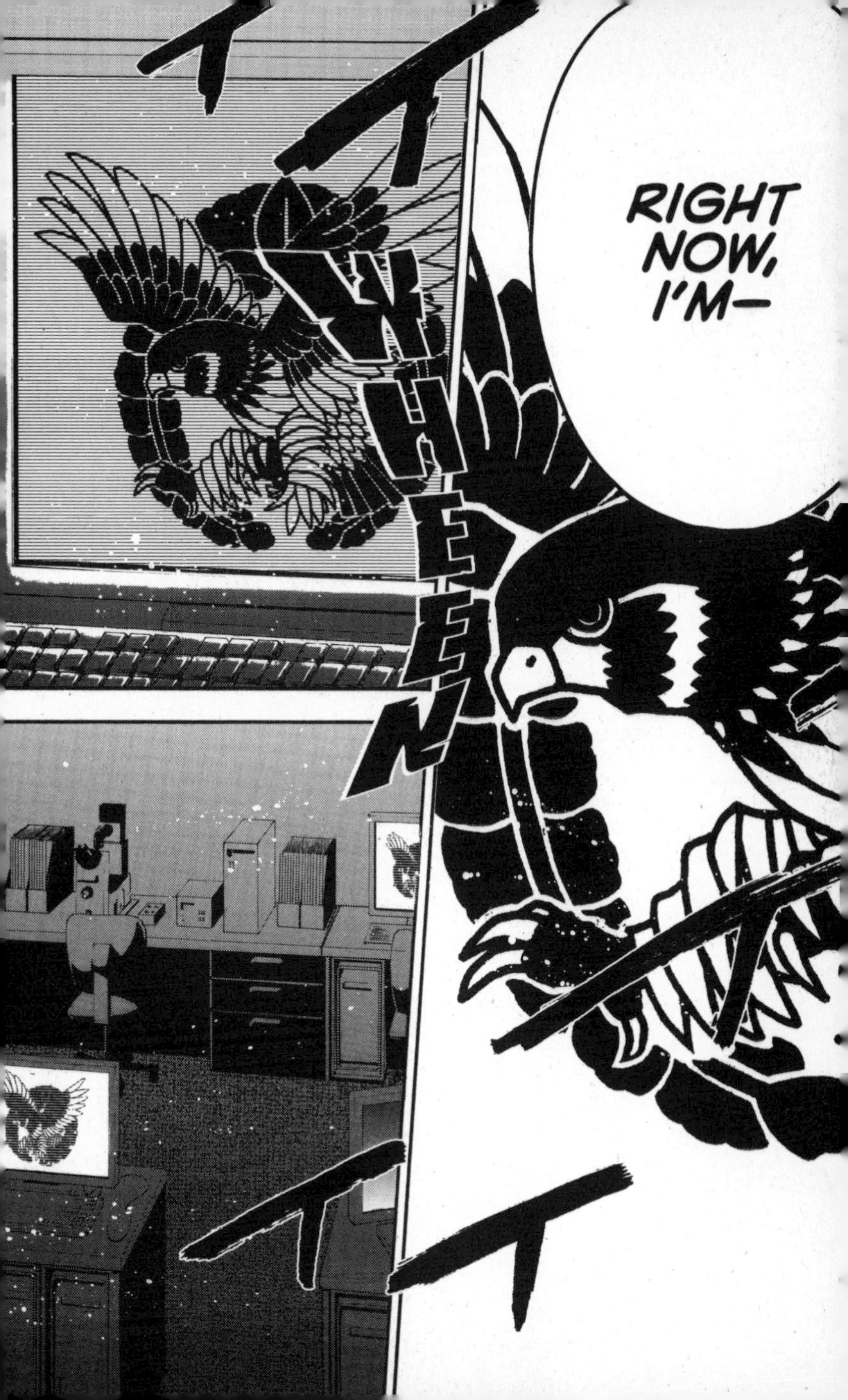
RIGHT NOW, I'M—
WHEEN

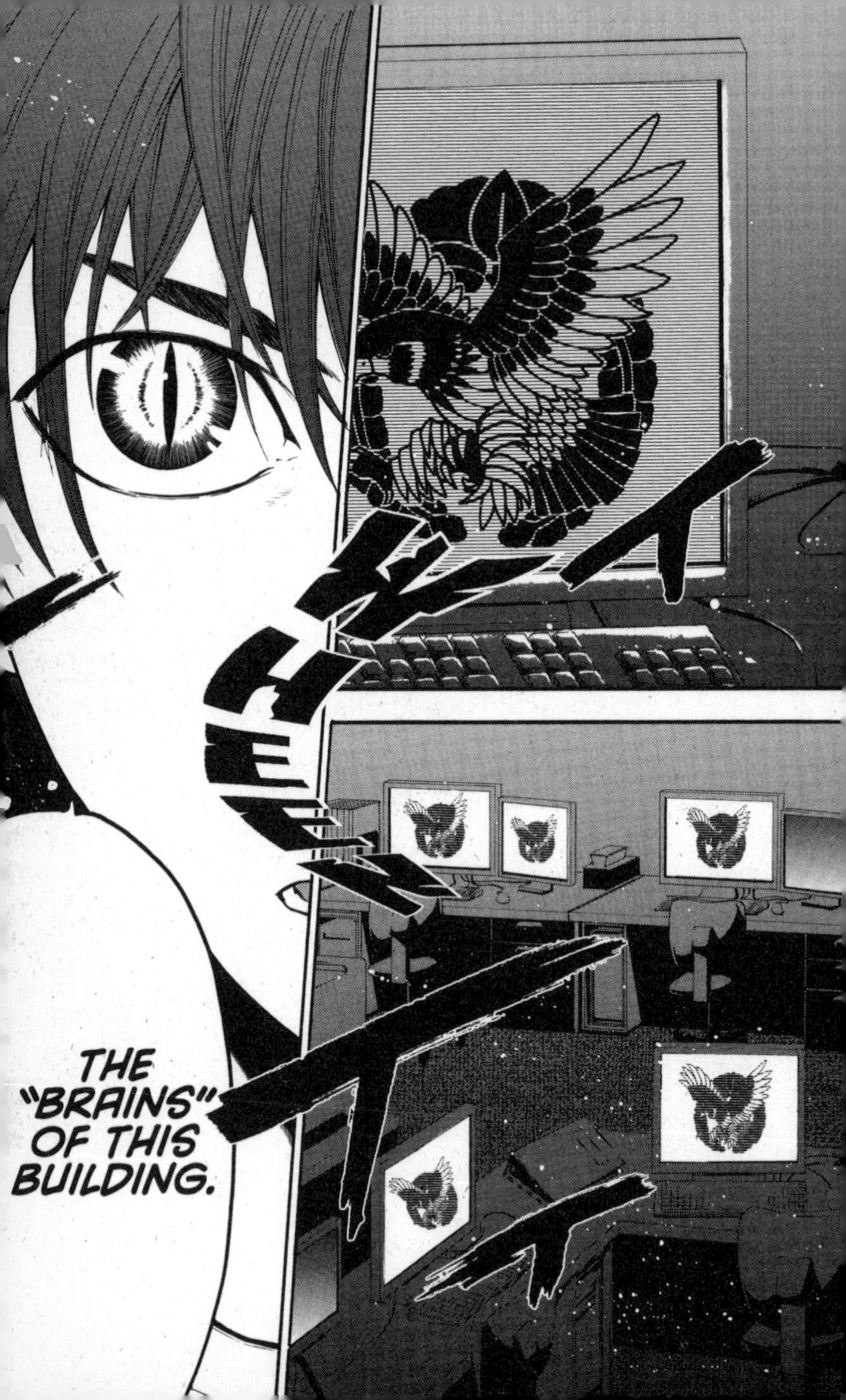
THE "BRAINS" OF THIS BUILDING.

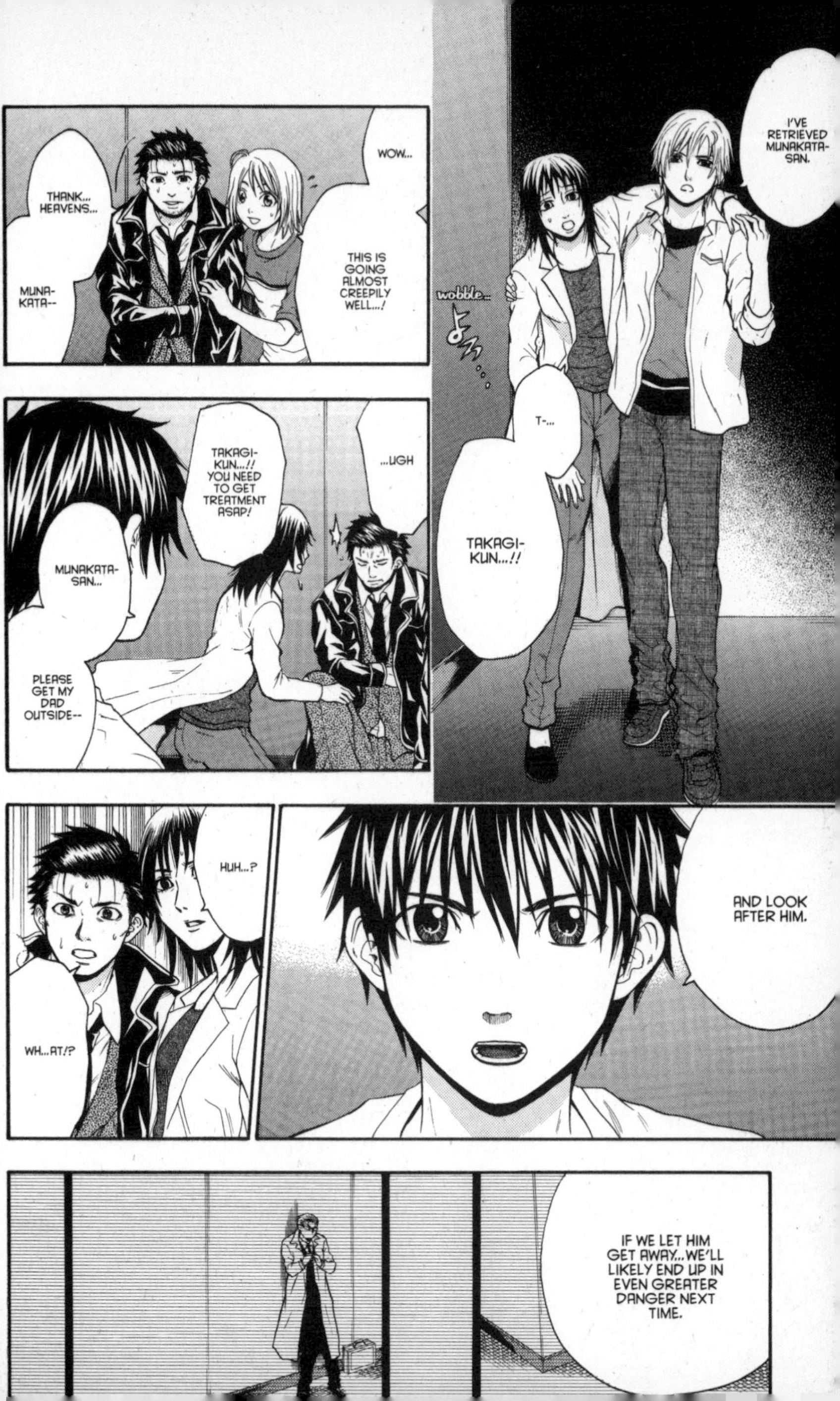
I'VE RETRIEVED MUNAKATA-SAN.
wobble...
よろ...
T-...
TAKAGI-KUN...!!
WOW...
THIS IS GOING ALMOST CREEPILY WELL...!
THANK... HEAVENS...
MUNAKATA--
...UGH
TAKAGI-KUN...!! YOU NEED TO GET TREATMENT ASAP!
MUNAKATA-SAN...
PLEASE GET MY DAD OUTSIDE--
AND LOOK AFTER HIM.
HUH...?
WH...AT!?
IF WE LET HIM GET AWAY...WE'LL LIKELY END UP IN EVEN GREATER DANGER NEXT TIME.

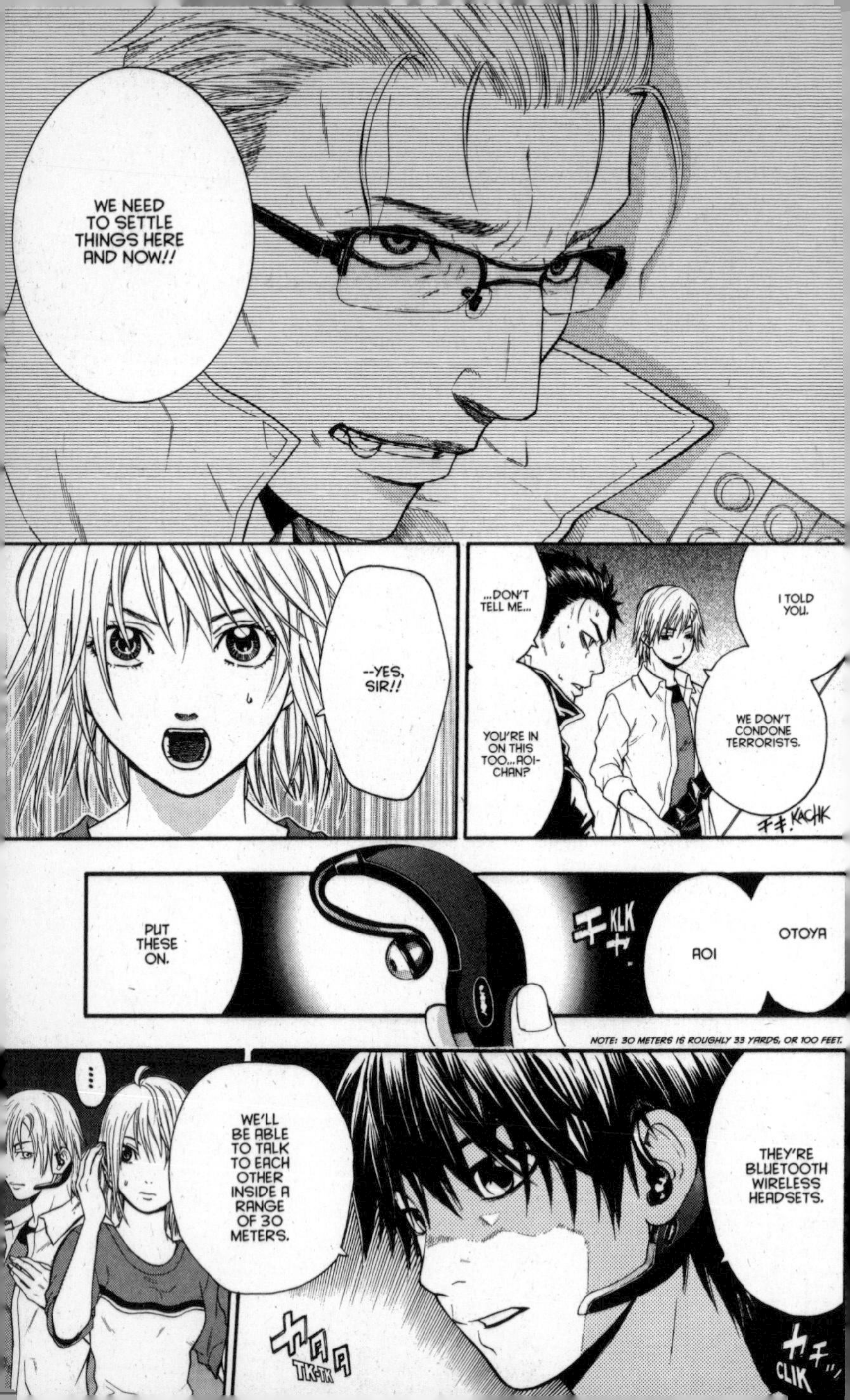

WE NEED TO SETTLE THINGS HERE AND NOW!!
I TOLD YOU.
WE DON'T CONDONE TERRORISTS.
...DON'T TELL ME...
YOU'RE IN ON THIS TOO...AOI-CHAN?
KACHK
--YES, SIR!!
OTOYA
AOI
KLK
PUT THESE ON.
NOTE: 30 METERS IS ROUGHLY 33 YARDS, OR 100 FEET.
THEY'RE BLUETOOTH WIRELESS HEADSETS.
CLIK
WE'LL BE ABLE TO TALK TO EACH OTHER INSIDE A RANGE OF 30 METERS.
TK-TK
....

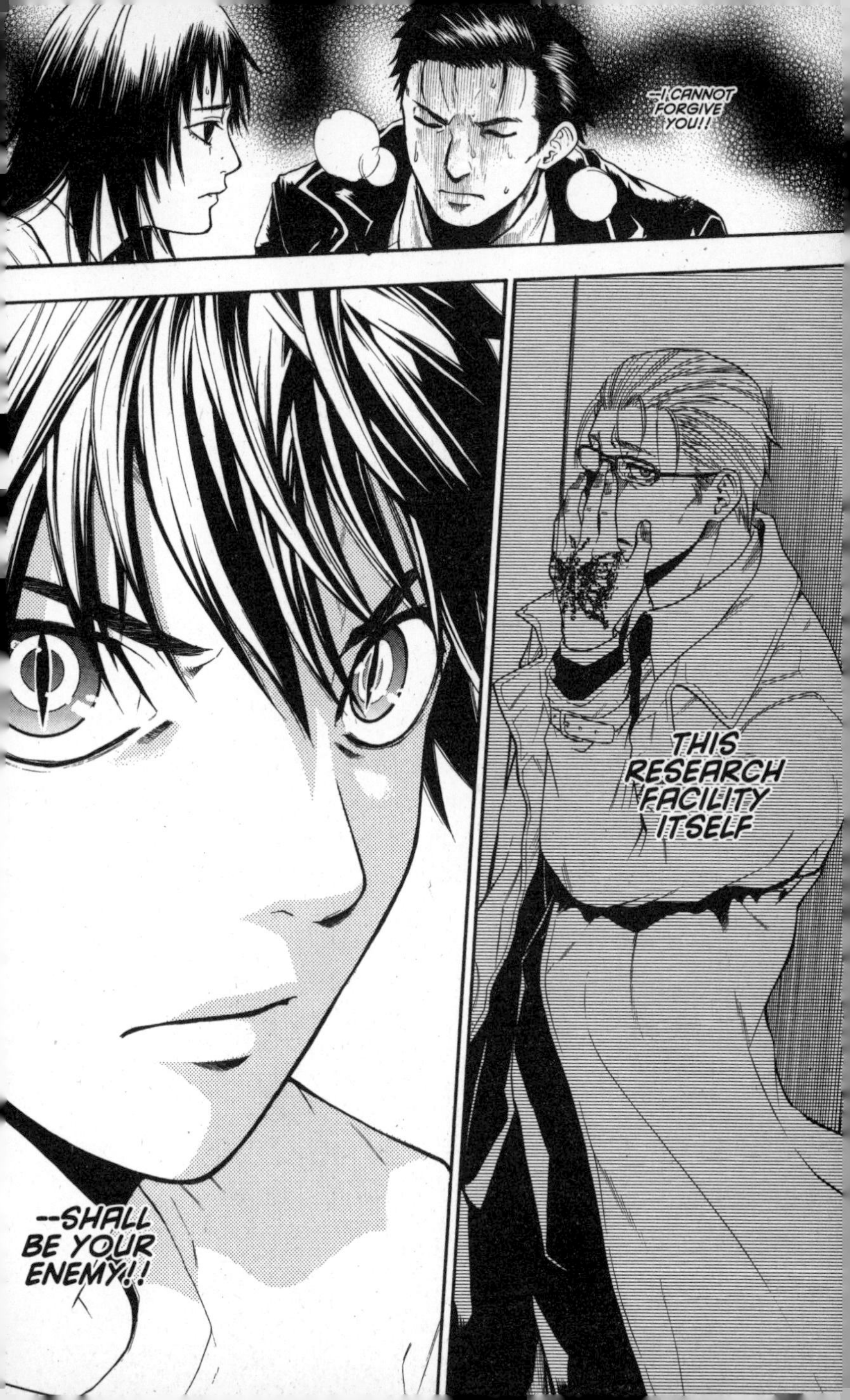
--I CANNOT FORGIVE YOU!!
THIS RESEARCH FACILITY ITSELF
--SHALL BE YOUR ENEMY!!

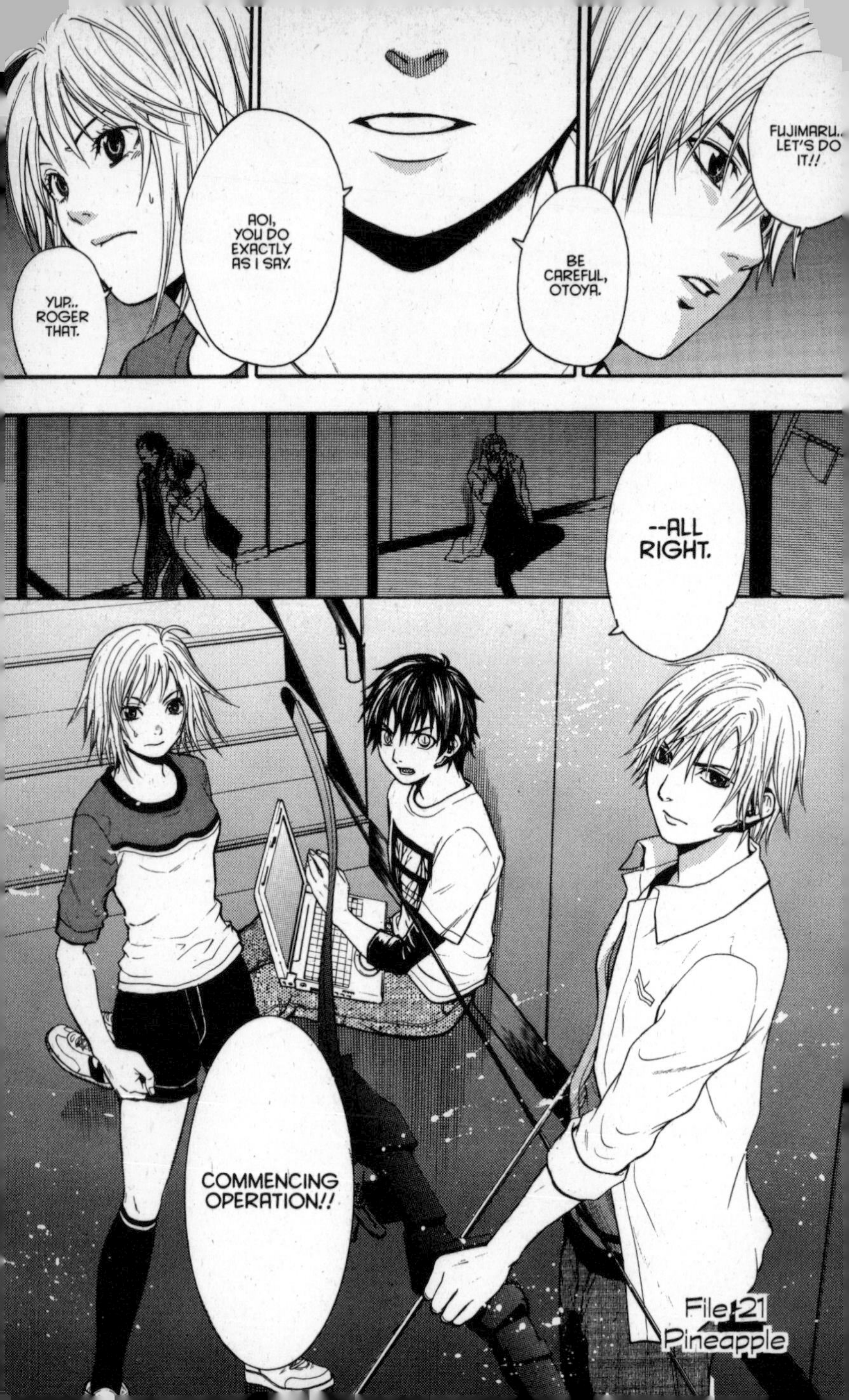
FUJIMARU.. LET'S DO IT!!
BE CAREFUL, OTOYA.
AOI, YOU DO EXACTLY AS I SAY.
YUP.. ROGER THAT.
--ALL RIGHT.
COMMENCING OPERATION!!
File 21
Pineapple

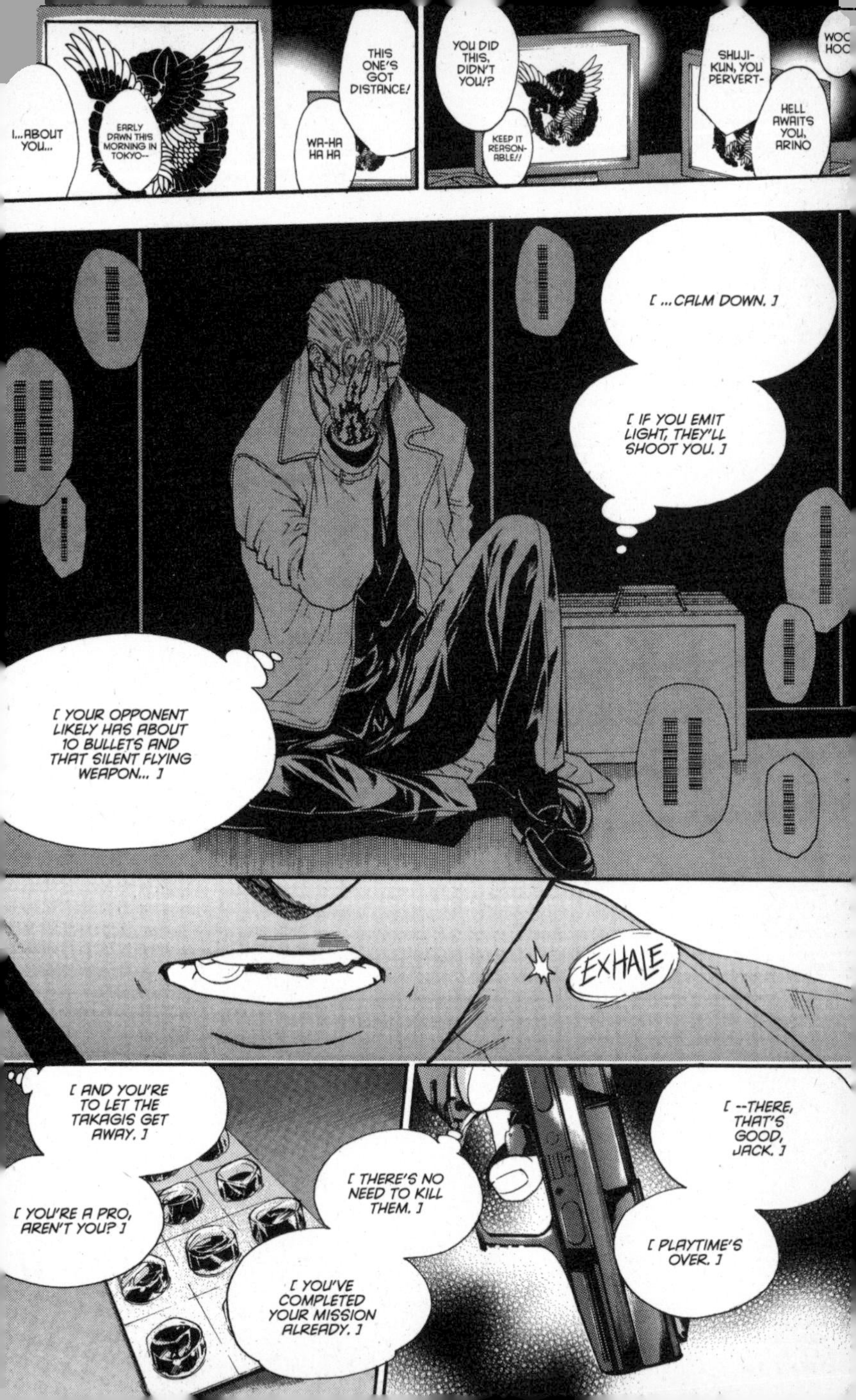
SHUJI-KUN, YOU PERVERT-
HELL AWAITS YOU, ARINO
YOU DID THIS, DIDN'T YOU!?
KEEP IT REASONABLE!!
THIS ONE'S GOT DISTANCE!
WA-HA HA HA
EARLY DAWN THIS MORNING IN TOKYO--
I...ABOUT YOU...
[...CALM DOWN.]
[IF YOU EMIT LIGHT, THEY'LL SHOOT YOU.]
[YOUR OPPONENT LIKELY HAS ABOUT 10 BULLETS AND THAT SILENT FLYING WEAPON...]
EXHALE
[--THERE, THAT'S GOOD, JACK.]
[PLAYTIME'S OVER.]
[AND YOU'RE TO LET THE TAKAGIS GET AWAY.]
[THERE'S NO NEED TO KILL THEM.]
[YOU'RE A PRO, AREN'T YOU?]
[YOU'VE COMPLETED YOUR MISSION ALREADY.]

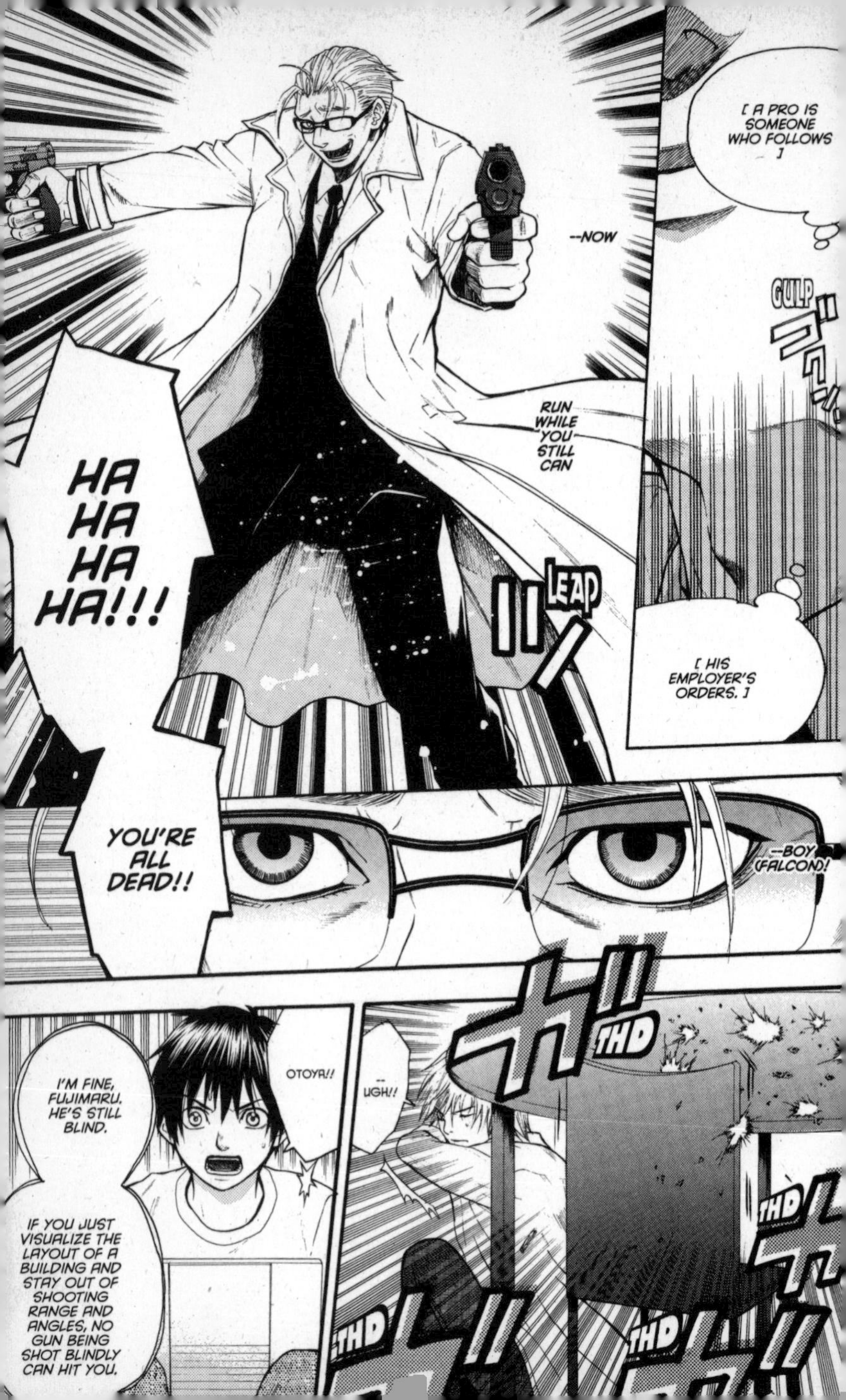
[A PRO IS SOMEONE WHO FOLLOWS]
GULP
[HIS EMPLOYER'S ORDERS.]
--NOW
RUN WHILE YOU STILL CAN
LEAP
HA HA HA HA!!!
--BOY (FALCON)!
YOU'RE ALL DEAD!!
THD
THD
THD
THD
--UGH!!
OTOYA!!
I'M FINE, FUJIMARU. HE'S STILL BLIND.
IF YOU JUST VISUALIZE THE LAYOUT OF A BUILDING AND STAY OUT OF SHOOTING RANGE AND ANGLES, NO GUN BEING SHOT BLINDLY CAN HIT YOU.

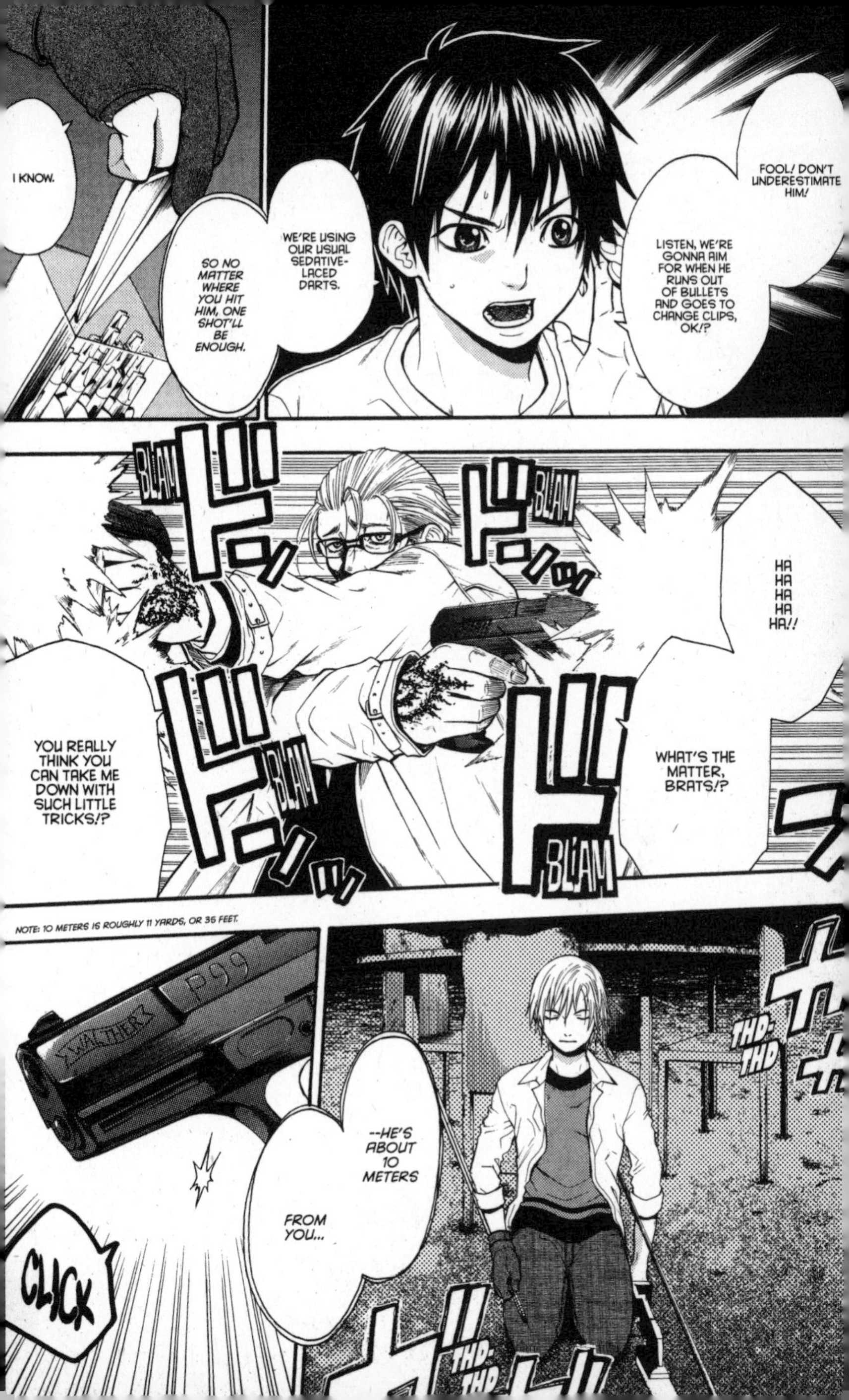
FOOL! DON'T UNDERESTIMATE HIM!
LISTEN, WE'RE GONNA AIM FOR WHEN HE RUNS OUT OF BULLETS AND GOES TO CHANGE CLIPS, OK!?
WE'RE USING OUR USUAL SEDATIVE-LACED DARTS.
SO NO MATTER WHERE YOU HIT HIM, ONE SHOT'LL BE ENOUGH.
I KNOW.
BLAM
BLAM
HA HA HA HA HA!!
WHAT'S THE MATTER, BRATS!?
BLAM
BLAM
YOU REALLY THINK YOU CAN TAKE ME DOWN WITH SUCH LITTLE TRICKS!?
NOTE: 10 METERS IS ROUGHLY 11 YARDS, OR 35 FEET.
THD-THD
--HE'S ABOUT 10 METERS
FROM YOU...
CLICK
THD-THD

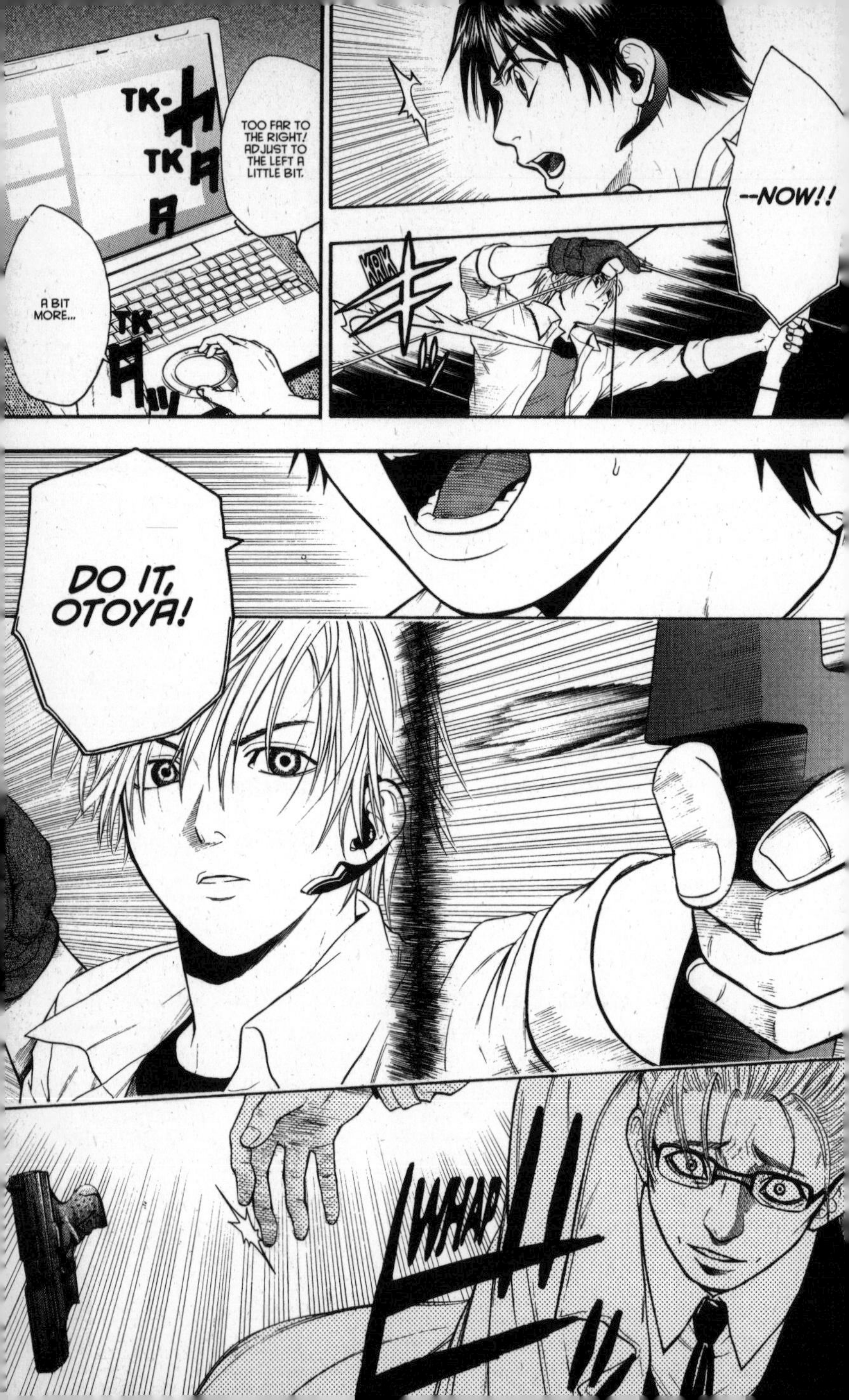
--NOW!!
KRIK
TOO FAR TO THE RIGHT! ADJUST TO THE LEFT A LITTLE BIT.
TK-
TK
TK
A BIT MORE...
DO IT, OTOYA!
WHAP

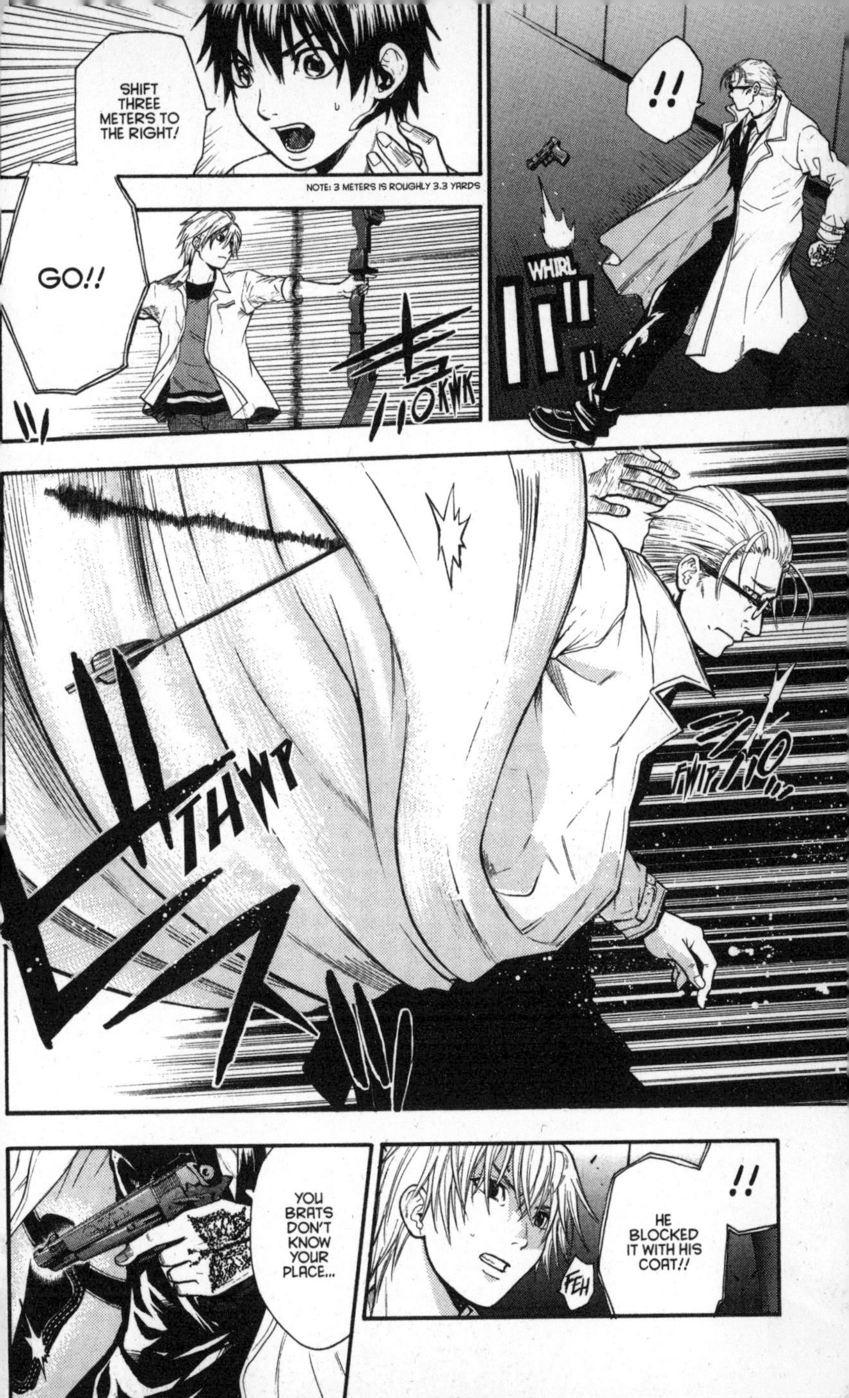
!!
WHIRL
SHIFT THREE METERS TO THE RIGHT!
NOTE: 3 METERS IS ROUGHLY 3.3 YARDS
GO!!
KWK
FWIP
THWP
!!
HE BLOCKED IT WITH HIS COAT!!
FEH
YOU BRATS DON'T KNOW YOUR PLACE...

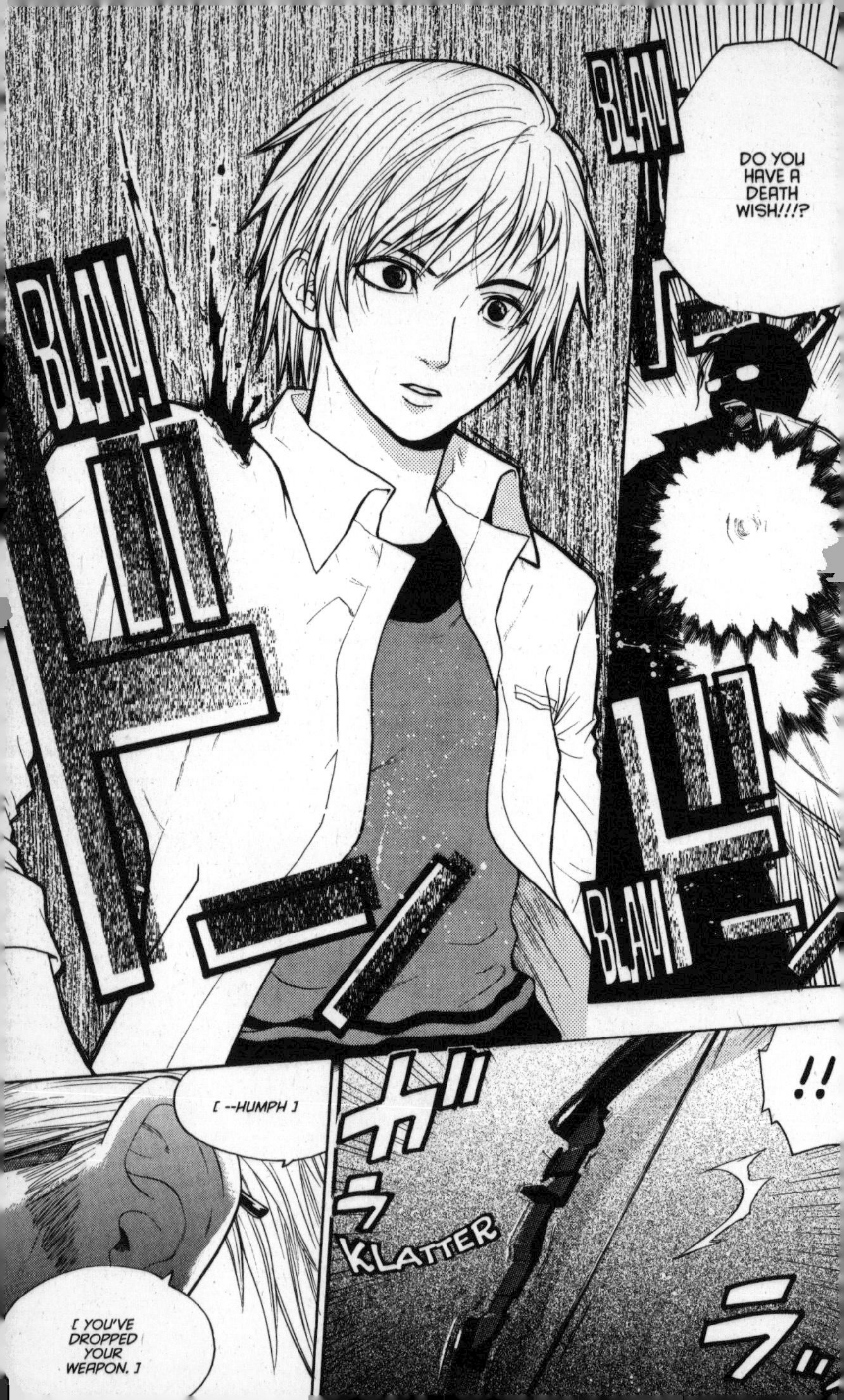
BLAM
DO YOU HAVE A DEATH WISH!!!?
BLAM
BLAM
!!
KLATTER
[--HUMPH]
[YOU'VE DROPPED YOUR WEAPON.]

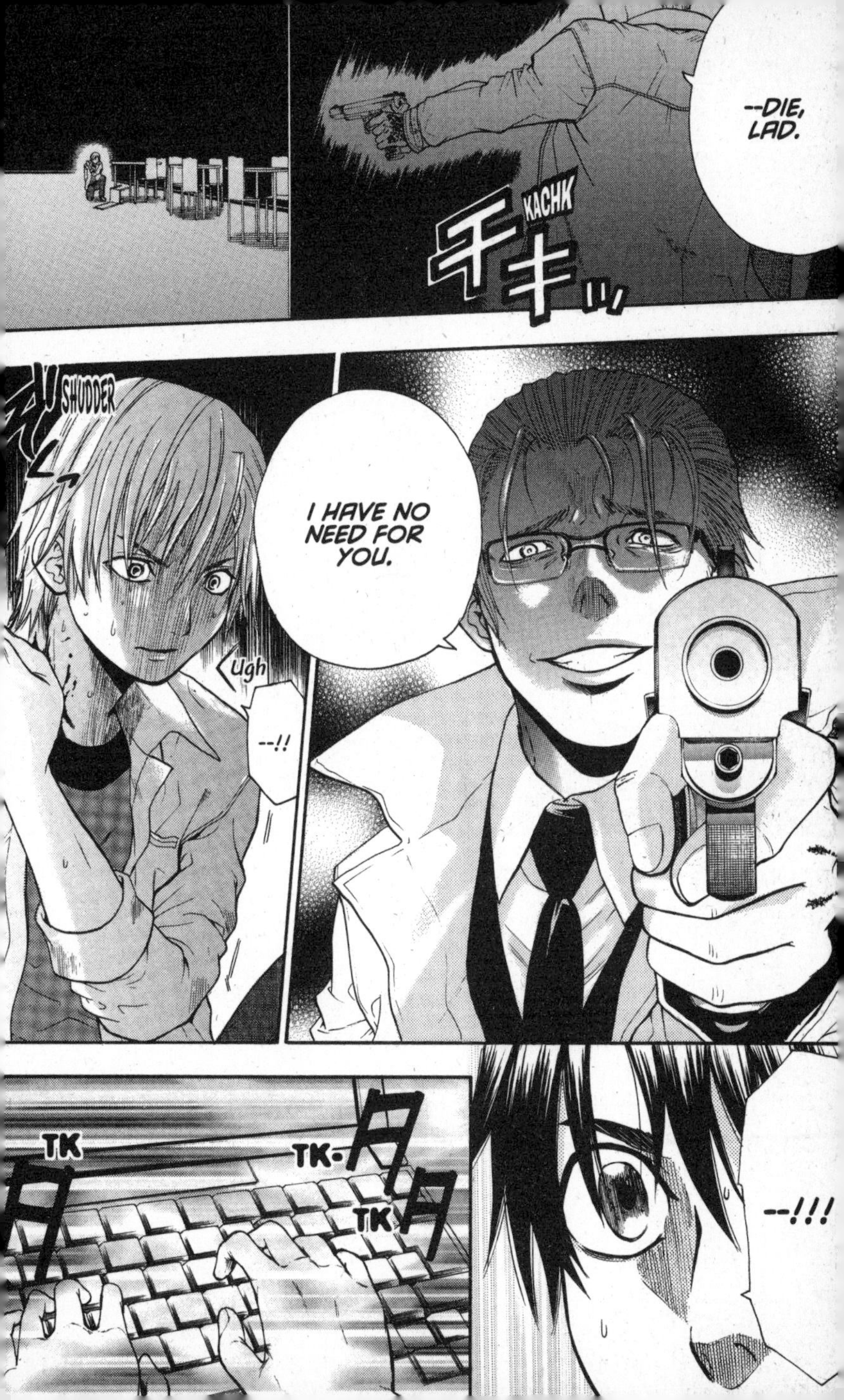
--DIE, LAD.
KACHK
I HAVE NO NEED FOR YOU.
SHUDDER
Ugh
--!!
--!!!
TK-
TK
TK

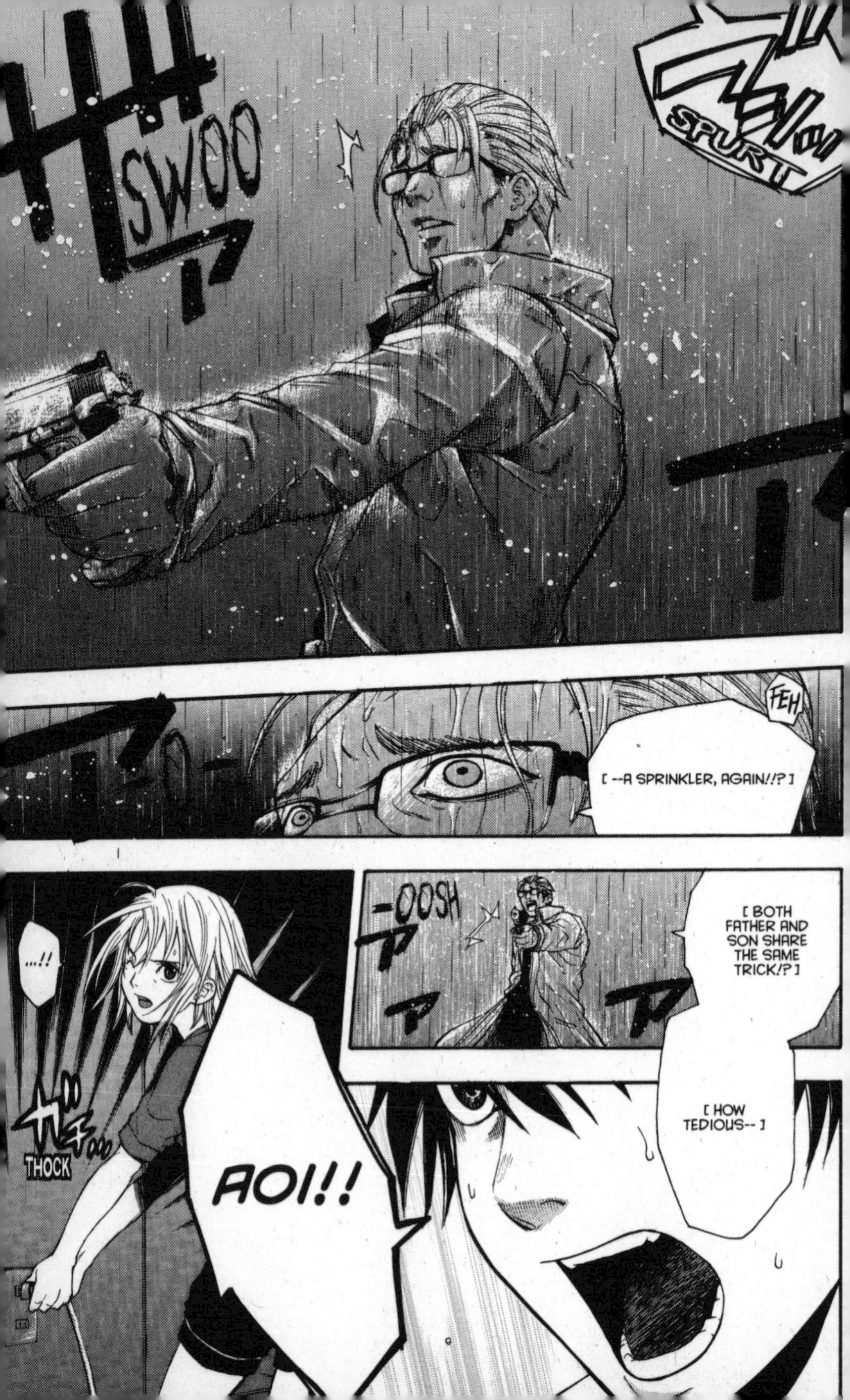
SPURT
SWOO
FEH
[--A SPRINKLER, AGAIN!!?]
[BOTH FATHER AND SON SHARE THE SAME TRICK!?]
-OOSH
[HOW TEDIOUS--]
AOI!!
...!!
THOCK

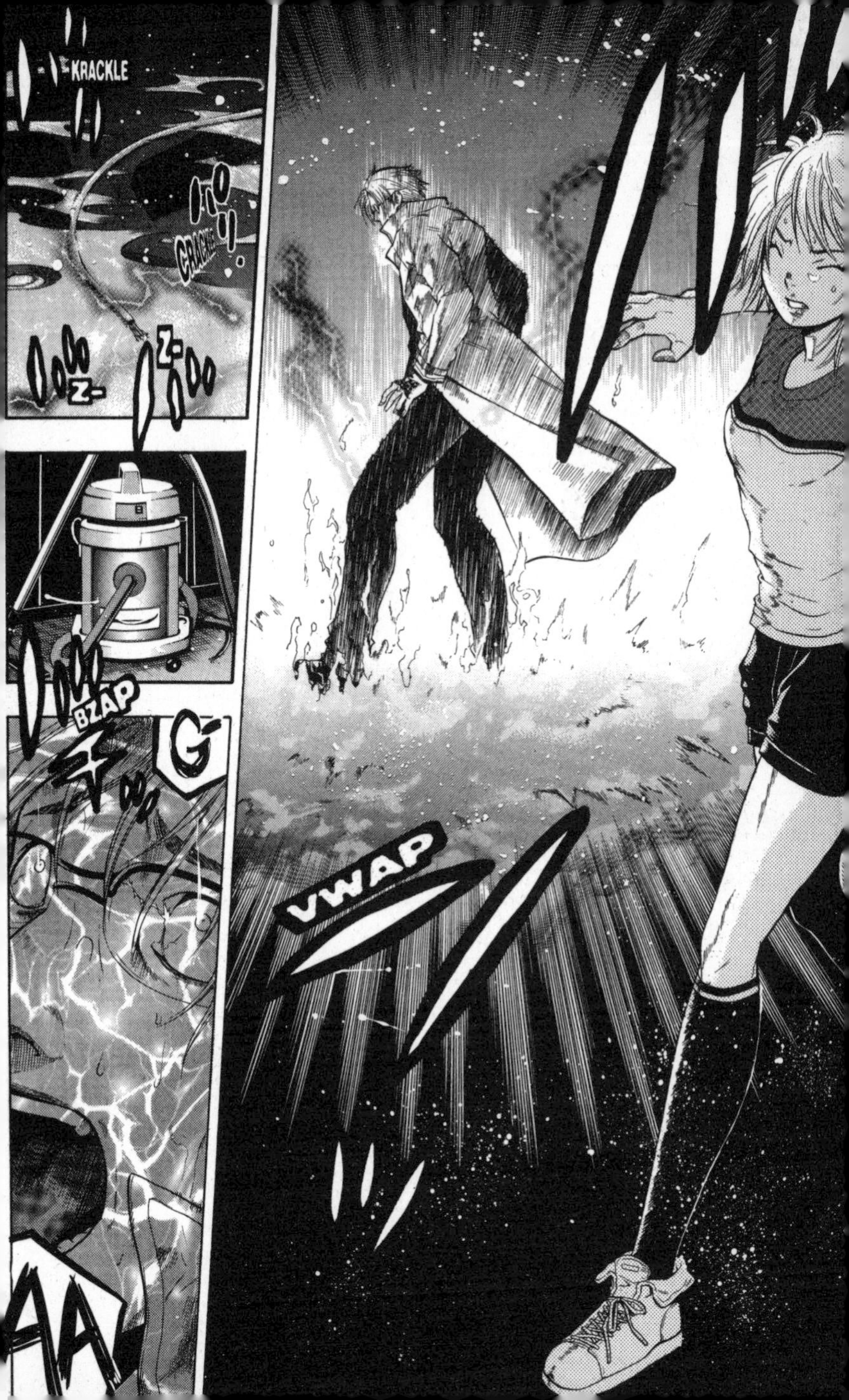
VWAP
KRACKLE
CRACKLE
Z-
Z-
BZAP
G-

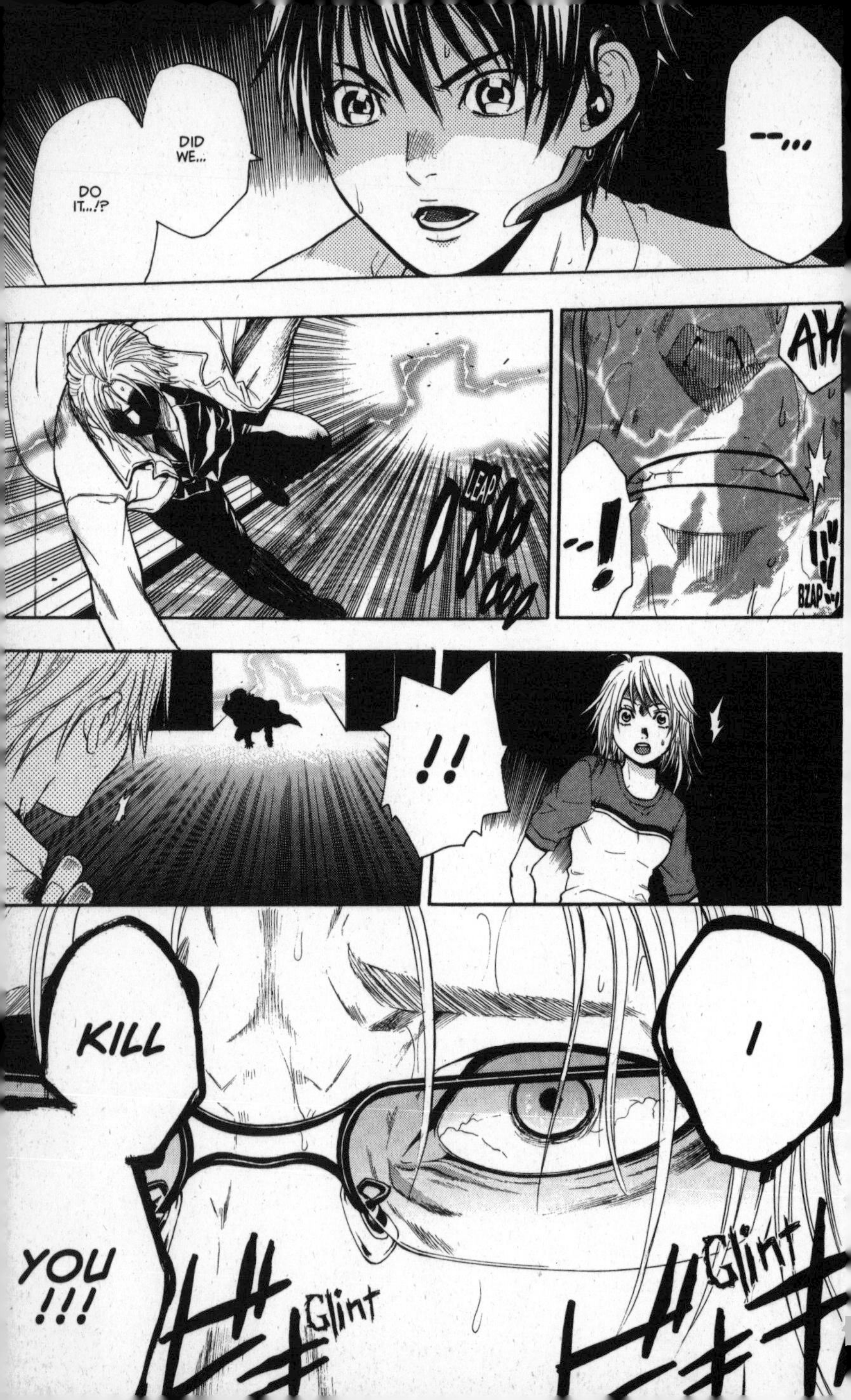
--...
DID WE... DO IT...!?
AH
--!
BZAP
LEAP
!!
I
KILL
YOU!!!
Glint
Glint

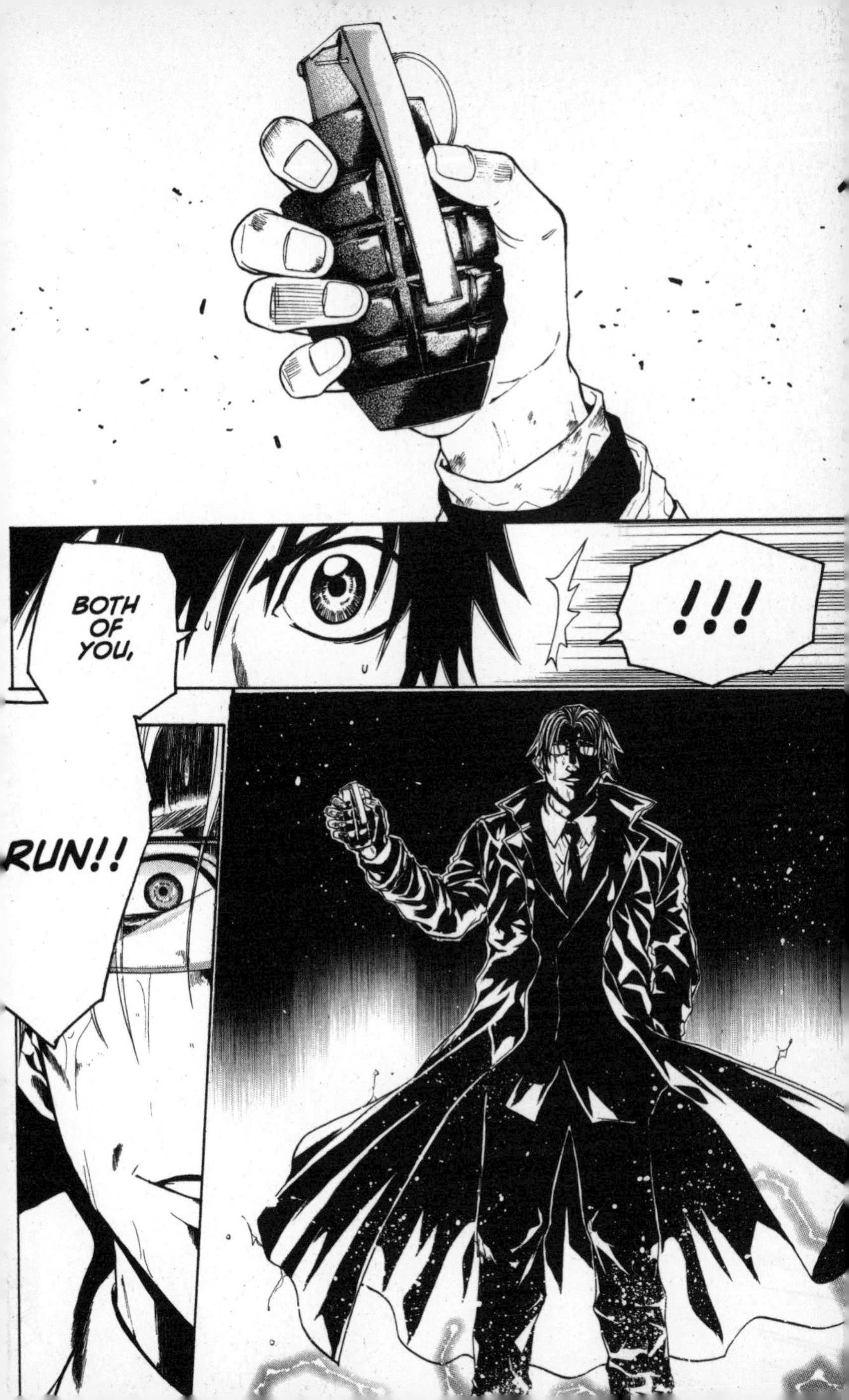
!!!
BOTH OF YOU,
RUN!!

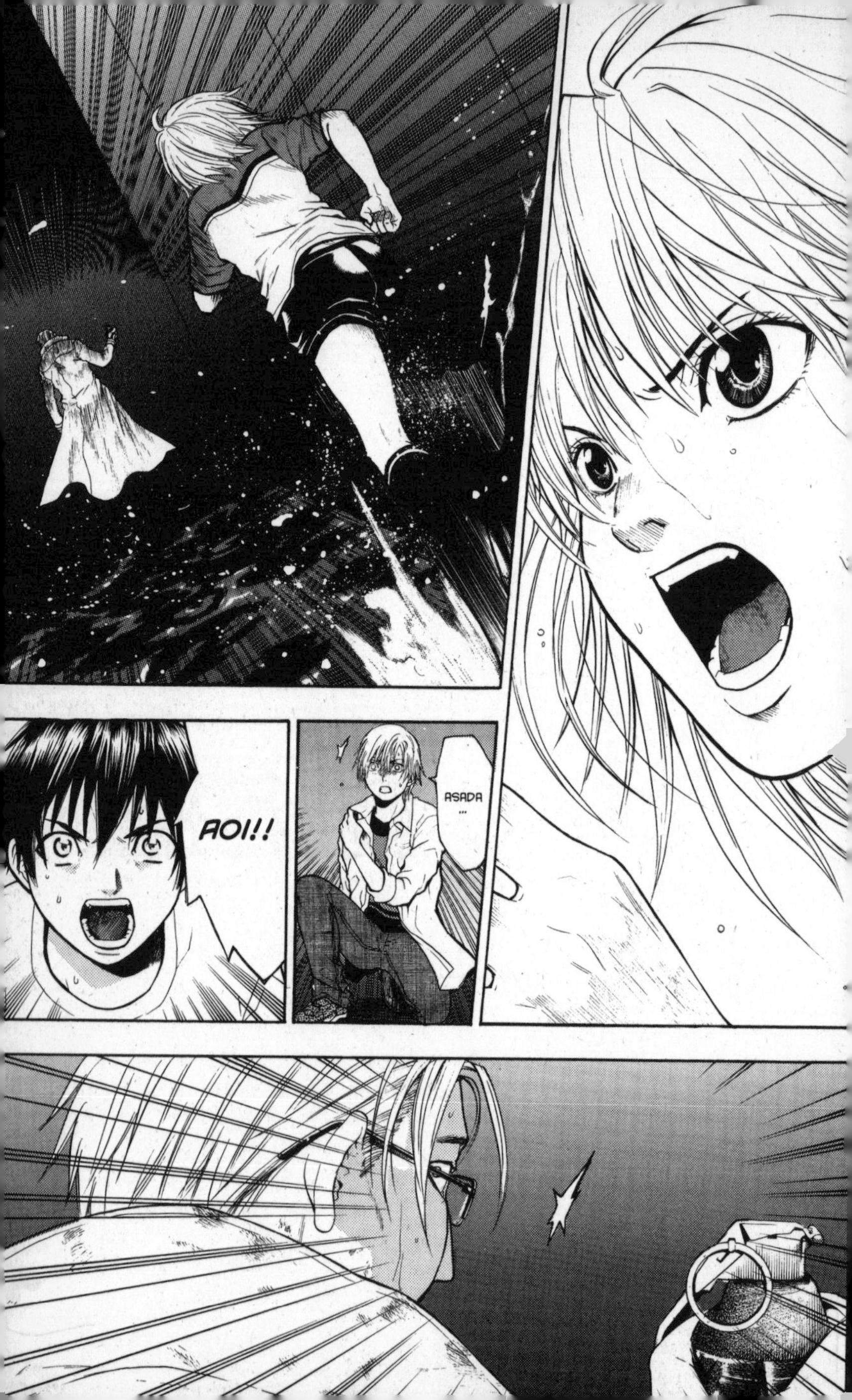
ASADA ...
AOI!!

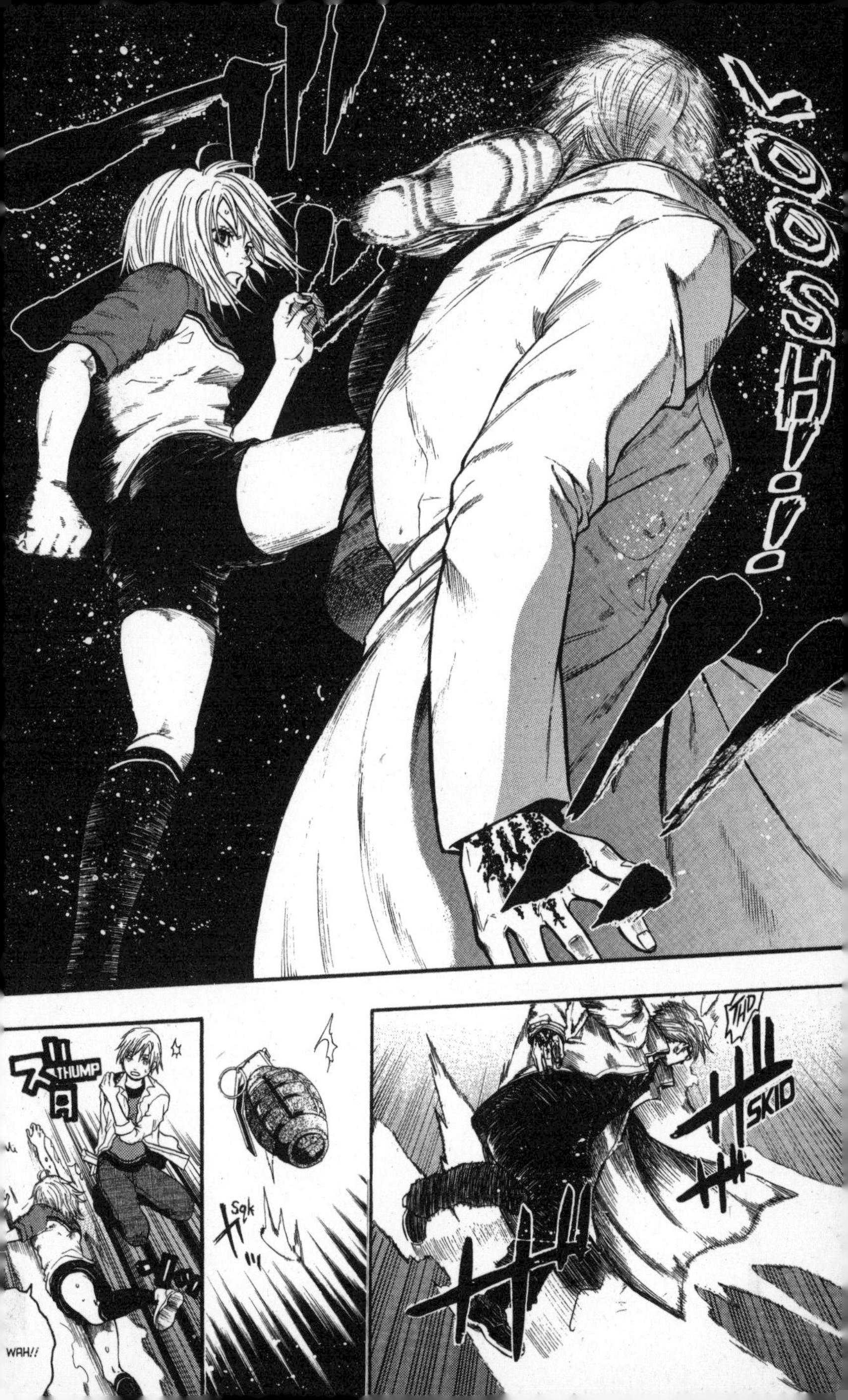
WHOOSH!!!
THD
SKID
Sqk
THUMP
WAH!!

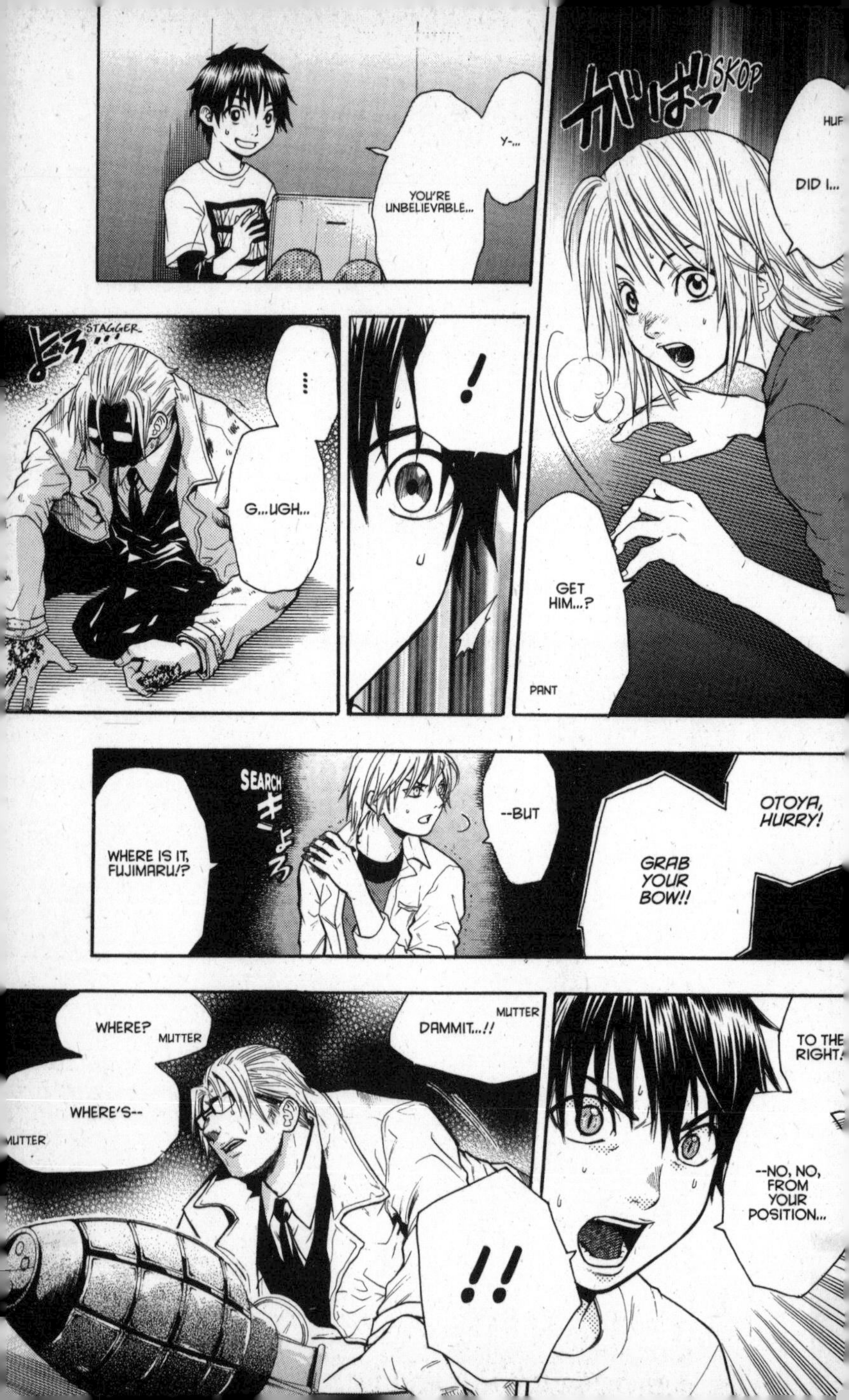
SKOP
HUF
DID I...
GET HIM...?
PANT
Y-...
YOU'RE UNBELIEVABLE...
!
STAGGER
...
G...UGH...
OTOYA, HURRY!
GRAB YOUR BOW!!
--BUT
SEARCH
WHERE IS IT, FUJIMARU!?
TO THE RIGHT.
--NO, NO, FROM YOUR POSITION...
!!
MUTTER
DAMMIT...!!
WHERE? MUTTER
WHERE'S--
MUTTER

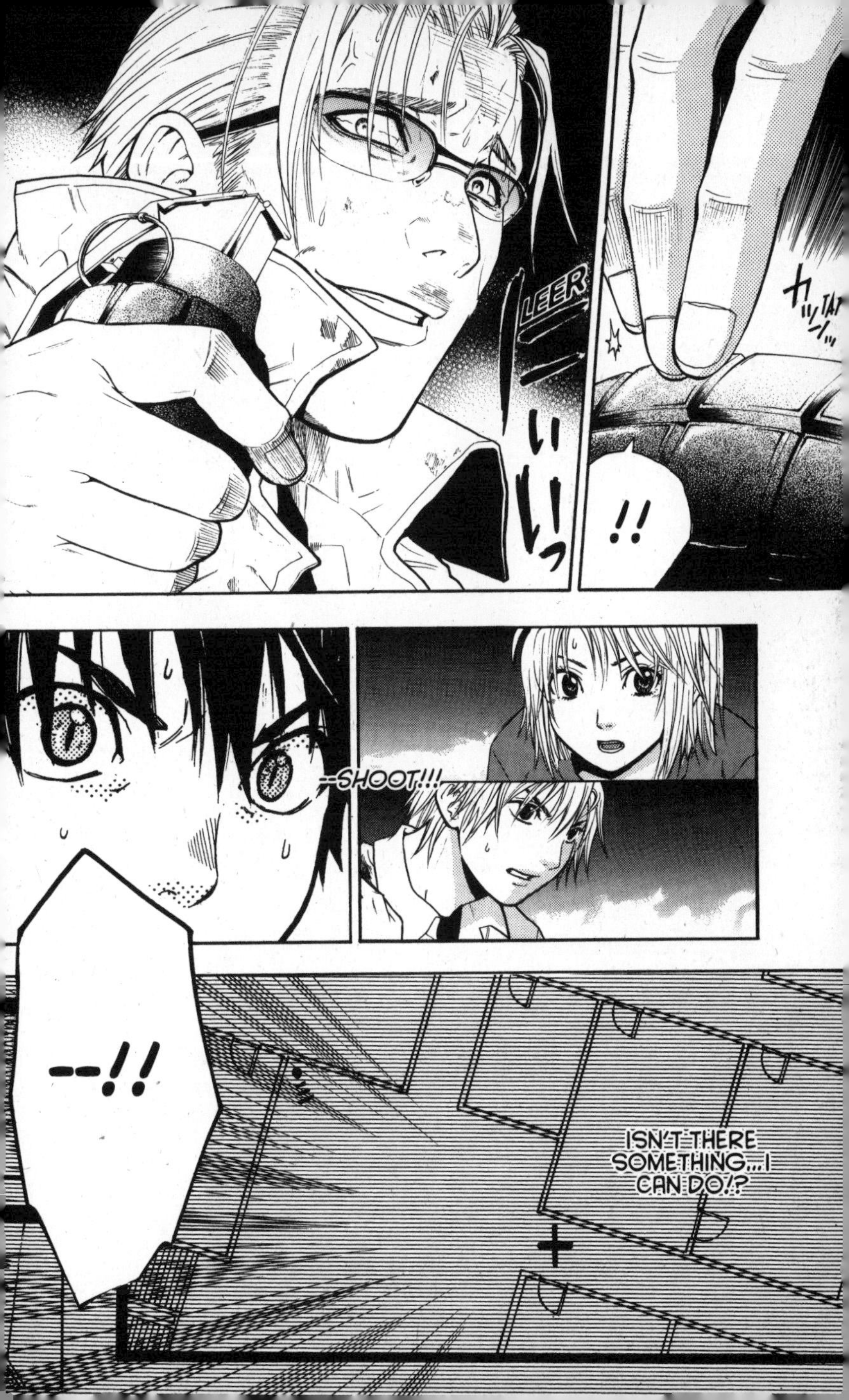
カッ TAT
!!
LEER
--SHOOT!!!
--!!
ISN'T THERE SOMETHING...I CAN DO!?

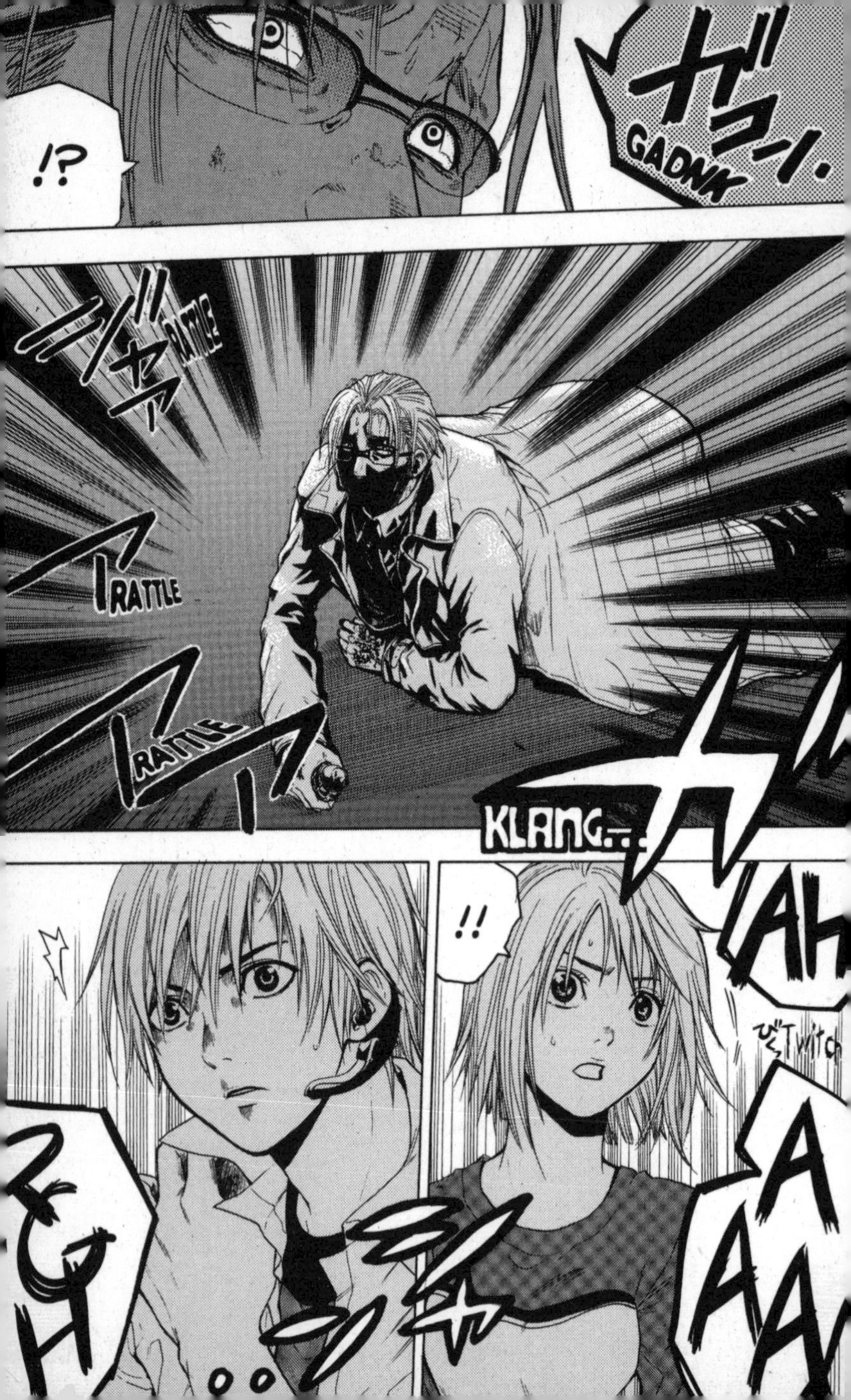
GADNK
!?
RATTLE
RATTLE
RATTLE
KLANG...
AH AAAA
Twitch
!!
...

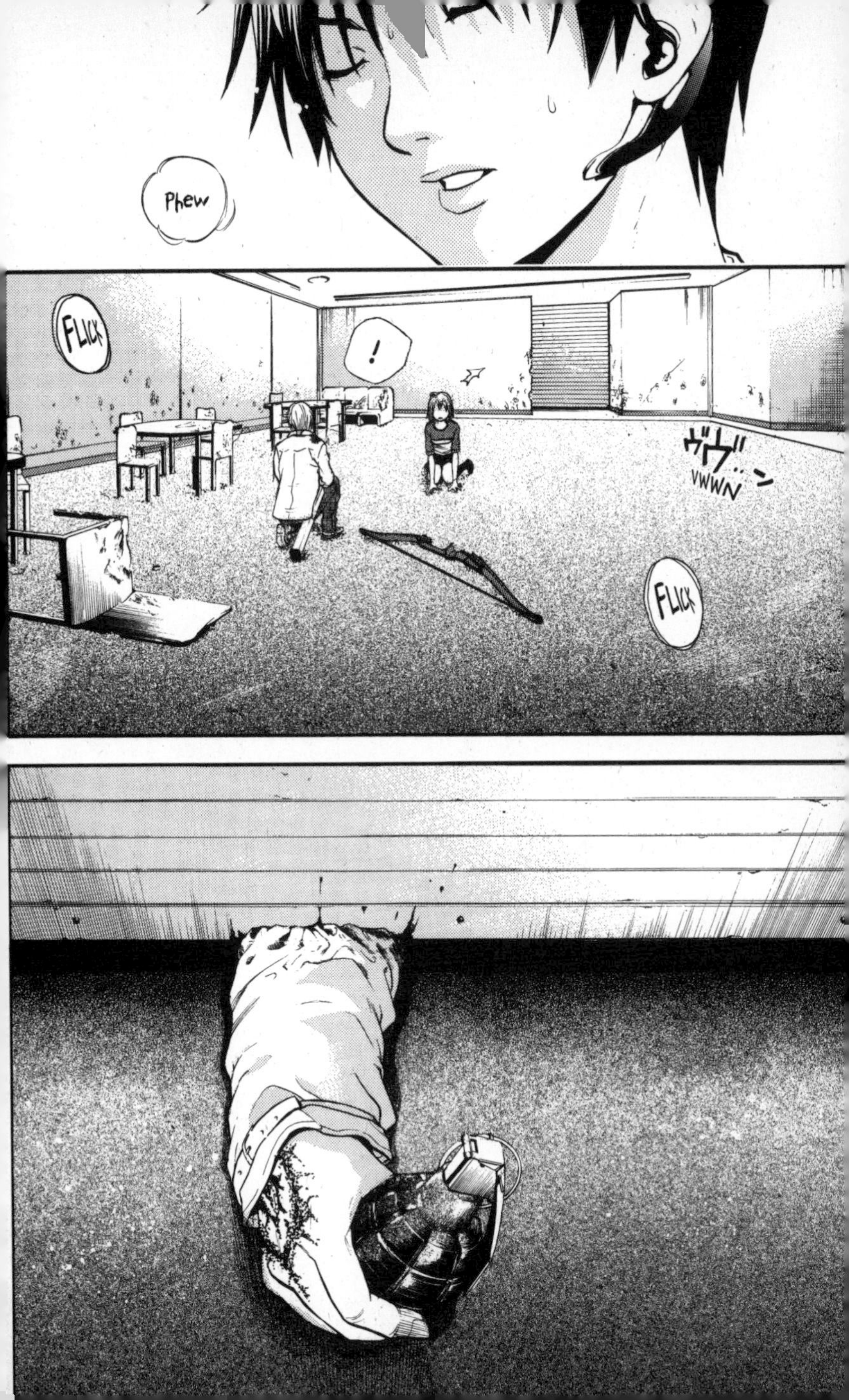

Phew
ヴヴ‥ン
VWWN
!
FLICK
FLICK

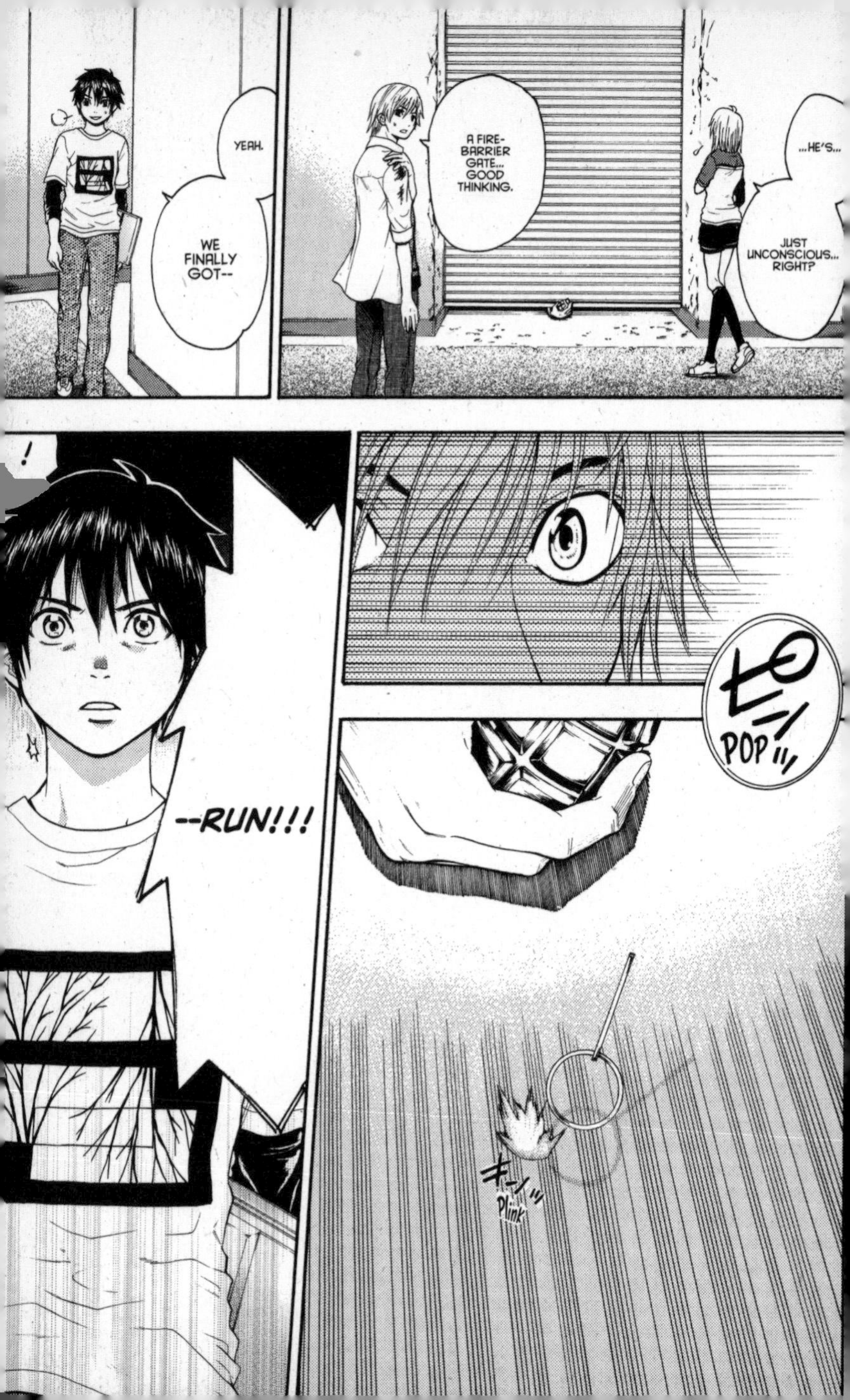
...HE'S...
JUST UNCONSCIOUS... RIGHT?
A FIRE-BARRIER GATE... GOOD THINKING.
YEAH.
WE FINALLY GOT--
POP
Plink
!
--RUN!!!

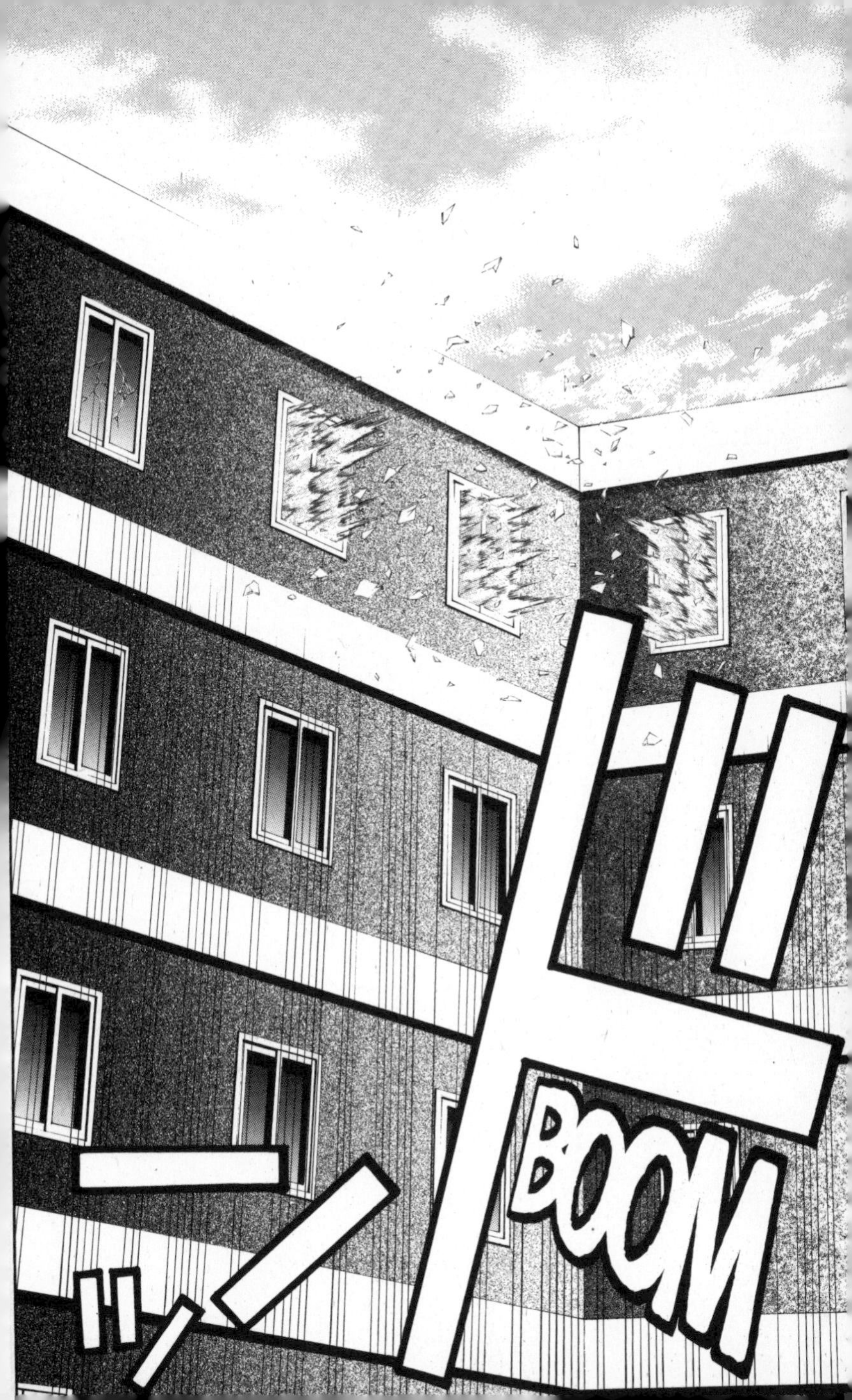
BOOM

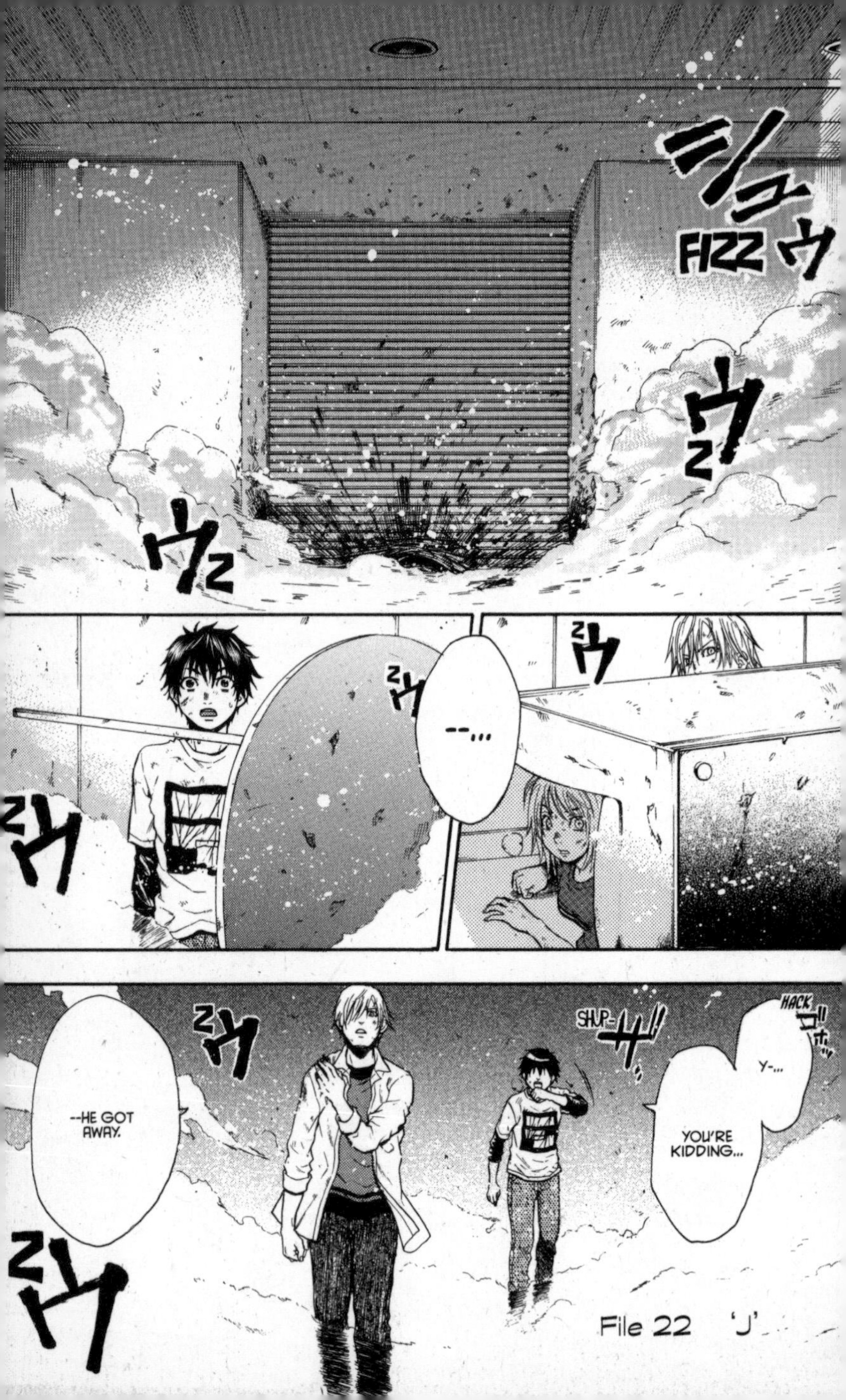
シュウ
FIZZ
--...
SHUP-
HACK
Y-...
YOU'RE KIDDING...
--HE GOT AWAY.

File 22 'J'

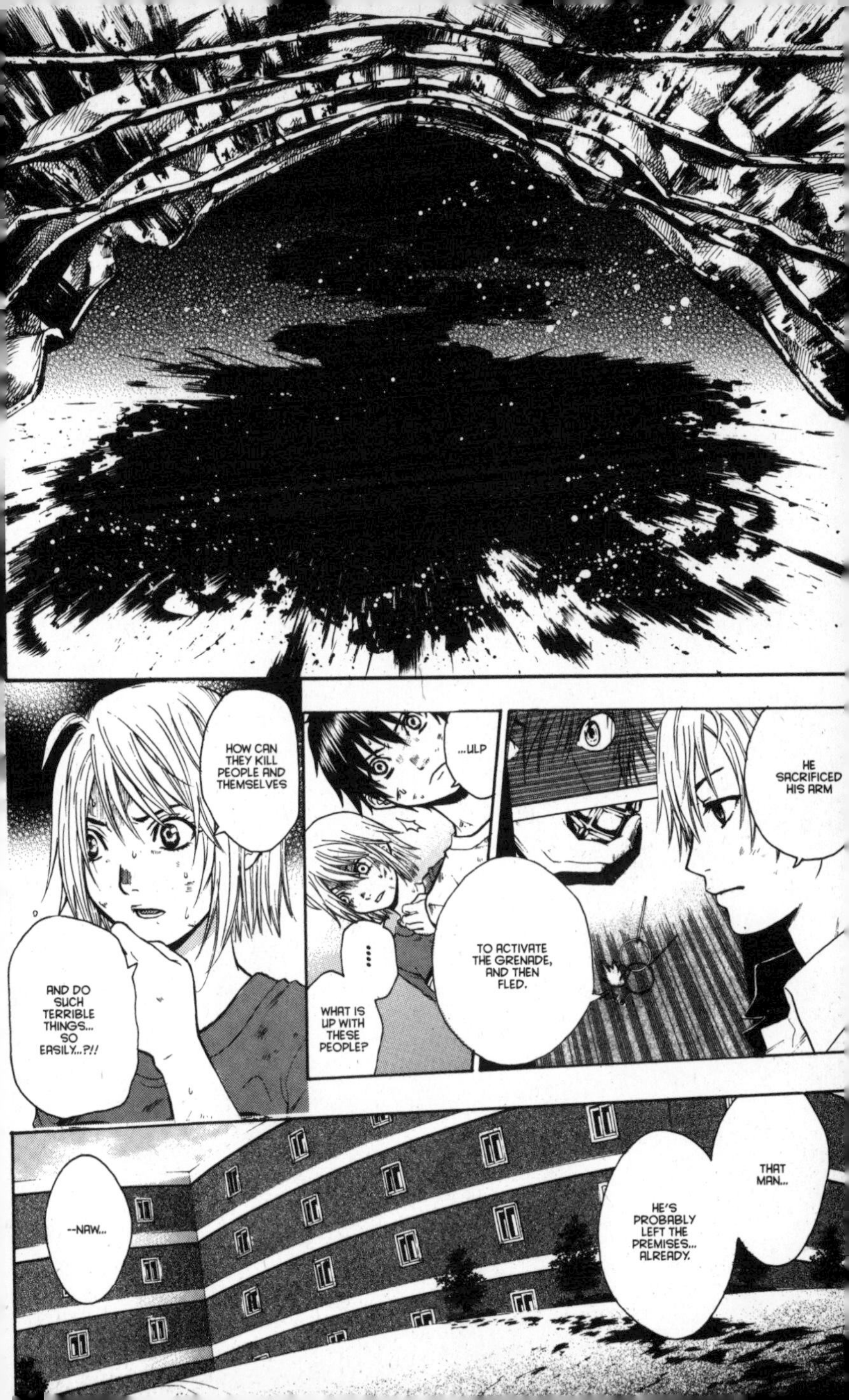
HE SACRIFICED HIS ARM
TO ACTIVATE THE GRENADE, AND THEN FLED.
...ULP
....
WHAT IS UP WITH THESE PEOPLE?
HOW CAN THEY KILL PEOPLE AND THEMSELVES
AND DO SUCH TERRIBLE THINGS... SO EASILY...?!!
THAT MAN...
HE'S PROBABLY LEFT THE PREMISES... ALREADY.
--NAW...

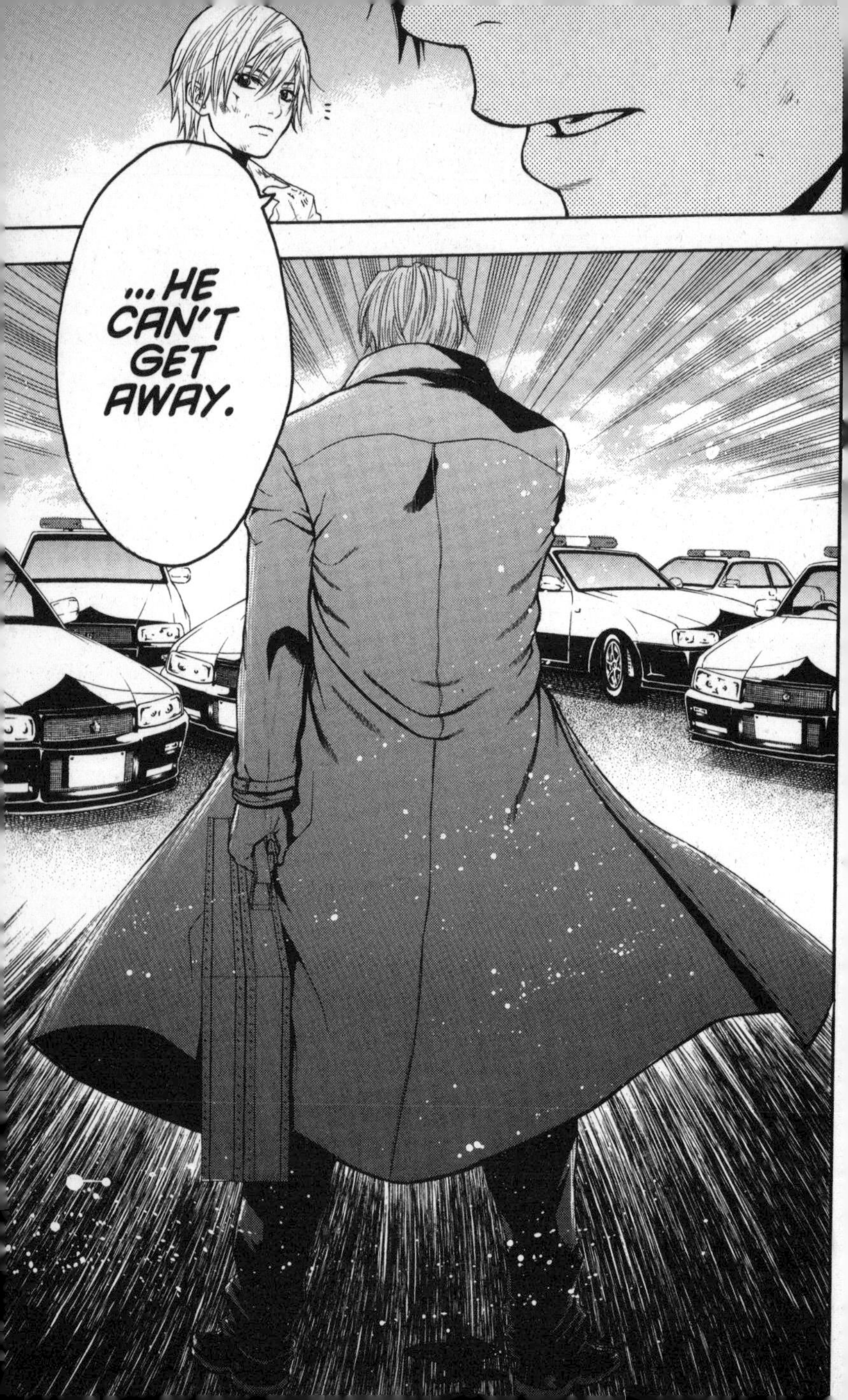
...HE CAN'T GET AWAY.

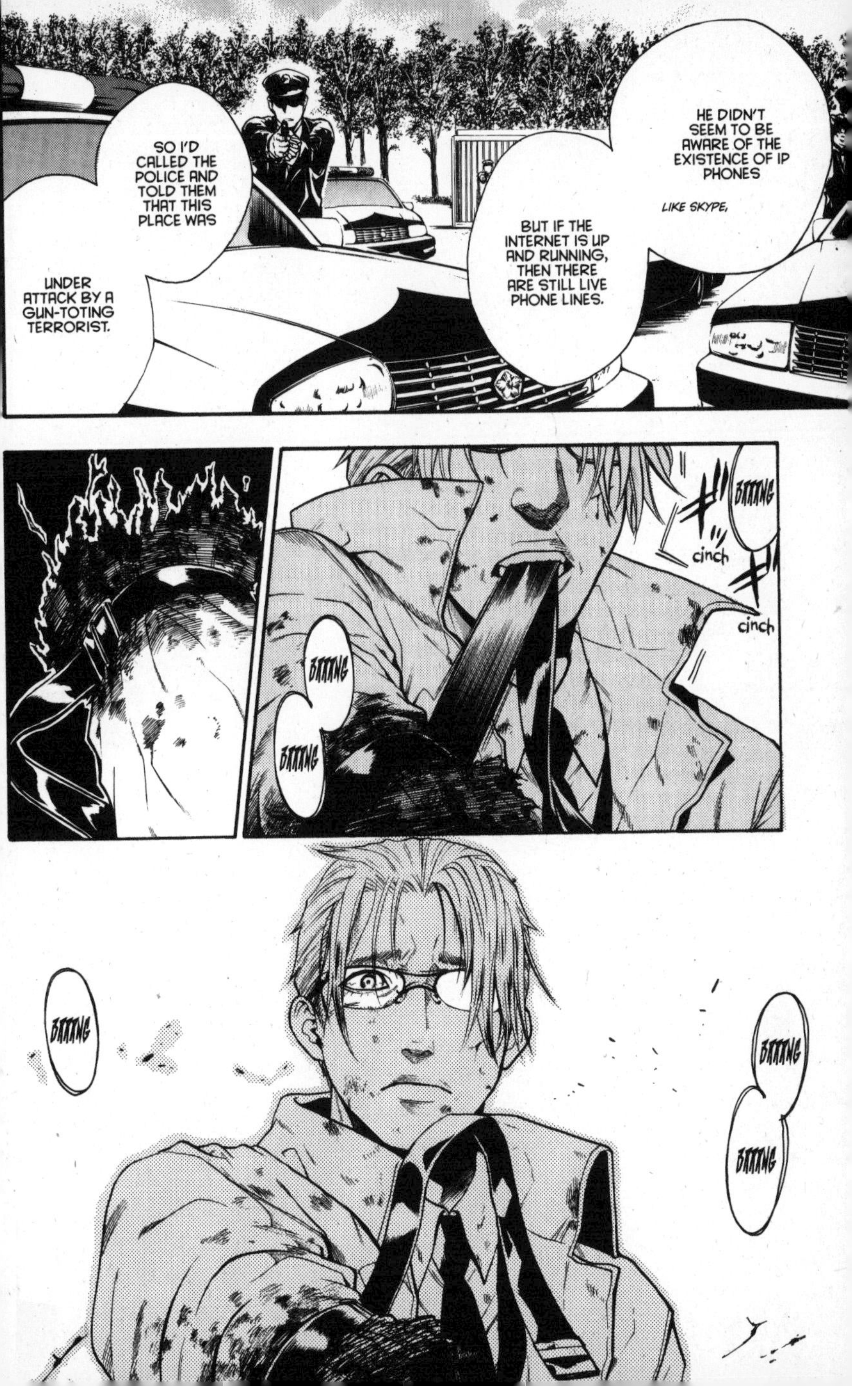
HE DIDN'T SEEM TO BE AWARE OF THE EXISTENCE OF IP PHONES
LIKE SKYPE,
BUT IF THE INTERNET IS UP AND RUNNING, THEN THERE ARE STILL LIVE PHONE LINES.
SO I'D CALLED THE POLICE AND TOLD THEM THAT THIS PLACE WAS
UNDER ATTACK BY A GUN-TOTING TERRORIST.
BRRRNG
cinch
cinch
BRRRNG
BRRRNG
BRRRNG
BRRRNG
BRRRNG

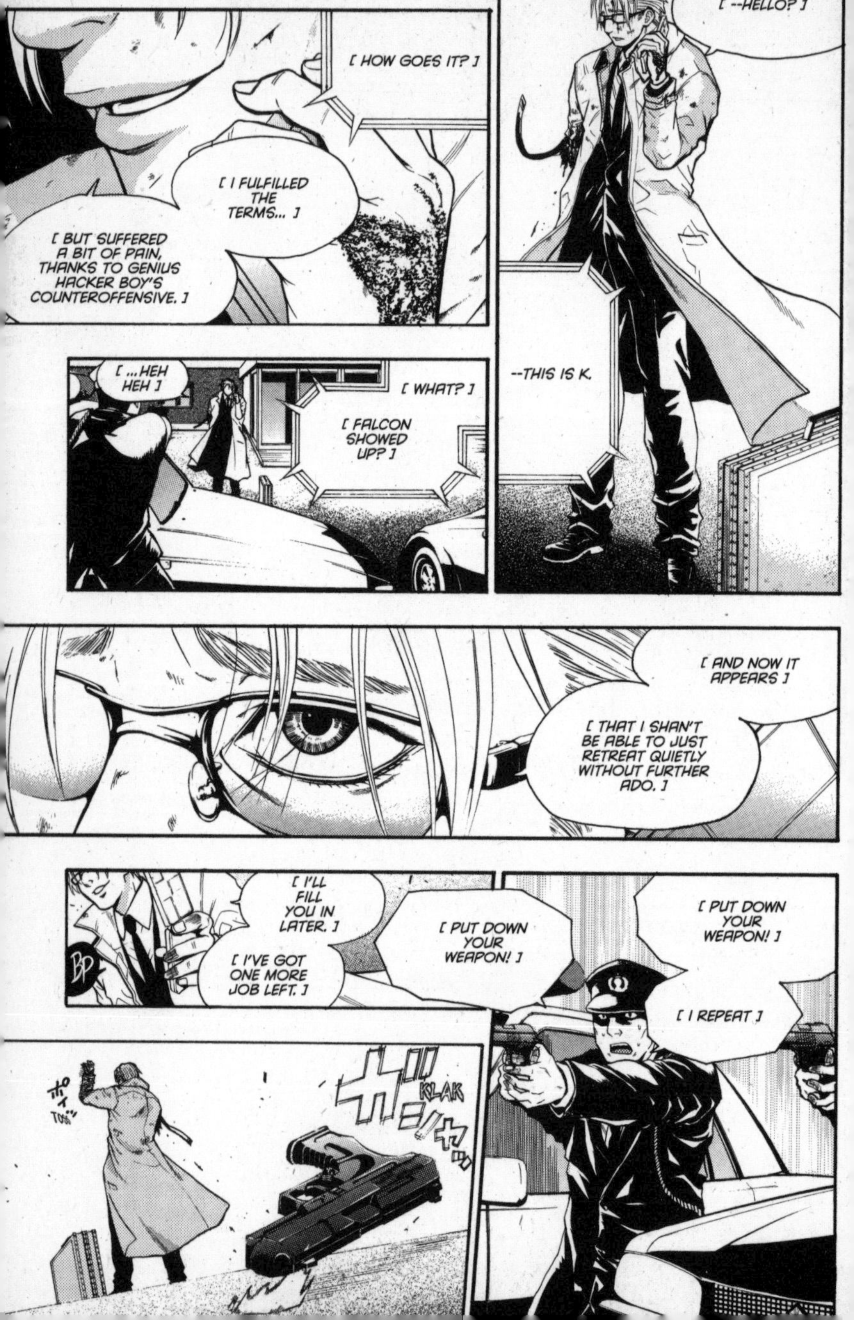
[--HELLO?]
--THIS IS K.
[HOW GOES IT?]
[I FULFILLED THE TERMS...]
[BUT SUFFERED A BIT OF PAIN, THANKS TO GENIUS HACKER BOY'S COUNTEROFFENSIVE.]
[WHAT?]
[FALCON SHOWED UP?]
[...HEH HEH]
[AND NOW IT APPEARS]
[THAT I SHAN'T BE ABLE TO JUST RETREAT QUIETLY WITHOUT FURTHER ADO.]
[PUT DOWN YOUR WEAPON!]
[I REPEAT]
[PUT DOWN YOUR WEAPON!]
[I'LL FILL YOU IN LATER.]
[I'VE GOT ONE MORE JOB LEFT.]
KLAK
TOSS

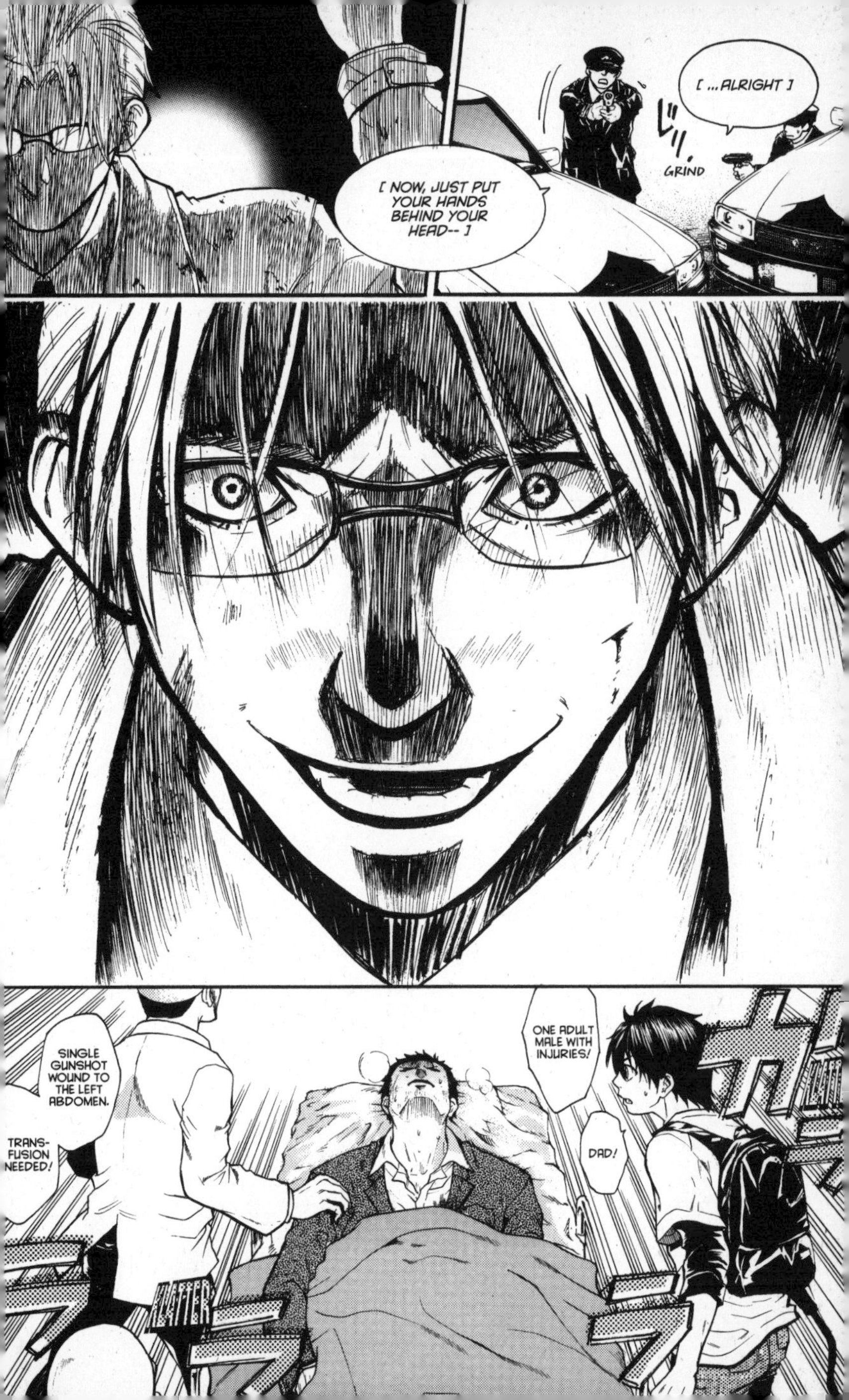
[...ALRIGHT]
GRIND
[NOW, JUST PUT YOUR HANDS BEHIND YOUR HEAD--]
ONE ADULT MALE WITH INJURIES!
DAD!
SINGLE GUNSHOT WOUND TO THE LEFT ABDOMEN.
TRANS-FUSION NEEDED!

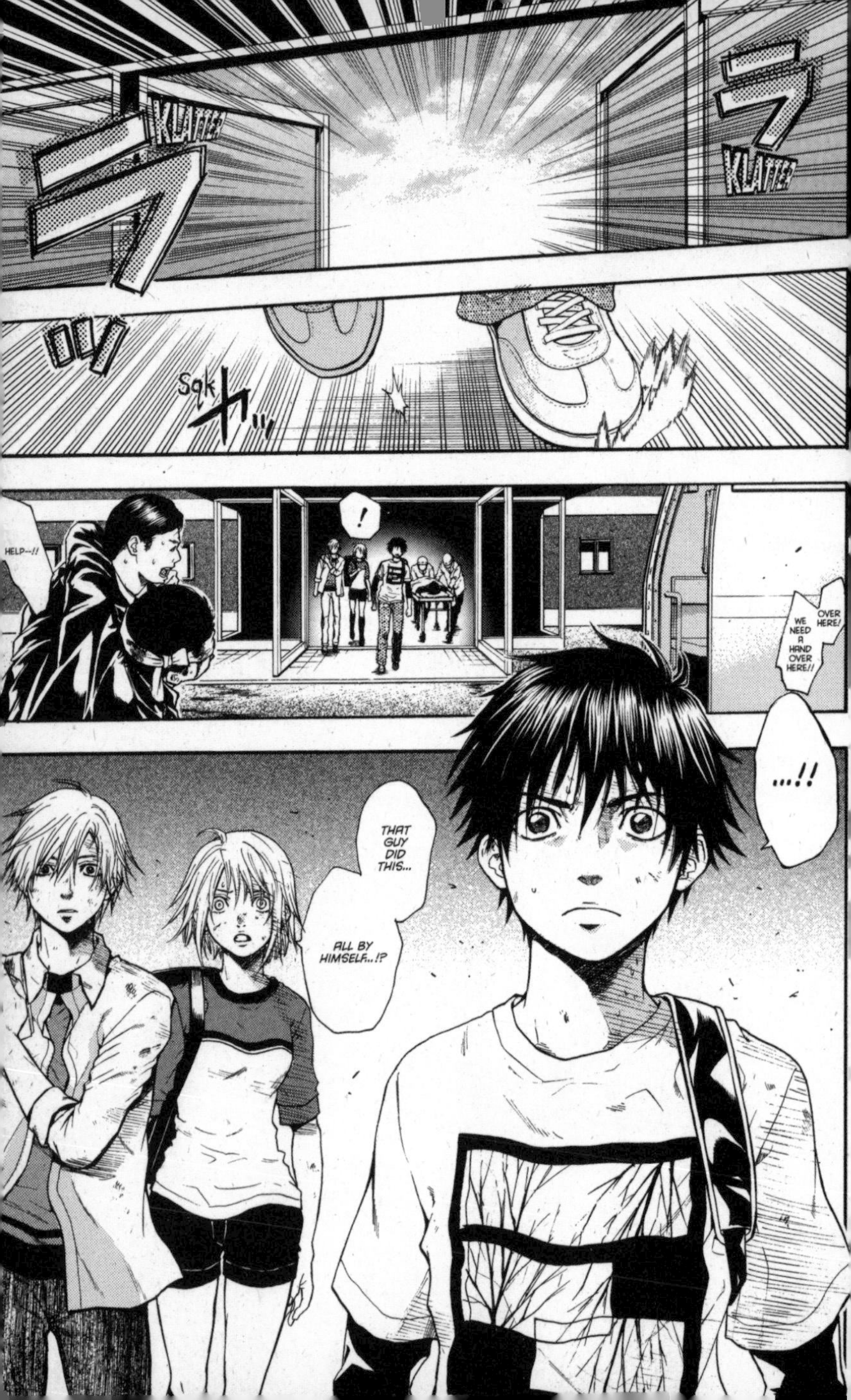
KLATTER
KLATTER
Sqk
!
OVER HERE! WE NEED A HAND OVER HERE!!
HELP--!!
...!!
THAT GUY DID THIS...
ALL BY HIMSELF...!?

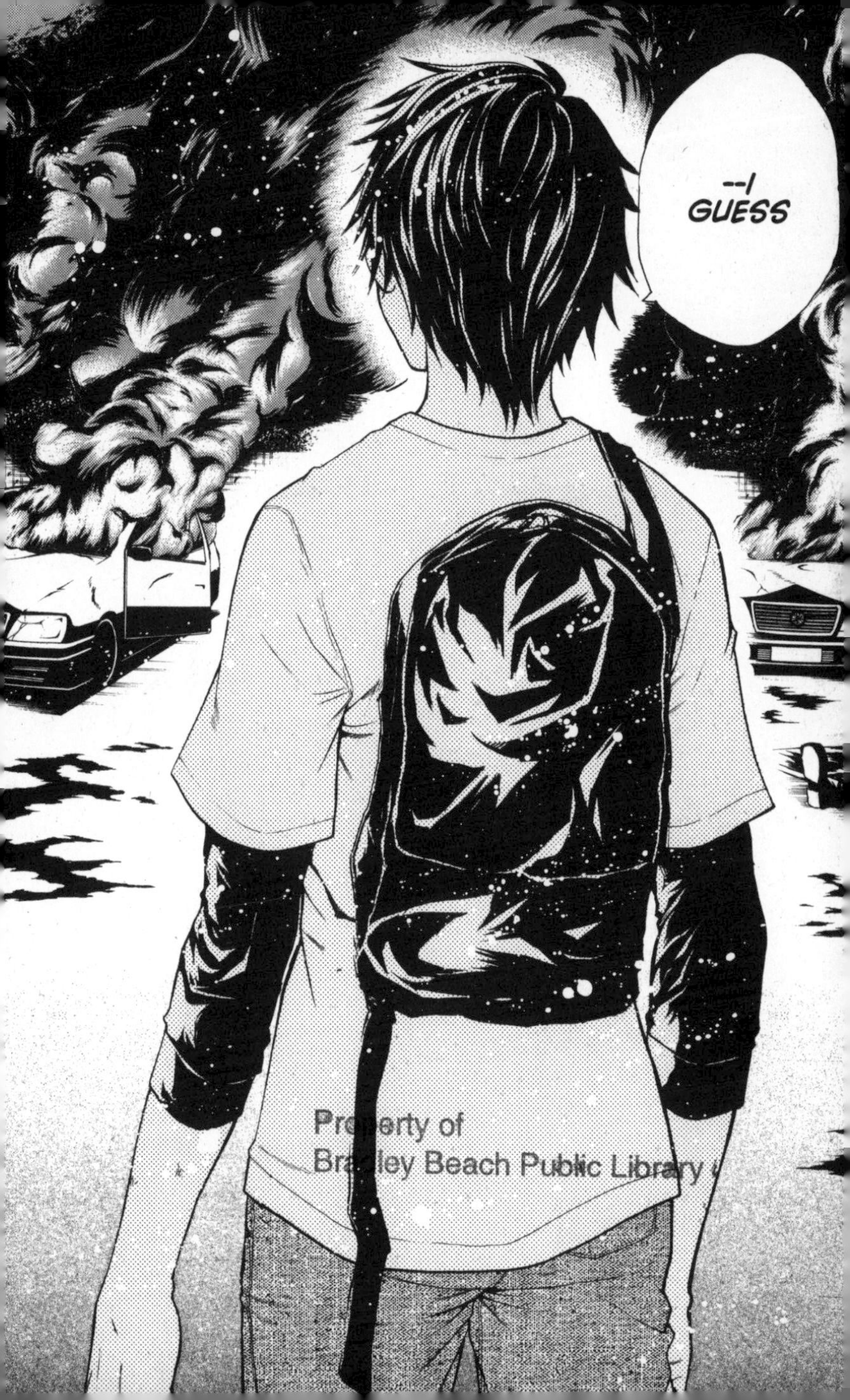
--I GUESS

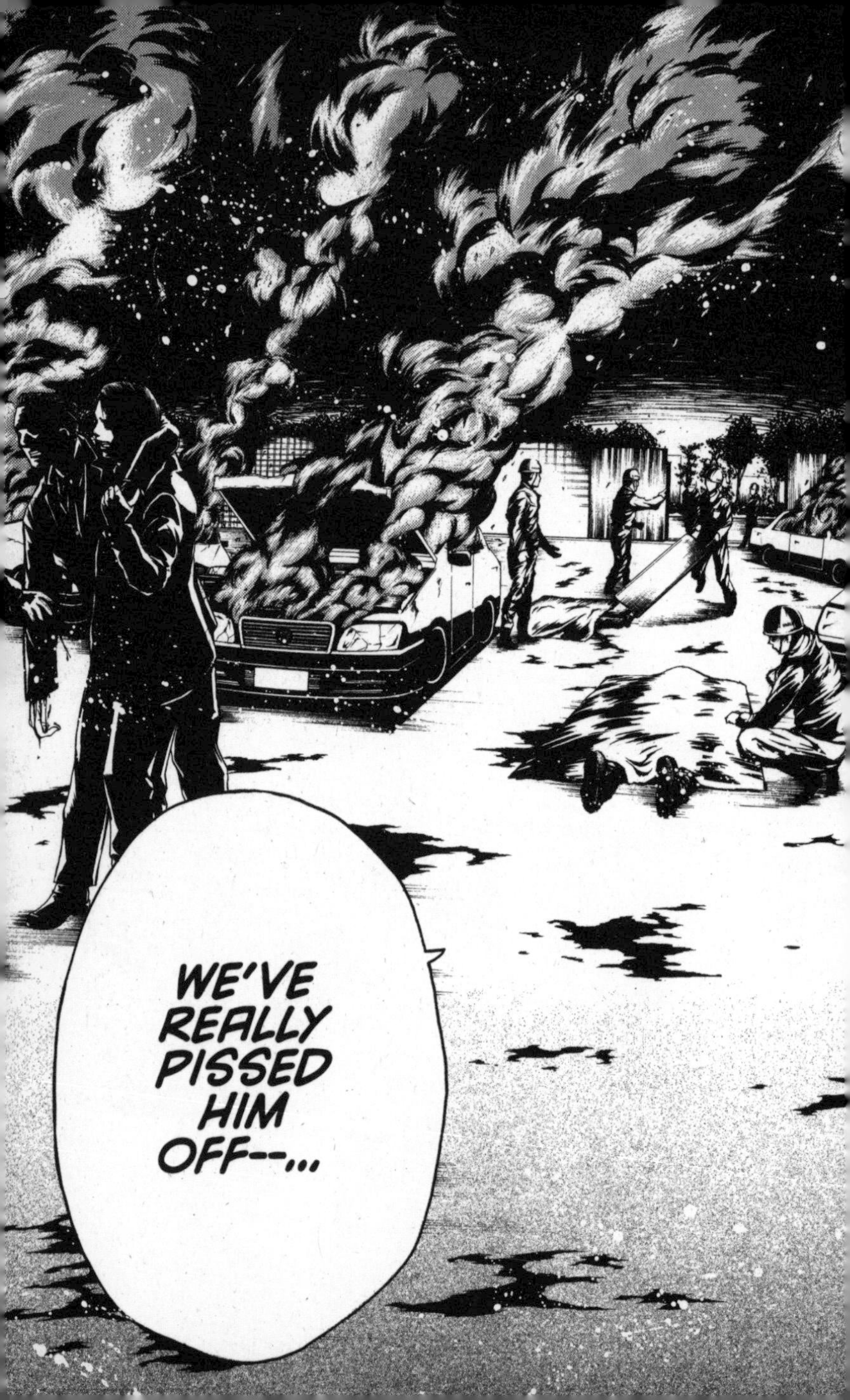
WE'VE REALLY PISSED HIM OFF--...

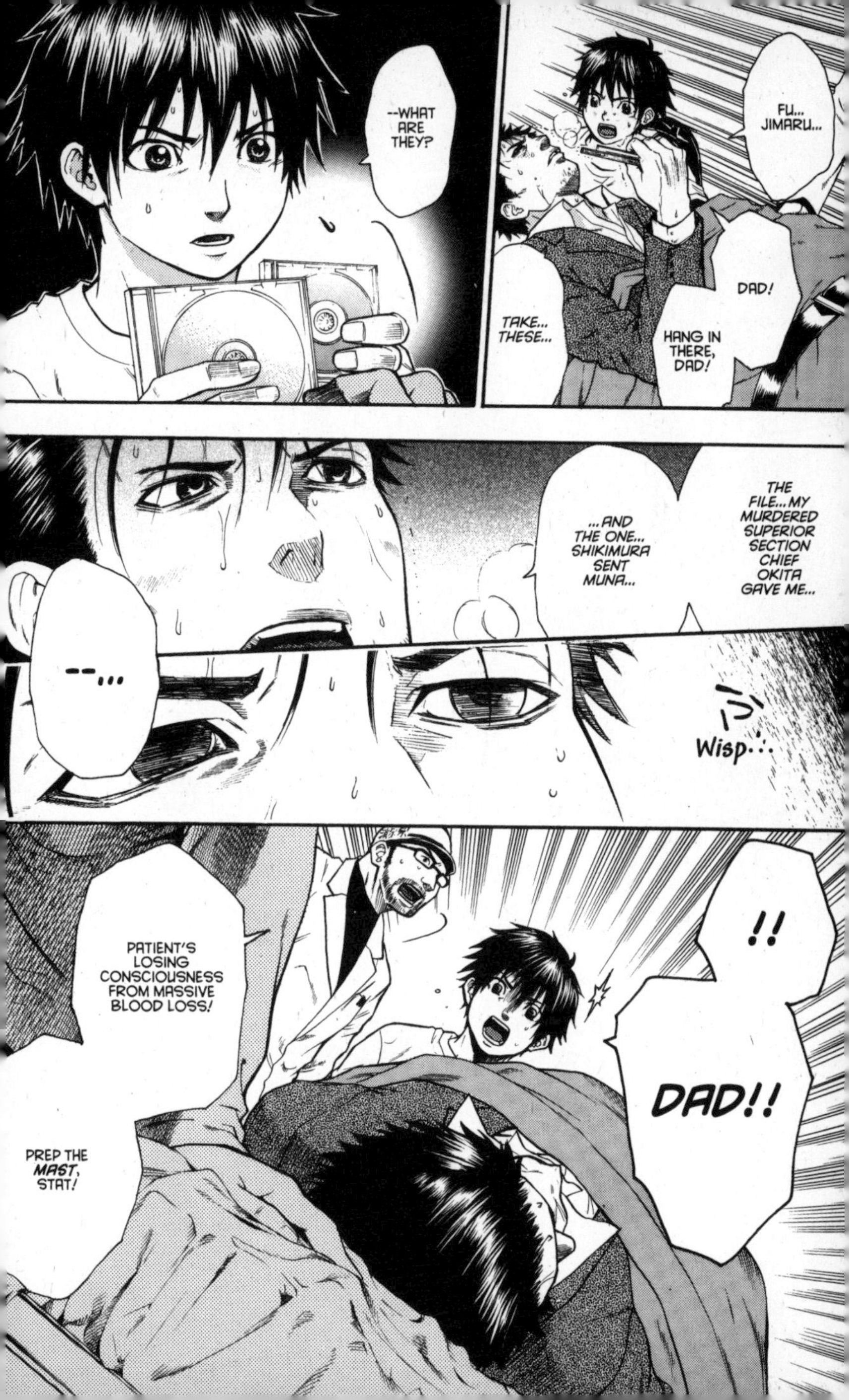
FU... JIMARU...
DAD!
HANG IN THERE, DAD!
TAKE... THESE...
--WHAT ARE THEY?
THE FILE...MY MURDERED SUPERIOR SECTION CHIEF OKITA GAVE ME...
...AND THE ONE... SHIKIMURA SENT MUNA...
Wisp...
--...
!!
DAD!!
PATIENT'S LOSING CONSCIOUSNESS FROM MASSIVE BLOOD LOSS!
PREP THE MAST, STAT!

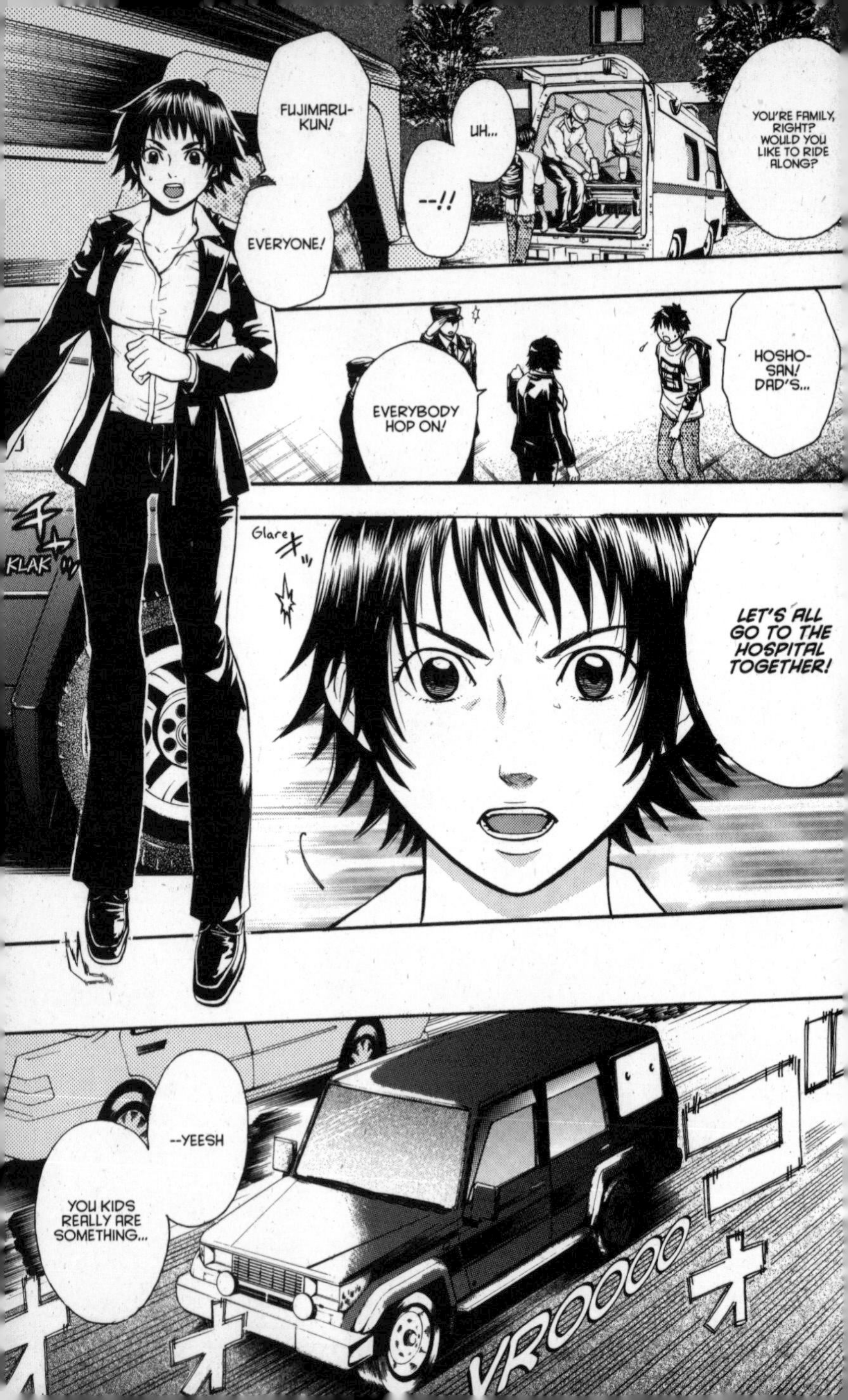
YOU'RE FAMILY, RIGHT? WOULD YOU LIKE TO RIDE ALONG?
UH...
--!!
HOSHO-SAN! DAD'S...
EVERYBODY HOP ON!
Glare
LET'S ALL GO TO THE HOSPITAL TOGETHER!
FUJIMARU-KUN!
EVERYONE!
KLAK
--YEESH
YOU KIDS REALLY ARE SOMETHING...
VROOOOO

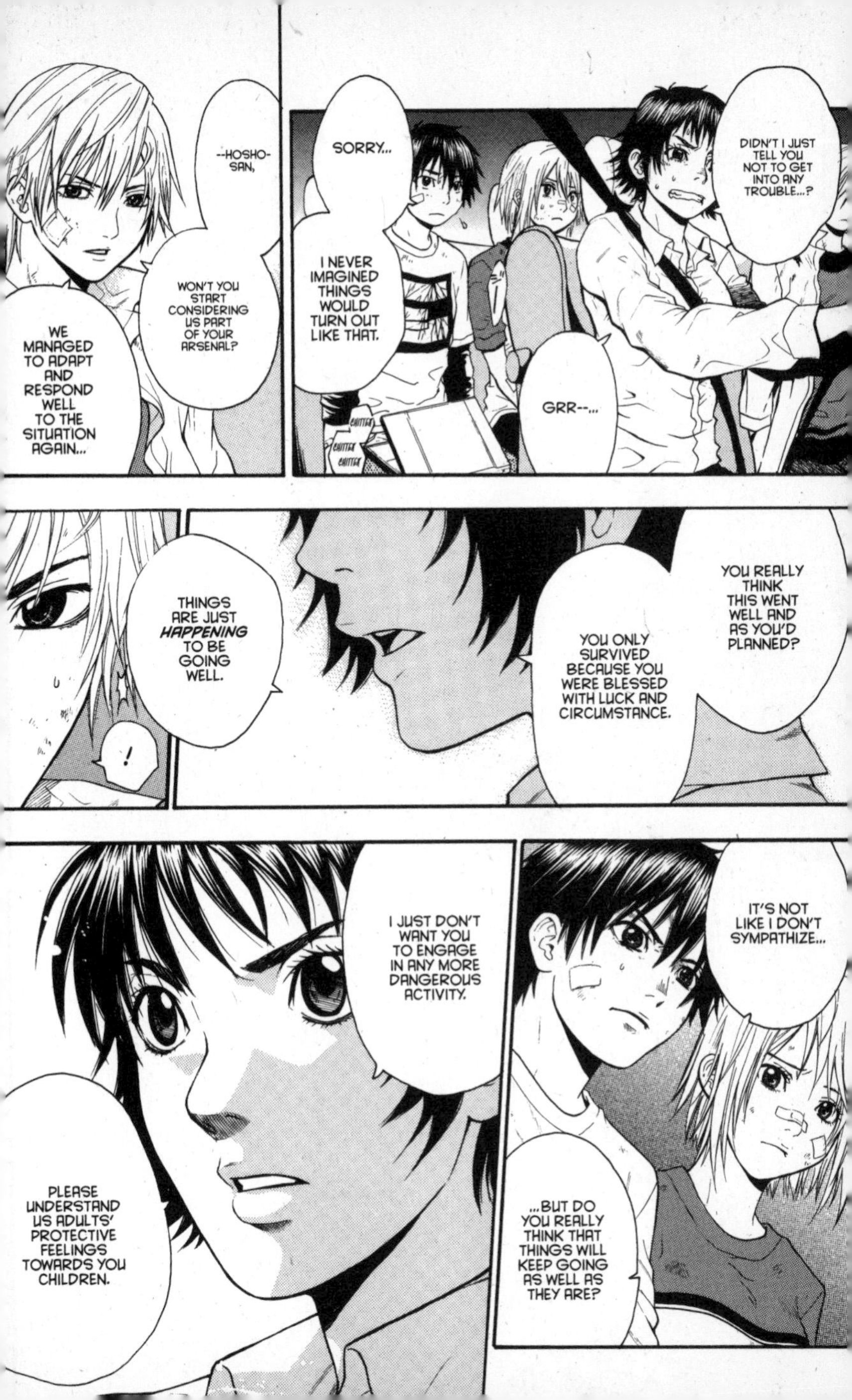
DIDN'T I JUST TELL YOU NOT TO GET INTO ANY TROUBLE...?
GRR--...
SORRY...
I NEVER IMAGINED THINGS WOULD TURN OUT LIKE THAT.
CHITTER CHITTER CHITTER
--HOSHO-SAN,
WON'T YOU START CONSIDERING US PART OF YOUR ARSENAL?
WE MANAGED TO ADAPT AND RESPOND WELL TO THE SITUATION AGAIN...
YOU REALLY THINK THIS WENT WELL AND AS YOU'D PLANNED?
YOU ONLY SURVIVED BECAUSE YOU WERE BLESSED WITH LUCK AND CIRCUMSTANCE.
THINGS ARE JUST *HAPPENING* TO BE GOING WELL.
!
IT'S NOT LIKE I DON'T SYMPATHIZE...
...BUT DO YOU REALLY THINK THAT THINGS WILL KEEP GOING AS WELL AS THEY ARE?
I JUST DON'T WANT YOU TO ENGAGE IN ANY MORE DANGEROUS ACTIVITY.
PLEASE UNDERSTAND US ADULTS' PROTECTIVE FEELINGS TOWARDS YOU CHILDREN.

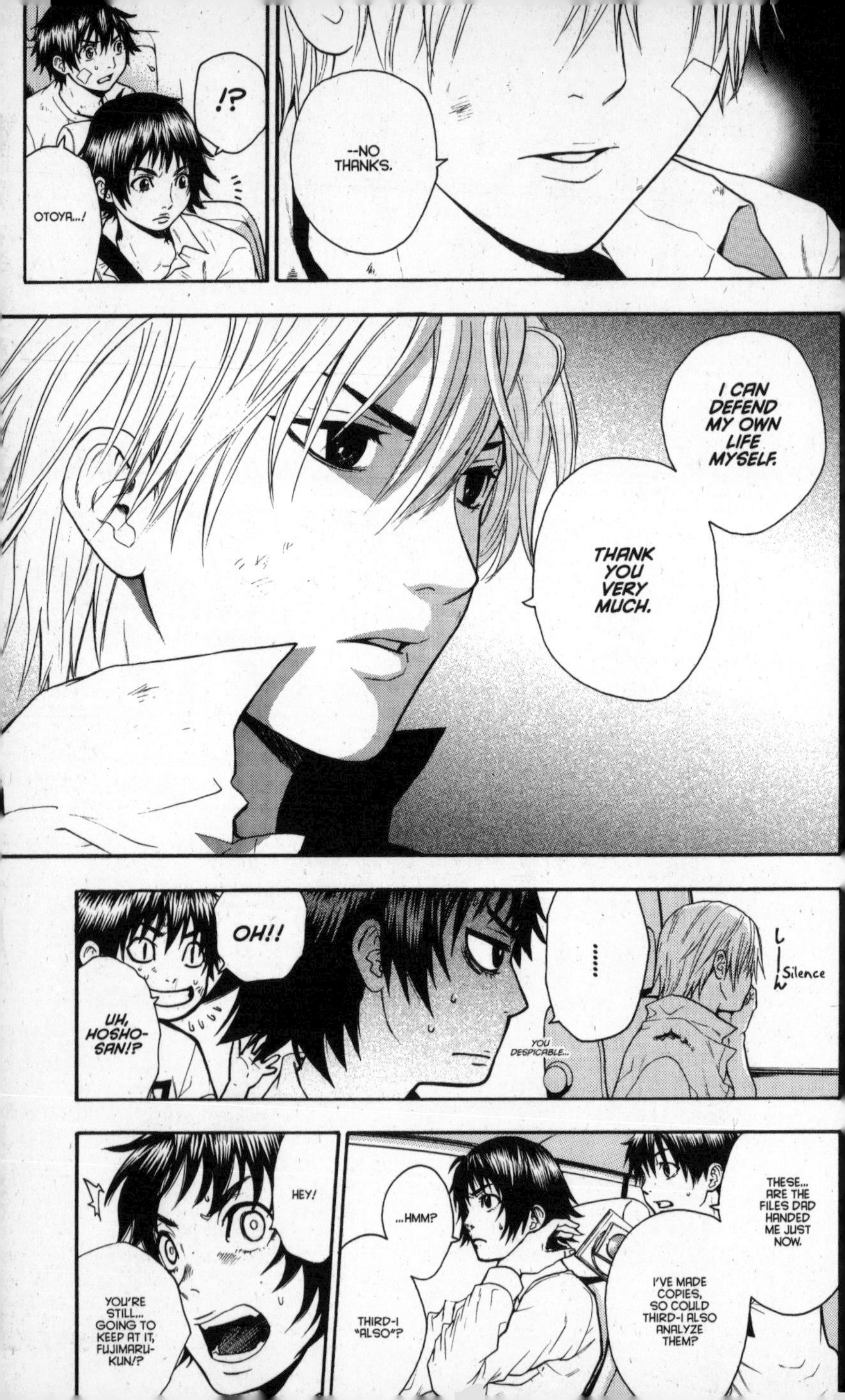
--NO THANKS.
!?
OTOYA...!
I CAN DEFEND MY OWN LIFE MYSELF.
THANK YOU VERY MUCH.
しーん
Silence
......
YOU DESPICABLE...
OH!!
UH, HOSHO-SAN!?
THESE... ARE THE FILES DAD HANDED ME JUST NOW.
I'VE MADE COPIES, SO COULD THIRD-I ALSO ANALYZE THEM?
...HMM?
THIRD-I "ALSO"?
HEY!
YOU'RE STILL... GOING TO KEEP AT IT, FUJIMARU-KUN!?

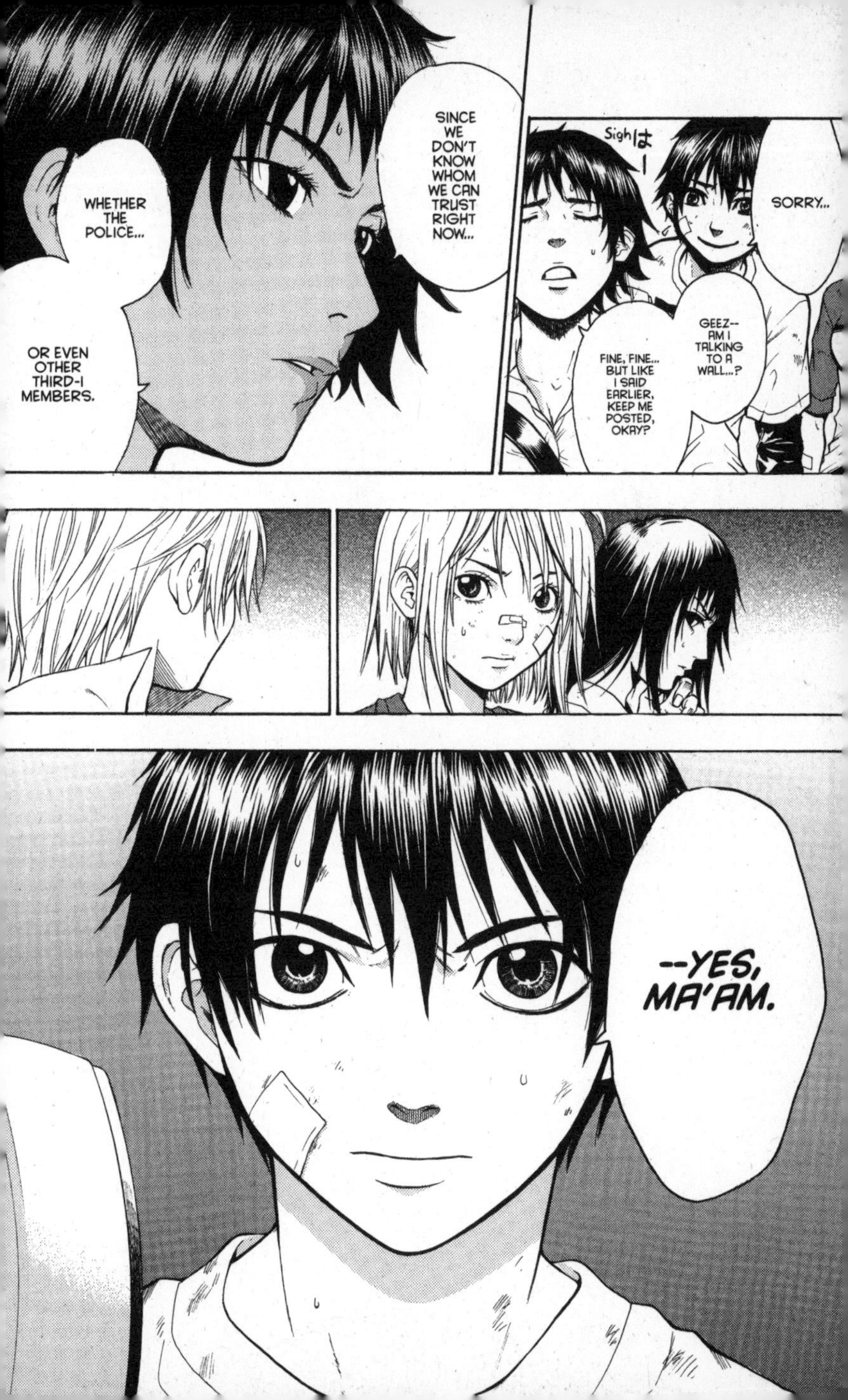
SORRY...
Sigh はー
GEEZ-- AM I TALKING TO A WALL...?
FINE, FINE... BUT LIKE I SAID EARLIER, KEEP ME POSTED, OKAY?
SINCE WE DON'T KNOW WHOM WE CAN TRUST RIGHT NOW...
WHETHER THE POLICE...
OR EVEN OTHER THIRD-I MEMBERS.
--YES, MA'AM.

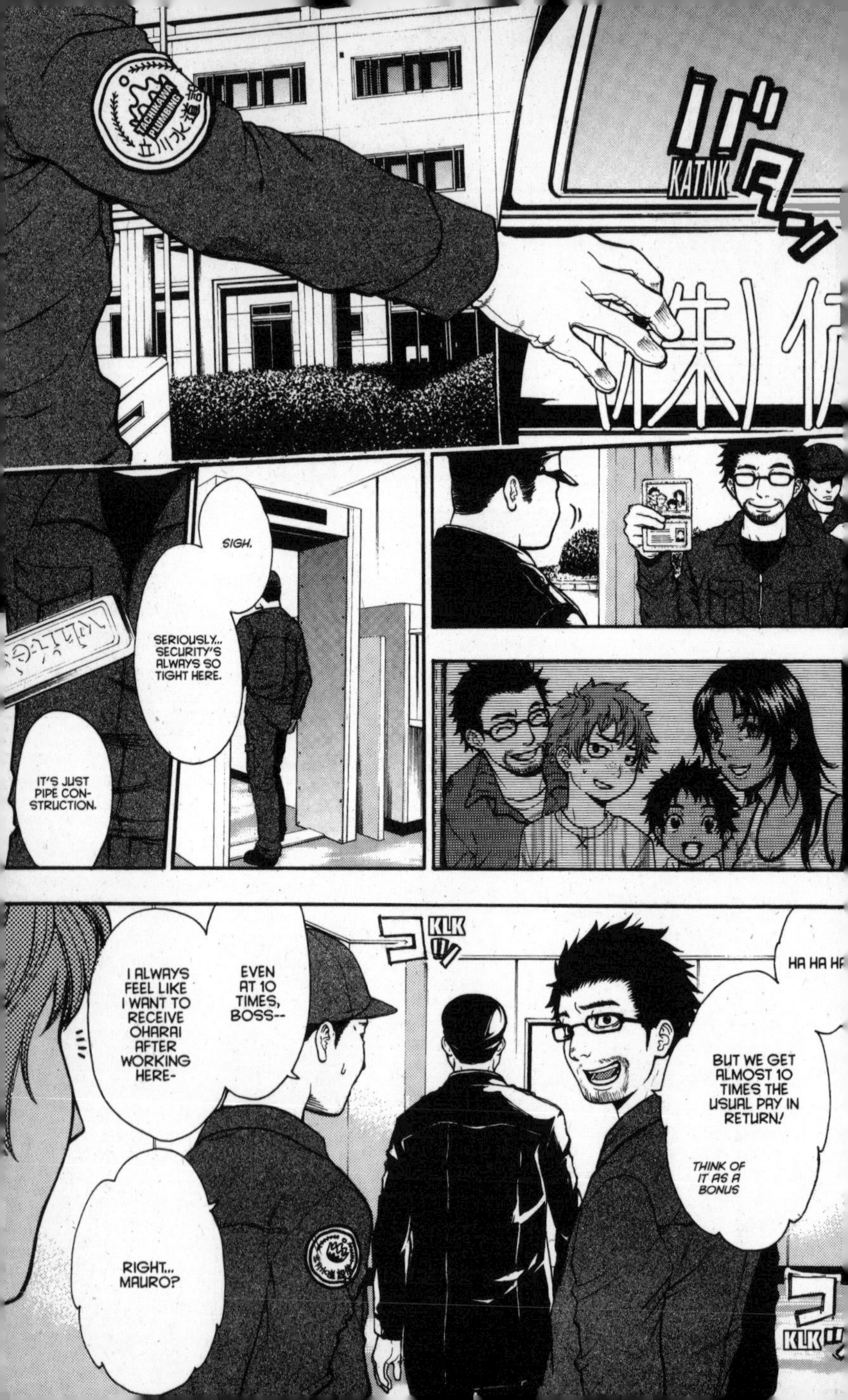

TACHIKAWA PLUMBING
立川水道部
バタッ
KATNK
SIGH.
SERIOUSLY... SECURITY'S ALWAYS SO TIGHT HERE.
IT'S JUST PIPE CONSTRUCTION.
KLK
HA HA HA
BUT WE GET ALMOST 10 TIMES THE USUAL PAY IN RETURN!
THINK OF IT AS A BONUS
EVEN AT 10 TIMES, BOSS--
I ALWAYS FEEL LIKE I WANT TO RECEIVE OHARAI AFTER WORKING HERE-
RIGHT... MAURO?
KLK

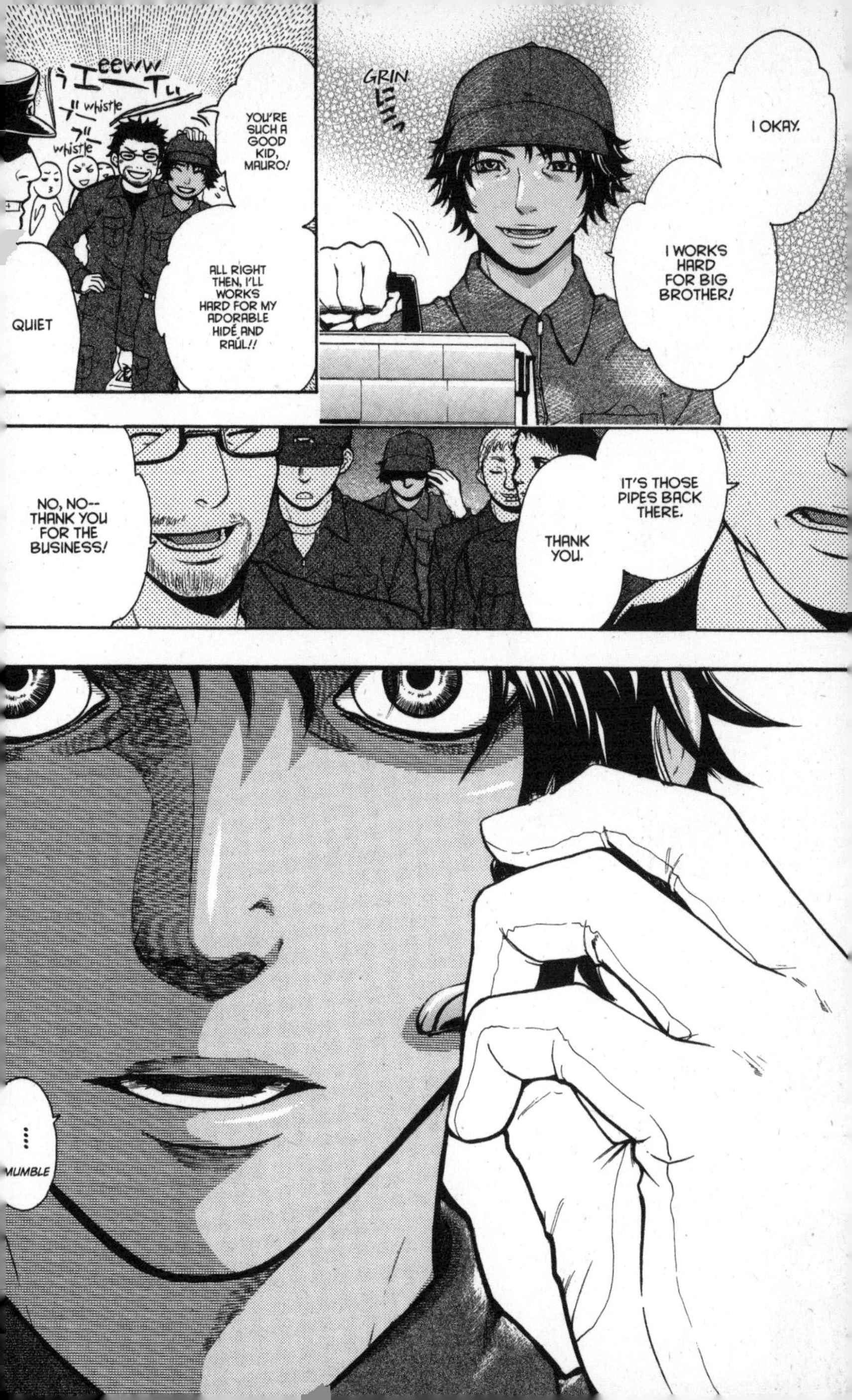
GRIN
I OKAY.
I WORKS HARD FOR BIG BROTHER!
YOU'RE SUCH A GOOD KID, MAURO!
EEWW
whistle
whistle
ALL RIGHT THEN, I'LL WORKS HARD FOR MY ADORABLE HIDÉ AND RAÚL!!
QUIET
IT'S THOSE PIPES BACK THERE.
THANK YOU.
NO, NO-- THANK YOU FOR THE BUSINESS!
....
MUMBLE

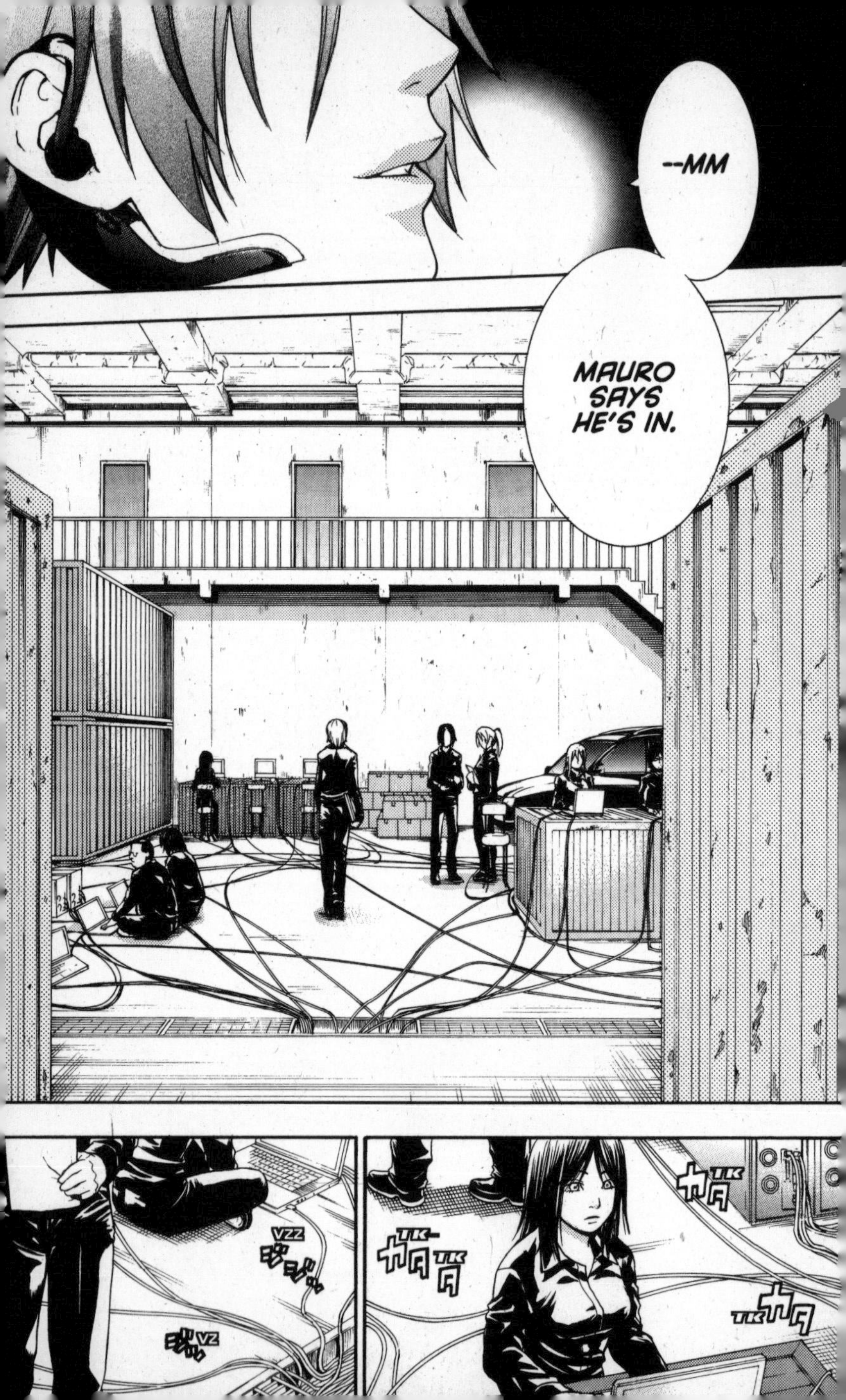
--MM
MAURO SAYS HE'S IN.
TK
TK-
TK
TK
VZZ
VZ

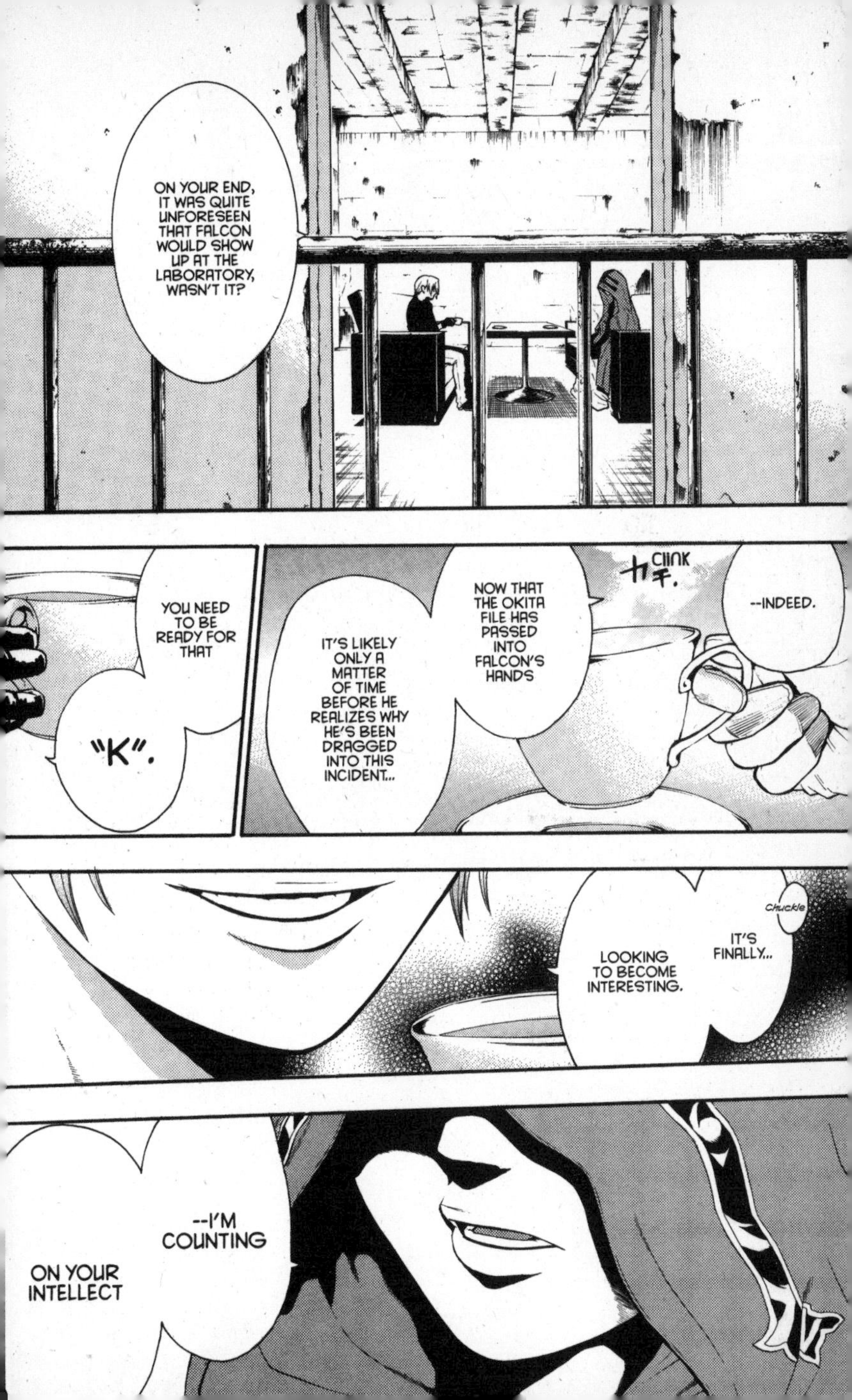
ON YOUR END, IT WAS QUITE UNFORESEEN THAT FALCON WOULD SHOW UP AT THE LABORATORY, WASN'T IT?
カチ CLINK
--INDEED.
NOW THAT THE OKITA FILE HAS PASSED INTO FALCON'S HANDS
IT'S LIKELY ONLY A MATTER OF TIME BEFORE HE REALIZES WHY HE'S BEEN DRAGGED INTO THIS INCIDENT...
YOU NEED TO BE READY FOR THAT
"K".
Chuckle
IT'S FINALLY...
LOOKING TO BECOME INTERESTING.
--I'M COUNTING
ON YOUR INTELLECT

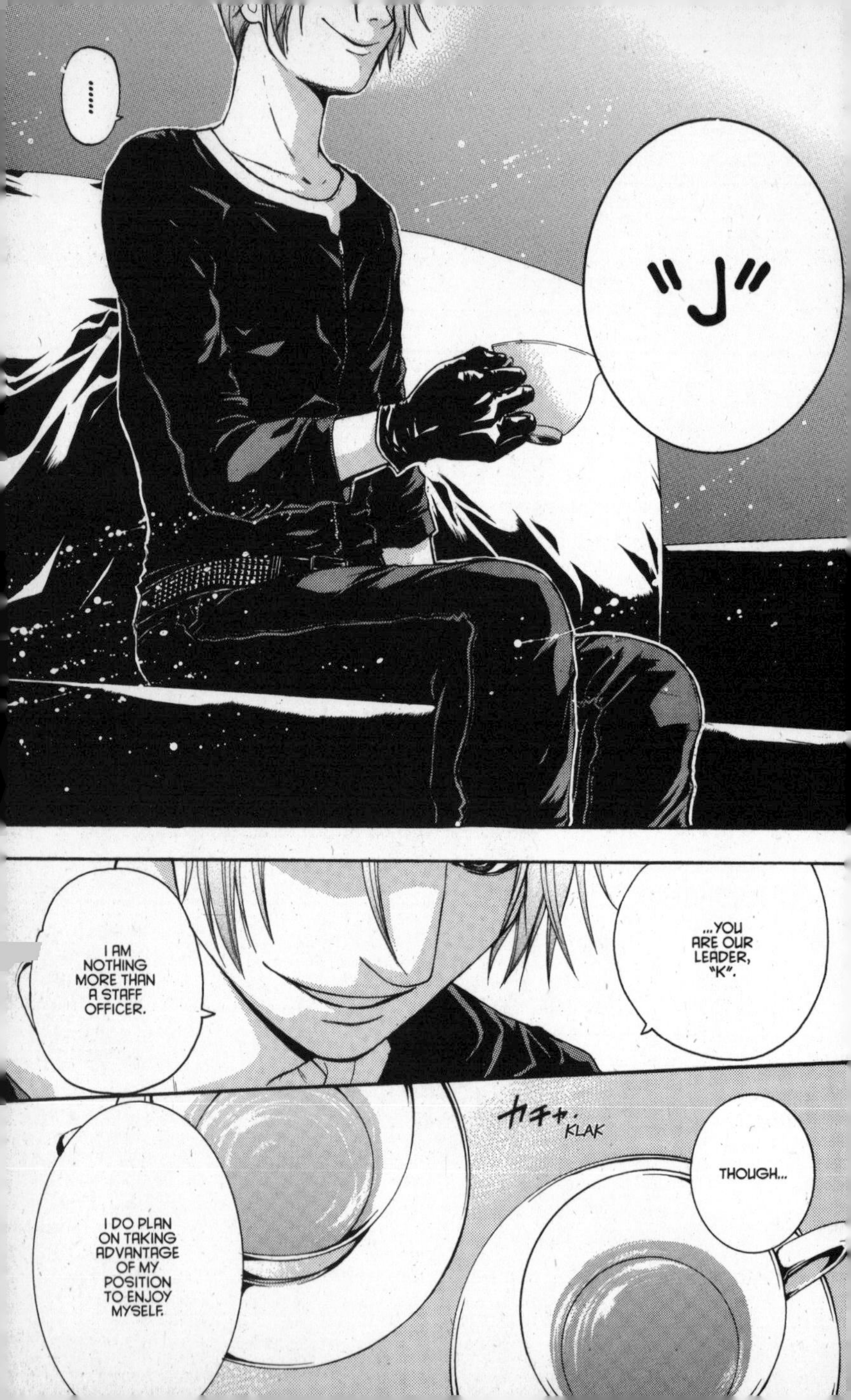
"J"
......
...YOU ARE OUR LEADER, "K".
I AM NOTHING MORE THAN A STAFF OFFICER.
カチャ KLAK
THOUGH...
I DO PLAN ON TAKING ADVANTAGE OF MY POSITION TO ENJOY MYSELF.

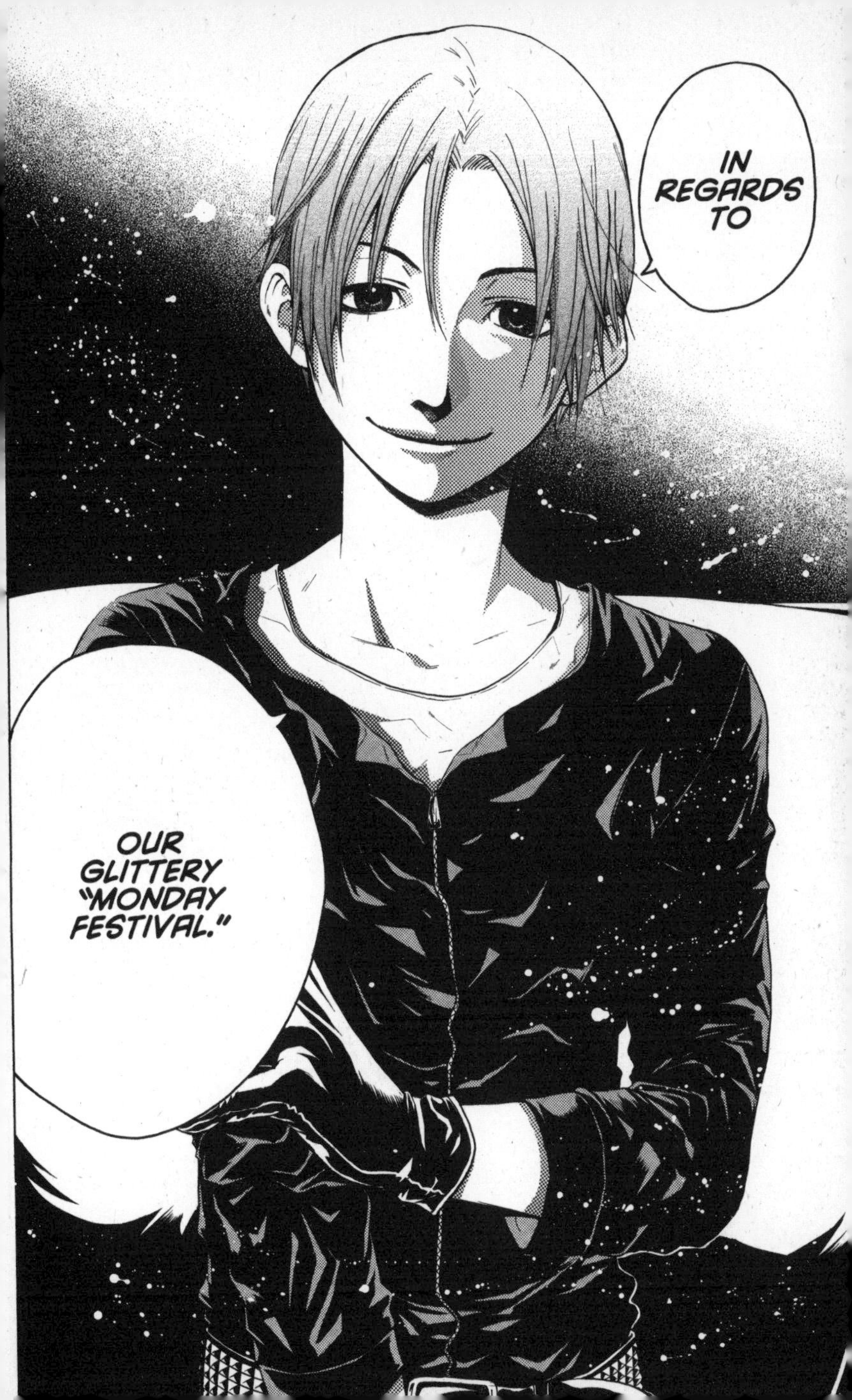
IN REGARDS TO
OUR GLITTERY "MONDAY FESTIVAL."

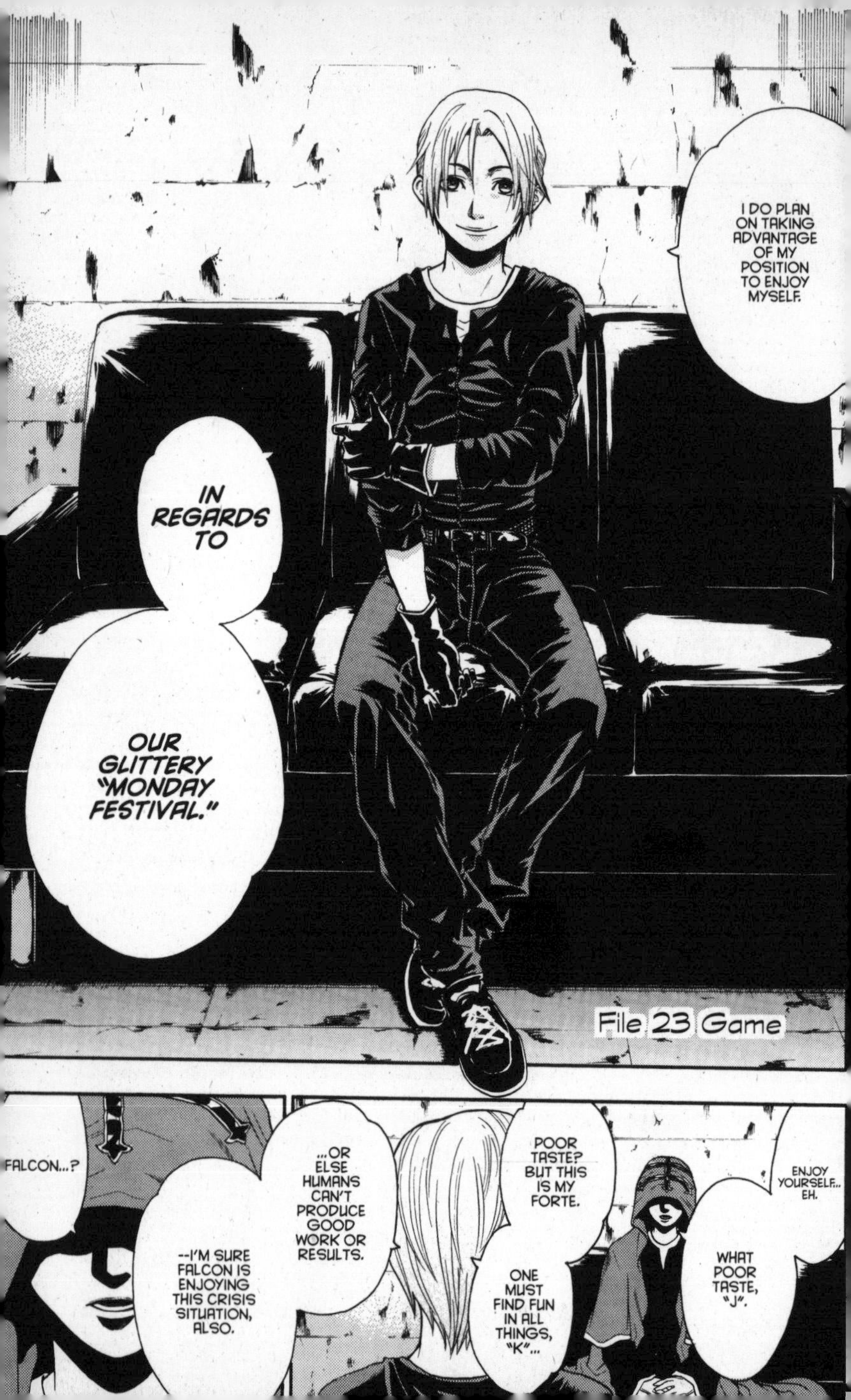
I DO PLAN ON TAKING ADVANTAGE OF MY POSITION TO ENJOY MYSELF.
IN REGARDS TO
OUR GLITTERY "MONDAY FESTIVAL."
File 23 Game
ENJOY YOURSELF... EH.
WHAT POOR TASTE, "J".
POOR TASTE? BUT THIS IS MY FORTE.
ONE MUST FIND FUN IN ALL THINGS, "K"...
...OR ELSE HUMANS CAN'T PRODUCE GOOD WORK OR RESULTS.
--I'M SURE FALCON IS ENJOYING THIS CRISIS SITUATION, ALSO.
FALCON...?

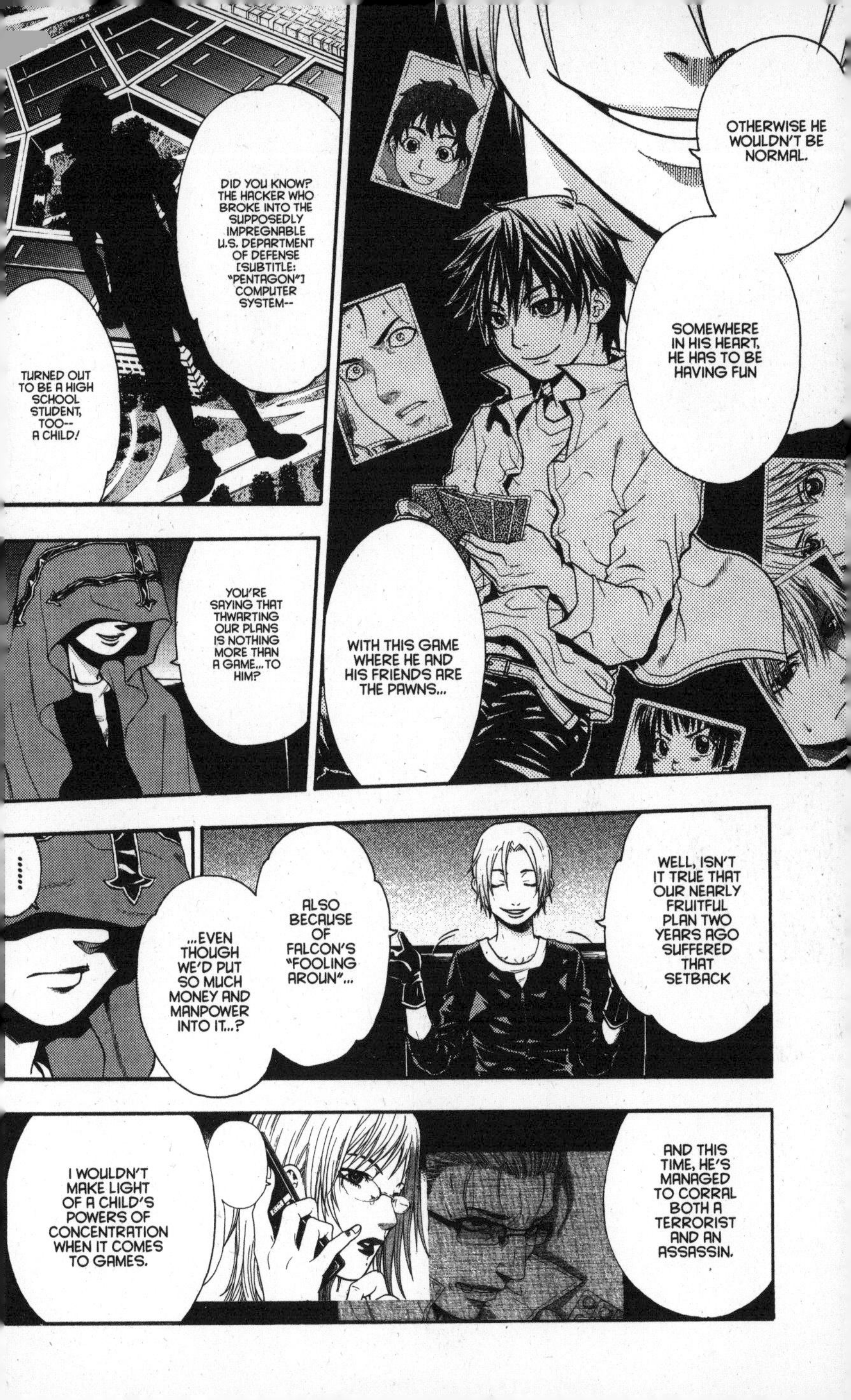
OTHERWISE HE WOULDN'T BE NORMAL.
SOMEWHERE IN HIS HEART, HE HAS TO BE HAVING FUN
WITH THIS GAME WHERE HE AND HIS FRIENDS ARE THE PAWNS...
DID YOU KNOW? THE HACKER WHO BROKE INTO THE SUPPOSEDLY IMPREGNABLE U.S. DEPARTMENT OF DEFENSE [SUBTITLE: "PENTAGON"] COMPUTER SYSTEM--
TURNED OUT TO BE A HIGH SCHOOL STUDENT, TOO-- A CHILD!
YOU'RE SAYING THAT THWARTING OUR PLANS IS NOTHING MORE THAN A GAME...TO HIM?
WELL, ISN'T IT TRUE THAT OUR NEARLY FRUITFUL PLAN TWO YEARS AGO SUFFERED THAT SETBACK
ALSO BECAUSE OF FALCON'S "FOOLING AROUN"...
...EVEN THOUGH WE'D PUT SO MUCH MONEY AND MANPOWER INTO IT...?
......
AND THIS TIME, HE'S MANAGED TO CORRAL BOTH A TERRORIST AND AN ASSASSIN.
I WOULDN'T MAKE LIGHT OF A CHILD'S POWERS OF CONCENTRATION WHEN IT COMES TO GAMES.

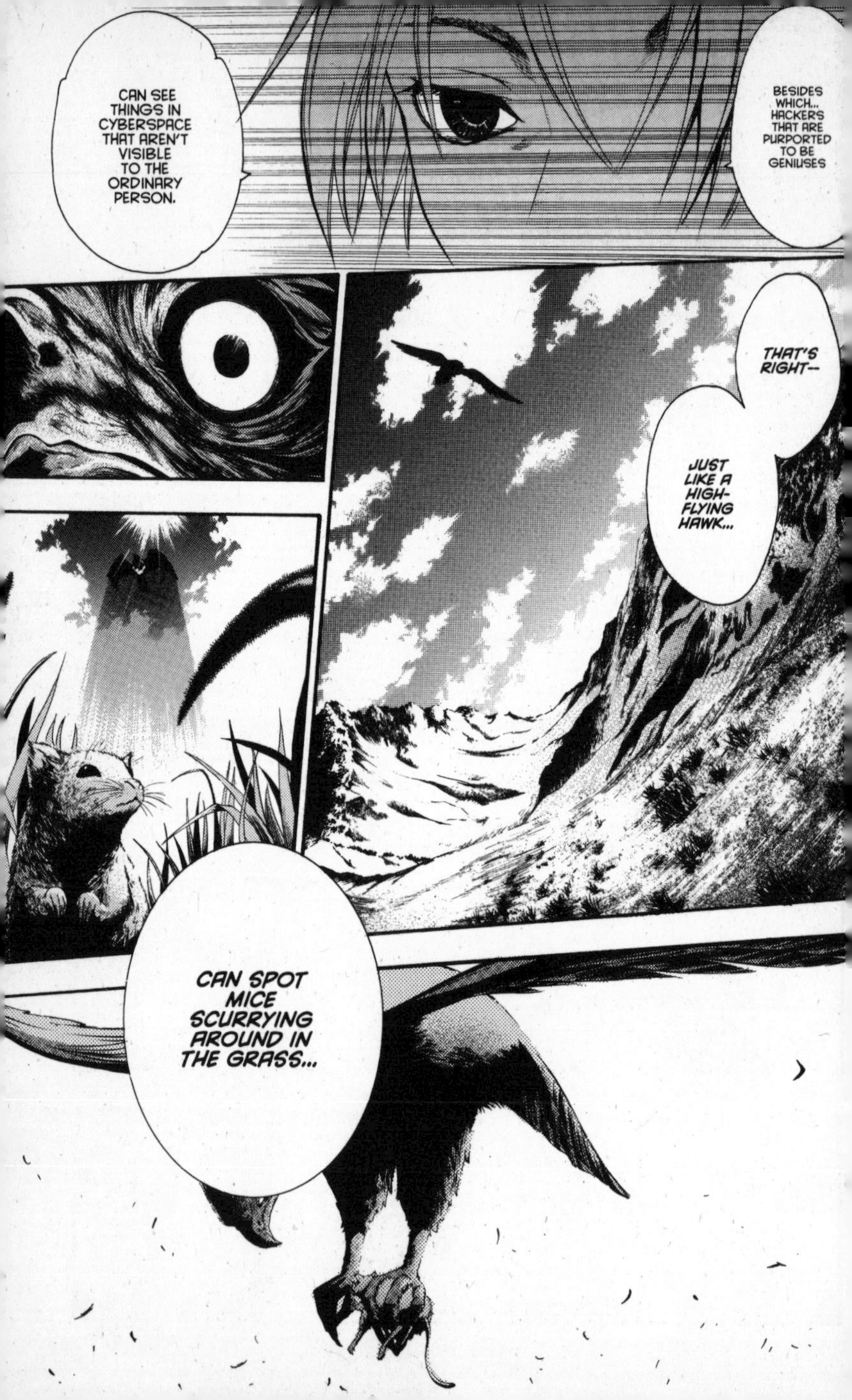
BESIDES WHICH... HACKERS THAT ARE PURPORTED TO BE GENIUSES
CAN SEE THINGS IN CYBERSPACE THAT AREN'T VISIBLE TO THE ORDINARY PERSON.
THAT'S RIGHT--
JUST LIKE A HIGH-FLYING HAWK...
CAN SPOT MICE SCURRYING AROUND IN THE GRASS...

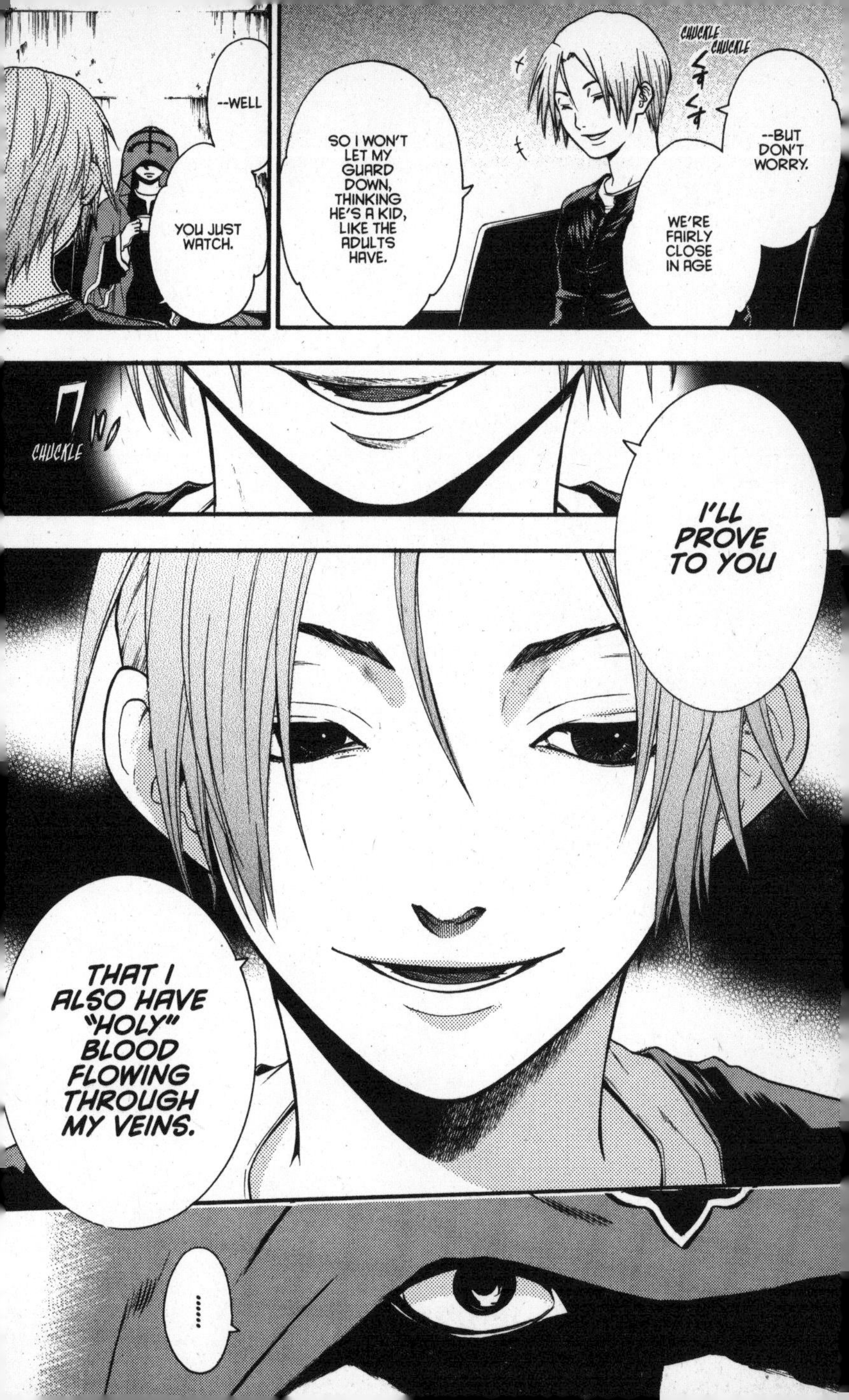
CHUCKLE CHUCKLE
くすくす
--BUT DON'T WORRY.
WE'RE FAIRLY CLOSE IN AGE
SO I WON'T LET MY GUARD DOWN, THINKING HE'S A KID, LIKE THE ADULTS HAVE.
--WELL
YOU JUST WATCH.
CHUCKLE
I'LL PROVE TO YOU
THAT I ALSO HAVE "HOLY" BLOOD FLOWING THROUGH MY VEINS.
......

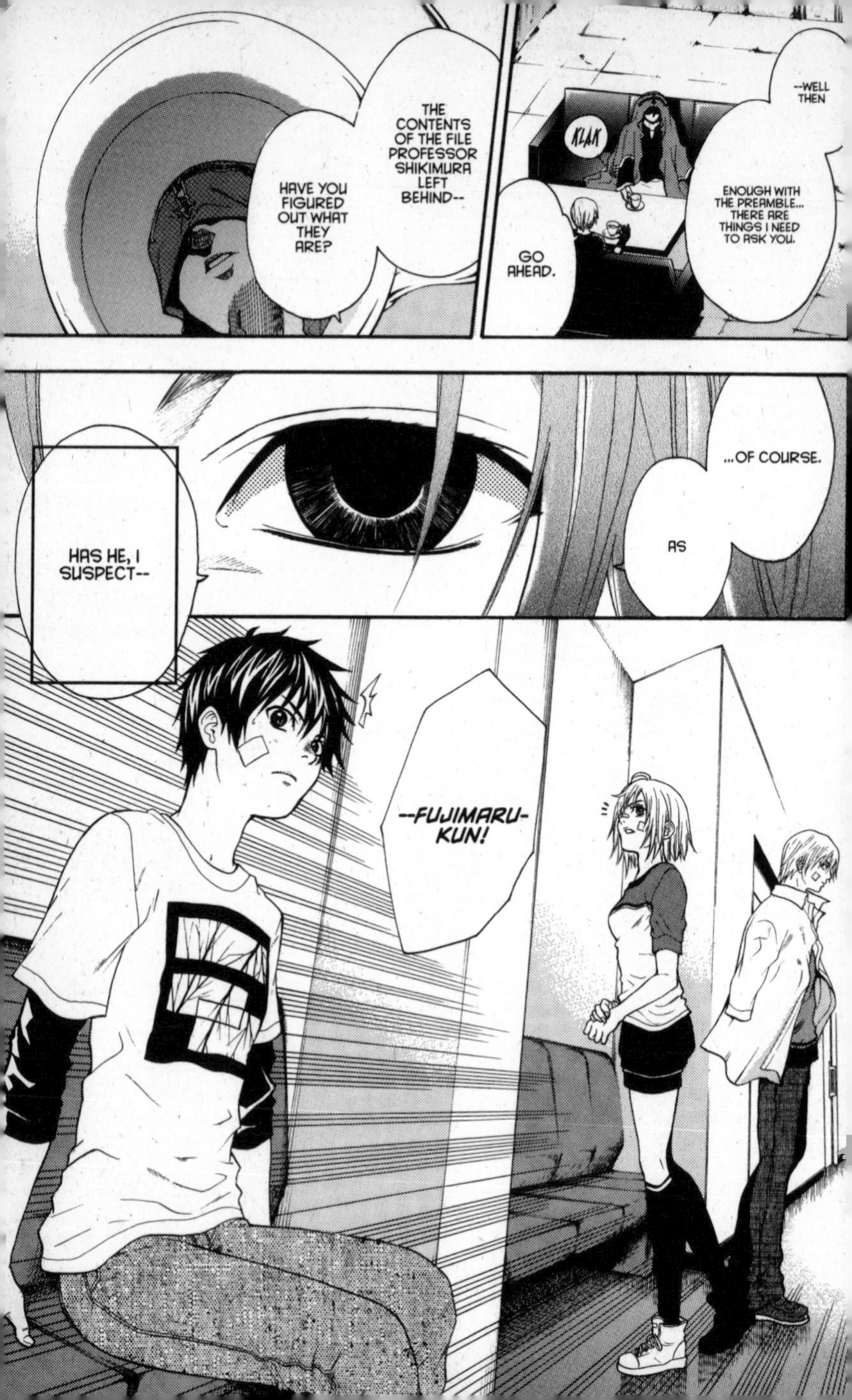
--WELL THEN
ENOUGH WITH THE PREAMBLE... THERE ARE THINGS I NEED TO ASK YOU.
KLAK
GO AHEAD.
THE CONTENTS OF THE FILE PROFESSOR SHIKIMURA LEFT BEHIND--
HAVE YOU FIGURED OUT WHAT THEY ARE?
...OF COURSE.
AS
HAS HE, I SUSPECT--
--FUJIMARU-KUN!

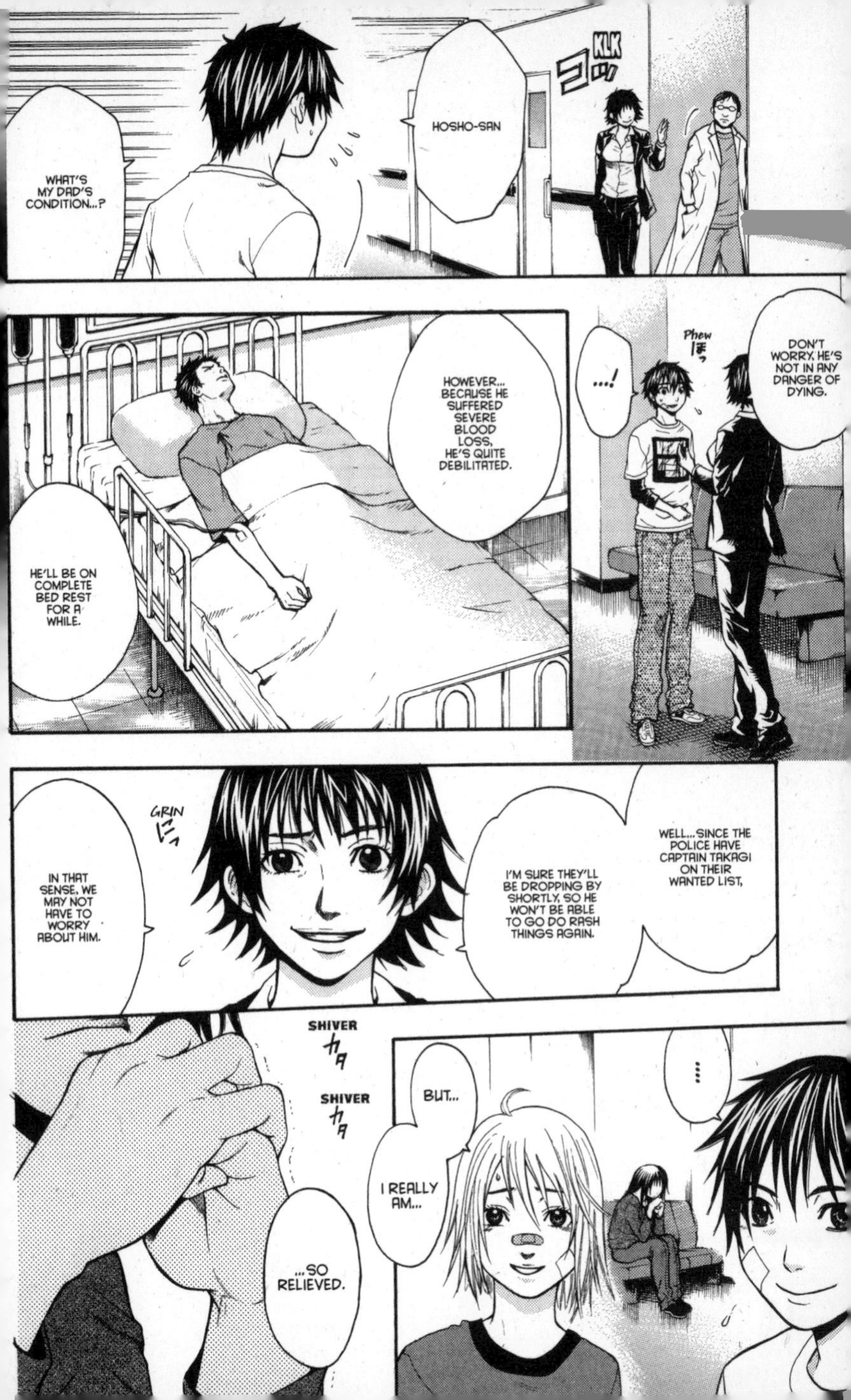
KLK
コッ
HOSHO-SAN
WHAT'S MY DAD'S CONDITION...?
DON'T WORRY. HE'S NOT IN ANY DANGER OF DYING.
Phew
ほっ
...!
HOWEVER... BECAUSE HE SUFFERED SEVERE BLOOD LOSS, HE'S QUITE DEBILITATED.
HE'LL BE ON COMPLETE BED REST FOR A WHILE.
WELL... SINCE THE POLICE HAVE CAPTAIN TAKAGI ON THEIR WANTED LIST,
I'M SURE THEY'LL BE DROPPING BY SHORTLY, SO HE WON'T BE ABLE TO GO DO RASH THINGS AGAIN.
GRIN
にっ
IN THAT SENSE, WE MAY NOT HAVE TO WORRY ABOUT HIM.
....
BUT...
I REALLY AM...
SHIVER
カタ
SHIVER
カタ
...SO RELIEVED.

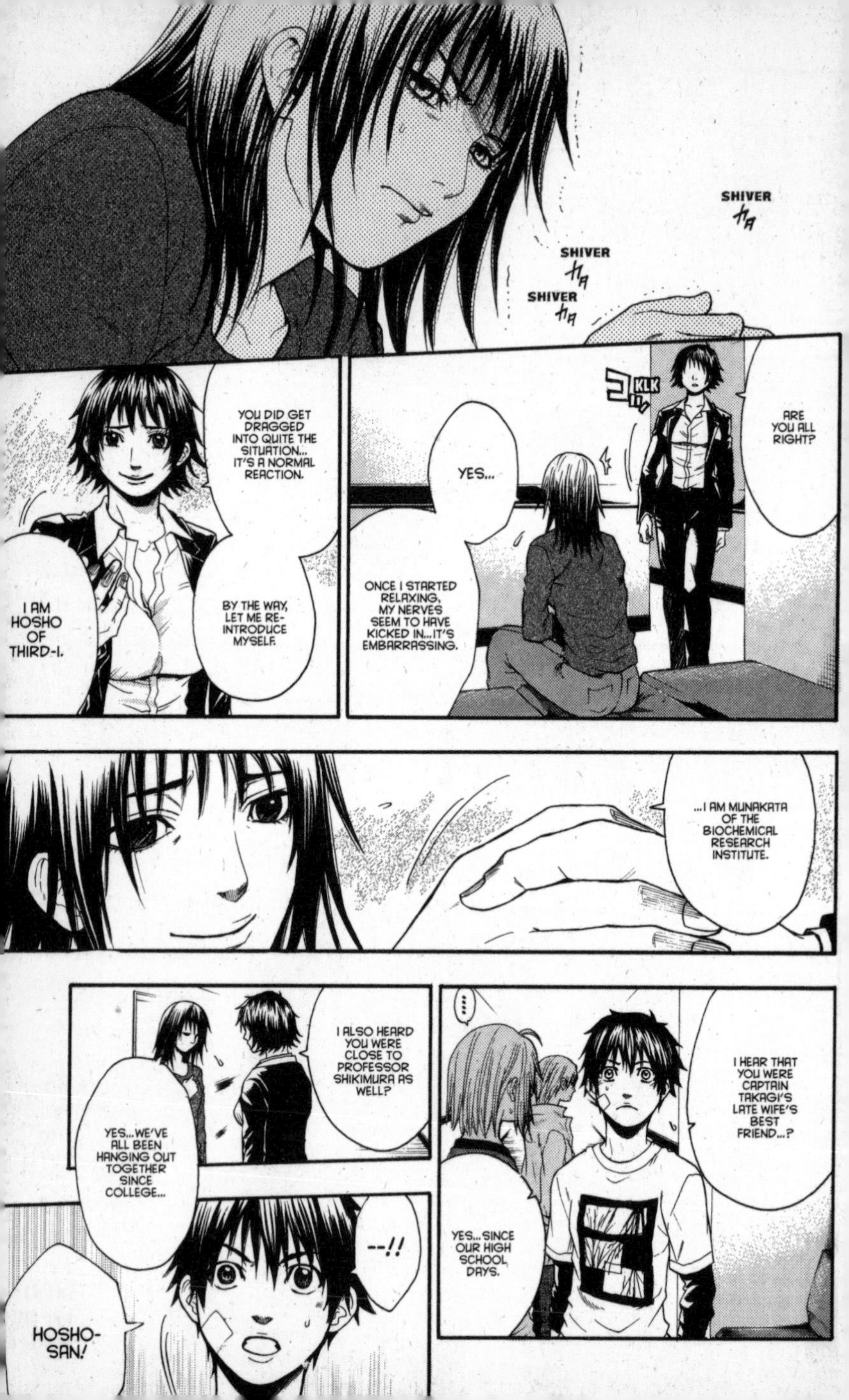
SHIVER
SHIVER
SHIVER
KLK
ARE YOU ALL RIGHT?
YES...
ONCE I STARTED RELAXING, MY NERVES SEEM TO HAVE KICKED IN...IT'S EMBARRASSING.
YOU DID GET DRAGGED INTO QUITE THE SITUATION... IT'S A NORMAL REACTION.
BY THE WAY, LET ME RE-INTRODUCE MYSELF.
I AM HOSHO OF THIRD-I.
...I AM MUNAKATA OF THE BIOCHEMICAL RESEARCH INSTITUTE.
....
I HEAR THAT YOU WERE CAPTAIN TAKAGI'S LATE WIFE'S BEST FRIEND...?
YES... SINCE OUR HIGH SCHOOL DAYS.
I ALSO HEARD YOU WERE CLOSE TO PROFESSOR SHIKIMURA AS WELL?
YES...WE'VE ALL BEEN HANGING OUT TOGETHER SINCE COLLEGE...
--!!
HOSHO-SAN!

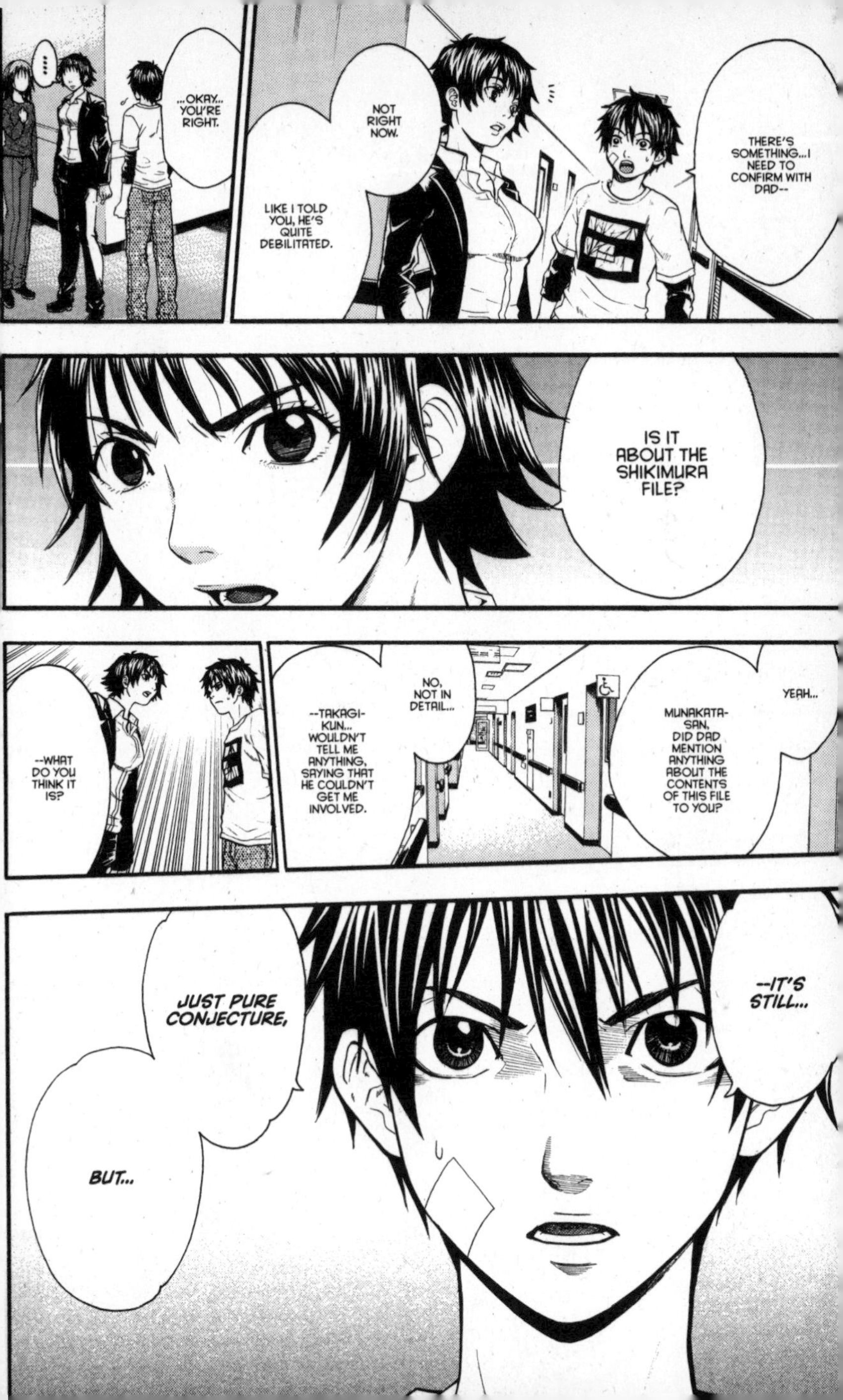
THERE'S SOMETHING...I NEED TO CONFIRM WITH DAD--
NOT RIGHT NOW.
LIKE I TOLD YOU, HE'S QUITE DEBILITATED.
...
...OKAY... YOU'RE RIGHT.
IS IT ABOUT THE SHIKIMURA FILE?
YEAH...
MUNAKATA-SAN, DID DAD MENTION ANYTHING ABOUT THE CONTENTS OF THIS FILE TO YOU?
NO, NOT IN DETAIL...
--TAKAGI-KUN... WOULDN'T TELL ME ANYTHING, SAYING THAT HE COULDN'T GET ME INVOLVED.
--WHAT DO YOU THINK IT IS?
--IT'S STILL...
JUST PURE CONJECTURE,
BUT...

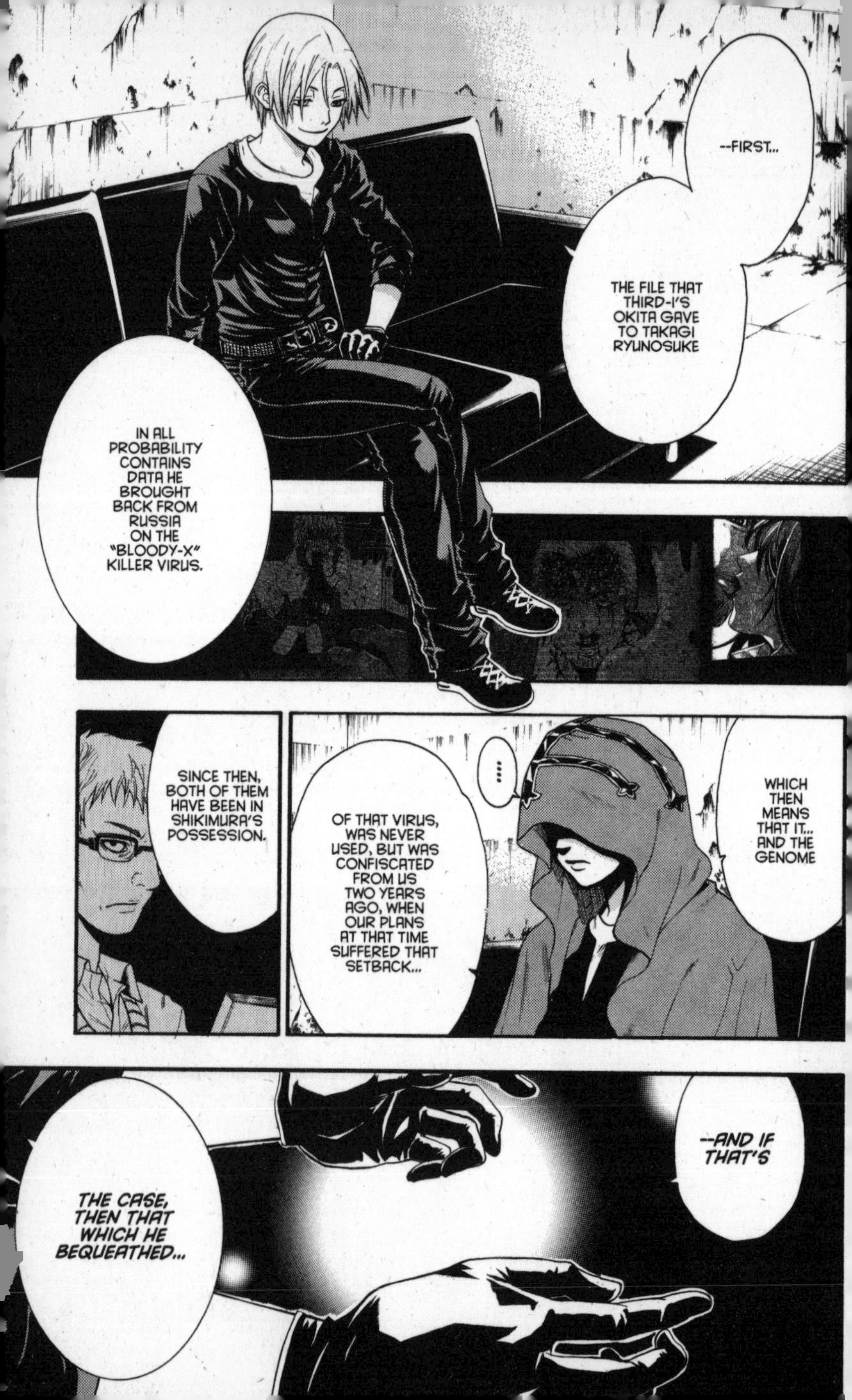
--FIRST...
THE FILE THAT THIRD-I'S OKITA GAVE TO TAKAGI RYUNOSUKE
IN ALL PROBABILITY CONTAINS DATA HE BROUGHT BACK FROM RUSSIA ON THE "BLOODY-X" KILLER VIRUS.
WHICH THEN MEANS THAT IT... AND THE GENOME
....
OF THAT VIRUS, WAS NEVER USED, BUT WAS CONFISCATED FROM US TWO YEARS AGO, WHEN OUR PLANS AT THAT TIME SUFFERED THAT SETBACK...
SINCE THEN, BOTH OF THEM HAVE BEEN IN SHIKIMURA'S POSSESSION.
--AND IF THAT'S
THE CASE, THEN THAT WHICH HE BEQUEATHED...

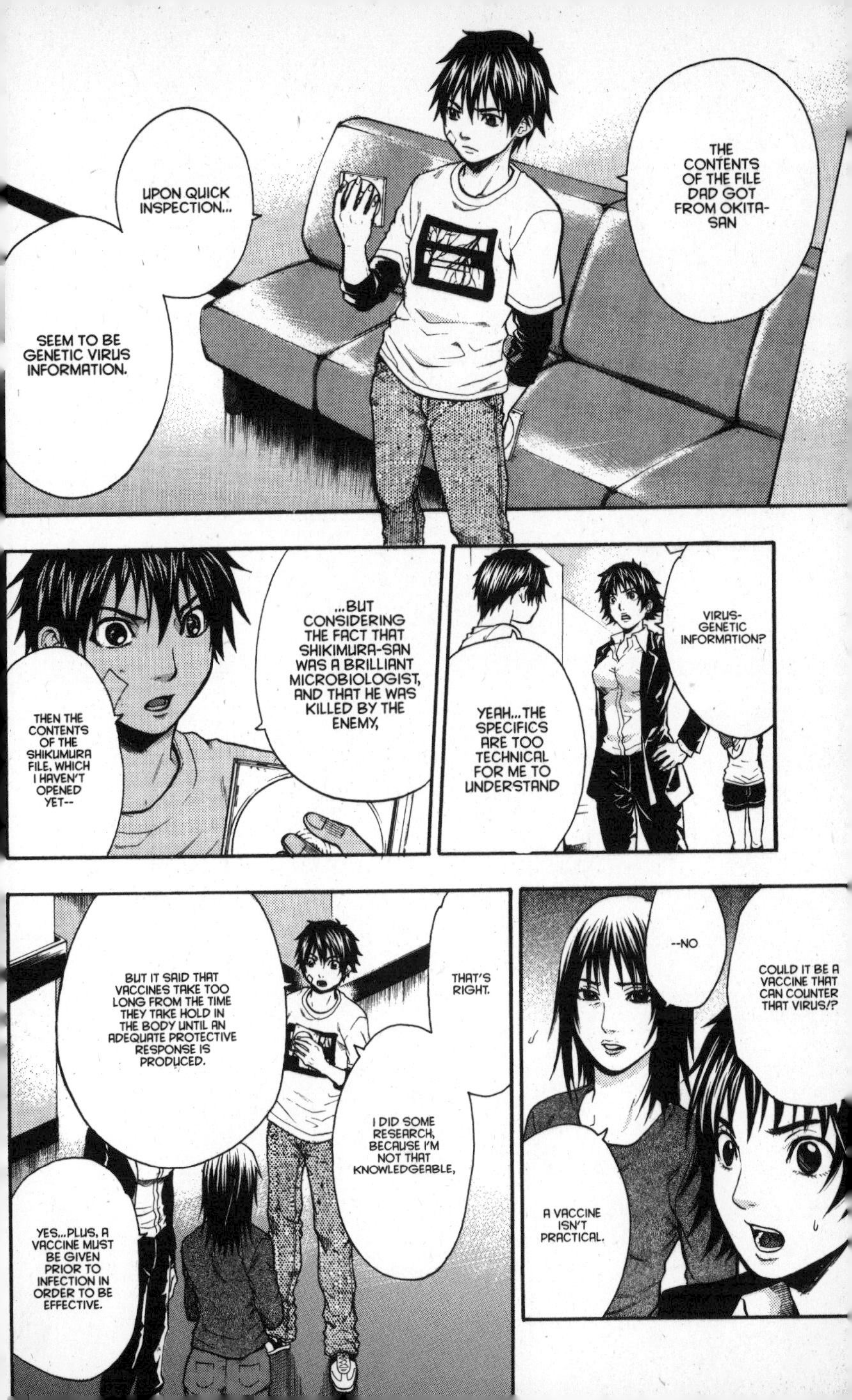
THE CONTENTS OF THE FILE DAD GOT FROM OKITA-SAN
UPON QUICK INSPECTION...
SEEM TO BE GENETIC VIRUS INFORMATION.
VIRUS-GENETIC INFORMATION?
YEAH...THE SPECIFICS ARE TOO TECHNICAL FOR ME TO UNDERSTAND
...BUT CONSIDERING THE FACT THAT SHIKIMURA-SAN WAS A BRILLIANT MICROBIOLOGIST, AND THAT HE WAS KILLED BY THE ENEMY,
THEN THE CONTENTS OF THE SHIKUMURA FILE, WHICH I HAVEN'T OPENED YET--
COULD IT BE A VACCINE THAT CAN COUNTER THAT VIRUS!?
--NO
A VACCINE ISN'T PRACTICAL.
THAT'S RIGHT.
I DID SOME RESEARCH, BECAUSE I'M NOT THAT KNOWLEDGEABLE,
BUT IT SAID THAT VACCINES TAKE TOO LONG FROM THE TIME THEY TAKE HOLD IN THE BODY UNTIL AN ADEQUATE PROTECTIVE RESPONSE IS PRODUCED.
YES...PLUS, A VACCINE MUST BE GIVEN PRIOR TO INFECTION IN ORDER TO BE EFFECTIVE.

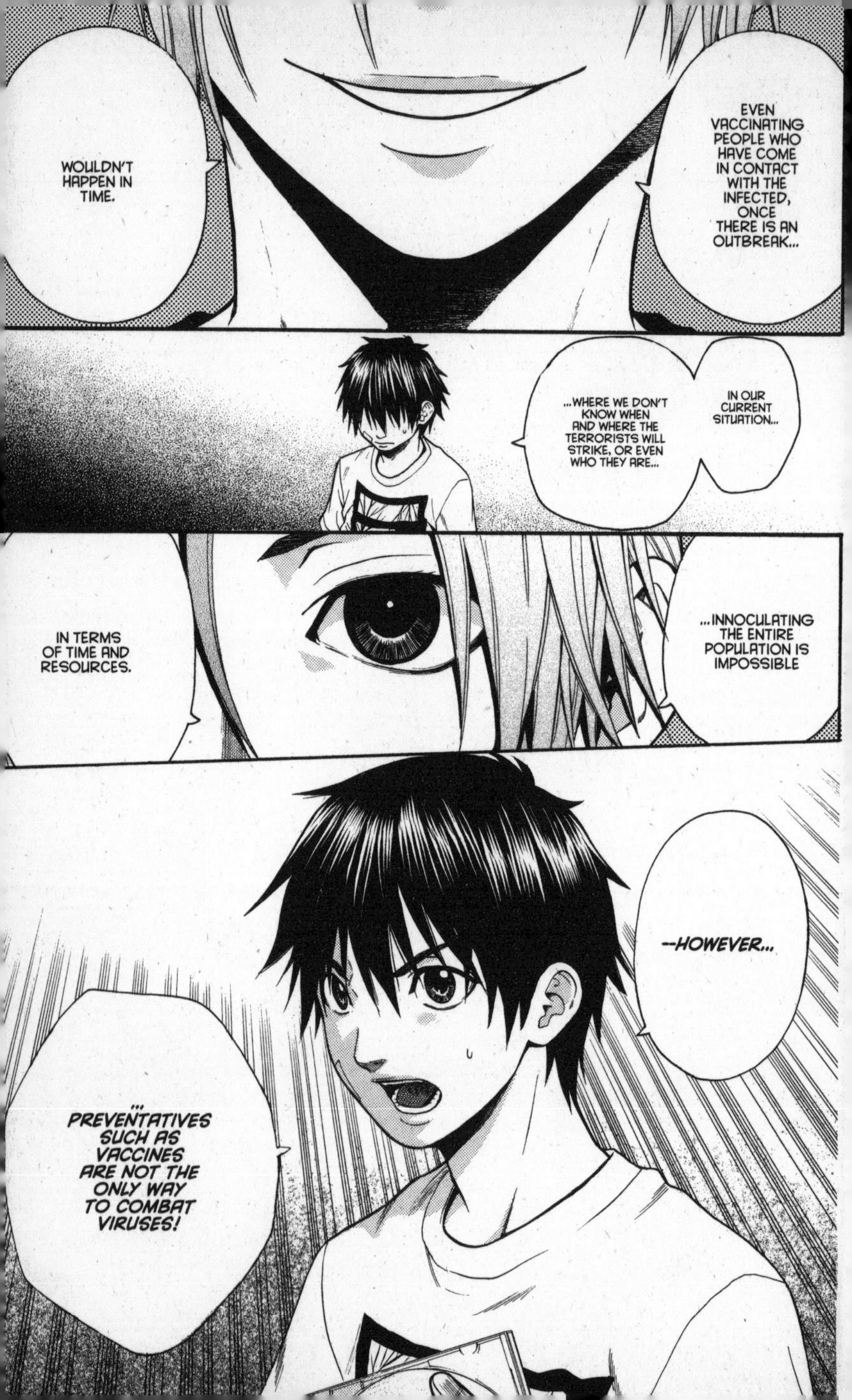
EVEN VACCINATING PEOPLE WHO HAVE COME IN CONTACT WITH THE INFECTED, ONCE THERE IS AN OUTBREAK...
WOULDN'T HAPPEN IN TIME.
IN OUR CURRENT SITUATION...
...WHERE WE DON'T KNOW WHEN AND WHERE THE TERRORISTS WILL STRIKE, OR EVEN WHO THEY ARE...
...INNOCULATING THE ENTIRE POPULATION IS IMPOSSIBLE
IN TERMS OF TIME AND RESOURCES.
--HOWEVER...
...PREVENTATIVES SUCH AS VACCINES ARE NOT THE ONLY WAY TO COMBAT VIRUSES!

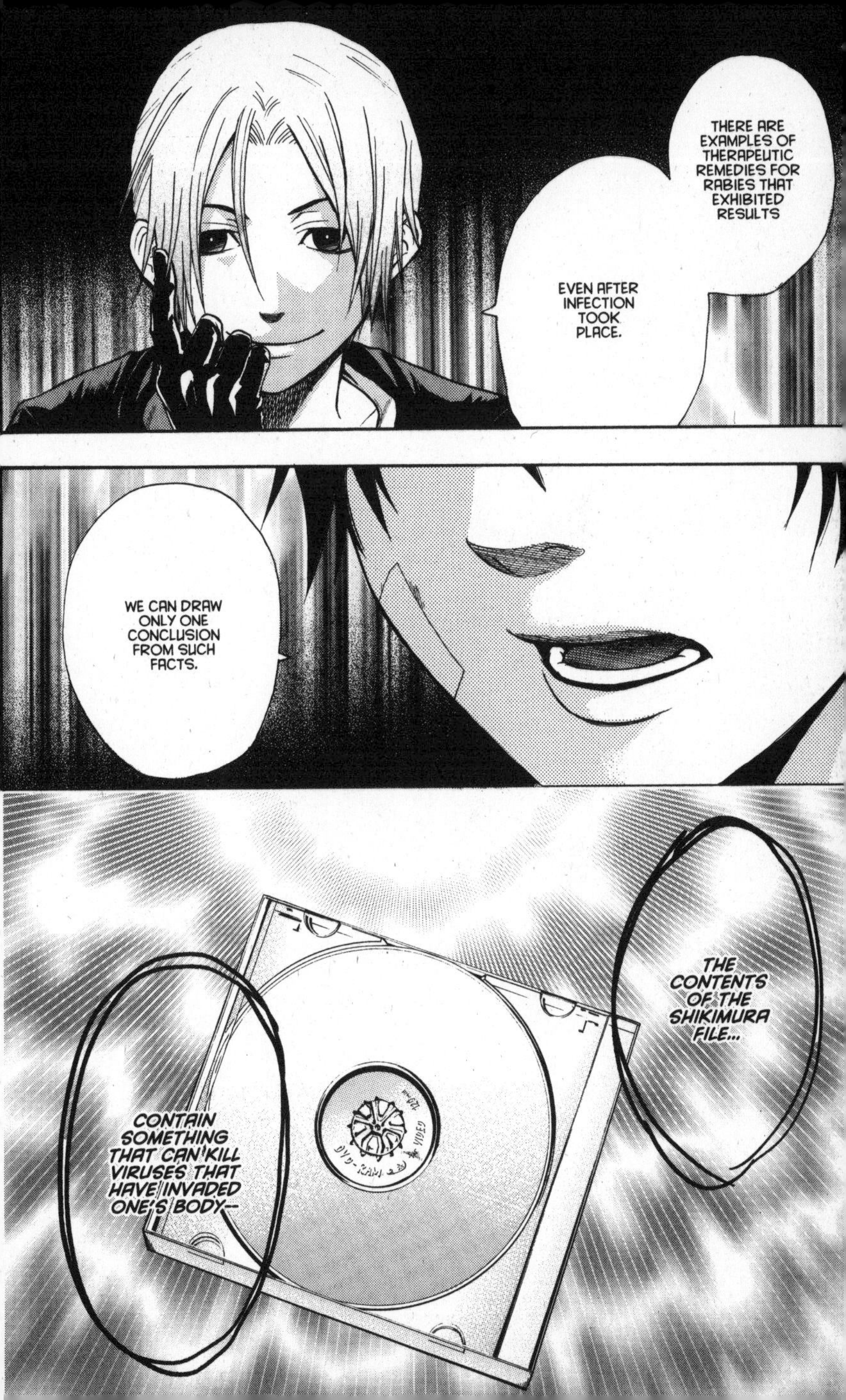
THERE ARE EXAMPLES OF THERAPEUTIC REMEDIES FOR RABIES THAT EXHIBITED RESULTS
EVEN AFTER INFECTION TOOK PLACE.
WE CAN DRAW ONLY ONE CONCLUSION FROM SUCH FACTS.
THE CONTENTS OF THE SHIKIMURA FILE...
CONTAIN SOMETHING THAT CAN KILL VIRUSES THAT HAVE INVADED ONE'S BODY--

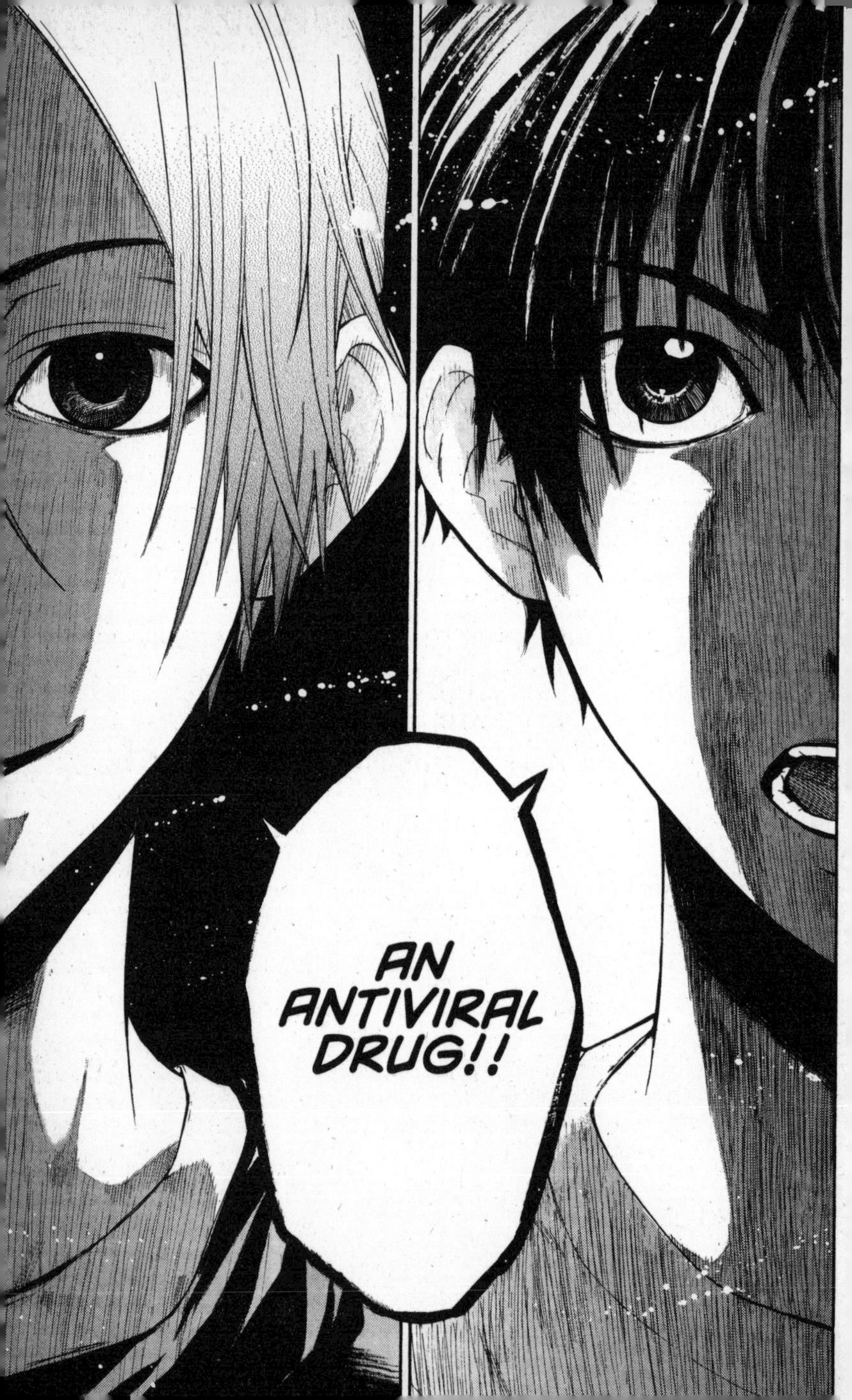
AN ANTIVIRAL DRUG!!

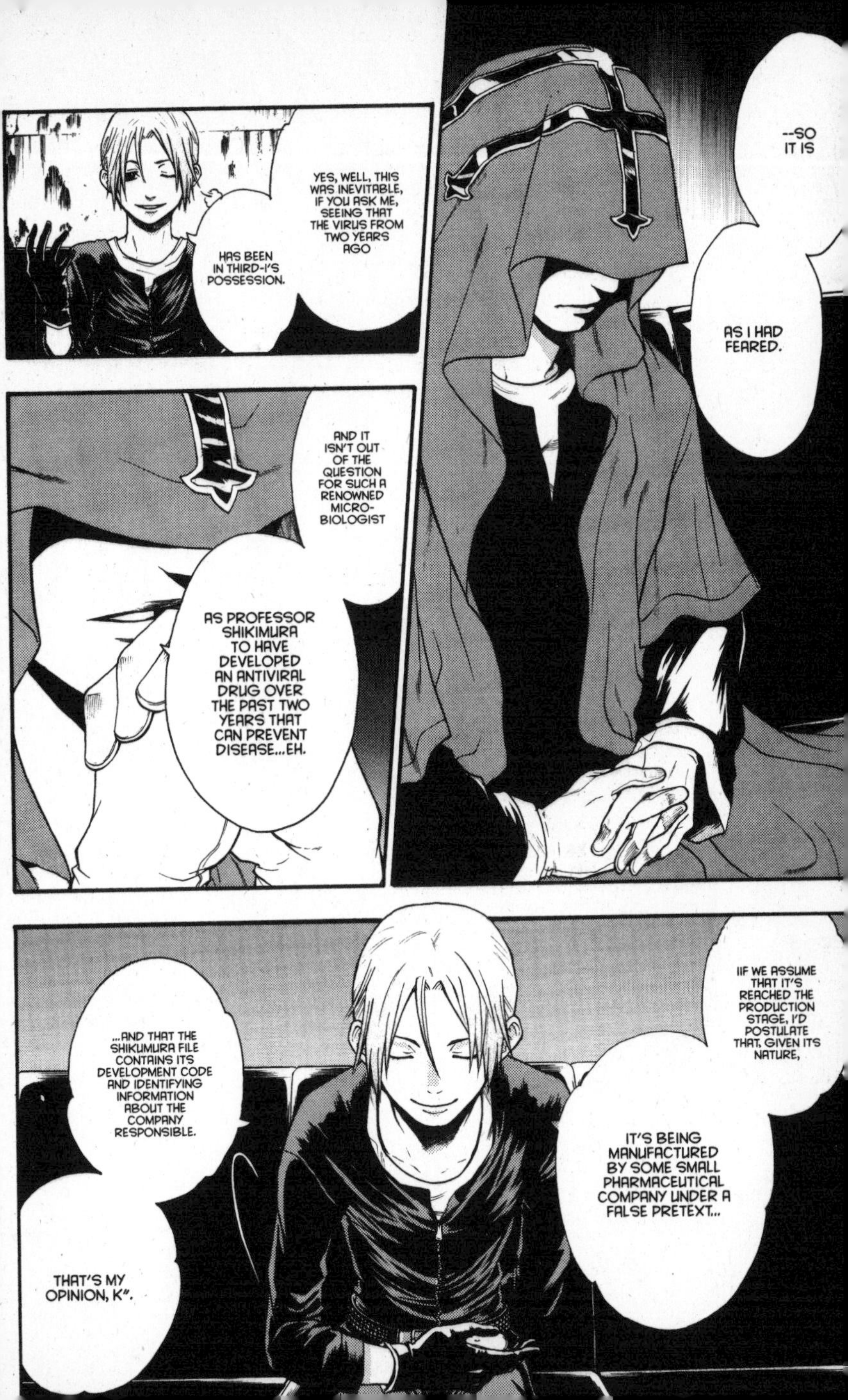
--SO IT IS
AS I HAD FEARED.
YES, WELL, THIS WAS INEVITABLE, IF YOU ASK ME, SEEING THAT THE VIRUS FROM TWO YEARS AGO
HAS BEEN IN THIRD-I'S POSSESSION.
AND IT ISN'T OUT OF THE QUESTION FOR SUCH A RENOWNED MICRO-BIOLOGIST
AS PROFESSOR SHIKIMURA TO HAVE DEVELOPED AN ANTIVIRAL DRUG OVER THE PAST TWO YEARS THAT CAN PREVENT DISEASE...EH.
IIF WE ASSUME THAT IT'S REACHED THE PRODUCTION STAGE, I'D POSTULATE THAT, GIVEN ITS NATURE,
IT'S BEING MANUFACTURED BY SOME SMALL PHARMACEUTICAL COMPANY UNDER A FALSE PRETEXT...
...AND THAT THE SHIKUMURA FILE CONTAINS ITS DEVELOPMENT CODE AND IDENTIFYING INFORMATION ABOUT THE COMPANY RESPONSIBLE.
THAT'S MY OPINION, K".

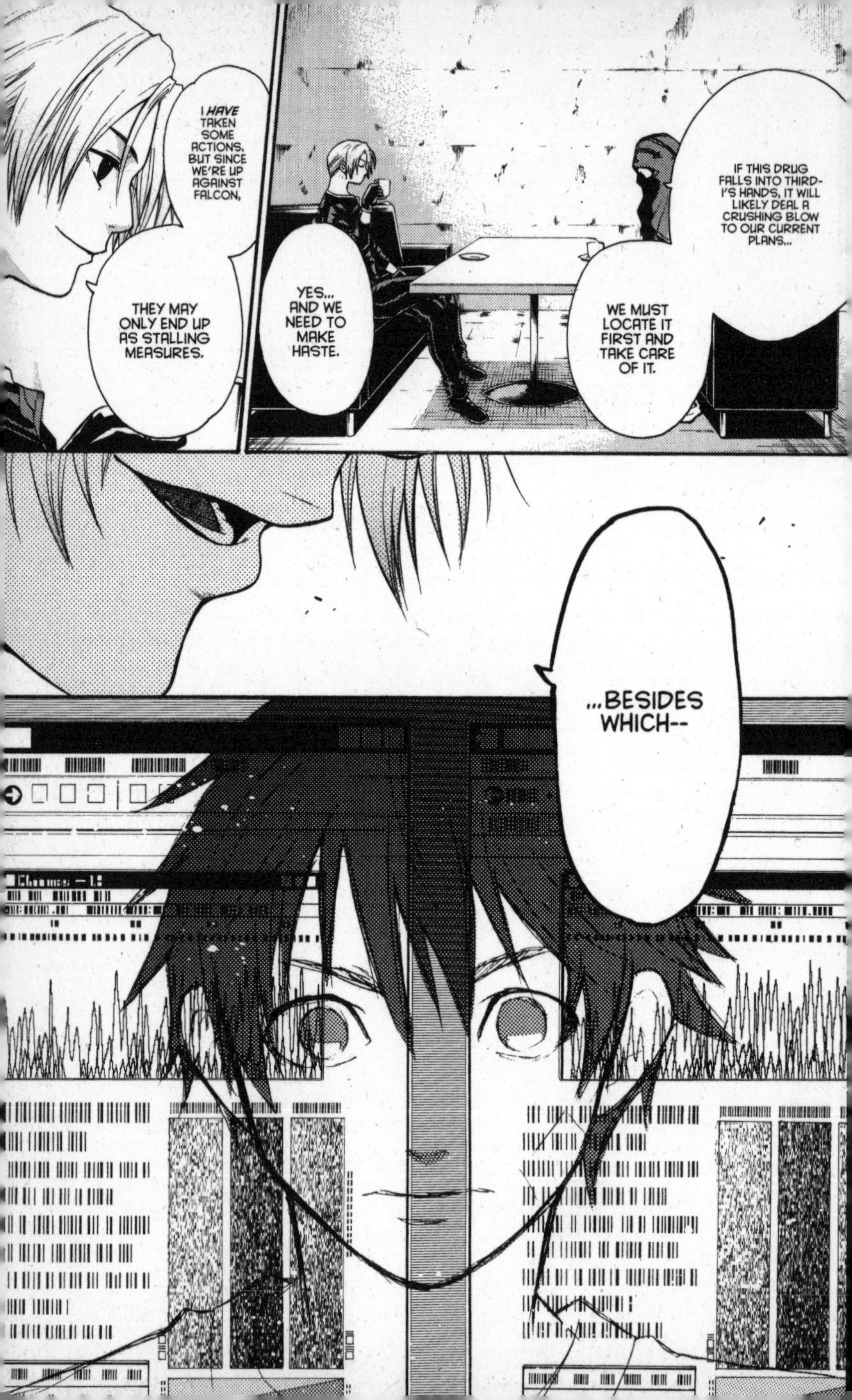
IF THIS DRUG FALLS INTO THIRD-I'S HANDS, IT WILL LIKELY DEAL A CRUSHING BLOW TO OUR CURRENT PLANS...
WE MUST LOCATE IT FIRST AND TAKE CARE OF IT.
YES... AND WE NEED TO MAKE HASTE.
I *HAVE* TAKEN SOME ACTIONS, BUT SINCE WE'RE UP AGAINST FALCON,
THEY MAY ONLY END UP AS STALLING MEASURES.
...BESIDES WHICH--

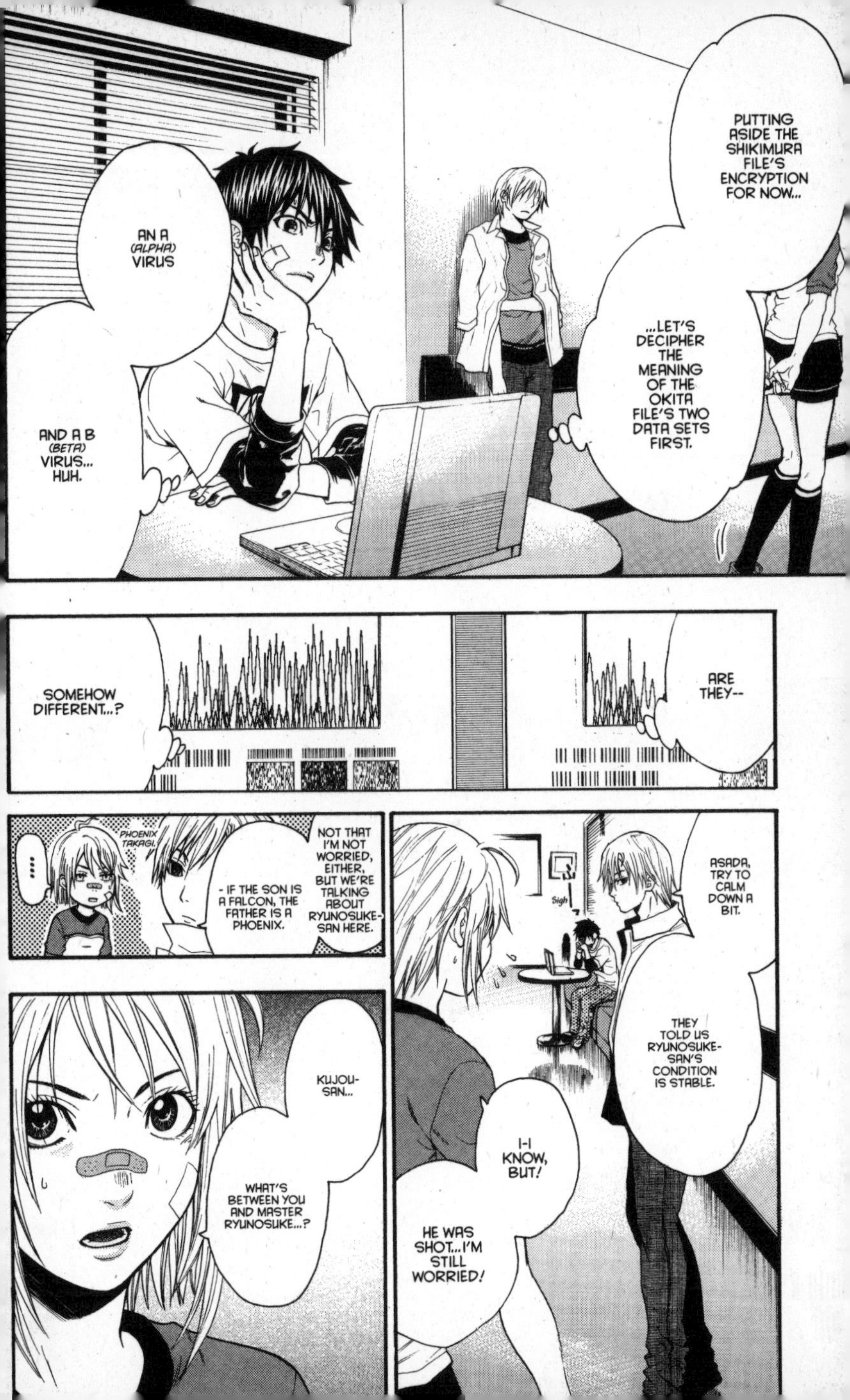
PUTTING ASIDE THE SHIKIMURA FILE'S ENCRYPTION FOR NOW...
...LET'S DECIPHER THE MEANING OF THE OKITA FILE'S TWO DATA SETS FIRST.
AN A (ALPHA) VIRUS
AND A B (BETA) VIRUS... HUH.
ARE THEY--
SOMEHOW DIFFERENT...?
ASADA, TRY TO CALM DOWN A BIT.
Sigh
THEY TOLD US RYUNOSUKE-SAN'S CONDITION IS STABLE.
I-I KNOW, BUT!
HE WAS SHOT... I'M STILL WORRIED!
NOT THAT I'M NOT WORRIED, EITHER, BUT WE'RE TALKING ABOUT RYUNOSUKE-SAN HERE.
- IF THE SON IS A FALCON, THE FATHER IS A PHOENIX.
PHOENIX TAKAGI.
....
KUJOU-SAN...
WHAT'S BETWEEN YOU AND MASTER RYUNOSUKE...?

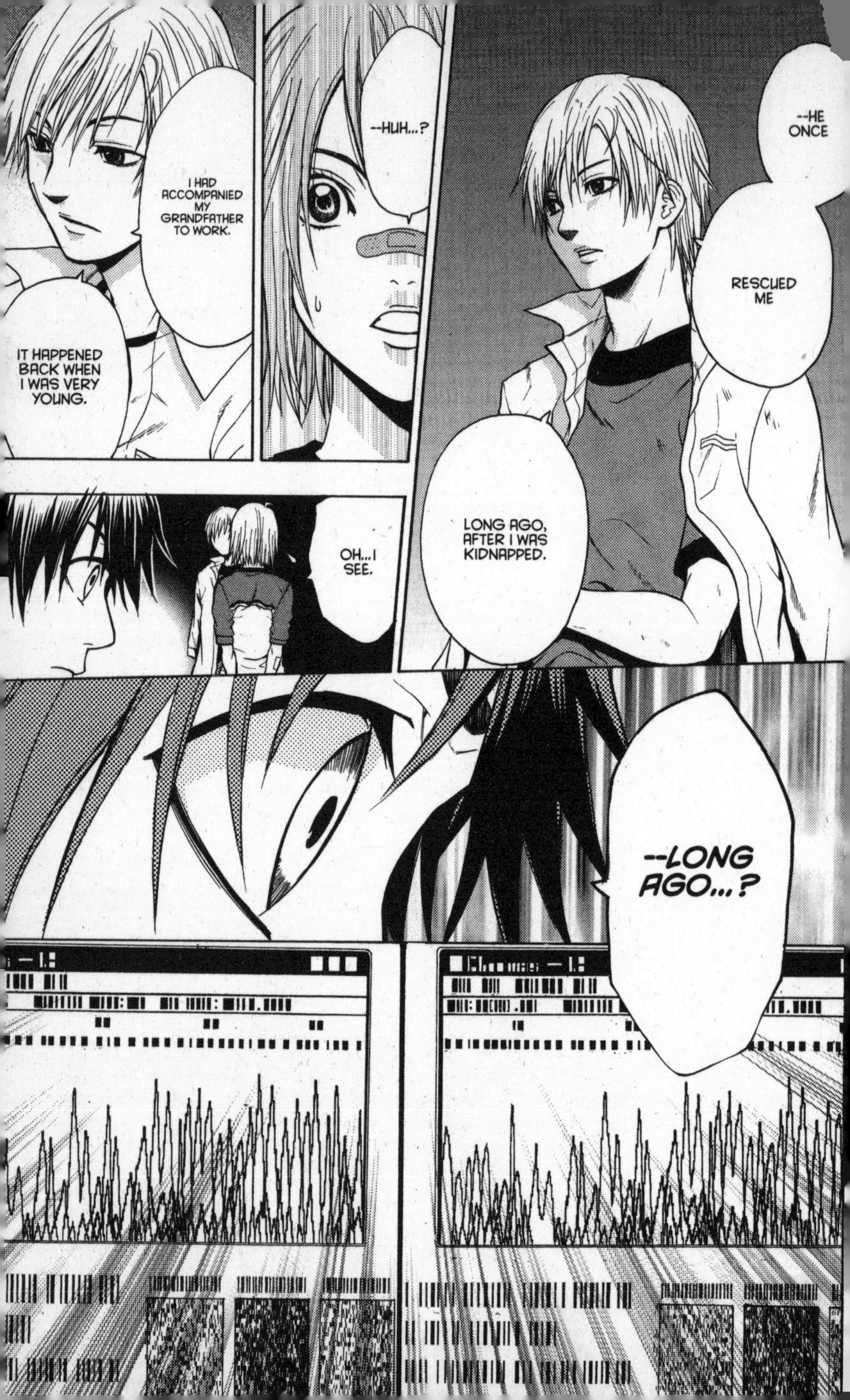
--HE ONCE
RESCUED ME
LONG AGO, AFTER I WAS KIDNAPPED.
--HUH...?
I HAD ACCOMPANIED MY GRANDFATHER TO WORK.
IT HAPPENED BACK WHEN I WAS VERY YOUNG.
OH...I SEE.
--LONG AGO...?

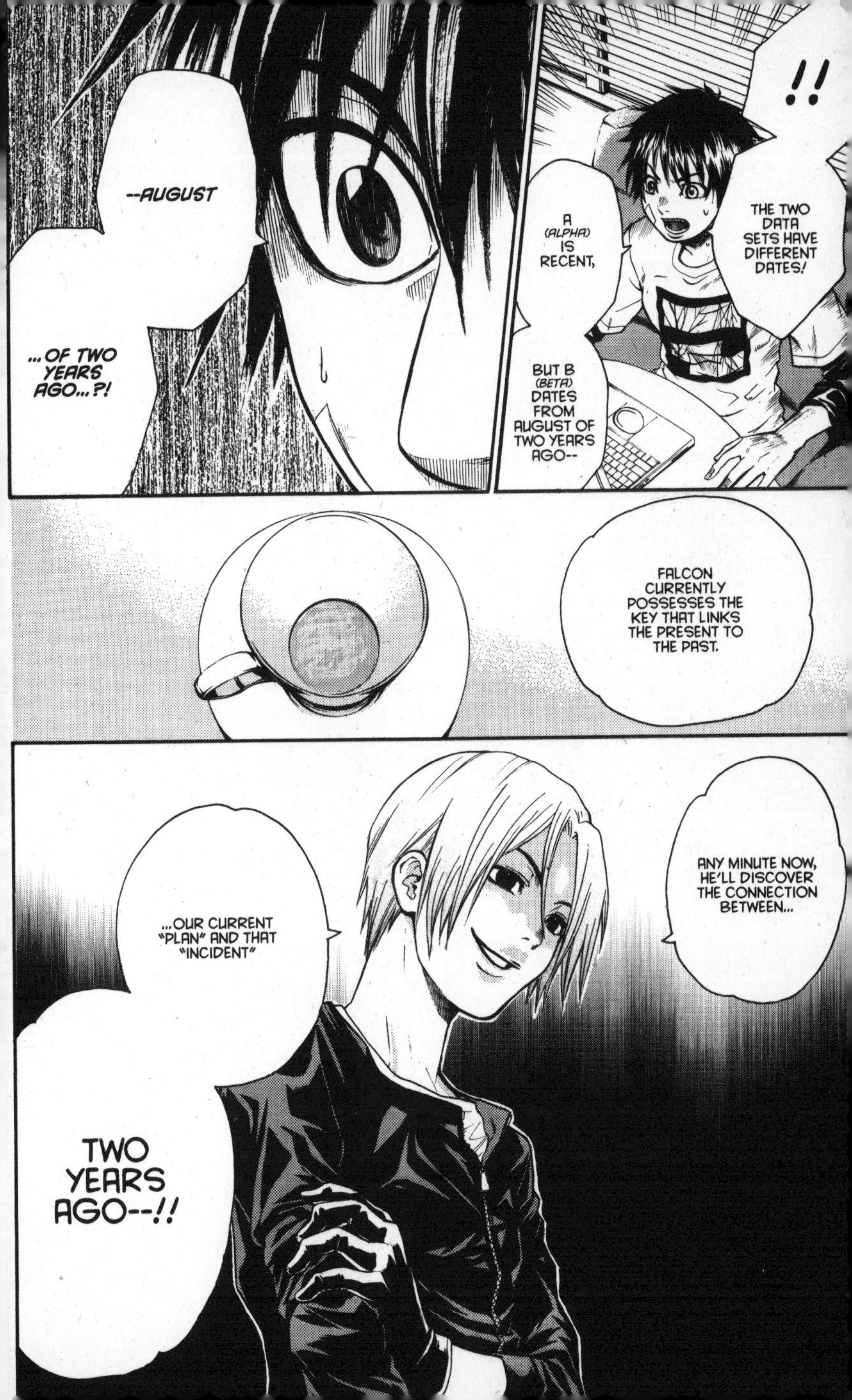
!!
THE TWO DATA SETS HAVE DIFFERENT DATES!
A (ALPHA) IS RECENT,
BUT B (BETA) DATES FROM AUGUST OF TWO YEARS AGO--
--AUGUST
...OF TWO YEARS AGO...?!
FALCON CURRENTLY POSSESSES THE KEY THAT LINKS THE PRESENT TO THE PAST.
ANY MINUTE NOW, HE'LL DISCOVER THE CONNECTION BETWEEN...
...OUR CURRENT "PLAN" AND THAT "INCIDENT"
TWO YEARS AGO--!!

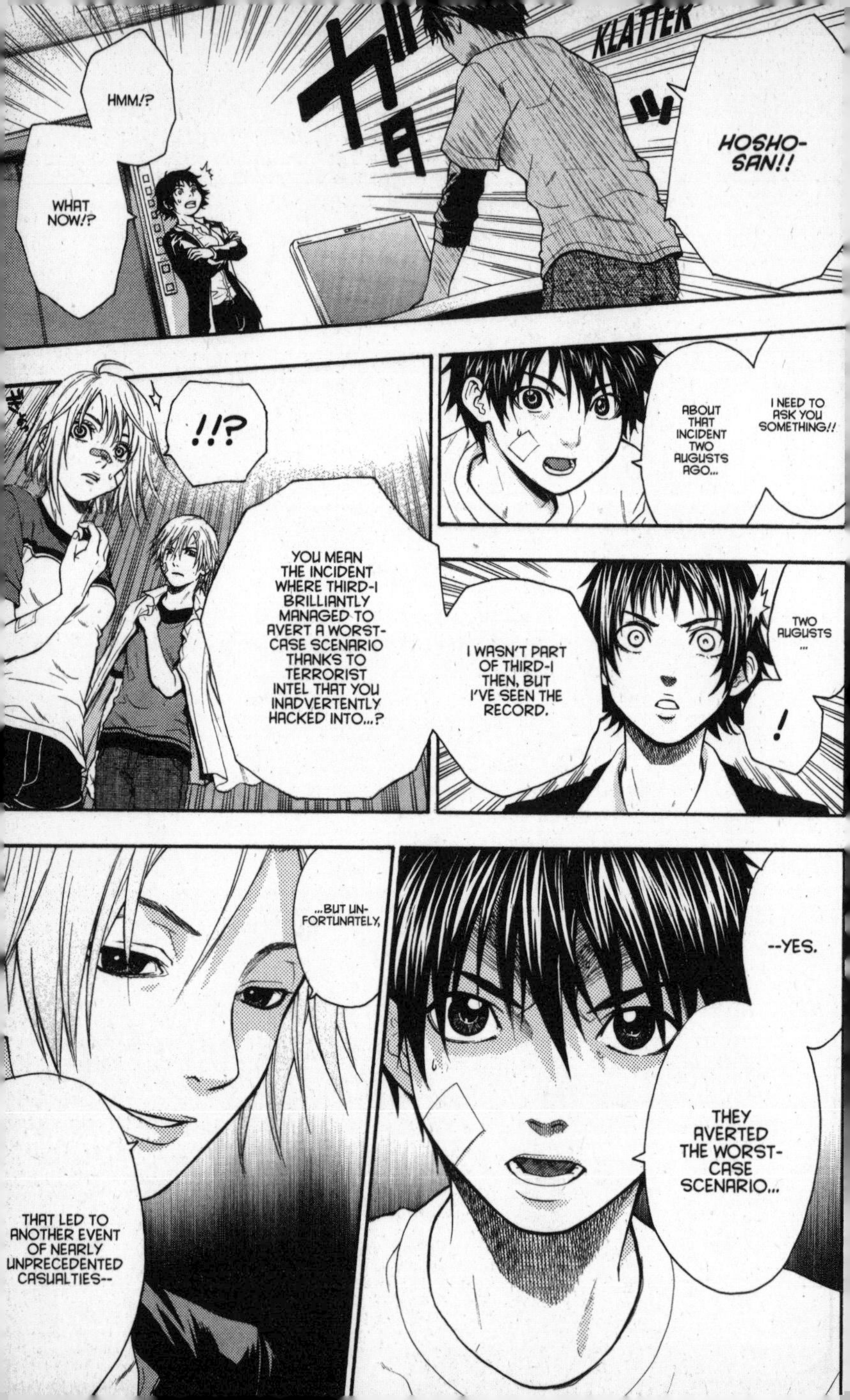
KLATTER
HOSHO-SAN!!
HMM!?
WHAT NOW!?
I NEED TO ASK YOU SOMETHING!!
ABOUT THAT INCIDENT TWO AUGUSTS AGO...
TWO AUGUSTS ...
!
I WASN'T PART OF THIRD-I THEN, BUT I'VE SEEN THE RECORD.
!!?
YOU MEAN THE INCIDENT WHERE THIRD-I BRILLIANTLY MANAGED TO AVERT A WORST-CASE SCENARIO THANKS TO TERRORIST INTEL THAT YOU INADVERTENTLY HACKED INTO...?
--YES.
THEY AVERTED THE WORST-CASE SCENARIO...
...BUT UN-FORTUNATELY,
THAT LED TO ANOTHER EVENT OF NEARLY UNPRECEDENTED CASUALTIES--

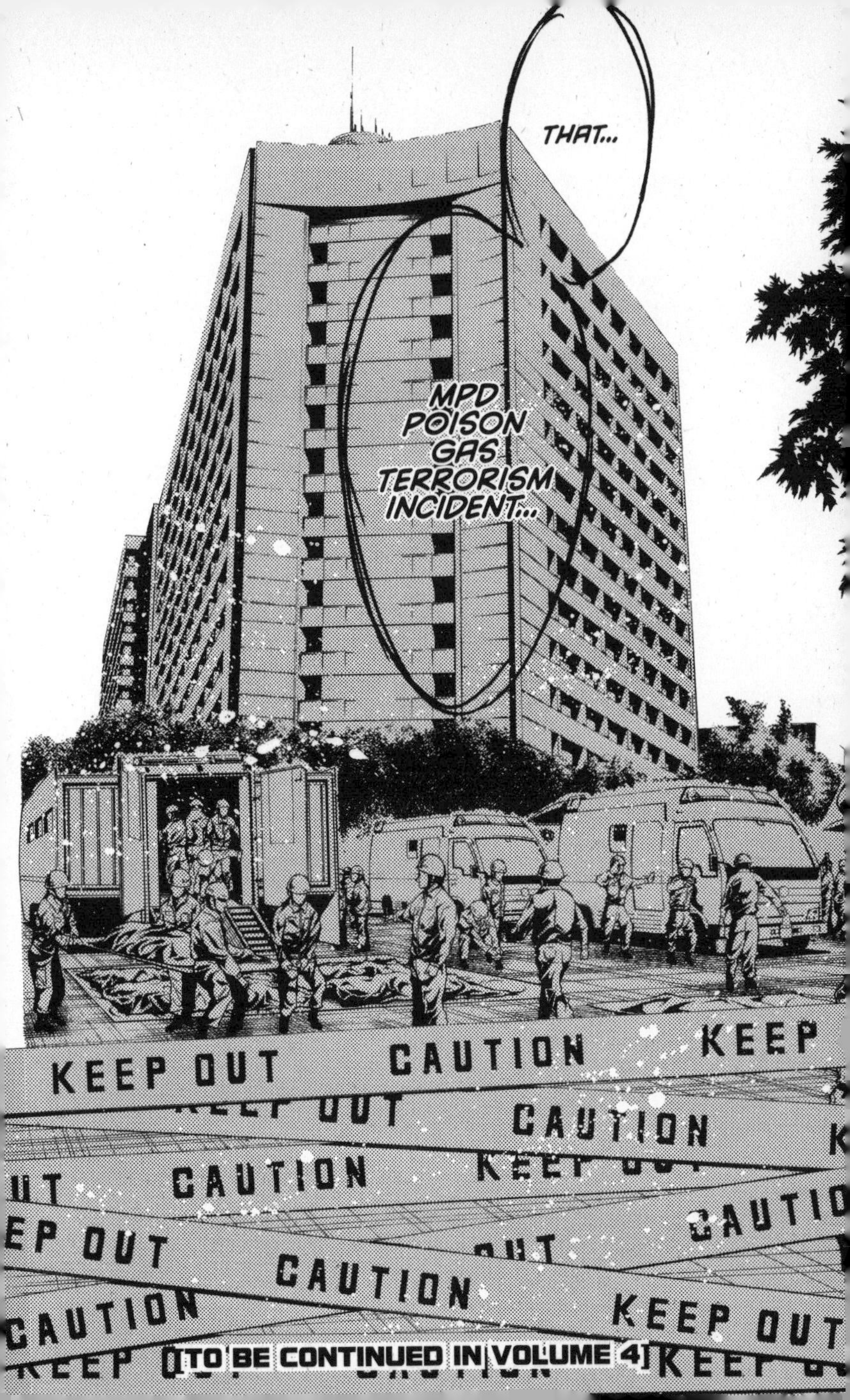
THAT...
MPD POISON GAS TERRORISM INCIDENT...
KEEP OUT
CAUTION
KEEP
CAUTION
CAUTION
CAUTION
KEEP OUT
[TO BE CONTINUED IN VOLUME 4]

BLOODY MONDAY 3

- **Many thanks**
  Daiwa Mitsu   Kawabata Kunihiro   Takeda Manabu   Mattsun

- **Editorial**
  Sugawara-san   Sato-san   Kawakubo-san   Nakata-san

- **Manga**
  Ryumon Ryou X Megumi Kouji

TRANSLATION NOTES

Japanese is a tricky language for most Westerners, and translation is often more art than science. For your edification and reading pleasure, here are notes on some of the places where we could have gone in a different direction with our translation of the work, or where a Japanese cultural reference is used.

Kakubaku (Internet slang), inside cover

Japanese people love their Internet slang just as much as Americans. (笑), or (*Shô*), means "laugh" and is the Japanese equivalent of "LOL". (爆笑), or (*bakushô*), means "explosive laughter", and (核爆), or (*kaku-baku*), means "nuclear explosive (laughter)".

Onigiri, inside cover

Onigiri are rice balls, usually wrapped in or with a rectangular piece of seaweed to provide a non-sticky surface to grip it with. They may or may not also contain one or more fillings such as pickled plum paste, bonito shavings, preserved kelp, shredded salmon, tuna salad, or shrimp tempura.

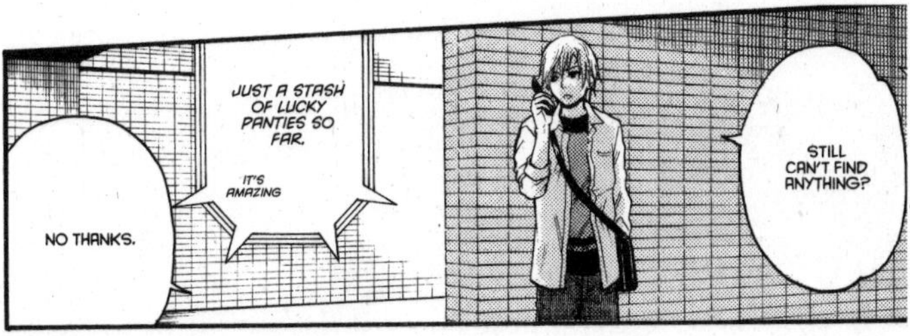
STILL CAN'T FIND ANYTHING?
JUST A STASH OF LUCKY PANTIES SO FAR.
IT'S AMAZING
NO THANKS.

Lucky panties, page 7

Underwear worn to bring luck or success, especially in the context of romantic conquest. If indeed set aside for special dates, they are usually colorful and sexy.

"Falcon", page 29

Fujimaru's alter ego and hacker name. A phonetic pun, derived from the first part of his last name "Takagi"… it is only phonetic because his name uses a different kanji than that of the "taka" that means "hawk" or "falcon".

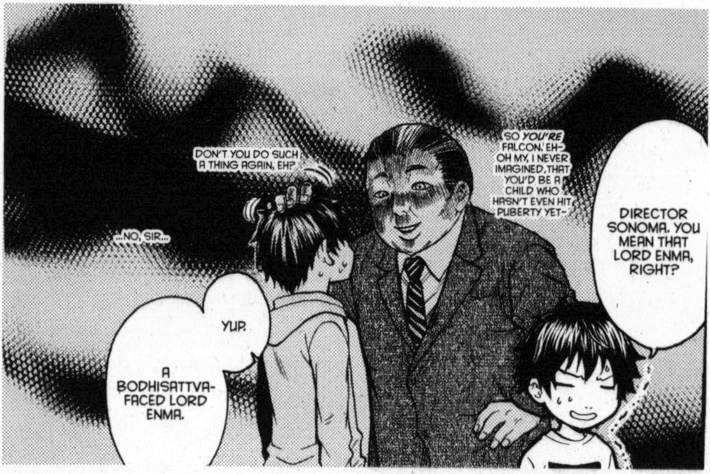

DIRECTOR SONOMA. YOU MEAN THAT LORD ENMA, RIGHT?
SO *YOU'RE* FALCON. EH~ OH MY, I NEVER IMAGINED, THAT YOU'D BE A CHILD WHO HASN'T EVEN HIT PUBERTY YET~
DON'T YOU DO SUCH A THING AGAIN, EH?
...NO, SIR...
YUP.
A BODHISATTVA-FACED LORD ENMA.

Lord Enma, page 61

Enma is the Japanese name for Yama, the Buddhist ruler of the underworld and judge of the dead. He is usually portrayed as a towering, scowling man with a red face, protruding eyes, and a black beard, wearing robes and a crown with the kanji for "king" written on it. He pops up in numerous anime and manga, sometimes as a satirical caricature, but here it is the nickname that THIRD-i members have given their fearsome Director Sonoma.

Bodhisattva-faced, page 61

Also called "Buddha-faced", but refers to someone with a gentle-looking face, often with a slight smile. In this case, Director Sonoma is referred to as a "bodhisattva-faced Lord Enma" because his fearsome demeanor is masked by his gentle-looking face.

"Anko", page 71

Fujimaru's nickname for Mako. It is derived from the first syllable of her last name (Anzai) and the last syllable of her first name (Mako), but Mako's objection is likely due to the fact that "anko" is also the Japanese word for "red bean paste".

PHS, page 90

EVEN THE LOW-POWER TRANSMISSION PHS SIGNAL IS OUT, BUT THE WIRELESS LAN IS UP AND RUNNING.

DOESN'T THAT SEEM A BIT WEIRD?

PHS stands for "Personal Handy-phone System", a short-range mobile network system whose units are basically cordless telephones. Initially nicknamed "Pitch", its onomatopoeia, by Japanese youth (especially girls), the moniker has since been picked up and adopted by mainstream society, including the cellular industry.

Daruma doll, page 117

Daruma dolls are round Japanese dolls said to be representations of Bodhidharma, the founder of Zen Buddhism. Typically red and a symbol of good luck and perseverance, they are usually sold without the eyes painted in, as one is supposed to color in the first eye upon setting a desired goal and the second after achieving it. In this case, Fujimaru is referring to the fact that Daruma dolls also lack ears and limbs, and thus could be considered helpless.

Oharai, page 163

Shito purification rituals whose purpose is to remove sin or uncleanliness, including disease, ill fortune, spirit possession, curses, baleful divinations, and blood-spilling. Locations, animals, and inanimate objects can also receive oharai, not just people.

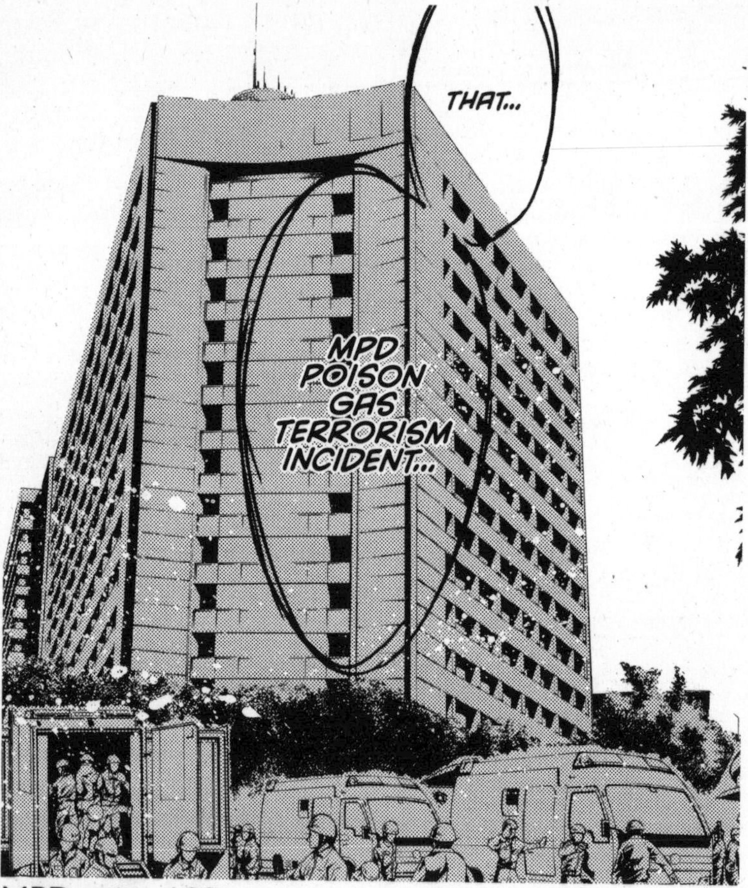
THAT...
MPD POISON GAS TERRORISM INCIDENT...

MPD, page 188

MPD is short for Metropolitan Police Department, the police force that serves the entire city of Tokyo and is the largest municipal law enforcement agency in the world.

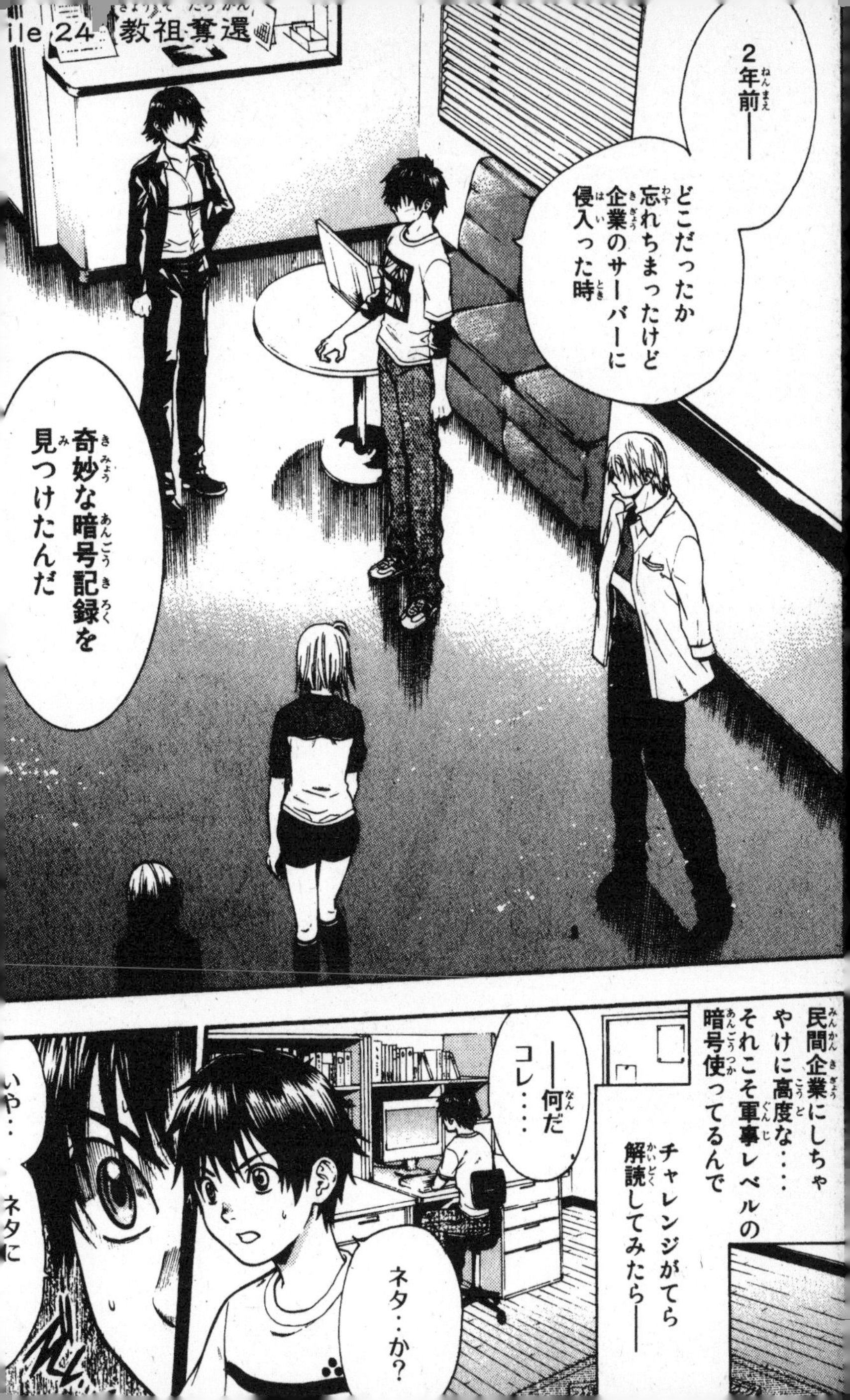
2年前——
どこだったか忘れちまったけど企業のサーバーに侵入った時
奇妙な暗号記録を見つけたんだ
民間企業にしちゃやけに高度な‥‥それこそ軍事レベルの暗号使ってるんで
チャレンジがてら解読してみたら——
——何だコレ‥‥
ネタ‥‥か？
いや‥ネタに

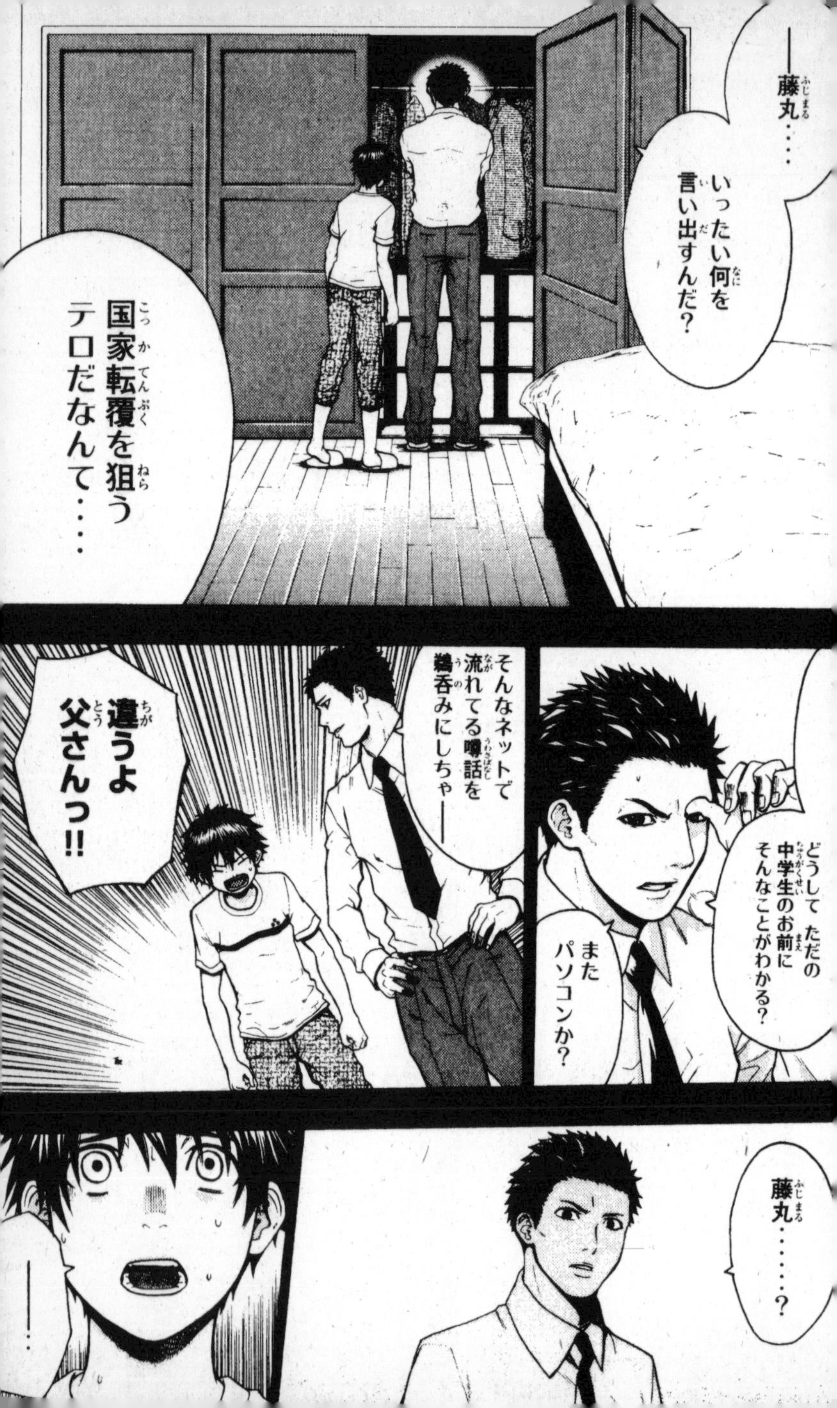
——藤丸・・・・
いったい何を言い出すんだ？
国家転覆を狙うテロだなんて・・・・
どうしてただの中学生のお前にそんなことがわかる？
またパソコンか？
そんなネットで流れてる噂話を鵜呑みにしちゃ——
違うよ父さんっ!!
藤丸・・・・・・？
——・・・

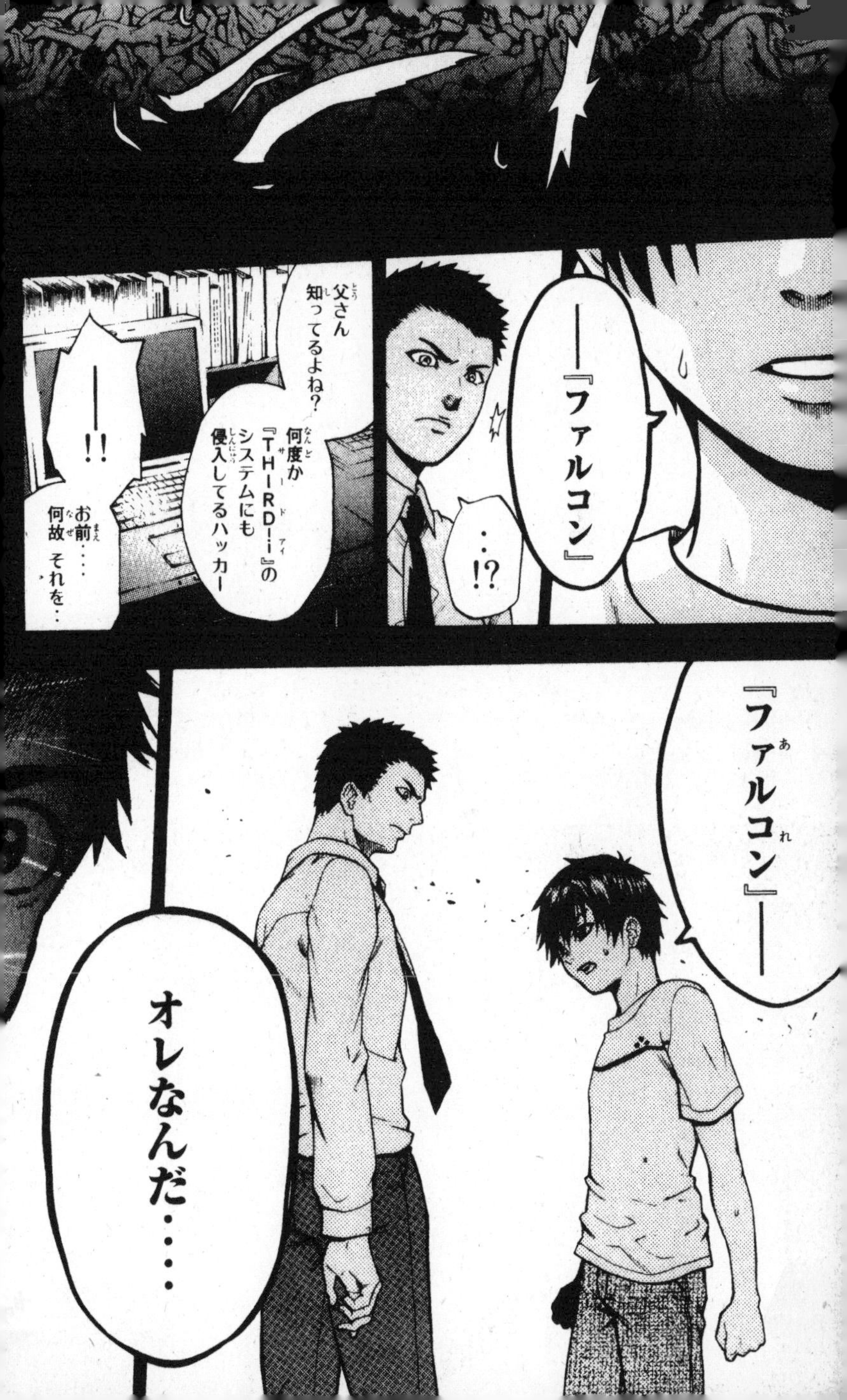
――『ファルコン』
・・・!?
父さん知ってるよね？何度か『THIRD-i』のシステムにも侵入してるハッカー
――!!
お前・・・・何故 それを・・
『ファルコン』――
オレなんだ・・・・

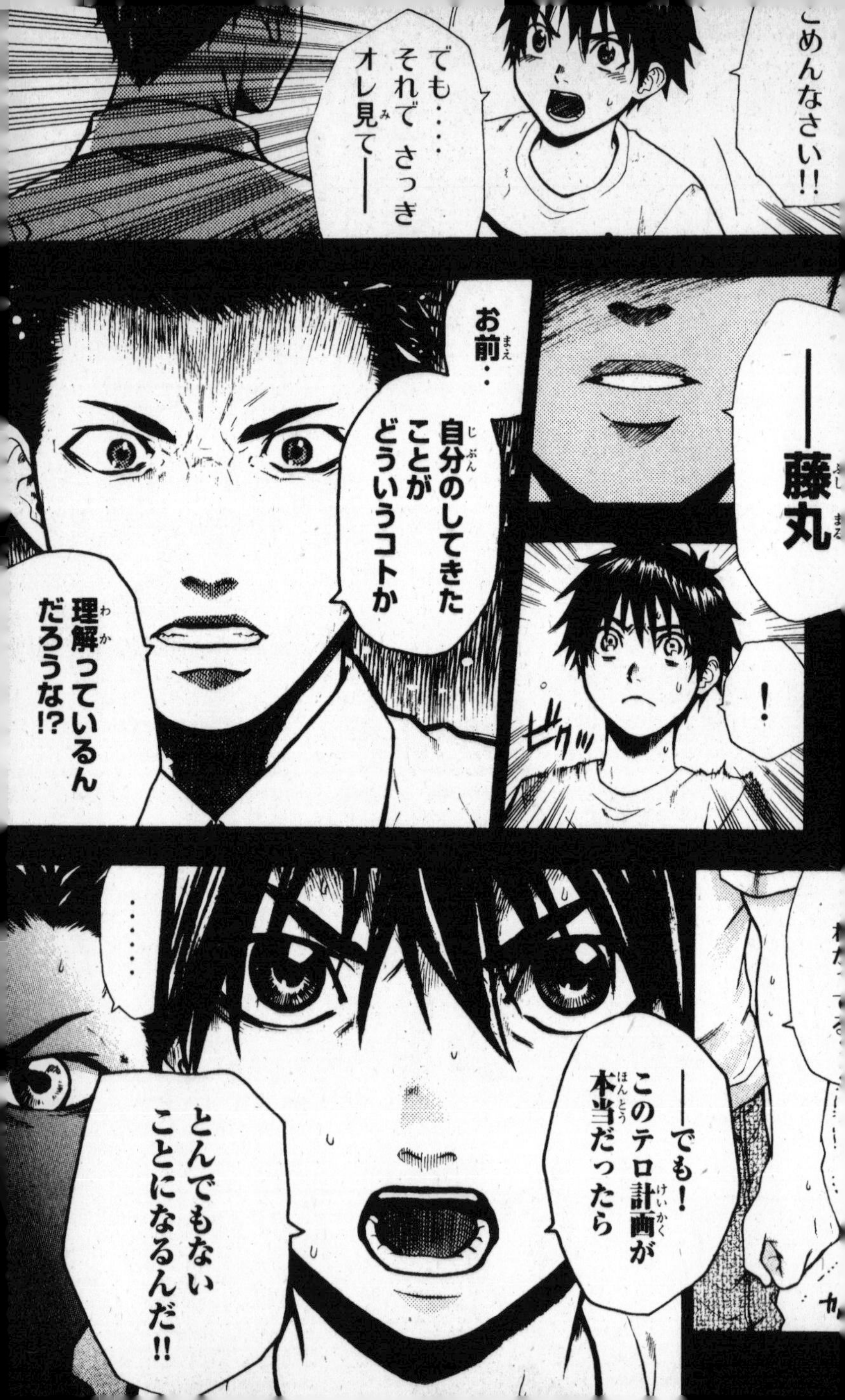
こめんなさい!!
でも・・・それで さっきオレ見て——
——藤丸
!
ビクッ
お前・・・
自分のしてきたことがどういうコトか
理解っているんだろうな!?
——でも!このテロ計画が本当だったら
とんでもないことになるんだ!!
……

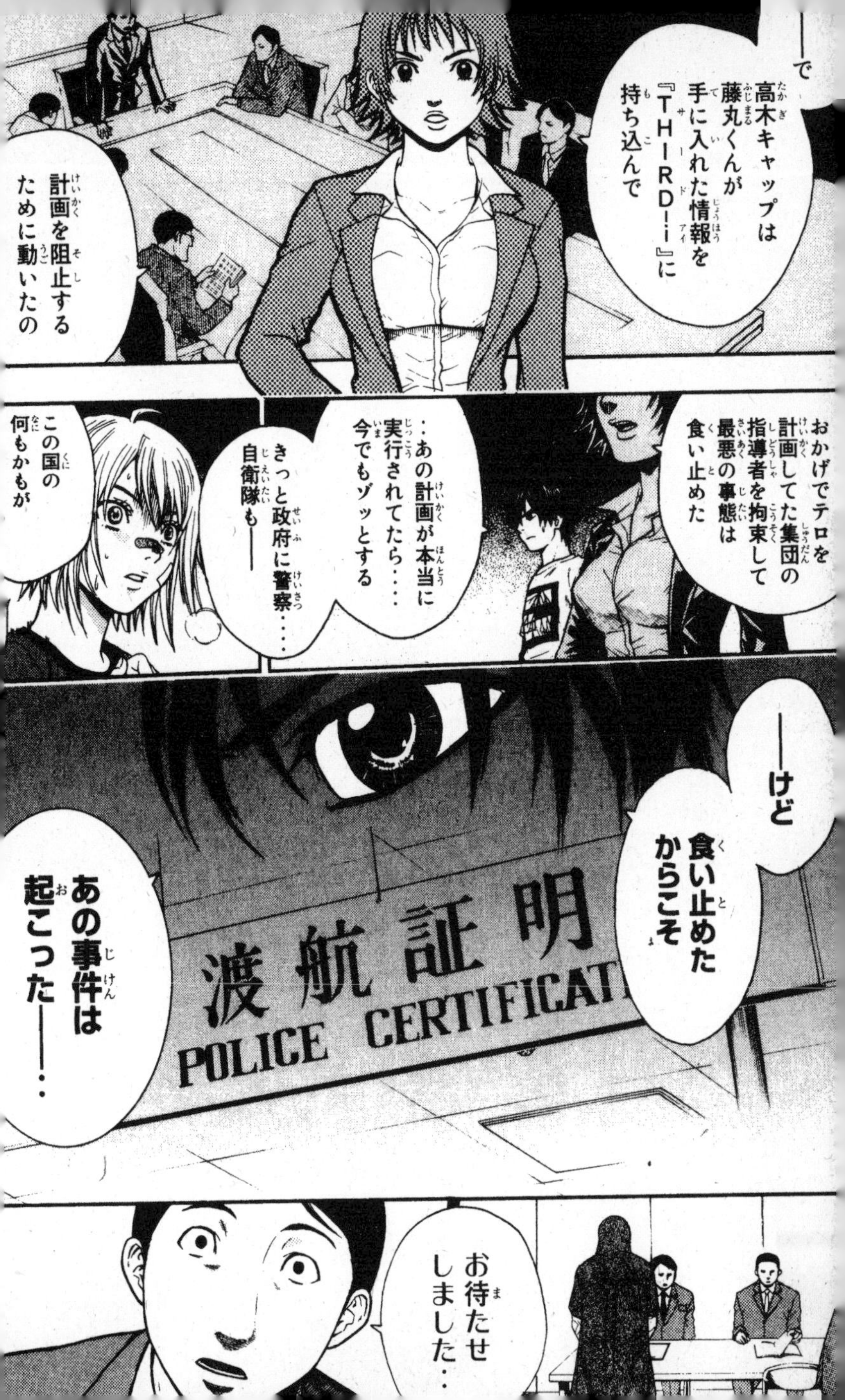
――で 高木キャップは 藤丸くんが 手に入れた情報を 『THIRD-i』に 持ち込んで
計画を阻止する ために動いたの
おかげでテロを 計画してた集団の 指導者を拘束して 最悪の事態は 食い止めた
…あの計画が本当に 実行されてたら…… 今でもゾッとする
きっと政府に警察…… 自衛隊も――
この国の 何もかもが
――けど
食い止めた からこそ
渡航証明
POLICE CERTIFICAT
あの事件は 起こった――……
お待たせ しました……

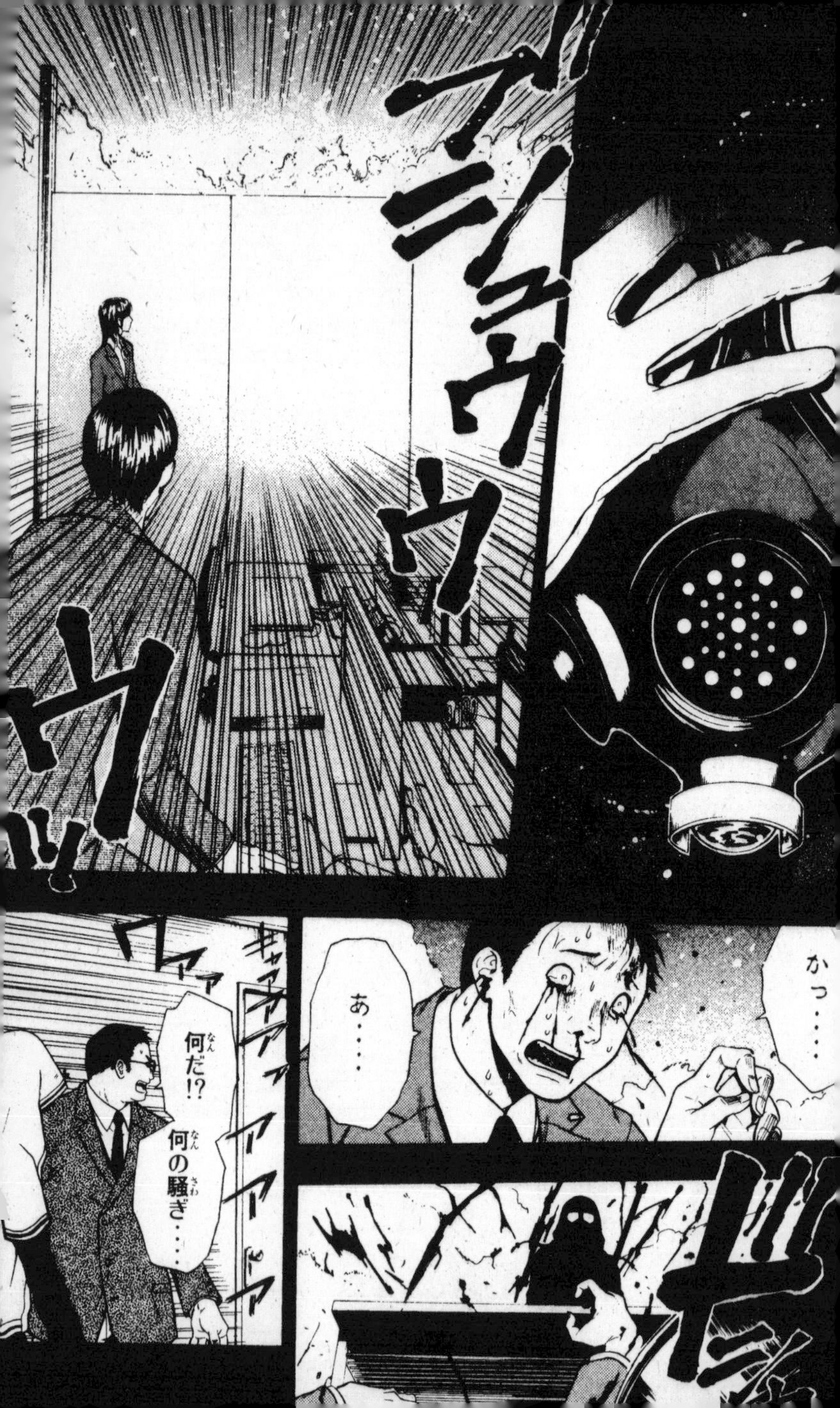
かつ・・・・
あ・・・・
何だ!?
何の騒ぎ・・・・

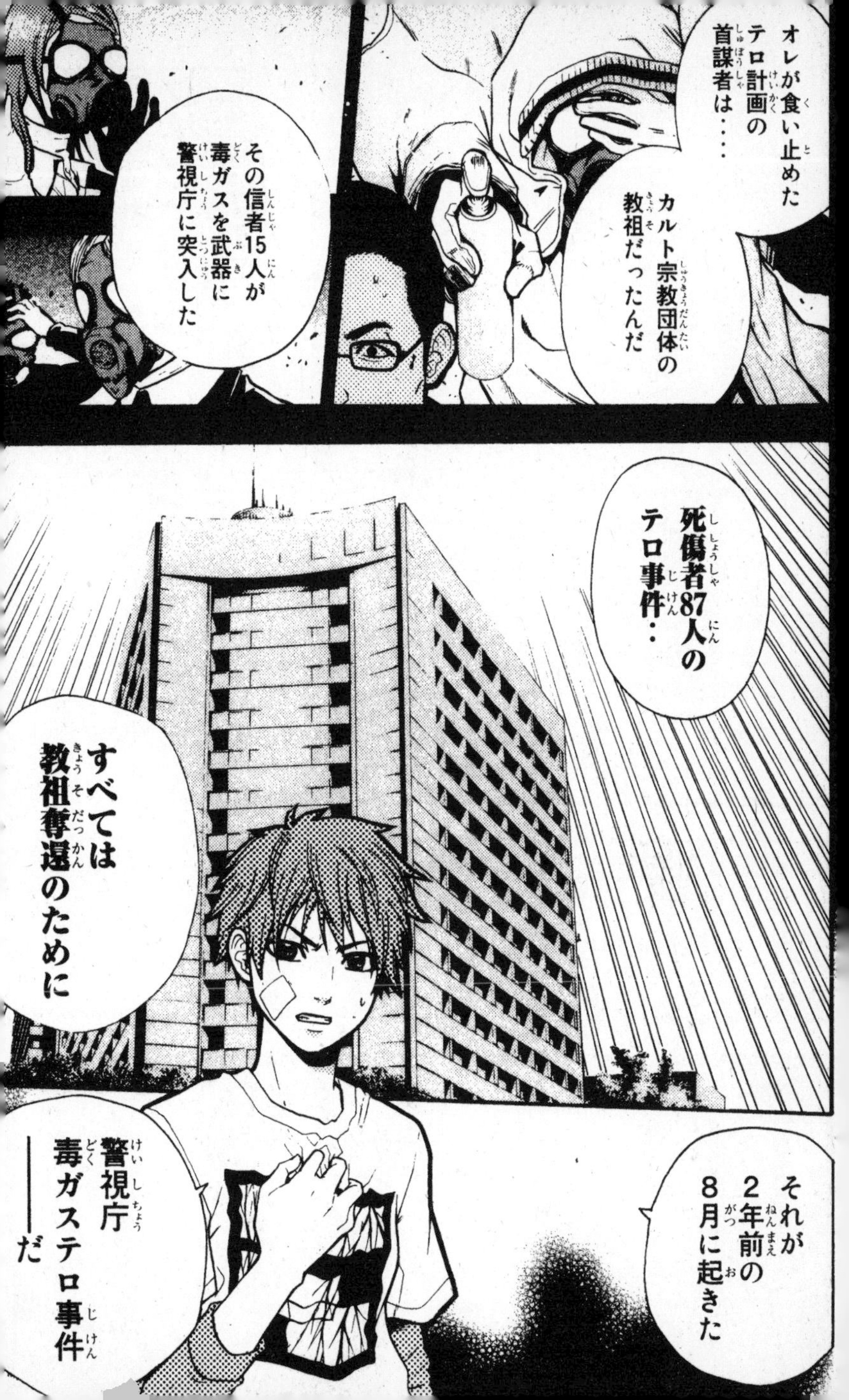
オレが食い止めたテロ計画の首謀者は‥‥
カルト宗教団体の教祖だったんだ
その信者15人が毒ガスを武器に警視庁に突入した
死傷者87人のテロ事件‥
すべては教祖奪還のために
それが2年前の8月に起きた
警視庁毒ガステロ事件——だ

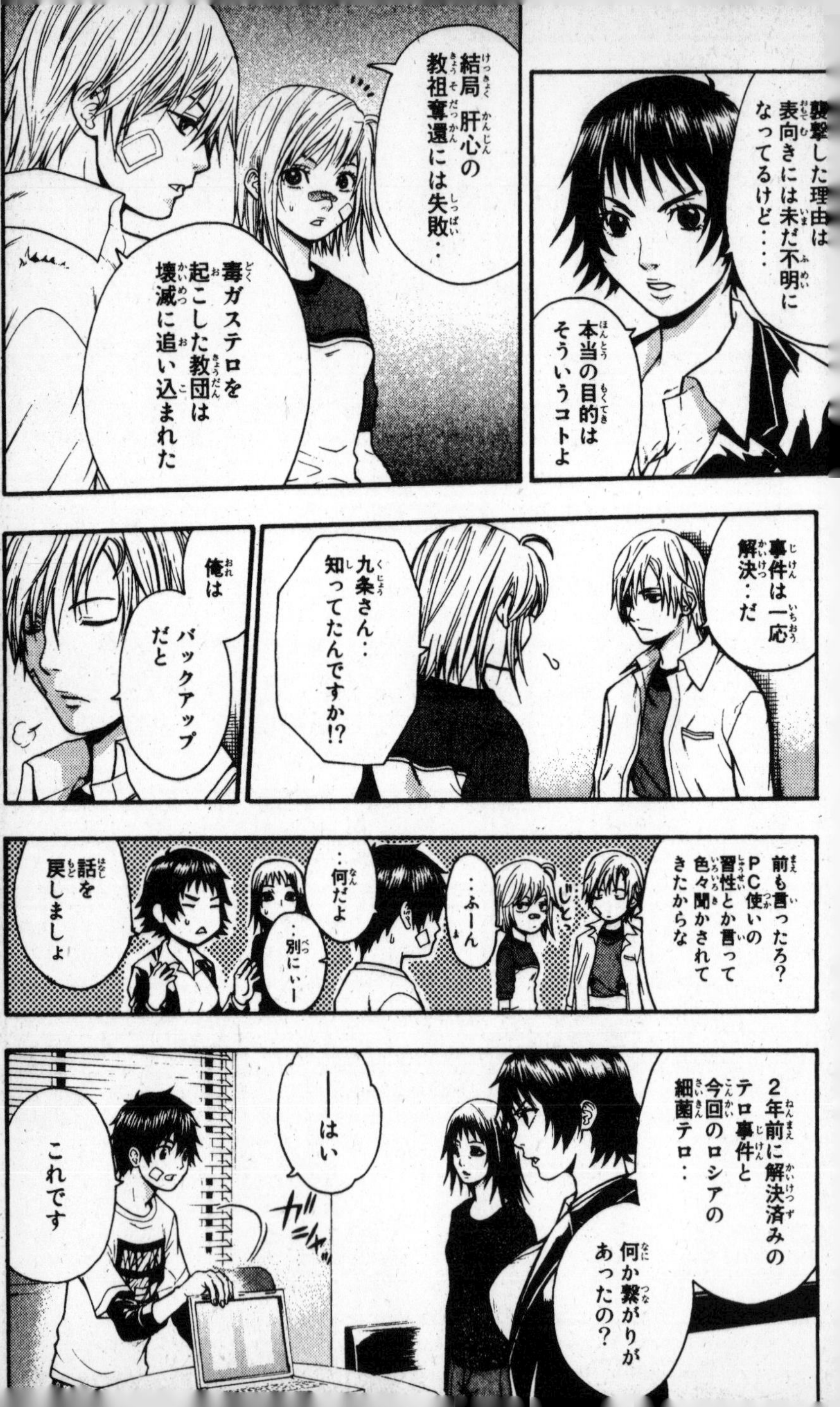

襲撃した理由は表向きには未だ不明になってるけど・・・・
本当の目的はそういうコトよ
結局肝心の教祖奪還には失敗・・
毒ガステロを起こした教団は壊滅に追い込まれた
事件は一応解決・・だ
九条さん・・知ってたんですか!?
俺はバックアップだと
前も言ったろ? PC使いの習性とか言って色々聞かされてきたからな
じとっ
・・ふーん
・・何だよ
・・別にぃー
話を戻しましょ
2年前に解決済みのテロ事件と今回のロシアの細菌テロ・・
何か繋がりがあったの?
――はい
ガシャ
これです

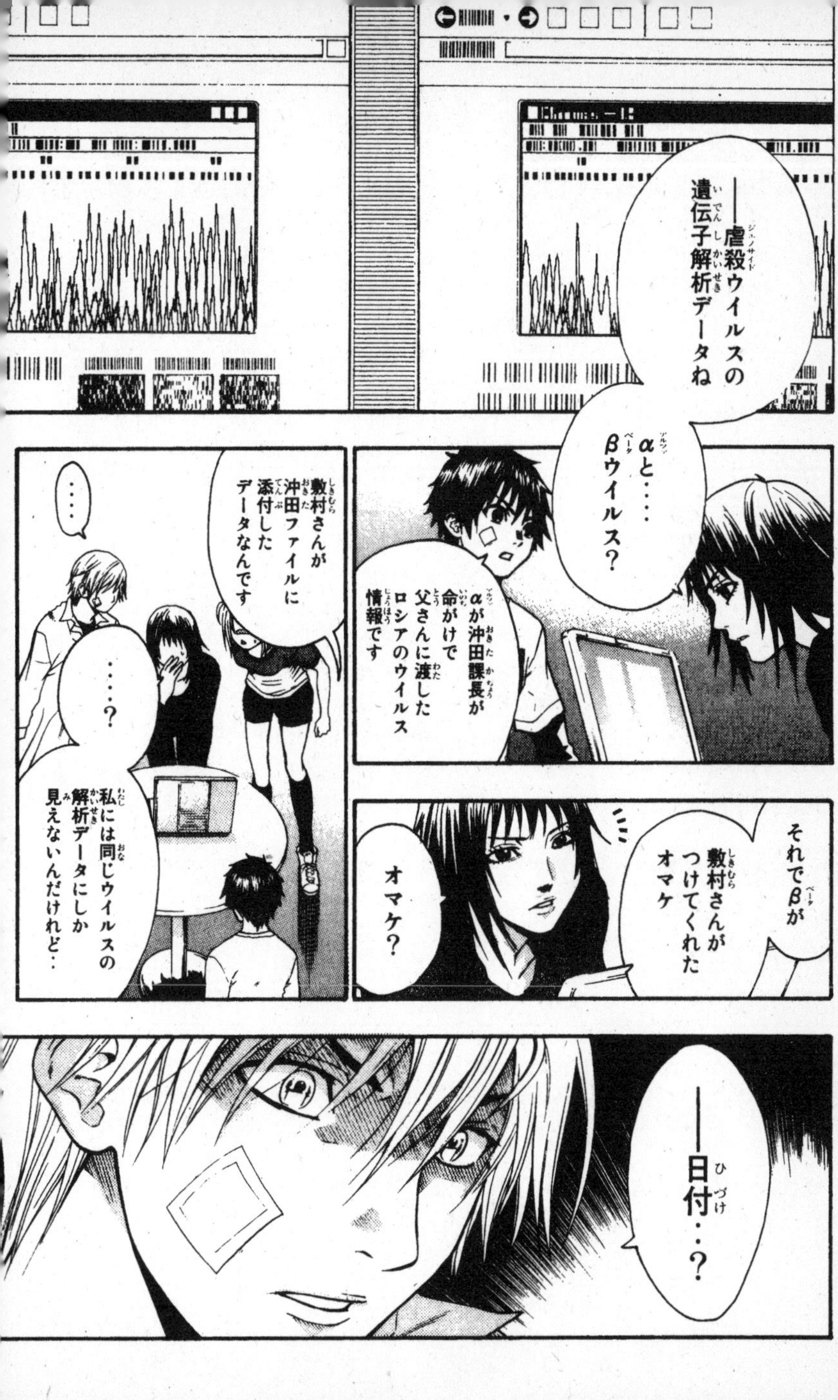
――虐殺ウイルスの遺伝子解析データね
αと・・・・βウイルス?
αが沖田課長が命がけで父さんに渡したロシアのウイルス情報です
それでβが敷村さんがつけてくれたオマケ
オマケ?
敷村さんが沖田ファイルに添付したデータなんです
・・・・
・・・・?
私には同じウイルスの解析データにしか見えないんだけれど・・
――日付・・?

HONORIFICS EXPLAINED

Throughout the Kodansha Comics books, you will find Japanese honorifics left intact in the translations. For those not familiar with how the Japanese use honorifics and, more important, how they differ from American honorifics, we present this brief overview.

Politeness has always been a critical facet of Japanese culture. Ever since the feudal era, when Japan was a highly stratified society, use of honorifics—which can be defined as polite speech that indicates relationship or status—has played an essential role in the Japanese language. When addressing someone in Japanese, an honorific usually takes the form of a suffix attached to one's name (example: "Asuna-san"), is used as a title at the end of one's name, or appears in place of the name itself (example: "Negi-sensei," or simply "Sensei!").

Honorifics can be expressions of respect or endearment. In the context of manga and anime, honorifics give insight into the nature of the relationship between characters. Many English translations leave out these important honorifics and therefore distort the feel of the original Japanese. Because Japanese honorifics contain nuances that English honorifics lack, it is our policy at Kodansha Comics not to translate them. Here, instead, is a guide to some of the honorifics you may encounter in Kodansha Comics.

-san: This is the most common honorific and is equivalent to Mr., Miss, Ms., or Mrs. It is the all-purpose honorific and can be used in any situation where politeness is required.

-sama: This is one level higher than "-san" and is used to confer great respect.

-dono: This comes from the word "tono," which means "lord." It is an even higher level than "-sama" and confers utmost respect.

-kun: This suffix is used at the end of boys' names to express familiarity or endearment. It is also sometimes used by men among friends, or when addressing someone younger or of a lower station.

-chan: This is used to express endearment, mostly toward girls. It is also used for little boys, pets, and even among lovers. It gives a sense of childish cuteness.

Bozu: This is an informal way to refer to a boy, similar to the English terms "kid" and "squirt."

Sempai/
Senpai: This title suggests that the addressee is one's senior in a group or organization. It is most often used in a school setting, where underclassmen refer to their upperclassmen as "sempai." It can also be used in the workplace, such as when a newer employee addresses an employee who has seniority in the company.

Kohai: This is the opposite of "sempai" and is used toward under-classmen in school or newcomers in the workplace. It con-notes that the addressee is of a lower station.

Sensei: Literally meaning "one who has come before," this title is used for teachers, doctors, or masters of any profession or art.

-[blank]: This is usually forgotten in these lists, but it is perhaps the most significant difference between Japanese and English. The lack of honorific means that the speaker has permission to address the person in a very intimate way. Usually, only family, spouses, or very close friends have this kind of permission. Known as *yobisute*, it can be gratifying when someone who has earned the intimacy starts to call one by one's name without an honor-ific. But when that intimacy hasn't been earned, it can be very insulting.

A Kodansha Comics Trade Paperback Original

Bloody Monday volume 3 copyright © 2007 Ryou Ryumon and Kouji Megumi
English translation copyright © 2011 Ryou Ryumon and Kouji Megumi

Published in the United States by Kodansha Comics,
an imprint of Kodansha USA Publishing, LLC, New York.

Publication rights for this English edition arranged through Kodansha Ltd, Tokyo.

First published in Japan in 2007 by Kodansha Ltd., Tokyo.

ISBN 978-1-935-42924-1
Original cover design by Takashi Shimoyama (Red Rooster)

Printed in the United States of America.

www.kodanshacomics.com

9 8 7 6 5 4 3 2 1

Translator: Mari Morimoto
Lettering: Karl Felton

TOMARE!

[STOP!]

You are going the wrong way!

Manga is a completely different type of reading experience.

To start at the *beginning*, go to the *end*!

That's right! Authentic manga is read the traditional Japanese way—from right to left, exactly the opposite of how American books are read. It's easy to follow: Just go to the other end of the book, and read each page—and each panel—from the right side to the left side, starting at the top right. Now you're experiencing manga as it was meant to be.